*Some other books by*

*All Through the Night* (C
Westminster John Knox Press)

*Every Pilgrim's Guide to the Journeys of the Apostles*
(Canterbury Press)

*The Little Book of Heavenly Humour* by Syd Little with
Chris Gidney and Michael Counsell (Canterbury Press)

*Every Pilgrim's Guide to England's Holy Places*
(Canterbury Press)

*A Basic Bible Dictionary* (Canterbury Press)

*A Basic Christian Dictionary* (Canterbury Press)

# The Canterbury Preacher's Companion 2008

*Sermons for Sundays, Holy Days,*
*Festivals and Special Occasions*
*Year A*

## Michael Counsell

CANTERBURY
PRESS
Norwich

First published in 2007 by the Canterbury Press Norwich
(a publishing imprint of Hymns Ancient & Modern Limited,
a registered charity)
9–17 St Alban's Place, London N1 0NX


www.scm-canterburypress.co.uk

British Library Cataloguing in Publication data

A catalogue record for this book is available
from the British Library


Scripture quotations are mainly drawn from the New Revised
Standard Version Bible © 1989 by the Division of Christian
Education of the National Council of Churches of Christ in
the USA.
Readings are from *The Christian Year: Calendar, Lectionary
and Collects*, which is copyright © The Archbishops'
Council of the Church of England: extracts and
edited extracts are used by permission.

Readings for days not covered by that book are from *Exciting
Holiness*, second edition 2003, edited by Brother Tristram,
copyright © European Province of the Society of Saint
Francis, 1997, 1999, 2003, published by Canterbury Press,
Norwich; see www.excitingholiness.org


ISBN 978-1-85311-793-0


Typeset by Regent Typesetting, London
Printed and bound in Great Britain by
William Clowes Ltd, Beccles, Suffolk

# LIST OF ADVERTISERS

# Contents

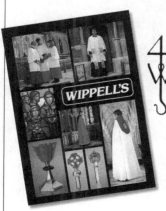

x

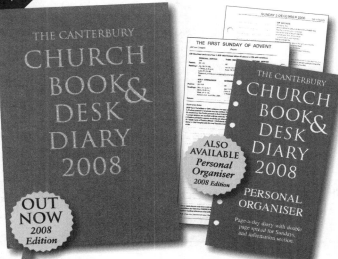

xi

Readings are from *Common Worship,* or from *Exciting Holiness* by Brother Tristam SSF, second edition, Canterbury Press, 2003.

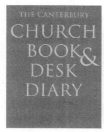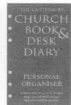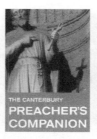

## Advance order for the 2009 editions

Avoid disappointment by ordering the 2009 editions now ! *(All to be published in May 2008)*    *quantity*

CANTERBURY CHURCH BOOK & DESK DIARY 2009 - *Cased* ............ £16.99 + p&p* .........

CANTERBURY CHURCH BOOK & DESK DIARY 2009 - *Personal Organiser*...£17.99 + p&p* .........

CANTERBURY PREACHERS COMPANION 2009 .............................. £16.99 + p&p* .........

ORDER FOR THE EUCHARIST 2009 .......................................... £7.99 + p&p* .........

Order a complete set of CANTERBURY CHURCH BOOK AND DESK DIARY *(either cased or personal organiser edition)*, CANTERBURY PREACHERS COMPANION and ORDER FOR THE EUCHARIST at the combined **advance order price of £34.00** + p&p*

## Order additional copies of the 2008 editions
*Subject to stock availability*

Desk Diary £16.99* .........    Organiser £17.99* .........    Preacher's Companion £16.99* .........    Order for the Eucharist £7.99* .........

**Ask for details of discounted prices for bulk orders of 6+ copies of any individual title when ordered direct from the Publisher.**

Sub-total:   £............

\* Plus **£2.50** per order to cover post and packing (UK only):   £............

All orders over £50 are sent POST FREE to any UK address.
Contact the Publishers office for details of overseas carriage.

**TOTAL AMOUNT TO PAY:**   £............

I wish to pay by...

...**CHEQUE** for £ .................... made payable to **SCM-Canterbury Press Ltd**

...**CREDIT CARD**   Visa, Delta, MasterCard and Switch accepted (please delete as appropriate)
Your credit card will not be debited until the books are despatched.

Card number: ....................................................................    Expiry: ___ / ___

Switch Issue No: ___   Valid from: ___ / ___

Signature of
cardholder: ..................................................................    Security code: ___ ___ ___

Last three digits on signature panel

Please **PRINT** all details below.

Title: ............... Name: ..................................................

Delivery address: ......................................................

.......................................................................................

.......................................................................................

.......................................................................................

....................................................... Post Code: ...............

Telephone: ........................................ Date: ......................

Return this order form - with details of payment - to
Canterbury Press Norwich, St Mary's Works, St Mary's Plain, Norwich NR3 3BH, UK

Telephone: 01603 612914    Fax: 01603 624483    Website: www.scm-canterburypress.co.uk

# PUBLISHERS
# ANNOUNCEMENT

To advertise your product or service in
**Canterbury Preacher's Companion**
or other annual publications, please contact

## The Advertising Department
## Church Times

Telephone
**020 7359 4570**

e-mail
**advertising@churchtimes.co.uk**

for details of rates and advertising specification.

Please remember that the order and copy
deadline will be in early March 2008.

Canterbury Press and Church Times are divisions of
Hymns Ancient & Modern Ltd, a registered charity

# Preface

I am grateful for the warm welcome given to last year's volume in this series, and I am still happy to receive suggestions as to how these books could be improved. It has been an interesting experience to hear some of my own sermons from that volume preached by other preachers. They have been most successful when they borrowed my ideas, structure and quotations, but spoke them in their own words; it takes longer in preparation, but where there is time, this is the best way to do it. I have found that where I stick too closely to the printed text, my sermons can sound lifeless even when I preach them myself. Those who have not yet found the confidence to preach from notes are encouraged to use these sermons as a stepping stone until they are ready to preach in their own words. Of course, the printed word is still valuable also to those who have no time to prepare, or for those who wish to read a sermon silently at home.

The suggestions for all-age worship have been especially welcomed. Further ideas can be found in *Crafts for Creative Worship* by Jan Brind and Tessa Wilkinson, published by Canterbury Press. The suggested hymns after each of my sermons offer four hymns which are directly relevant to the subject of the sermon. They have been taken from sources old and new, and I doubt if it would be advisable to use more than one unfamiliar hymn at any service. Canterbury Press have brought out a new edition of *Sing God's Glory: Hymns for Sundays and Holy Days, Years A, B & C*, which suggests a large number of hymns related to the readings at the Principal Service; and most hymnals have an index of hymns by subject or by Bible reference.

For seasonal liturgies, see *Common Worship: Times and Seasons*, published by Church House Publishing in 2006.

I have kept the same features as last year, with a colour liturgical calendar and the introductions to the seasons, as well as sermons for special occasions. In place of the chapter on 'How to Preach', I offer this year a paper on 'How to Pray', which could form the basis for a series of sermons, study groups or Lent talks.

Preaching is a great adventure. Preachers should be excited at the opportunity of making their hearers as moved as they themselves are by the word of God and the love of God. I hope those who use this book will find preaching as enjoyable as I do.

*Michael Counsell*
*Birmingham 2006*

# How to Pray

## Why pray?

Prayer is a form of communication, between a human or humans and God. The Bible gives us many examples of private prayer and public prayer, and Jesus encourages us to be persistent in prayer; gives us the example of his own prayers; and teaches us the art of prayer by giving us the Lord's Prayer. Jesus called God 'Abba', the word children used for speaking to their father, and prayer should be as natural as a friendly chat. Every child likes to talk to a well-loved parent, and every father wants his children to talk to him – and not only when they want something from him! 'Owls', who work best in the evening, should pray before they go to bed; 'larks', who are at their best in the morning, should pray as soon as they wake up. Resolve to pray at least once every day, to begin with, for as long as it takes to tell God all you want to say; then sit quietly for a while, listening to God and working out if there's anything God wants to say to you. Then just quietly enjoy God's love. Prayer is one of the means of grace, through which God draws us to himself, and gives us the power to live our Christian lives.

## When and where?

Jesus said:

> Whenever you pray, go into your room and shut the door and pray to your Father who is in secret; and your Father who sees in secret will reward you.

You can pray to God anywhere: in the garden, in the country, on a mountaintop, in the bus or while you are working. But a regular time and place (perhaps with an icon or crucifix) for your prayers is a help. A busy mother used to pull her apron over her head when she prayed, so that the children playing round her knew she was not to be interrupted.

'Arrow prayers' are short memorized phrases, which you can shoot up to heaven while you're busy doing something else: 'Lord, have mercy'; 'My Lord and my God'; 'Father, forgive'; 'Healing, please'; 'Guidance, please'; 'Help, Lord!'

## Chatting with your dad

*'The one-way telephone'*. Prayer should be as natural as chatting to your dad. Yet imagine a faulty telephone, when you are pretty sure the person at the other end can hear you, but you can't hear them. Prayer is like that. It takes faith to believe that there is somebody listening: 'Is there anybody there?' The eventual aim is for spontaneity in prayer, but to get there you will need discipline.

*Tongues*. Charismatic Christians emphasize 'speaking in tongues', when your heart is so full that the sounds just tumble out of your mouth. This is a gift of the Holy Spirit, because it gives to ordinary Christians the confidence that even they can be inspired. St Paul spoke in tongues, but preferred people to use the gift in private prayer rather than in public worship, and warned against despising those who don't have this gift.

## Written prayers

When Christians pray together, if all pray spontaneously the result is chaos, as St Paul pointed out. They need written prayers to say together, known as 'Liturgy'. A parking attendant's kiosk seen in Greece had 'Hours of Liturgy' painted on the outside, because it means service to the public! Because you know what words to expect, you can let your mind wander where the Holy Spirit leads you, then return to the liturgy. But private prayer should ideally be spontaneous.

St Teresa of Avila wanted to pray naturally, but she could never think of the words to say. In frustration she wrote down what she wanted to say first, and always added, 'Please Lord, help me to pray spontaneously and naturally.' One day her carriage went off the road and threw her into a muddy ditch. As she crawled out she said angrily, 'Lord, it's no wonder you have so few friends when you treat the ones you have so badly!' Then she realized her prayer had been answered.

Beginners in prayer may need to read out written prayers; later you can make up your own words. The Collects or Opening Prayers for each Sunday are not too difficult to memorize, or you can read

# Your First Stop for
## Christian Books *is...*

## CHURCH HOUSE BOOKSHOP

We also accept orders by mail, phone, email or via the website at: **www.chbookshop.co.uk**

*Opening hours:*

| Monday | 9.30am - 5.00pm |
|--------|-----------------|
| Tuesday | 9.00am - 5.00pm |
| Wednesday | 9.00am - 5.00pm |
| Thursday | 9.00am - 6.00pm |
| Friday | 9.00am - 5.00pm |

**Church House Bookshop**, 31 Great Smith Street, London, SW1P 3BN
Tel. 020 7799 4064  Fax: 020 7340 9997
Email: bookshop@chbookshop.co.uk
Nearest underground station: Westminster.

them from a book. Many collections of prayers old and new have been published. Some traditional prayers are expressed in very beautiful language, and it seems appropriate to offer the best we have of everything to God.

## ACTS of prayer

Using the mnemonic ACTS reminds us that prayer should include Adoration, Confession (Penitence), Thanksgiving and Supplication (Intercession and Petition), like this:

- *A for Adore*: Praise God and tell him how much you love him.
- *C for Confess*: Go through the past day in your memory, recalling all the things you are ashamed about, and telling God that you are sorry. Then believe that he has forgiven you.
- *T for Thanks*: Go through the past day again, thanking God for all the good things that have happened to you. Thank him for sending Jesus to show how much he loves us.
- *S for Supplies and Service*: Look forward over the day to come. Ask God for all the supplies that are needed, first for other people (Intercession), then for yourself (Petition).

*Intercession.* It is good to write a list of the people you want to pray for, and then pray for a few of them each day. Think about each of them for a while, and try to imagine what they most need. You may sometimes realize that you yourself could do something to help them. If you cannot think what would be best for them, silently lift them up in your imagination before the Lord, and ask God to do what is best for them.

*Petition.* This includes food and home comforts, but also the fruit and gifts of the Spirit, like patience and wisdom. Then think about ways you can serve God in the coming day, and tell God that you're ready and willing to do all you can.

## The Lord's Prayer

The Lord's Prayer is the form of prayer that Jesus taught his disciples. When using the prayer privately it seems probable that Jesus intended us to use each phrase as a 'headline' to remind us what we should pray about. Here is an example, using the form in The Book of Common Prayer, for readers to adapt in their own words:

3

*Our Father, who art in heaven –*
I'm talking to you, God, because you're a Father who loves me. You're not just my Father, but everybody's Father. And because you're our heavenly Father, you have power to hear and answer our prayers.

*hallowed be thy name –*
May the name 'God' be made holy, treated with respect, by everyone. Father, I praise you.

*Thy kingdom come –*
Please make everyone in the world obey you as their king, so that the world may be filled with peace and justice.

*thy will be done, on earth as it is in heaven –*
Please make everyone in the world do what you want them to, beginning with me. Then earth will be like heaven.

*Give us this day our daily bread –*
Please give me enough to eat, clothes to wear and a house to live in, and sometimes a few luxuries. Show me how I can bring food to all the starving people.

*and forgive us our trespasses –*
I'm sorry for all the unkind things I've done today, but I know that as soon as I own up you'll forgive me and forget all about them.

*as we forgive those who trespass against us –*
If anybody has done anything today to make me cross, I here and now forgive them, and I'll try to become friends with them again as soon as I can.

*and lead us, not into temptation –*
Show me the way I should behave. Sometimes I want to do things I shouldn't do, so please help me to avoid situations where I might do wrong, and to say no if I'm tempted.

*but deliver us from evil –*
Please make me better if I'm ill, and help me to escape unharmed if I'm in danger.

*For thine is the kingdom, the power and the glory, for ever and ever. Amen.*
All the power in the world belongs to you, and I praise you because you're wonderful. Yes!

## Answers to prayer

Answers to prayer are sometimes direct, when God gives us exactly what we ask for, and sometimes indirect when we receive something even better. They may consist in the healing of sickness, or the grace needed to bear our suffering. Often answers do not come immediately, and are only recognizable in retrospect. Sometimes they are miracles, or nearly miraculous, and often they are so unexpected that we repent for praying with so little faith. We must always thank God for answers to prayer, but we also have to face the problem of unanswered prayer.

Unanswered prayer is a painful experience, like that which Jesus went through in the Garden of Gethsemane when he asked for the cup of suffering to be taken away from him. It is particularly difficult when we pray for healing for ourselves or someone we love. God needs us to be aware of our total dependence on him in trusting faith when we pray. But it is cruel to tell anyone whose prayers have not been answered that they did not have enough faith, for that may drive them away from God into despair. God always answers prayers, but the answer may be 'yes', 'wait' or 'no, but I will give you something better instead'. The time may not be ripe, and God will give us what we ask for, or something like it, later when he knows it would be most use to us, if we learn to wait in patience. We cannot have miracles on demand or the world would be unbearably unpredictable. In our prayer there must be a real search for the will of Jesus, and a determination to pray only for the things he would have prayed for, and which he knows would be good for us. We should ask for the simplest material things, and even for miracles, while being prepared for disappointment if they turn out not to be part of God's plan for us at this time. More often, we should pray for grace, to be given the strength to co-operate with God in bringing about the things we have asked for, and to bear our sorrow and suffering if we cannot have what we wish at this time.

## Meditation

Meditation is thinking about God in a structured way. A retreat is a wonderful opportunity to learn to meditate, but short periods of meditation can be included in the pattern of a busy week, such as on solitary walks, or before church worship begins. There is a long and little-known tradition of Christian teaching on meditation, which aims for a personal encounter with a personal God.

The Rosary is a form of structured prayer, meditating on events in the life of Jesus and Mary. Every group of ten beads is counted off while reciting ten 'Hail Marys' (or, if you prefer, the Jesus Prayer;

see below), preceded by the 'Our Father' and followed by 'Glory be to the Father'. Each of these twenty 'decades' is recited while meditating on one of twenty 'Mysteries': five each of the Joyful, Luminous, Sorrowful and Glorious Mysteries.

Among the most widely used methods of meditation are the Ignatian and Salesian methods. St Ignatius Loyola (1491–1556) described his method in the *Spiritual Exercises*. St Francis de Sales (1567–1622), in his *Introduction to the Devout Life,* recommends:

- *Preparation*: remembering the presence of God; prayer for inspiration.
- *Imagination*: reading a passage from the Bible, and using all the senses to imagine that you are there at the scene described.
- *Consideration*: using your mind to work out how the lessons of the passage can be applied to today.
- *Resolution*: using the will, deciding on a practical response to what you have learnt.
- *Conclusion*: thanksgiving, self-offering, asking for grace to carry out your resolutions, the Lord's Prayer and other vocal prayers.
- A *'spiritual nosegay'*: selecting a phrase from the reading, memorizing it, and recollecting it occasionally during the day to enjoy again what the meditation has given you.

Or you can use the word 'ACTS', as above, to meditate on your Bible reading.

## Listening to God

Listening to God is an important part of prayer. Some time in our personal prayers needs setting aside for silence. Before church worship begins there may also be a time to unwind. Rarely, we may have an 'audition', the aural equivalent of a vision, and hear the voice of God. Usually, listening means working out if there is anything God wants to say to us. In seeking God's guidance we need to read the Bible and listen to the advice of others. If we have a strong inner feeling that God is saying something, we must check it with Scripture, tradition and reason, to be sure it is not self-deception or wishful thinking.

## Contemplation

Meditation leads into contemplation, when the mind is so relaxed that it does not think at all, but rests in the presence of God.

The Jesus Prayer is a short prayer which was taught, especially in the Eastern Orthodox Church, as a method which will concentrate the mind on the presence of God. The repetition has a relaxing effect. The long form of the prayer is:

Lord Jesus Christ, Son of the living God,
have mercy on me, a sinner, now and in the hour of my death.

This is repeated, aloud or silently, in time with one's breathing, for several minutes. Then words are omitted, a few at a time, until the prayer is just 'Jesus, mercy'. You breathe Jesus into your soul, and then you breathe out his mercy onto the world around you. This becomes almost subconscious, until with practice it can continue as you go about your work, and you 'pray without ceasing'.

A retreat is a time for quiet reflection, developing the arts of prayer, meditation and contemplation. A retreat director may give a series of addresses, and the opportunity for personal interview, spiritual direction and absolution if required. Some retreats encourage quiet concentration by painting or calligraphy. The Retreat Association has an annual publication listing places and dates where individuals or groups can arrange a retreat (consult www.retreats.org.uk).

Contemplation is silence focused on the being of God, when the mind is relaxed and stops the effort to reason. Contemplation leads into mysticism, which seeks union with God by a bond of love. The 'purgative way' is the stage in which one seeks to be cleansed from all sin and everything that hinders us from the vision of God. The second stage is the 'illuminative way', in which the soul is cleansed from attachment to pleasures of the five senses; it is sometimes called the 'dark night of the senses'; and it may lead into the 'dark night of the soul', when we learn to dispense with even the awareness of the presence of God. This eventually leads to the 'unitive way', the 'vision of God' or 'beatific vision' and the 'mystical union' of the soul with God, lasting into eternal life

Prayer is selfish if only practised for our own benefit. The aim is to come so close to God that his love can flow through us and out into service and love to our neighbours.

# Starvation
## Exploitation
## Poverty
### Drought

#### Who cares?

## You do.
## And you're not alone.

Twenty-two thousand churches support Christian Aid's work to eradicate poverty. Why? Because we believe in a God of love and justice.

We're here to help you make an impact on poverty in communities all over the world.

**To find out more, call 020 7523 2014.**
**www.christianaid.org.uk**

We believe in life before death

UK registered charity number 1105851 Company number 5171525 Republic of Ireland charity number CHY 6998

# YEAR A, the Year of Matthew

*(Year A begins on Advent Sunday in 2007, 2010, 2013, etc.)*

---

**ADVENT**

Advent consists of the four Sundays leading up to Christmas. It is a penitential season, so altar frontals and vestments are purple, (except that the Third Sunday in Advent may be rose), and there needs to be an air of solemnity in the services. 'Glory to God in the highest' is often omitted. 'Advent' means 'coming'; there is a sense of eager expectancy looking forward to the coming of Christ into the world at Christmas, but, except in carol services, it is a shame to introduce many Christmas carols during Advent as this robs us of the chance to enjoy some splendid Advent music, and leads to a sense of anticlimax when Christmas comes. We also celebrate the coming of Jesus into our lives daily, at our death, and at the end of the world. Traditional themes for sermons on the four Sundays are Death, Judgement, Heaven and Hell. Candles can be lit, mounted on an Advent wreath, one on the first Sunday, two on the second, and so on, leading up to five on Christmas Eve.

---

## First Sunday of Advent   2 December 2007

*Principal Service*   **Death**

Isa. 2:1–5 Nations will seek the Temple; Ps. 122 Let us go up to the Temple; Rom. 13:11–14 Lay aside the works of darkness; Matt. 24:36–44 The coming of the Son of Man

> *'[Jesus said,] "Keep awake therefore, for you do not know on what day your Lord is coming."' Matthew 24:42*

9

## Be prepared

The Boy Scouts' motto is 'Be prepared'. Robert Baden-Powell, known as 'BP', the founder of the Scout movement, wrote in the 1908 edition of *Scouting for Boys*,

> The scouts' motto is founded on my initials, it is: BE PREPARED, which means, you are always to be in a state of readiness in mind and body to do your DUTY.

For instance, the neckerchief was designed so that in emergencies it could serve as a triangular bandage, if the Boy Scout met somebody who was injured. You never know when an emergency is going to happen. You hope it may never happen. But a good scout's ready for anything. There's nothing morbid in thinking about what you'd do in an emergency, before it happens; but to be unprepared is foolish and could be dangerous. We could all learn a lesson from the scouts.

## Planning for the worst

There's no harm in considering the fact that unexpected things do happen. We should always hope for the best and plan for the worst. Jesus put this idea in the form of a one-sentence story, a sort of mini-parable:

> 'Understand this,' he said: 'if the owner of the house had known in what part of the night the thief was coming, he would have stayed awake and would not have let his house be broken into. Therefore you also must be ready, for the Son of Man is coming at an unexpected hour.'

In other words, be prepared for anything.

## Prepared for his coming

Specifically, Jesus warns us to be prepared for the coming of the Son of Man:

> 'Keep awake therefore, for you do not know on what day your Lord is coming.'

The Jews in Jesus's time expected the resurrection of our physical bodies when God's rule begins on earth, so the first Christians expected that the coming of the Son of Man would be a physical return of Jesus to earth. That's the obvious literal meaning of the words. But then generation after generation passed, with all the Christians keeping themselves ready for this event to happen in their lifetime, and Jesus didn't come. Some therefore became disillusioned, saying that all this about the Second Coming was the ignorant superstition of primitive people. If Jesus does come again on earth, such sceptics will get a nasty shock. Nevertheless, perhaps we've been wrong to concentrate on the literal meaning of the words. Most Christians now regard what the Bible says about the beginning of the universe as poetry, explaining through metaphors *why* God created the earth – in order to have people to love – rather than *how* God created the earth. Apart, that is, from those who call themselves creationists or fundamentalists. Can't we apply the same reasoning to what the Bible says about the end of the world, also? Not *how,* but *why* the universe will end?

## Prepared for death

That doesn't mean we can ignore what Jesus says about the coming of the Son of Man. It could be true literally and physically, and it could also be true metaphorically. Jesus came to the people of the first century, and they 'didn't know the time of their visitation'. He comes to each one of us every day, offering blessings, challenging us to serve him. He comes to each one of us on the day we die. Death can come at any time. People say there are only two things that nobody can avoid: death and taxes! So we should be prepared for anything. To think about death isn't morbid. Perhaps it's only Christians who can say, 'Come, welcome death'; because for Christians death is the gateway to happiness, the entrance to eternal life. The season of Advent is all about the coming of Jesus, and traditionally there were four themes, one for each of the four Sundays of Advent: death and judgement, heaven and hell. Peter Pan says in J. M. Barrie's play, 'To die will be an awfully big adventure.' Jesus advises us to be prepared for that adventure to start at any time; or in the words of the hymn, 'to live this day as if thy last'.

## *All-age worship*

*List or draw some of the things:*

– *you would do if you knew a burglar was coming to your house tonight;*

11

- *you would do if you knew the world was coming to an end today;*
- *you would like to do before you die if you lived to be a hundred.*

### Suggested hymns

*Awake my soul, and with the sun; Come, living God, when least expected; Lo, he comes with clouds descending; Ye servants of the Lord.*

Not really

# First Sunday of Advent
## *Second Service* False Messiahs
Ps. 9 The Lord judges the world; Isa. 52:1–12 How beautiful upon the mountains; Matt. 24:15–28 False Messiahs

> '[Jesus said,] "If anyone says to you, 'Look! Here is the Messiah!' or 'There he is!' – do not believe it."' Matthew 24:23

### Dreaming of a leader

It's the nature of human beings to hope for the best and to fear the worst. Yet no matter how dark the day, there remains always a ray of hope that things will get better. No matter how appalling the kings of the Old Testament were, the people of Israel always clung to the hope that, one day, there'd be a good king, an ideal king: one who'd lead them to the longed-for world of peace and prosperity. They called this ideal leader 'The Anointed One'; in Hebrew, 'the Messiah'; in Greek, 'the Christ'. Thank God they did dream the impossible dream. For in this way God prepared them for the coming of Jesus. Had they not hoped against hope that a Messiah would one day come, they wouldn't have been willing to welcome Jesus and listen to his message. It was a difficult and demanding message, involving self-sacrifice and love, not the offer of easy paradise that they'd expected. But because they were waiting for the Messiah, some of them, at least, paid heed to what Jesus said.

### The danger of a despot

But with every good gift comes the opposite side of the coin: the danger that it'll be misused. In every age, because people dream of an ideal leader, they're like putty in the hands of a megalomaniac. Over and again, therefore, false Messiahs have arisen, and many people have followed them. It happened in the lifetime of Jesus. Messianic movements still arise today; most tragically in the events connected with Charles Manson in the USA, and with Waco, Texas, where dozens died because they had been duped into following a false Messiah. For a while, young people were willing to follow any Indian guru who promised them a way of meditation, without questioning the personal lives of the teachers they followed. And in some parts of the Christian Church, it's all too easy for a minister who's dissatisfied with taking orders from somebody else, to break away and set up a new church of his own. Usually he rules it with a rod of iron, controlling the lives of his followers in the attempt to manipulate them to his own purposes. With the dream of a Messiah, there always comes the danger of a despot.

## Telling the difference

How then can we tell the difference between a true Messiah and a false one? False leaders try to convert people to the truth as they see it, not to the truth as it is found in Jesus. Therefore they refuse to study other people's interpretation of the Scriptures, or to take advice from others on how the church should be run. The false Messiah takes more pleasure in making people do his bidding, than in winning them to obey God's will. The false Messiah pays very little attention to the historical Jesus. He promises instant gratification instead of the long haul, and directs his followers' attention away from Jesus to himself. Thus the false leader creates new divisions in the Church, and leads it away from that unity for which Jesus prayed.

## A likeness

The Church must have leaders to co-ordinate its actions. Otherwise our energies will be dissipated in a whole lot of individual initiatives. But good leaders will point their followers beyond themselves towards Jesus Christ. Good leaders won't draw attention to themselves. Daily they'll try to conform their own lives to the pattern set us by Jesus himself. Jesus is the true Messiah, the Good Shepherd, the model for what leadership should be. If anyone in a position of leadership bases their life on the teaching of Jesus, others will recognize their Christlike character and be willing to follow them.

If we all look to Jesus, the author and finisher of our faith, then we shall be less likely to be led astray by false Messiahs. We are God's chosen ones, his 'elect' – that's what the word means. Jesus warned us that

> 'False messiahs and false prophets will appear and produce great signs and omens, to lead astray, if possible, even the elect. Take note, I have told you beforehand.'

### Suggested hymns

*Come, thou long-expected Jesus; Hark, a thrilling voice is sounding; Lo, he comes with clouds descending; Thy way, not mine, O Lord.*

## Second Sunday of Advent    9 December
### Principal Service    Judgement    Small L.t

Isa. 11:1–10 A shoot from the stump of Jesse; Ps. 72:1–7, 18–19 Give the king your righteousness; Rom. 15:4–13 Hope from the Bible; Matt. 3:1–12 John the Baptist preaches repentance

> *'In those days John the Baptist appeared in the wilderness of Judea, proclaiming, "Repent, for the kingdom of heaven has come near."' Matthew 3:1–2*

### A God who cares

An idol can't see what happens outside its temple. So idol-worshippers can do just exactly what they like. If you bribe the idol with enough sacrifices, you can beat up your neighbours, rob them and starve their children with a clear conscience. The idol doesn't know, so it probably doesn't care. The Jews, however, believed in a God who does care how we treat each other. God's everywhere, and God sees everything we do, they taught. Judaism, and Christianity and Islam which are based on it, teach about a God who knows how we treat each other and judges us.

### Repentance

John the Baptist preached, 'Repent, for the kingdom of God has come near.' God's a king, he said, who expects you to obey him.

Examine yourselves: look to see what things you've done to displease God. Then own up to God, stop making excuses for yourself, and take responsibility for what you've done. Next, make up your mind to obey God as your king in the future, and love your neighbours because that's what God commands. All that's included in John's cry of 'Repent!' He was certain that God knows, and cares, how we treat each other. Everything we do is under God's judgement.

## Judgement Day

Some people think that God will judge us at some future cataclysmic event, which they call Judgement Day. Have you heard impatient parents telling their teenage children in the shops, 'Oh, hurry up and make up your mind, or we shall be here till Judgement Day!' Other people think that John's urgency sprang from something much more imminent: for John, the coming of Jesus was the arrival of the kingdom of God.

## We judge ourselves

Jesus said that we judge ourselves all the time:

'This is the judgement, that the light has come into the world, and people loved darkness rather than light because their deeds were evil. For all who do evil hate the light and do not come to the light, so that their deeds may not be exposed. But those who do what is true come to the light, so that it may be clearly seen that their deeds have been done in God.'

We can't put off the assessment until some far off global assize, because we've already been judged at the court of our own conscience. We know perfectly well which of our deeds were inspired by genuine generosity and Christian care, and which were selfish and unloving. If we're honest, we should all admit that the latter outweigh the former. Not only that, but our attitude much of the time's self-centred; we don't take the trouble to find out God's will and follow it. So we all need to heed John the Baptist's message: 'Repent!' Then we can benefit from the love of Jesus and the free forgiveness which he offers through his death on the cross. Then we can stand with our consciences washed clean before the judgement throne of God.

## Advent themes

The traditional themes for the four Sundays of Advent are death and judgement, heaven and hell. These subjects may seem a bit like 'doom and gloom' when everybody's beginning to get the happy Christmas spirit. But when Jesus died on the cross, the kingdom of God had come. Our good deeds and bad deeds are shown up for what they are in the light of his goodness and love. If we repent, the bad deeds can be forgiven. And we'd much better get this over before Christmas, because how can you have a happy Christmas when you've got a guilty conscience? John the Baptist's message, 'Repent, for the kingdom of heaven has come near,' implies the offer of forgiveness. It's what we mean when we wish each other a happy Christmas – only at a much deeper level.

### All-age worship

*Make a balance: a rod with a pivot in the middle, and a tray hanging from each end. Mark the balance, 'God's Judgement', with one tray marked 'Guilty' and the other 'Not Guilty'. Then make two blocks, a small one marked 'My Good Deeds' and a bigger one marked 'My Bad Deeds'. Then put a bigger block marked 'God's Love' in the tray with the Good Deeds and see how it comes down, 'Not guilty'.*

### Suggested hymns

*Hark, a thrilling voice is calling; In a world where people walk in darkness; On Jordan's bank the Baptist's cry; The kingdom of God is justice and joy.*

## Second Sunday of Advent   *last bit – ok*
### Second Service   Elijah and the Prophets of Baal
Ps. 11 The righteous Lord loves righteousness [28 The Lord has heard my prayer]; 1 Kings 18:17–39 Elijah and the prophets of Baal; John 1:19–28 The testimony of John the Baptist

> *'Elijah then came near to all the people, and said, "How long will you go limping with two different opinions? If the LORD is God, follow him; but if Baal, then follow him."' 1 Kings 18:21*

16

## Mount Carmel

At the northern end of the Judean hills, there's a sheer drop to what the Old Testament calls the Valley of Jezreel. Mount Carmel's at the west end of the valley and rises high over the Mediterranean. Elijah chose a dramatic spot to challenge the prophets of Baal.

## Prophets of Baal

'Baal' means husband; it was a general term for all the male fertility gods worshipped in that part of the world. Fertility goddesses were called Asherah. There was a group of men, 450 prophets of Baal and 400 prophets of Asherah, worshipping the Baals and forcing themselves into a frenzy. They danced themselves into a trance by prancing round a bull that had been sacrificed and laid on a pyre. They did a limping dance, cutting themselves with knives until they were covered in blood, and shouting, 'Baal, hear us' from dawn till midday. To test them, Elijah said they weren't to set light to the wood under the sacrifice, but wait to see whether Baal would send fire to set it alight. Of course nothing happened, and in the midday heat the smell of blood and sweat and meat and the sound of the shouting must have been appalling.

## Elijah's mockery

Then Elijah made fun of them. False gods probably don't exist at all; if they do, they're powerless compared to the one true God whom Elijah worshipped. So he mocked the Baals as though they were all too weak and human: 'At noon Elijah mocked them, saying, "Cry aloud! Surely he is a god; either he is meditating, or he has wandered away, or he is on a journey, or perhaps he is asleep and must be awakened."' Those are all things which his God, being a real God, has no need to do: 'Behold, he that keepeth Israel shall neither slumber nor sleep.'

The one true God of all the earth doesn't wander about or go on journeys.

## Fire from heaven

Next it was Elijah's turn. Elijah's maturity is shown by the dignity and restraint of his prayer. He didn't set light to his sacrifice; he even poured water all over it to make it harder to ignite. 'Then the fire of the LORD fell and consumed the burnt offering, the wood, the stones, and the dust, and even licked up the water that was in the trench.' Elijah's God wasn't only the God of the lightning, but also of the rain. From a cloud 'no bigger than a man's hand' a storm arose that broke the drought, and Elijah stripped off to his loincloth and ran joyfully through the rain, down the steep slope to the plain and all the way to Jezreel, quicker than King Ahab could keep up with him in his chariot.

## Indecision

It's a marvellous story, made even more dramatic in Mendelssohn's oratorio *Elijah*, but what's the point of it? Elijah's belief in one all-powerful God, who demands moral behaviour from his worshippers, was true; his opponents' belief in a multitude of little gods that they could twist any way they liked was untrue. The fire from heaven proved it. The challenge wasn't really to the prophets of Baal, as they limped round their altar. It was to the people of Israel, to whom Elijah said: ' "How long will you go limping with two different opinions? If the LORD is God, follow him; but if Baal, then follow him." The people did not answer him a word.'

Like so many people today, they couldn't make up their minds. Each of them believed one thing with one half of themselves, and the opposite with the other half. As a result, they were like someone walking along with one foot on the footpath and the other in the gutter. They were the ancestors of the people who answer 'Don't know' to all the public opinion polls. Some people today even make a virtue of this, and call themselves 'agnostics', as though to be a lifelong 'Don't know' were a virtue. Certainly you need to study the pros and cons, and take time before you make up your mind, but you can't put off decisions for ever. The decision as to whether or not God exists, and whether or not you'll obey him, is a matter of life and death. You can't go on for ever putting off the decision about your eternal future. One day it'll be too late.

## *Suggested hymns*

*Hark, a thrilling voice is sounding; I want to walk with Jesus Christ; O Jesus, I have promised; Who is on the Lord's side?*

## Third Sunday of Advent   16 December   ✓
*Principal Service*   **Hell**

Isa. 35:1–10 Healing in the desert; Ps. 146:4–10, Healing and salvation, *or Canticle*: Magnificat, God's Justice; James 5:7–10 Wait in patience; Matt. 11:2–11 Jesus' teaching about John the Baptist

> *'Jesus answered them, "Go and tell John what you hear and see."'*
> Matthew 11:4

### John is puzzled

Even John the Baptist was puzzled. He couldn't make Jesus out. John's own cousin, and Jesus was behaving in a most unexpected manner. John had announced that Jesus was the Messiah, coming to bring in the kingdom of God. Jesus, he said, would baptize the people 'with the Holy Spirit and fire'. And nobody was lighting the fire. Like most people then, John probably thought that the kingdom of God was political. God in charge of the land of Israel, ruling through the Messiah, and no foreign soldiers occupying God's land. But Jesus said, 'My kingdom is not of this world.' John began to wonder whether Jesus really was the Messiah. John was in prison, put there by King Herod, so he sent some of his own disciples to ask Jesus, 'Are you the one who is to come, or are we to wait for another?' John had been walking along fine in the way of the Lord which he had prepared. Then he tripped. He stumbled over the un-expected love and tolerance of Jesus's ministry, and the unexpected nature of the kingdom of God which Jesus brought.

### Have a good trip

It's like when you're walking along an uneven pavement, and you trip over something because you weren't looking down. Sometimes your friends are very rude to you, and they laugh at you saying, 'Have a good trip!' Jesus made it quite clear that he thought John had tripped up: 'Don't stumble because of me,' he said. Most Bibles translate this as 'Blessed is anyone who takes no offence at me.'

### The kingdom of God

So what is the kingdom of God? John thought it was hell-fire, with the wicked, and especially the Roman soldiers, being burnt up like

19

the rubbish on a farmer's bonfire. But it's not like that at all, said Jesus; tell John it's like this: in the kingdom of God, the blind receive their sight, the lame can walk, lepers are healed, the deaf enabled to hear, and the poor have good news announced to them. It means physical healing; Jesus was doing plenty of that. But at a deeper level it means a change in attitudes: people who are blind to the truth are seeing the meaning of life, people who are stumbling over their prejudices are helped to walk straight, captives to bad habits are set free from their addiction, social outcasts are readmitted to society, those who won't listen are hearing God speak through their neighbours, and those who thought they were unimportant are told the good news that God loves them. That's the kingdom of God, said Jesus: not the destruction of the wicked, but their conversion. This was the idea that John had tripped up over.

## Hell-fire

So did Jesus believe in hell-fire? It was a phrase that he used eight times in the four Gospels; typical are:

> 'Every tree that does not bear good fruit is cut down and thrown into the fire.'

> 'If your eye causes you to stumble, tear it out; it is better for you to enter the kingdom of God with one eye than to have two eyes and to be thrown into hell, where the worms never die, and the fire is never quenched.'

This sounds like a poetic image: selfish people are no better than the rubbish we tip onto the incinerator to be destroyed; the word translated as hell was the name of the Jerusalem rubbish-tip. Some people take these words literally. Others say the vivid imagery's meant to make us take seriously the consequences of our selfish actions. But more people are loved into heaven than are ever frightened into it. We may condemn ourselves to final destruction, however, by refusing to accept the eternal life God offers us. The love of Jesus is open to everyone. Only let's be careful we don't trip up over our prejudices on the way.

## *All-age worship*

*List examples today of how people who are blind to the truth are seeing the meaning of life, people who are stumbling over their prejudices are helped to walk straight, captives to bad habits are set free from their addiction, social outcasts are readmitted to society, those who won't listen are hearing God speak through their neighbours, and those who thought they were unimportant are told the good news that God loves them.*

## Suggested hymns

*Make way, make way for Christ the king; Hark! the glad sound! the Saviour comes; O for a thousand tongues to sing; Thy kingdom come, O God.*

## Third Sunday of Advent
*Second Service*   **A Lamp Showing Up the Truth**
Ps. 12 Social injustice [14 The fool has said]; Isa. 5:8–30 Social injustice; John 5:31–40 Jesus' teaching about John the Baptist

> '[Jesus said,] "You sent messengers to John, and he testified to the truth … He was a burning and shining lamp, and you were willing to rejoice for a while in his light."' John 5:33, 35

### Batu caves

Two people were visiting Batu caves in Malaya. For the man it was his first time, and he wanted to explore one of the less-visited caves. It was pitch-dark, and the woman, who'd been there before, called out, 'I shouldn't go in there without a torch, in some places the floor drops away suddenly.' 'Nonsense,' replied the man, groping his way forward, 'it's perfectly …' – but the end of his sentence came from six feet lower down! Fortunately he picked himself up unhurt. But he'd learnt two important lessons: you should always listen to the witness of somebody who knows the truth; and a torch or lantern is useful for showing up what the truth really is.

### A witness

Jesus called his cousin John the Baptist a witness and a lantern. Witnesses have to report what they've actually seen with their own eyes. Hearsay isn't evidence, you can't report what other people have told you. In *Pickwick Papers*, Charles Dickens has Sam

21

Weller joke about a comical remark made by an imaginary soldier.

> 'You must not tell us what the soldier, or any other man, said, sir' interposed the judge; 'it's not evidence.'

The Jewish law courts had very strict laws against people giving false witness: swearing in court that something's true when it isn't. So Jesus was appealing to a well-known standard when he talked about witnesses. A retranslation will make that clearer:

> [Jesus said,] 'If I give evidence about myself, my evidence isn't true. John the Baptist gives evidence on my behalf, and I know that his evidence about me is true. You sent messengers to John, and he gave evidence about the truth. Not that I need such human evidence, but I say these things so that you may be saved. John was a burning and shining lamp, and for a while you were happy in his light. But I have evidence to give more persuasive than John's. The things that my Father sent me to complete, the actual things that I'm doing, give evidence on my behalf that my Father's sent me. And my Father's himself given evidence on my behalf.'

## A lantern

John, said Jesus, is a witness to the truth and a lantern which shows up the truth. Suppose a child calls out in panic, 'Mummy, there's a bear in my bedroom!' His mother comes in and puts the light on and the child sees with relief that the dark shape's not a bear after all, but the child's dressing-gown hanging behind the door. Light shows up what things really are, and what we should do about them. John the Baptist said about Jesus:

> 'Here is the Lamb of God who takes away the sin of the world! This is he of whom I said, "After me comes a man who ranks ahead of me because he was before me." I myself did not know him; but I came baptizing with water for this reason, that he might be revealed to Israel ... And I myself have seen and have given evidence that this is the Son of God.'

The truth about Jesus is that he is the Son of God, and the sacrificial lamb who, by his death on the cross, wipes out the guilty record of your sins and my sins and everybody else's sins. We know this is true, because John gave it as the evidence of his own eyes, and he's a reliable witness.

## Listen to the witnesses, look at the evidence

It's crazy to step into the darkness if you ignore the witnesses who'll tell you the truth from their own experience. It's crazy not to take a torch to show up the dangers. Yet millions do it every day. In Psalm 119 we read, 'Your word, O God, is a lantern for my feet.' The Bible contains the witness of hundreds of people who experienced God's activity in their own lives, and saw Jesus at work. There are tens of thousands in this country alone who could tell you what they've experienced of the love of God, and how it's changed their lives. Listen to the witnesses, look at the evidence. What we say about God's love and power is true, because we've experienced it for ourselves.

### Suggested hymns

*Come, thou long-expected Jesus; Hark, a thrilling voice is sounding; I cannot tell why he, whom angels worship; On Jordan's bank the Baptist's cry.*

## Fourth Sunday of Advent  *23 December*  No.
*Principal Service*  **Emmanuel**

Isa. 7:10–16 The sign of Immanuel; Ps. 80:1–8, 18–20 Restore your people; Rom. 1:1–7 Sent to preach the gospel of salvation; Matt. 1:18–25 The birth of Jesus and Joseph's dream

> *'[The angel said to Joseph,] "Look, the virgin shall conceive and bear a son, and they shall name him Emmanuel," which means, "God is with us."' Matthew 1:23*

### Emmanuel

Emmanuel means 'God is with us.' When Joseph discovered that Mary was expecting a baby, an angel appeared to him in a dream and said:

> 'Joseph, son of David, do not be afraid to take Mary as your wife, for the child conceived in her is from the Holy Spirit. She will bear a son, and you are to name him Jesus, for he will save his people from their sins.'

Then St Matthew's Gospel goes on to explain:

All this took place to fulfil what had been spoken by the Lord through the prophet: 'Look, the virgin shall conceive and bear a son, and they shall name him Emmanuel,' which means, 'God is with us.'

## Isaiah

Matthew was quoting from the prophet Isaiah. The armies of Syria and the northern kingdom of Israel were attacking the southern kingdom of Judah, where Isaiah lived, and everyone was terrified. Isaiah went to reassure King Ahaz. He gave the king a sign, to prove that God was on their side:

'Therefore the LORD himself will give you a sign. Look, the young woman is with child and shall bear a son, and shall name him Immanuel.'

This isn't a direct prediction of the virgin birth, though Christians immediately recognized that it could be applied to the birth of Jesus from the Virgin Mary. The word Isaiah used, which the New Testament translates as 'virgin', could be used to apply to any young woman, perhaps even to King Ahab's new bride. She was already expecting a baby. By the time the child was born, in something under nine months, the nation would be victorious over their enemies, said Isaiah. They would be so happy, they'd go round saying to each other, 'Im-ahnu-el' – we've got God on our side, God is with us. And the Queen would name the new Prince 'Immanuel' to celebrate the victory.

'Therefore the LORD himself will give you a sign. Look, the young woman is with child and shall bear a son, and shall name him Immanuel.'

## Jesus, God with us

That's why the birth of Jesus, the Prince of Peace, was so important. God, by coming to earth and being born at Bethlehem, scored a notable victory over the forces of evil which attack us daily. God shows that he is on our side. But not only that, God comes and lives among us, as an ordinary human being, the same as you and me. At Bethlehem, God is with us – Im-ahnu-el. No matter how many times you say it, that's a quite astonishing statement. 'The Word became flesh'; 'Love came down at Christmas'; 'Behold, the great Creator makes himself a house of clay'; 'Veiled in flesh the godhead see'; God, himself, is with us.

## O come, O come Emmanuel

The great Advent hymn 'O come, O come Emmanuel' is based on 'The great Advent Os', seven wonderful anthems sung in the Middle Ages before the Magnificat on the days leading up to Christmas. Each verse addresses Jesus by one of the titles used to describe him in the Bible: God's *wisdom; Adonai,* the LORD; the *stem* from the stump of Jesse; the *key* to the palace of King David; the new *dawn;* the *king* of the nations. The last, used on the day before Christmas Eve, though it comes first in our hymnbooks, is *Emmanuel:* God is with us.

## How does that make you feel?

How does that message make you feel? That God should humble himself, come to earth and be born in a stable! God must love you, if he's willing to come to earth for your sake. You can't be as insignificant as you'd assumed, if God is with us. If heaven is where God lives, a little bit of heaven fell to earth at Bethlehem. Defeat isn't inevitable, victory's certain, God's on our side. And one day he'll take us all to live with him in heaven, where we can sing for evermore, 'Emmanuel, God is with us.'

### All-age worship

*Collect pictures of any churches near you dedicated to 'Emmanuel'. Make a collage and write underneath, 'God is with us.'*

### Suggested hymns

*Creator of the starry height; O come, O come Emmanuel; The great God of heaven is come down to earth; Sleepers wake! or Wake, O wake! With tidings thrilling (or other translations).*

# Fourth Sunday of Advent
## *Second Service*   Marana-tha   *grounding*

Ps. 113 God blesses the barren [126 Sow in tears, reap with joy];
1 Sam. 1:1–20 Hannah conceives Samuel; Rev. 22:6–21 Come,
Lord Jesus!; *Gospel at Holy Communion*: Luke 1:39–45 Mary visits
Elizabeth

> *'The one who testifies to these things says, "Surely I am coming
> soon." Amen. Come, Lord Jesus!' Revelation 22:20*

## A tee-shirt

A tee-shirt seen recently had, written across the front, 'Jesus is
coming!' Printed on the back was 'Try to look busy!' Behind the
jokiness is a serious point. If our loving heavenly Saviour did return
to earth today, we'd surely want him to be pleased with what we're
doing, because he's our friend, and we like to please our friends.
We don't know whether the world is going to end this week or in
thousands of years' time, so we should make long-term plans, build
churches that will last for centuries, plant woodland that won't be
mature until after our lifetime. Then if Jesus does come to us, or if
we come to him, we shall be proud of the things we've been doing
for him.

## Jesus is coming

Jesus is coming to each one of us soon, in some way or another. Of
course, he's here all the time, and watching us. But that's nothing to
be frightened about, because Jesus loves us. Sometimes we become
especially aware of his presence. Then we can say, 'Jesus came to
me in that moment.' Each of us will die one day, and Jesus will
come to us at our death and welcome us into a better and happier
world. Cosmologists agree that our solar system has a shelf-life of
only a few billions of years more, at best. So, one way or another,
Jesus is coming, and we should be glad.

## Come, Lord Jesus!

The first Christians could hardly wait for the coming of Jesus.
'Come, Lord Jesus!' they cried enthusiastically. Ideas change and
develop very rapidly in the first few years of any new movement,

and the Christian Church was no exception. Starting with a belief that Jesus would usher in a new earthly kingdom in their lifetime, they progressed to a belief in a heavenly kingdom. Whether this dream would find its fulfilment sooner or later, they would welcome it, and they longed for it with eager hope.

## You can speak Hebrew

So universal was this expectation that it became a greeting, a sort of catchphrase in Hebrew. Did you know that you can speak Hebrew? If you start to learn a foreign language, it's always an encouragement to discover that you already know some of the vocabulary. So from Hebrew, or it's later dialect of Aramaic which Jesus used, you already know 'Amen', meaning 'Yes, that's the truth, I agree'; 'Halleluiah' which means 'Praise the Lord', and probably a few others like 'Ephatha', 'Be opened'; and 'Talitha cum', 'Little girl, stand up'. In his first letter to the Corinthians, St Paul signs off with the Aramaic words, 'Marana-tha', meaning 'Our Lord, come!' Even the Greek-speaking Christians, who formed a majority in Corinth, and spoke no Hebrew, knew what that meant. So Paul had no need to translate it for them. However, the word could possibly be split in a different place, to read 'Maran-atha' instead of 'Marana-tha'; that would translate as 'Our Lord *has* come'. Perhaps it doesn't matter. Probably the first Christians were aware of the tension between rejoicing that God had come to earth in the birth of Jesus, and hoping that he will come to each of us again, collectively and individually, at the end of our lives when time has merged into eternity.

## The Revelation to John

The Book of the Revelation to John, the last book in the Bible, is in the style of what we call 'apocalyptic literature'. There have been many different interpretations. Now that we've found a lot of other books in the same style from the same period, however, many people are coming to regard Revelation as a vision of the ideal world, the world as God would like it to be. Through the coming of Jesus at Bethlehem, and his coming into our lives to transform us, gradually we're beginning to transform the world. If we let Jesus control our lives, we can make a difference. Gradually the world becomes more and more like the heavenly Jerusalem of John's vision. And, of course, the process culminates in heaven, which is 'out of this world'. So St John ends his book with the same words that St Paul used, only in Greek this time, 'Come, Lord Jesus!' With those words and a short grace, the Bible ends on a note of Christmas joy and hope: Jesus has come, Jesus comes to us daily, and we shall all come to Jesus in heaven. How can you help having a happy Christmas if you believe that?

## Suggested hymns

*Come, thou long-expected Jesus; Hark, a thrilling voice is sounding; Hark, the glad sound! the Saviour comes; Soon and very soon.*

### CHRISTMAS, EPIPHANY AND CANDLEMAS

In spite of our weariness from all the preparations, Christmas retains its magic as a season of joy. The churches are brightly decorated, vestments and hangings are gold, if possible, on Christmas Day and white on the Sundays following. On 6 January we celebrate the Epiphany, which means the revelation or revealing of who Jesus really is. On that day we read about the visit of the Wise Men, who were the first non-Jews to recognize Jesus as 'King, and God, and Sacrifice'. The following Sundays have readings about other occasions when Jesus was 'manifest': when the Father spoke at his Baptism, when he 'revealed his glory' at the wedding in Cana, when he proclaimed his programme in Nazareth, when Nathanael (and the demons!) recognized him as Son of God, and when he called the first disciples and sent them out as 'fishers' to reveal him to all races. The Epiphany season is a time therefore to remember our own missionary task of evangelism. Then on 2 February comes 'The Presentation of Christ in the Temple', when old Simeon recognized Jesus as the Messiah, and sang of him as 'a Light to lighten the Gentiles'. This is therefore also called 'Candlemas', and candle-ceremonies are held in some churches (see *Common Worship: Times and Seasons*, pp. 203–7).

Simeon also predicted that a sword would pierce Mary's heart, looking onward to the crucifixion; so Candlemas is a watershed between the Sundays following Christmas and those leading up to Holy Week, and is often celebrated on the Sunday falling between 28 January and 3 February. From then until Ash Wednesday there are a number of 'Sundays before Lent', using, if necessary, readings for Propers 1–3 in Ordinary Time.

# Christmas Day   25 December   *multiol*

*Any of the following sets of readings may be used on the evening of Christmas Eve and on Christmas Day. Set III should be used at some service during the celebration.*

*Set I*   **A Child is Born**   Isa. 9:2–7 A child is born; Ps. 96 Tell of his salvation; Titus 2:11–14 Salvation has come; Luke 2:1–14 [15–20] The birth and the shepherds

> *'For a child has been born for us, a son given to us; authority rests upon his shoulders; and he is named Wonderful Counsellor, Mighty God, Everlasting Father, Prince of Peace.' Isaiah 9:6*

## Happy birthday

Happy birthday, Jesus! And happy 'rebirth-day' to all of you who are here. For the Bible says that because of the child who was born on this day, 'to all who received him, who believed in his name, he gave power to become children of God, who were born, not of blood or of the will of the flesh, but of God'. So this is your birthday too, if you believe in Jesus.

## A child is born

> For a child has been born for us, a son given to us; authority rests upon his shoulders; and he is named Wonderful Counsellor, Mighty God, Everlasting Father, Prince of Peace.

What a wealth of images are included in that single verse! We know it by heart, of course, because of its use in Handel's *Messiah*: 'For unto us a child is born …'. Let's go through the picture which Isaiah draws word by word. Like all the Old Testament's dreams of the Messiah, it grew out of a particular political situation. The king of Judah at the time was turning out to be a disaster. But a new prince had just been born. So there was fresh hope for the future: perhaps this would be the ideal king who would put everything right. He wasn't, of course. But the idea grew that one day the ideal king, the Messiah, would come. Thus people had some idea what to expect of Jesus, when he was born seven hundred years later.

## Authority

First, *authority* rests on Jesus's shoulders. The image is of a large and heavy sceptre, the rod which symbolized the authority of the king. Or even of a key; we're told that keys in those days were big heavy things, which could only be carried round by shouldering them like a rifle. Isaiah says about a royal steward, who had the sole authority to go into the store-rooms of the palace:

> I will place upon his shoulder the key of the house of David; he shall open, and no one shall shut; he shall shut, and no one shall open.

So Jesus has the authority to rule the world; he has the key to 'open the kingdom of heaven to all believers'. Jesus, who was born on this day, shoulders that authority confidently, gives us just laws, and admits us to the kingdom of heaven.

## Wonderful Counsellor

Second, the new king will be a *Wonderful Counsellor*. A counsellor is somebody who gives advice. Jesus, who was born on this day, gives us wonderful advice. If only everybody would obey his advice, the world would be a better place.

## Mighty God

Third, Jesus, who was born on this day, is the *Mighty God*. Jewish readers have great problems with these words: how can any man be described as God when God is one? Christians know that the answer is that the God who is one-in-three became human at Christmas.

## Everlasting Father

For Jesus, who was born on this day, is, fourth, one with the *Everlasting Father*. Isaiah may have been thinking merely of the king as 'father' of the nation; we know that God's our loving heavenly Father, and Jesus is his Son.

## Prince of Peace

Lastly, Jesus, who was born on this day, is the *Prince of Peace*. If people will listen to him.

> Yet with the woes of sin and strife
> The world has suffered long;
> Beneath the angel strain have rolled
> Two thousand years of wrong.

But although wars continue, some of them caused by sinful so-called Christians, still there has been progress: at least now most people realize that war is wrong.

> For lo, the days are hastening on
> by prophet-bards foretold,
> when, with the ever-circling years,
> comes round the age of gold;
> when peace shall over all the earth
> its ancient splendours fling,
> and the whole world give back the song
> which now the angels sing.

Welcome the Prince of Peace, who was born on this day, to rule in your hearts. Then work that he may be king over all the world. Happy birthday, Prince of Peace, and to all of you who serve in his army!

### All-age worship

*Make a Christmas card showing Jesus with a crown on, breaking a gun in half; write on it, 'Happy Birthday, Prince of Peace'.*

### Suggested carols

*Hark, the herald angels sing; I cannot tell why he, whom angels worship; It came upon the midnight clear; Joy to the world, the Lord is come!*

## Christmas Day   25 December   ~~more rubbish~~

*Set II*   **Shepherds** Isa. 62:6–12 Prepare a way; Ps. 97 God comes to rescue his people; Titus 3:4–7 Salvation by grace; Luke 2:[1–7] 8–20 Shepherds go to Bethlehem

> *'The angel said to [the shepherds,] "… I am bringing you news of great joy for all the people: to you is born this day in the city of David a Saviour, who is the Messiah, the Lord."'* Luke 2:10–11

### Shepherds are people

Shepherds are people. Perfectly ordinary people, like you and me. They eat when they're hungry, they fall asleep when they're tired. No different from the rest of us. They have an unusual job to do, looking after sheep. They have to turn out in the middle of the night in all weathers to care for their sheep. They have to learn certain skills which the rest of us don't need, like managing a sheepdog, using a sheep dip, and how to cut the wool off the sheep's back at shearing time. But ask shepherds and they'll tell you, they're just ordinary people.

### Marie Antoinette

You remember hearing about Marie Antoinette? The Queen of France at the time of the French Revolution, who was alleged to have been told that the people had no bread, and replied, 'Then let them eat cake!' She and her friends, the lords and ladies of the court, used to like to dress up as shepherds, and pretend that they were ordinary people. Which, of course, they weren't; she was the Queen of France. That's why she knew so little about ordinary people, that she thought that if they had no bread they could go to the cupboard and bring out a fruitcake. She was a bit of a fruitcake herself; she certainly knew nothing about how ordinary people live.

### The shepherds of Bethlehem

So when the King of kings came to earth, in Bethlehem, the town where King David had been born centuries earlier, to whom did he first appear? To kings and queens, or to ordinary people? Well, if the three wise men were really kings, they didn't arrive till later; the first on the scene were the shepherds of Bethlehem. Shepherds.

32

Perfectly ordinary people, like you and me. They eat when they're hungry, they fall asleep when they're tired. No different from the rest of us. Why did the angels send mere shepherds to see the new-born king and to tell their neighbours about him? Surely it would have been better to send the rich and the famous to listen to them. But no, God chose shepherds, ordinary people. And the angels said to them,

> 'I am bringing you news of great joy for all the people: to you is born this day in the city of David a Saviour, who is the Messiah, the Lord.'

## Joyful news for all people

'Joyful news for *all* people.' The coming of God to earth as a perfectly ordinary baby was good news for everybody. Not just for kings and queens; not just for the rich and famous; not just for television and sporting personalities; but for perfectly ordinary people like the shepherds. Like you. Like me. That's why God chose ordinary people to bring us the joyful news. So that we should realize that it's important for us, too. After all, we think, the birth of a new king, what's that got to do with people like us? But Jesus was a very special sort of king. He was a king of the people, a king for the people, the ordinary people, like us. He is our Saviour, to save us from the guilt of our sins, from slavery to bad habits, and from the fear of death. To reveal to us the love of God, and God's plan for the world. We might not have realized that all those wonderful things applied to ordinary people like us, if God hadn't chosen ordinary people like the shepherds to tell us. You and I ought to be grateful to the shepherds of Bethlehem, and to God for choosing them. So to all of you perfectly ordinary people here, God wishes you a joyful Christmas. And so do I. Happy Christmas, *everybody*!

### All-age worship

*Make a Christmas banner reading GOD LOVES ORDINARY PEOPLE.*

### Suggested carols

*Away in a manger; Christians awake, salute the happy morn; See him lying on a bed of straw; While shepherds watched their flocks by night.*

## Christmas Day   25 December

*yet more nd'/.2*

*Set III*   **Speaking through a Son** Isa. 52:7–10 The messenger
of peace; Ps. 98 God's victory; Heb. 1:1–4 [5–12] God speaks
through a Son; John 1:1–14 The Word became flesh

> 'Long ago God spoke to our ancestors in many and various ways
> by the prophets, but in these last days he has spoken to us by a
> Son.' Hebrews 1:1–2

### Carol singers

Imagine a church choir's going round the houses singing Christmas
carols at the door. At one house there are lights on, so they know
there must be people inside, and they sing one carol outside in the
cold before they ring the bell. Then a young lad answers the door.
The choirmaster asks him, 'Can we speak to your father, sonny?'
The boy answers, 'Dad said I'm to tell you he's busy at the moment
and can't come to the door himself. But I'm to tell you that you
sing very beautifully, and give you this pound.' The choirmaster
accepts the money with a smile, saying, 'Thank you very much, my
boy. You make a good spokesman for your father.' But the boy
has something more to say: 'And Dad says if you could come back
again in an hour's time, he'd like you to sing for the people who are
coming for supper. You can come in where it's warm, and he says
he'll give you some mince pies.' The whole choir accepts this invitation, once food and drink are mentioned. If the boy says his father
told him to say this, who are they to doubt him? They turn up later,
meet the father, sing carols to his guests, and receive the reward
they were promised. End of story. It's only a little made-up story for
Christmas, but it illustrates the idea that a son is entitled to speak
on behalf of his father, and be believed. The very first words of the
Letter to the Hebrews, in the Bible, are, 'Long ago God spoke to
our ancestors in many and various ways by the prophets, but in
these last days he has spoken to us by a Son.'

### What God wants

That's what Christmas is all about: God speaking to us through
Jesus, his Son. The Bible assumes God wants to speak to us. Now
that's a pretty amazing suggestion. Up until then, most people
thought their god was an idol of wood or bronze, stuck in a temple.

Now, ears made of bronze or wood don't hear very well, and you have to shout and jump up and down to attract the attention of their owners! Or else they thought the gods lived on top of Mount Olympus, and only spoke to human beings when they had bad news for us. But the Bible says that God actually wants to speak to us, and is trying to attract our attention, not the other way round. What does he want to say to us, basically? The Bible says God wants to tell us he loves us. He also wants to tell us how we should treat each other lovingly, because God loves everybody equally and cares what we do to other people.

## How can God speak?

So how can God speak to us? How can he tell us he loves us? God can't come to the door himself; if God appeared to us directly we'd all shrivel up with shame and fear. So first he tried to speak through people he called 'prophets'. They all came proclaiming, 'Thus saith the LORD'. And nobody listened to them. 'How do we know that you have the authority to speak on behalf of God?' they asked. Prophets were a good idea, but not good enough; God would have to find another way to tell us that he loves us.

## Speaking through a Son

So, like the father in the story, God sends his Son to speak for him, to be his representative. Surely everybody will listen to God's Son, and trust him to have the authority to speak on behalf of his Father. This time God's plan worked better. Some people just wouldn't listen. But many did, and they formed a society of people who are willing to listen to the Son of God and do what he tells us to do – it's called the Christian Church. And you and I are here today because we want to listen when God tells us he loves us, and when he tells us to love each other for his sake. Happy Christmas!

## *All-age worship*

*Make a model of the Christmas crib in a shoebox, and wrap it in Christmas gift-wrap paper and ribbon. Then partially unwrap it so that people can see the contents, and put it at the front of the church with a label on it reading: THIS IS MY CHRISTMAS GIFT TO MY PEOPLE, WITH LOVE FROM GOD.*

35

*In the bleak midwinter; Long ago, prophets knew; Love came down at Christmas; Thou who wast rich beyond all splendour.*

# Christmas Day
## Second Service   The Mouths of Babes

Morning Ps. 110 This day of your birth, 117 Steadfast love; Evening Ps. 8 Out of the mouths of babes; Isa. 65:17–25 A new creation; Phil. 2:5–11 Jesus emptied himself; *or* Luke 2:1–20 (*if it has not been used at the Principal Service of the day*)

> *'Your majesty above the heavens is praised, out of the mouths of babes at the breast.' Psalm 8:2* (Common Worship*)*

### Familiar words

What comes out of the mouths of babes? Most parents, and some uncles and aunts, will answer, 'That smelly stuff that makes a mess on your shoulder when you bring up their wind!' Then there's that loud bawling noise that wakes you up in the middle of the night. But those who are familiar with the Psalms in The Book of Common Prayer will have a different answer:

> Out of the mouths of very babes and sucklings hast thou ordained strength, because of thine enemies; that thou mightest still the enemy, and the avenger.

Beautiful words, and in this form they are quoted in the Authorised Version of Jesus's reply to the priests when they object to the children crying Hosanna as he entered Jerusalem:

> And Jesus saith unto them, 'Yea; have ye never read, Out of the mouth of babes and sucklings thou hast perfected praise?'

But just a minute; in the Psalm it says that out of the mouths of babes comes strength; Jesus says that out of the mouths of babes there comes praise. The *Common Worship* version of the Psalms is on the side of Jesus in this argument:

> Your majesty above the heavens is praised, out of the mouths of babes at the breast.

## A problem in translation

Do we have a translation problem here? Sure enough, we do, and it affects the choice of this Psalm for Christmas Day. Basically, we know a lot more about the structure of Hebrew poetry than when the old translations were made, and the early translations got the verse divisions wrong. And that's on top of the problem that 'sucklings' immediately makes us today think of pigs, whereas it's correctly translated into modern English as 'babes at the breast'.

## Our place in nature

But whether it should be translated as praise or strength, it's a pretty remarkable thing to come out of a baby's mouth. The answer is that the whole of Psalm 8 is about the human race and its place in nature. In terms of the age of the universe we are mere newborn babes. And yet God has given us the amazing dignity that he communicates with us. For to *Homo sapiens,* alone of all the species, God has given the power of speech. Parents treasure the moment their babies utter their first words: 'My baby's talking to me!' What do you think God feels the first time any of us speaks to him and calls him 'Father'?

## Baby-power

We're talking baby-power here. Babies may be weak and dependent, but compared with any other creature they are immensely powerful, because they possess the possibility of speech. When babies grow up, they can tame horses with bit and bridle, they can move mountains with JCBs, they can discuss the meaning of life and they can argue with their Creator. Such strength! They can praise their Creator too, and pray to God and worship him, in words as well as by their actions. Alone of all creation. And all this power and praise is lying latent in the mouth of every baby in the cradle.

## The baby of Bethlehem

So God chose to become a baby: the baby of Bethlehem. What a compliment to pay to babies! What a revelation of baby-power! For by becoming a baby, who can't talk, God communicated, as he could have in no other way, the vulnerability of love. To love is to make yourself dependent on others. To love is to trust other people. To love is to make your deepest feelings open to public gaze. To love is to give yourself completely to those you love. That's how God loves us, and what he proclaimed by coming to earth as a helpless baby. Out of the mouth of the baby of Bethlehem, God proclaimed the strength of baby-power, and led us to praise the majesty of God in heaven.

## Suggested carols

*See, amid the winter's snow; Silent night, holy night; Where is this stupendous stranger?; Who would think that what was needed?*

# First Sunday of Christmas   30 December
## *Principal Service*   Egypt
Isa. 63:7–9 God's presence brings salvation; Ps. 148 Let all creation praise the Lord; Heb. 2:10–18 The suffering of Jesus brings salvation; Matt. 2:13–23 Flight into Egypt

> 'This was to fulfil what had been spoken by the Lord through the prophet, "Out of Egypt I have called my son." ' *Matthew 2:15*

## The flight into Egypt

Mary, Joseph and little Jesus, who was almost two years old by now, fled from King Herod's anger and sought safety in a foreign land. The land they chose was Egypt, and it was a hard journey on a donkey. This was traditionally called 'the flight into Egypt'. A child was once asked to draw the flight into Egypt, and he drew an aeroplane. 'Who are these four people in the aeroplane, Johnny?' asked the astonished teacher. 'That's Mary, and Joseph, and Jesus, on the flight into Egypt,' Johnny replied. 'And the fourth one is Pontius, the pilot!'

## Refugees

So they became foreigners, in a strange land, far away from home and the people they loved. They didn't know the language, and nobody could speak theirs. They didn't know the customs or understand the laws. They felt lost and afraid; the only thing they knew for certain was that if they went back to their own country they would be killed. They were refugees, and asylum-seekers. When-ever anyone speaks about refugees and asylum-seekers today, they should stop and remember that Jesus was one when he was a helpless child. If anyone's living in a country which is not the land of their birth, they may be comforted to remember that Jesus understands their loneliness and deprivation, because he's known the experience at first hand.

## The Exodus

The Jewish people had themselves been foreigners in Egypt. The sons of Jacob and their families had gone there when Joseph was chief adviser to the Pharaoh. Gradually they sank from a position of privilege into slavery and abject poverty. Then Moses led them out of Egypt, across the sea and the desert and into their promised land. They never forgot this; it was then that they learnt that God is a God who saves. The prophet Hosea appealed to this experience, when he wanted to show his people that they were behaving as rebellious children to God their loving father. In a uniquely touch-ing expression of God's fatherly love, Hosea imagines God describ-ing his care for his people as being like a father teaching his son to walk, taking them in his arms, lifting them to his cheek; bending down and feeding them:

> When Israel was a child, I loved him,
> and out of Egypt I called my son.

So Matthew was able to use the experience of Jesus in Egypt as a way of showing that Jesus is God's Son.

## The Son of God

What does it mean to say that Jesus is the Son of God? Many books have been written about this term, and of course words are never adequate to give us more than hints of the nature of God. The Hebrew language has no words for 'human' or 'divine'; it can only talk about 'one like a son of man' or 'all the sons of God shouted for joy'. So to say that Jesus is the Son of God means that he is divine, but it says more than that. In a sense we are all sons and daughters of God, because God loves us as his children. But Jesus is unique. He has a special relationship with God the Father, so that he could say: 'Do you not believe that I am in the Father and the

Father is in me? The words that I say to you I do not speak on my own; but the Father who dwells in me does his works.' What Jesus does, his Father does, because he is the unique Son of God. Yet that closeness to the Father's breast that he knows, he wants to share with all of us. From the depths of slavery in Egypt God called the people of Israel, his son – with a small 's'. From the lowly status of a refugee in Egypt, God called Jesus, his Son – with a capital 'S'. No matter what depths of misery or despair we ourselves sink to, God can call us out of them and welcome us to the proud status of sons and daughters of our God.

### All-age worship

*Draw Mary and two-year-old Jesus on a donkey, led by Joseph, on their way to Egypt. Can you find on a map Old Cairo, where the Holy Family is supposed to have rested, and measure how far it is from Bethlehem?*

### Suggested hymns

*Lully, lulla; Our Saviour's infant cries were heard; Unto us a boy is born; Who would think that what was needed?*

## First Sunday of Christmas

*Second Service* **The Son of David** Ps. 132 The Son of David; Isa. 49:7–13 These shall come from far away; Phil. 2:1–11 Born in human likeness; *Gospel at Holy Communion*: Luke 2:41–52 Jesus aged twelve.

*'Of the fruit of your body shall I set upon your throne.' Psalm 132:12* (Common Worship)

### Lord, remember David

A bride and groom were discussing with the vicar the choice of music for their wedding. This was in the days when it was usual to include a psalm from the Book of Common Prayer. The groom, whose first name was David, was flicking through the pages. 'This will do for my wedding day,' he said, with a cheeky grin. 'The psalm begins, "Lord, remember David and all his trouble"!' If you look at the whole of Psalm 132 you see it isn't actually about the tribulations of getting married. It's about the trouble that King David took to find a place to build a permanent Temple for the Lord. In return, the Lord makes a promise to David: 'Of the fruit of your body shall I set upon your throne.' This is poetic language for saying that one of David's own children will succeed him as king in Jerusalem. It was fulfilled when Solomon, the son of David, inherited the kingdom.

## A succession of kings

God's promise didn't stop there.

'If your children keep my covenant,
  and my testimonies that I shall teach them,
their children also shall sit upon your throne for evermore.'

God promises a non-stop succession of descendants, one after another inheriting the title of King of the Jews, for ever and ever, Amen. Only it didn't happen. When King Zedekiah was taken into exile in Babylon in 587 BC, his sons were all slaughtered before his eyes, and he 'died without issue', as the lawyers say. After the exile there was an abortive attempt to create a new royal family with Zerubbabel as the new king, but the Persian King Darius wouldn't allow it. So from then on the Jews had no legitimate king, descended from David: King Herod was a foreigner, imposed on them by the Romans.

## Jesus, the Son of David

A strong hope persisted, however, that one day a descendant of David would once again be anointed as King of the Jews. So they dreamed of a Messiah – the word means 'anointed' – who would be called the 'Son of David'. Now, Jesus had problems with the word 'Messiah', because of its militaristic overtones. He also argued that calling the Messiah 'David's son' didn't imply that he was inferior to King David in any way. But the gospel writers emphasized that the birth of Jesus fulfilled all the old prophecies of a Messiah, that he was the new leader they'd longed for, and was descended from King David. Actually he was descended from the royal family through Joseph, whom, I suppose, you'd call his adoptive father, but that was perfectly legal. Jesus was born in Bethlehem, where his ancestor King David was born: 'Once in royal David's city ...'.

The angel told Mary that 'The Lord God shall give to him the throne of his ancestor David.'

The angel said to the shepherds, 'To you is born this day in the city of David a Saviour, who is the Messiah, the Lord.'

The wise men frightened Herod with the threat of a rival when they asked, 'Where is the child who has been born king of the Jews?' and his scribes told him that the Messiah was to be born in Bethlehem, the birthplace of King David.

Pontius Pilate asked Jesus, 'Are you the king of the Jews?'

So Jesus was seen as the Son of David whom God had promised so many years before.

## What does it mean to us?

What does it mean to us today that Jesus was born 'King of the Jews'? After all, most of us are not Jews. First, it means that God always keeps his promises. If you find anything promised in the Bible, you can be sure it will one day come true. Often the promises are fulfilled in a way we didn't expect. Jesus wasn't the military Messiah they'd been waiting for to drive out the occupying army of the Romans. God came to earth as a helpless baby. God doesn't save us from suffering; instead, he suffers alongside us. But after we get over our initial shock, we gradually realize that the fulfilment is even better than we'd expected. So, secondly, calling Jesus the Son of David reminds us that Jesus fulfils all our dreams. All of them. It doesn't get any better than this. Whatever you've longed and hoped for, dreamt of and looked forward to, you can find it right there in the baby in the manger. Not, perhaps, in the form you'd expected. But even better. The stable at Bethlehem is where all our dreams come true.

## Suggested carols

*Long ago, prophets knew; Once in royal David's city; Unto us a boy is born; While shepherds watched their flocks by night.*

# Epiphany   6 January 2008
## *Principal Service*   Gold, Frankincense and Myrrh
Isa. 60:1–6 Bringing gold and incense; Ps. 72:[1–9] 10–15 Kings will bow before him; Eph. 3:1–12 Preaching to Gentiles; Matt. 2:1–12 Visit of the Magi

> *'On entering the house, they saw the child with Mary his mother; and they knelt down and paid him homage. Then, opening their treasure chests, they offered him gifts of gold, frankincense, and myrrh.' Matthew 2:11*

### 'Frank sends this'

In the nativity play, a small boy was given the part of one of the wise men, who brought gifts of gold, frankincense and myrrh. He was a little uncertain of his lines, which he didn't understand, anyway. The other wise men said, 'I bring this, which is gold', and 'I bring this, which is myrrh'. Groping for inspiration, the third boy blurted out, 'And Frank sends this.'

### Fulfilment of prophecy

The story of the wise men in Matthew's Gospel tells of star-gazers from eastern lands, come to honour baby Jesus, bringing gifts which were symbolic, and a fulfilment of prophecy. Isaiah wrote, 'All those from Sheba shall come. They shall bring gold and frankincense, and shall proclaim the praise of the Lord.'

Frankincense was one of the spices in the incense offered in the Temple; it's a resin formed from the sap of a tree; its name comes from the freedom or 'frankness' with which it gives off a beautiful perfume when burnt. Liquid myrrh was made from the sap of another plant, dissolved in oil. It was used in the oil for anointing priests and kings. The perfume of myrrh is also mentioned several times in that great biblical love-poem called the Song of Songs, or the Song of Solomon. The wise men were fulfilling the scriptural prophecy that people would come from the East to offer gifts to the Messiah. The Gospel doesn't say there were three of them, but it seems logical since there were three gifts. Neither does it say they were kings, but that's taken from Psalm 72 which says of the Messiah: 'May the kings of Tarshish and of the isles render him tribute, may the kings of Sheba and Seba bring gifts.'

## Gold

Christians give symbolic meanings to the three gifts, in several popular Christmas, or Epiphany, carols; see if you can recognize which carols these quotations come from. In the first Caspar sings:

> Born a king on Bethlehem plain,
> gold I bring to crown him again,
> king for ever, ceasing never
> over us all to reign.

The wise men recognized in the Baby of Bethlehem a newborn king. Jesus, our king, must be obeyed, even if we'd rather not do what he tells us. 'Gold of obedience' is what we must offer to Jesus; not actual gold, but our obedience to Jesus includes using what money we have to help those worse off than ourselves.

## Incense

Melchior sings:

> Frankincense to offer have I,
> incense owns a deity nigh,
> prayer and praising, all men raising,
> worship him, God most high.

In God's presence there can be no pride. We must offer to Jesus the 'incense of lowliness', coming to church not just when we feel like it, but every week if at all possible.

## Myrrh

Balthazar sings:

> Myrrh is mine, its bitter perfume
> breathes a life of gathering gloom;
> sorrowing, sighing, bleeding, dying,
> sealed in the stone-cold tomb.

Spices were used for anointing a body for burial, and burnt as incense on the altar in the Temple. So myrrh symbolizes the sacrifice of Jesus's life on the cross. There can be no love without sacrifice. God doesn't save us from suffering. The Bible promises that Jesus saves us from sin, and the fear of death. When people die, Jesus welcomes them into heaven. And when we suffer, Jesus is beside us, suffering with us.

## Our offering

'King and God and sacrifice' sing the three kings. This is what the gold, frankincense and myrrh symbolize.

> Solemn things of mystic meaning:
> Incense doth the God disclose,
> Gold a royal child proclaimeth,
> Myrrh a future tomb foreshows.

So what do we do about it?

> What can I give him, poor as I am? ...
> if I were a wise man I would do my part;
> yet what I can I give him, give my heart.

All we can offer the Christ-child is obedience to our king; worship to our God. But above all we offer self-sacrificing love to Jesus. Oh, and the answers to the carol quiz? The quotations were from: 'We three kings of orient are'; 'O worship the Lord in the beauty of holiness'; 'Bethlehem, of noblest cities'; and 'In the bleak mid-winter'.

### All-age worship

*Act the story of the wise men as told in Matthew 2.*

### Suggested hymns

*Bethlehem, of noblest cities; In the bleak mid-winter; O worship the Lord in the beauty of holiness; We three kings of orient are.*

## Epiphany
### Second Service   People, Look East!

Ps. 98 In the sight of the nations, 100 All the earth; Baruch 4:36—5:9 Look towards the east; *or* Isa. 60:1–9 Kings shall come; John 2:1–11 Jesus reveals his glory

> *'Look toward the east, O Jerusalem, and see the joy that is coming to you from God.' Baruch 4:36*

## Orientation

Are you one of those people who can never remember the points of the compass? Do you have to mutter to yourself, 'West is on the left, when you're facing north'? Do you find it difficult to get yourself orientated? Ah, there's a clue there. *Oriens* is the Latin for 'rising'. An oriental is someone who comes from the east, where the sun rises. If it's morning, the sun will be in the east and in the evening in the west. There's a sport called 'orienteering': it's the art of making your way quickly across country with the aid of a map and a compass. So long as you've fixed where the east is, you can get oriented.

## The Middle East

In the UK we think of the people of Israel or Palestine as living in what we call 'The Middle East' – they think of us as 'the near west'. For them, 'the near east' is Syria, Iraq, Iran and Saudi Arabia. In Bible times these eastern nations were called Assyria and Persia. When the Jews were exiled to Babylon, that was in the east; when Jerusalem hoped that her exiled people would return, they were told to look east. When Persian astrologers came to worship baby Jesus in Bethlehem, they were called 'wise men from the east'. And when they told Herod 'we have seen his star in the east' – the Orient – that could equally be translated as 'we have seen his star at its rising', or even 'in the ascendant'.

## Baruch

There's a striking phrase in the book of Baruch: 'Look toward the east, O Jerusalem, and see the joy that is coming to you from God.' Here the people of Jerusalem are told to look for the exiles returning from Babylon, in the east. Baruch was the name of the scribe who copied down the words of the prophet Jeremiah in around 600 BC. But the book of Baruch is in what Protestants call the Apocrypha, not the Old Testament, and dates from much later than Jeremiah's time, probably about 150 BC. Yet this reading's appropriate for Epiphany, when we think about the wise men from the east bringing their riches to Baby Jesus.

## Different cultures

There's a real difference between the cultures of people who live in the eastern and western hemispheres. Eastern people, in general, think mystically; western people think materialistically. Oriental philosophy's concerned with states of being, in the West we think in terms of laws and logic. Oriental religions provide for peasants scraping a meagre living year after year from the soil, and think of time going round in an unending circle. Western religion's for pioneers striking out to discover ever new frontiers, and thinks of time as a straight line. Westerners think of Orientals as having no sense of time; Chinese and Indians pity British and North American people going round, as they put it, 'strapped to a wrist watch'! These are rather superficial distinctions for a very complex subject. Judaism and Christianity, although they pioneered the western idea of time as progress, are in other respects basically eastern religions. Or they were, until St Paul and others started translating them into Greek ideas.

## Never the twain shall meet?

So we of the West have much to learn from the people of the East. We've forgotten our traditions of mystical prayer, so that young people look to eastern religions, unaware that mysticism's there already in Christianity. Brooke Fosse Westcott, the author of the greatest commentary on St John's Gospel in the English language, wrote that we must wait for someone from the East, who understands St John's mystical outlook, to write the really definitive commentary on his Gospel. People from the East who've become Christians have brought great riches of music, dance, literary form, art and architecture, and laid them at the feet of the infant Christ. Rudyard Kipling was only partially right when he wrote:

> Oh, East is East, and West is West, and never the twain shall meet,
> till Earth and Sky stand presently at God's great Judgement Seat.

In Christianity, the best of eastern and western cultures have already met.

## People, look east

Eleanor Farjeon wrote a great hymn, looking towards Christmas, which begins, 'People, look East'. We need to keep our eyes fixed to the east, towards Bethlehem, where the love of God came to earth as a babe in a manger. Perhaps we should also look further east, to that great world of oriental culture which the Persian magi brought into the Christian faith. We need to get oriented.

### Suggested hymns

*From the eastern mountains; Hills of the North, rejoice; In Christ there is no east or west; People, look east.*

## The Baptism of Christ 13 January
### *Principal Service* Anointing with the Holy Spirit

Isa. 42:1–9 God gives his Spirit to his Servant; Ps. 29 The voice of the Lord is over the waters; Acts 10:34–43 Anointing by the Holy Spirit; Matt. 3:13–17 The Baptism and anointing of Jesus

> *'God anointed Jesus of Nazareth with the Holy Spirit and with power; … he went about doing good and healing all who were oppressed by the devil, for God was with him.' Acts 10:38*

### Doing good

In a Victorian cartoon in *Punch* magazine, the master of the house is seen instructing the nanny to investigate his little girl's behaviour: 'Go directly – see what she's doing, and tell her she mustn't.' He assumed that, if the child was doing anything at all, it must be something mischievous or bad. Sir A. P. Herbert parodied the killjoy Puritanical attitude when he wrote,

> Let's find out what everyone is doing,
> And then stop everyone from doing it.

But St Peter said that Jesus of Nazareth 'went about doing good'. Mahatma Gandhi, when he first read that, is said to have exclaimed, 'Jesus went about doing good; I regret that I waste so much time just going about.' Later, Gandhi did a great deal of good, partly inspired by the example of Jesus. Although Gandhi never became a

Christian, he greatly admired the founder of Christianity. St Peter said that Jesus did kind things because he was inspired by the Holy Spirit: 'God anointed Jesus of Nazareth with the Holy Spirit and with power; ... he went about doing good and healing all who were oppressed by the devil, for God was with him.'

## Anointed at baptism

God anointed Jesus at his baptism, when the Spirit came down on him in the shape of a dove. When Peter spoke those words, he was talking to Cornelius, the Roman centurion, a non-Jew. So Peter talked about something which everyone, of any faith or none, understands: doing good. Almost everyone wants to do good, but, sadly, very few of us achieve very much in that direction. St Peter says we can do good, but only with the help of God's Holy Spirit.

## Anointing for everyone

We can all be anointed with the Holy Spirit at our baptism. Or, as a consequence of our baptism, if not visibly at the time we are baptized. To St Peter's astonishment, no sooner had he proclaimed the good news of God's love for everybody than Cornelius and his friends began praising God and speaking in tongues. As St Paul later pointed out, not everybody speaks in tongues, but on this occasion it was very obvious to Peter that these non-Jews had received the power of the Holy Spirit. Then, after that, they were baptized: first the Spirit, then the baptism, in their case. For most of us today, baptism happens when we're wee squalling babies; then we're confirmed; and then gradually we realize that God has given us the power to go about, doing good.

## Use what you're given

The power to do good is the proof that you've been anointed with the Holy Spirit. It's offered to everyone. You don't have to assent to certain doctrines. You don't need a particular type of conversion experience. If you were baptized, even as a baby, and took the promises for yourself at confirmation, God will anoint you with the power to do good to others. Peter understood that. When Jesus met him, Peter was a rough fisherman, and could hardly string a coherent sentence together; he was always blurting out the wrong thing. But on the day of Pentecost Peter knew without any doubt that he'd been anointed with the Holy Spirit of power. This wasn't for his own benefit, but for the sake of others. He couldn't just sit there and enjoy having the Holy Spirit, he had to go out and speak for Jesus. Suddenly he found he could speak rather well. The power hadn't come from within him; he'd had no lessons in elocution and rhetoric; it was the power of the Holy Spirit. That same Spirit is given to everyone who's baptized. Only, you've got to use what you're given. Use it or lose it. 'You may not pray like Peter, you may not preach like Paul', but still you can bear witness to what you've seen and heard: that Jesus went about doing good; that millions of others have done the same in his name; and that the power to go about doing good is given to anyone who's willing to use it. Even to me; even to you. Just think what the world would be like if we *all* went about doing good!

### All-age worship

*Draw a Christening service, with the dove of the Holy Spirit hovering over the font.*

### Suggested hymns

*Christ, when for us you were baptized; Go, tell it on the mountain; O thou who camest from above; When Jesus came to Jordan.*

## The Baptism of Christ

*Second Service*    **Deep River** Ps. 46 There is a river, 47 King over the earth; Joshua 3:1–8, 14–17 Crossing the Jordan; Heb. 1:1–12 Superior to angels; *Gospel at Holy Communion*: Luke 3:15–22 Baptism with the Spirit

> '*While all Israel were crossing over on dry ground, the priests who bore the ark of the covenant of the LORD stood on dry ground in the middle of the Jordan, until the entire nation finished crossing over the Jordan.*' *Joshua 3:17*

### Deep River

Deep river, my home is over Jordan,
Deep river, Lord, I want to cross over into campground.

Oh, don't you want to go to that gospel feast,
That promised land where all is peace?
Oh don't you want to go to that promised land,
That land where all is peace?
Deep river, my home is over Jordan,
Deep river, Lord, I want to cross over into campground.

The well-known spiritual expresses the longings of the Africans who had been shipped across the ocean and taken into slavery in the Americas. There is, as always, a double meaning. The longing for freedom combines a yearning to return over the waters of the Atlantic, home to Africa, a continent which, of course, most of them had never seen; together with a longing for heaven, passing through the deep waters of death. Both of these dreams are combined under the imagery of Joshua leading the people of Israel through the waters of the River Jordan into the Promised Land, and they're there too in the Baptism of Jesus in the River Jordan: entry to heaven through the brave bearing of the cross.

## Joshua

Both stories, Joshua and Jesus, remind us of Moses leading the Israelites through the waters of the Red Sea. Whether it's historical or not, the book of Joshua is obviously written to teach the twelve tribes the importance of being loyal to each other and loyal to the one God. God has led them through various dangers and adversities to where they stand, and bound them in a covenant to each other and to the Lord. There can be no national life, and no church life, without the will for unity; there can be no rejoicing without passing bravely through suffering.

## Suffering

The idea of passing through the waters to the promised land of heaven helps us to bear all kinds of suffering in our lives. It would not be true to say the imagery makes sense of suffering, for perhaps we shall never understand with our minds why it is that we have to suffer. But it enables us to bear suffering because we know that we are bound to God in a covenant. Jesus said of the wine at the Last Supper, 'This is my blood of the covenant.' Everyone who's bound to Jesus in sacrament and faith is bound for life to God the Father. God binds himself by a solemn promise to care for us in this life,

51

and lead us to another better life where there is no more pain and all wrongs are righted. In return we bind ourselves at our baptism willingly to obey God, and to co-operate with our neighbours, as the children of Israel did.

## Waters of death

The waters of the River Jordan, then, also symbolize for us the deep waters of death. As the waters of the stream stood 'rising up in a single heap' to allow the Israelites to walk across the riverbed dry-shod, thus the pains of dying, which we so much fear, will abate, so that we can pass through in peace to a better life. Wordsworth, in his *Intimations of Immortality from Recollections of Early Child-hood,* uses the imagery of water for our entry into life and our passage into immortality:

> Hence in a season of calm weather
>     Though inland far we be,
> Our Souls have sight of that immortal sea
>     Which brought us hither,
>     Can in a moment travel thither,
> And see the Children sport upon the shore,
> And hear the mighty waters rolling evermore.

Through the resurrection of Jesus, the waters of death are presented to us as a passage to eternal joy. The verse to the Spiritual *Swing Low, Sweet Chariot* runs:

> I looked over Jordan,
> And what did I see,
> Comin' for to carry me home?
> A band of angels comin' after me,
> Comin' for to carry me home.

Turning, then, from the Afro-American musical tradition to the Welsh, part of the popularity of 'Guide me, O thou great Redeemer' is due to the wonderful tune 'Cwm Rhondda', but partly also to the imagery of the third verse:

> When I tread the verge of Jordan,
> Bid my anxious fears subside;
> Death of death, and hell's destruction,
> Land me safe on Canaan's side ...

What a lot of comforting images come from that one little story in the Book of Joshua!

## Suggested hymns

*Guide me, O thou great Redeemer/Jehovah; Jesu, lover of my soul; Let saints in earth in concert sing; There is a land of pure delight.*

# Third Sunday of Epiphany  20 January

*See also 'Week of Prayer for Christian Unity', p. 298.*  WW 20/1/13

*Principal Service*  **Called to be Saints** Isa. 49:1–7 The Servant a Light to the nations; Ps. 40:1–12 I spoke of your salvation; 1 Cor. 1:1–9 Called to be saints; John 1:29–42 Andrew brings Peter

> *'Paul ... to the church of God that is in Corinth, to those who are sanctified in Christ Jesus, called to be saints.' 1 Corinthians 1:1–2*

## What sort of place?

St Paul wrote at least two letters 'to the church of God which is at Corinth ... together with all those who in every place call on the name of our Lord Jesus Christ'. He was writing primarily to a specific group of people living in a quite unique city; but also to you and me. To understand what the Apostle was saying to us, we need to understand something about the city and the people he was focusing on. Corinth in those days was a large commercial centre and a busy seaport. It lay by a narrow strip of land, an 'isthmus', which divided the Gulf of Corinth, bringing commercial shipping in from Rome, from the Saronic Gulf which connected with the Eastern Mediterranean nations. Time is money, and to save precious days of sailing, the ships would travel down one Gulf, carry the cargo over the isthmus, and put it in other ships which sailed out of the other Gulf. Nowadays you can sail through the isthmus by the Corinth Ship Canal. In St Paul's day, thousands of slaves were needed to lift the cargo out of one boat, push it in a cart over the isthmus, and load it into another boat on the other side. In many cases they actually dragged the whole boat onto a cart, pushed it up one side of the hill and down the other. On this trade Corinth grew rich. The Isthmian Games were second only to the Olympics: the finishing line was in the centre of the city of Corinth. On top of a nearby mountain, which they called Acro-Corinth, they built a Temple to Aphrodite, with a thousand sacred prostitutes. Corinth was famous for its wealth, its vice, and its quarrelsome inhabitants.

## Who were the Christians?

Among this population was a small number of Christians. Paul wrote 'to the church of God which is at Corinth'. Of course there were no church buildings, 'the church' means the people. They met in private houses. They must have thought they were quite insignificant. Paul writes, no, you have been made holy, you are called to be saints, set apart for God's purposes, an essential part of his plan.

## Jews and Gentiles

Now that's surprising, because Paul grew up thinking that God's plan was to choose the Jewish nation, and make an exclusive covenant or contract with them. Paul, like other Pharisees, believed that God would soon send the Messiah, defeat their enemies and bring about the resurrection. The enemies of the Jews were all the non-Jews, whom they called 'Gentiles'. In most places, Jews and Gentiles hated each other. Yet in the tiny Christian community in Corinth, Greek slaves, Jewish traders and Roman officials were trying to worship together. Paul wrote to say, you are part of God's plan.

## This is where we come in

This is where we come in. You, who've been baptized, are the new covenant community. The first covenant was signed by sprinkling the blood of an animal. Jesus is the Lamb of God, who takes away the sin of the world, and at the Last Supper he took wine and said, 'This is my blood of the new covenant.' When you drink the wine in Holy Communion you sign up to a contract with God. Simply to be faithful to Jesus. Then, few as we Christians are, we have a vital part in God's plan to tell the whole world that he loves them.

## How can we do this?

How can we do this? You'd need to be a saint to make an impact on this unbelieving world. Paul writes that this is just we are called to be. The Christians at Corinth weren't perfect. In fact the Apostle rebukes them for sins we've never even thought of, for quarrelsomeness and lack of love. Then he says an unexpected thing. However unfaithful the Christians are, God is faithful. He'll never let us down or fail us or desert us. God will strengthen you to the end. Because you have entered the covenant community by baptism, confessed your failures and signed up again in Holy Communion, God will be faithful to you, and give you the strength to lead a better life from now on.

### All-age worship

*Practise making a church with your fingers: 'Here's the church, and here's the steeple; open the doors and here's all the people.' The people are the church.*

### Suggested hymns

*Hail to the Lord's Anointed; Lord of the Church, we pray for our renewing; O worship the Lord in the beauty of holiness; Restore, O Lord, the honour of your Name.*

## Third Sunday of Epiphany

*Second Service*    **Ezekiel** Ps. 96 Among the nations; Ezek. 2:1—3:4 Eating the scroll; Gal. 1:11–24 Proclaiming God's Son to the Gentiles; *Gospel at Holy Communion*: John 1:43–51 The call of Nathanael

   *'[God] said to me, O mortal, eat what is offered to you; eat this scroll, and go, speak to the house of Israel.' Ezekiel 3:1*

### Mad?

An old American spiritual runs,

> Ezekiel saw the wheel of time –
> Wheel in the middle of a wheel –
> Every spoke was a human kind,
> Way in the middle of a wheel.
> The big wheel runs by faith,

The little wheel runs by the grace of God.
Wheel in a wheel,
Way in the middle of the air.

The black people who wrote that put their own interpretation on one of the most puzzling visions of the prophet Ezekiel, the vision of the flying wheels in chapters 1 and 10. He had many visions: he saw a scroll of parchment which he had to eat; he imagined himself being lifted up by his hair to get an aerial view of the Temple; and, most famously, he saw the valley of dry bones which sprang to life. Some of his visions he acted out dramatically: he shaved his head with a sword; he clapped his hands and stamped his foot; he refused to mourn when he was bereaved. If he'd behaved like that today, he'd be considered mad.

## Wouldn't listen

The people of Ezekiel's day wouldn't listen to him. He brought them a message which was challenging, but full of hope. The only way he knew to express it was through symbols: symbolic pictures and symbolic actions. They never heard the message of hope, because they didn't want to listen to the challenge. Ezekiel lived through the time when the Jews were taken into exile in Babylon. They thought their God had let them down by allowing them to be defeated. They'd left God behind in his Temple in Jerusalem; he belonged to the past. God had lost interest in them, so they lost interest in God. But Ezekiel's vision proclaimed that God's got wheels: God's mobile. He doesn't stay behind in Jerusalem; God comes with them to Babylon. God hasn't lost interest; he still has a plan for them.

## Western Europe

We have a similar situation in Western Europe today. Many people think God belongs to the past, so they've lost interest in religion. There are other things to do on Sunday, like visiting the relations or 'retail therapy', and therefore many of them have stopped going to church. They feel a bit guilty about this, so the newspapers and the television calm their consciences by attacking the Church. After all, if they can show that the Church belongs to the past, is corrupt and irrelevant, then people will feel better about ignoring God, or even imagining that he doesn't exist. A wise person said, 'When I see human beings debating the existence of God it reminds me of a shoal of fish debating the existence of water – it surrounds them and they depend on it, but they can't see it.'

## Internalizing

The decline of religion is a Western European problem: in the USA, Asia and Africa Christianity is growing fast. Maybe, here, things will have to get worse before they get better. Not until we realize that we're no longer a Christian country shall we be ready to receive missionaries from Africa to tell us once again the good news of God's love for us. But it doesn't seem to do any good to address the hard-hearted people around us in clever words and symbolic language. Ezekiel was told to eat the scroll containing God's message for the people. Maybe we, too, have to 'internalize the message'. Not talking about love, but showing it in action. The love of God has to become an integral part of every Christian's life before the world will hear what we say. For God has wheels; God comes with us, suffers with us in our exile, and still has a purpose, even for the godless nations of Western Europe.

## Witnessing is enough

In the end, Ezekiel had to be satisfied with knowing that he'd done what he had to do, and leaving the outcome to God. God said to Ezekiel:

'Go to the exiles, to your people, and speak to them. Say to them, "Thus says the LORD GOD"; whether they hear or refuse to hear.'

And:

'Whether they hear or refuse to hear (for they are a rebellious house), they shall know that there has been a prophet among them.'

There are many prophets today, proclaiming to the people of Western Europe that God still cares about them and has a purpose for them. Maybe we shan't see the results in our lifetime, but if we remain faithful, one day they'll turn back to the God they've forsaken.

## Suggested hymns

*My God, how wonderful thou art; O Lord, the clouds are gathering; Take my life, and let it be; Thou who wast rich beyond all splendour.*

## Fourth Sunday of Epiphany   27 January
*Principal Service*   **God's Publicity Agents**

Isa. 9:1–4 Those who walked in darkness have seen light; Ps. 27:1, 4–12 The Lord is my light and my salvation; 1 Cor. 1:10–18 Unity through baptism; Matt. 4:12–23 Call of the fishermen

> '[Jesus said to the disciples,] "Follow me, and I will make you fish for people" ... So his fame spread throughout all Syria.' Matthew 4:19, 24

### Publicity

The Irish dramatist Brendan Behan once said that 'There's no such thing as bad publicity, except your own obituary.' Of course, he could afford to say that because he made a living of sorts by being notorious. Others, who've suffered from bad publicity, might disagree. But he was emphasizing a truism: anyone who wants to influence a lot of people has to make sure their name is in front of the public at all times. Nowadays every business of any size, every organization and every political party has to pay a staff of publicity agents or public relations officers to make sure that their message is constantly being quoted in the media. They will try to make sure that all the publicity is good publicity; but publicity of some sort there must be. In the days before the television, radio and newspapers, this had to be done by word of mouth. If you wanted to make a difference in the world, you had to get yourself talked about.

### The disciples

Jesus certainly wanted to make a splash. He wanted to change the course of world events; he wanted to make such an impression on people that it would change their whole attitude and behaviour. So he called some fishermen to be his disciples. An unlikely choice, you'd think; they had no technical training or experience in the art of publicity management. But they were effective. They gossiped about Jesus; spoke breathlessly to the people they met about what an impression Jesus had made on them; and the word spread like wildfire. Soon everybody in the land of the Jews and the other countries around the eastern Mediterranean region had heard about Jesus – the whole Roman Province of Syria.

## Fishing for people

Yet the choice of fishermen to be Jesus's publicity agents was a canny one. As William Barclay pointed out in *The Daily Study Bible,* there are six characteristics which are needed in those who would catch fish, which are also required in a disciple who wants to attract people to Jesus:

- First, they must have *patience*, not expecting immediate results.
- Second, they must have *perseverance,* prepared to keep trying to influence others until the results come.
- Third, they must have *courage*. The fisherman may meet a storm; the Christian disciple may meet a storm of opposition.
- Fourth comes the *recognition of the right moment*. The fisherman knows when to cast his net; the Christian must know when to speak and when to keep silent.
- Fifth is the skill to *choose the right bait for each type of fish*. There are as many ways of coming to Christ as there are human beings, and we mustn't expect any sort of 'one-size-fits-all' approach to attract the person we're talking to.
- Sixth and last, fishermen must *keep themselves out of sight*. So must Christians. It's not ourselves that we're trying to draw attention to, but Jesus.

## Every Christian is a publicity agent

I'm no longer talking about those original disciples. They've done their work in attracting us to Jesus; that's why we're here. Now it's our turn. We've been chosen, as they were, but not for our own benefit; not so that we can just sit back and enjoy being a Christian. We're chosen for service, not for privilege. We have a job of work to do. For in the eyes of Jesus, every Christian is a publicity agent. Each one of us, in our own way, must gossip the gospel, and spread the good news about Jesus and his love. We must use, of course, those qualities of tact and timing that the fishermen learnt. But every word you say about what your faith means to you is judged by others, and you can be sure they'll notice if you don't talk about it. If God means anything to you, you can't keep it to yourself, you'll want to share it with others. Not to do so would be indescribably selfish. You become Christ's fisher-folk, not by great gifts of oratory, but by choosing the right moment to speak sincerely about your own experience. Willy-nilly, we're God's publicity agents.

## All-age worship

*Make a poster telling people what fun it is coming to church.*

## Suggested hymns

*And can it be; One shall tell another; O for a thousand tongues to sing; Tell out, my soul.*

# Fourth Sunday of Epiphany
## *Second Service*   Family Values
Ps. 33 All the children of earth; Eccles. 3:1–11 A time for everything; 1 Peter 1:3–12 Family values; *Gospel at Holy Communion*: Luke 4:14–21 To bring good news

> *'All of you, have unity of spirit, sympathy, love for one another, a tender heart, and a humble mind. Do not repay evil for evil or abuse for abuse; but, on the contrary, repay with a blessing.' 1 Peter 3:8–9*

## A baptism sermon

Some people think that what we call the First Letter of Peter was actually the text of a sermon he preached in Rome, soon after he arrived there, possibly at an Easter baptism service. The adult converts, drawn from all races in the multicultural society of the capital city, had decided to become Christians; now he was going to tell them how a Christian should live. As he well knew, Christian life and morality begins in the home. So St Peter wanted to teach the new converts something about Christian family values.

## Family values

Naturally Peter didn't use the term 'family values'. The term was probably invented by the politically right-wing North American fundamentalists. It's been parodied as a belief in the death penalty, military strength, and real-estate growth, and opposition to abortion, adultery, homosexuality, masturbation and long hair! Use of the term will probably make some people think of the television series, *Addams Family Values*. But in its origins it must have been an appeal to the importance of the family as a place where we feel loved and secure, and where children can learn right behaviour.

## Husbands and wives

The ordinary people of Rome were well aware how important the family is, and how fragile. They were afraid that the new religion of Christianity might bring in dangerous ideas which would lead to the break-up of the family. Like Confucius, they knew that stable families lead to a stable nation. So St Peter teaches that wives, just because they have become Christians, must not walk out and leave their husbands. The time was not ripe yet to talk about equality. But Peter does say a very surprising thing. He says that husbands must show consideration for their wives and honour them, because they too are human beings with an eternal future, and you will live together in the next life with those you love and with those you've harmed. In the Roman Empire, to say that husbands had duties towards their wives was quite revolutionary enough to be going on with.

## Mutual love

Then the Apostle goes on to give a clearer definition of the love which lies at the heart of Christian family values. All of you, he says, must 'have unity of spirit, sympathy, love for one another, a tender heart, and a humble mind. Do not repay evil for evil or abuse for abuse; but, on the contrary, repay with a blessing.' This mutual love is obviously the foundation of happy family life: there must be no one-sided grasping selfishness or everything will collapse. But what's learnt in the family is carried out to be practised in the world outside.

## The family of Christ

So St Peter, who has taught the newly baptized that they have become members of the Christian Church, now compares the Church to a family. We are the family of Christ. That same spirit of mutual love, tolerance and self-sacrifice which is needed to build happy families is needed also in our relations with each other in the Church. Then, if the people round us see that this is how Christians treat each other, they may begin to treat their neighbours, other nations, even their enemies with these same Christian family values.

## Revenge

For St Peter finishes by telling us how to treat people who've offended us or harmed us. Yes, even in the family, we get upset sometimes; so what should we do about it? Tit-for-tat, like-for-like, getting-our-own-back? No, says Peter, if someone does something evil to you, there's no place for revenge or retribution. Instead, return the offence with a blessing. Say, 'God bless you, I love you, and I hope you'll soon be feeling less angry.' What a surprise that would be! A policy of no revenge, turning the other cheek, and returning hatred with a blessing. It might actually work. It might produce reconciliation in family rows. It might reform those who have a grudge against society. It might actually enable us to live at peace with other nations in the world. For those are the true Christian family values, and we're gradually realizing that the human race is a global family. Every family has quarrels; the question is, how do you kiss and make up?

### Suggested hymns

*For the beauty of the earth*; *'Forgive our sins as we forgive'*; *In Christ there is no east or west*; *Love came down at Christmas.*

## Sunday next before Lent (or Candlemas; see p. 302)
### 3 February
### *Principal Service*   **A Voice from Heaven**
Ex. 24:12–18 God appears to Moses on Mount Sinai; Ps. 2 You are my son, *or* Ps. 99 A pillar of cloud; 2 Peter 1:16–21 We ourselves heard this voice; Matt. 17:1–9 The transfiguration

*'While [Peter] was still speaking, suddenly a bright cloud over-shadowed them, and from the cloud a voice said, "This is my Son, the Beloved; with him I am well pleased; listen to him!"'* Matthew 17:5

## 'Damn, I missed!'

This week's joke: the vicar and the general were playing golf. The general kept missing the ball, and swore: 'Damn, I missed.' The vicar gave him a warning, 'Mind your language, General, or God will strike you dead.' The general took another swing, missed, swore, and there was a flash of lightning, a loud bang ... and the vicar lay dead on the grass. With that there came a voice from heaven, which said, 'Damn, I missed!'

## The heavenly voice

The heavenly voice is a useful tool in fiction; by imagining a heavenly voice, a writer can help you to imagine God's view of things. Fiction is a necessary part of our culture; a regular diet of novel-reading is good for a Christian. You can learn things from fiction that naked history will never tell you: how you should behave, how you should not behave, human weakness. That's why dramatic stories, in a book, in a film or on the television are so popular. When we assert that the Bible is all true, we forget that some of it may be the truth of fiction. The parables of Jesus are the most obvious examples of stories that aren't literally true. There may be other stories in the Bible which are fictional, but tell you things about human nature – and the nature of God – which mere naked history could never reveal.

## Transfiguration

The Gospel today tells of the transfiguration of Jesus on the mountain-top. Greek people today still use the same word that's in the Gospels: *Metamorphosis*. It means changing form: Jesus appeared in a new way. The story's undoubtedly true, but it can hardly be historical truth in the way that the crucifixion story is. It tells of a vision seen by Peter, James and John: suddenly they saw through into what they recognized was the 'real world'. They saw that Jesus was far more than just human. He was the culmination of the process that began with Moses and Elijah, the law and the prophets. They heard a voice. Then they tried explaining that to other people. Trying to explain a vision is as difficult as explaining a dream: it's full of symbols and you have to guess at their meaning. Is this history or fiction? Whichever it is, it's true because it reveals a deep truth, which is that *the character of Jesus reveals the character of God.*

63

## God quotes from Scripture

The voice of God in the story quotes from Scripture. He quotes 'This is my Son' from the second psalm, where God speaks those words to King David. The name of David means 'the Beloved'. But 'the beloved son' also means 'the first-born son', the most important one, though there will be others. The words 'With him I am well pleased' come from one of the Servant Songs in Isaiah; they warn us that Jesus is the Suffering Servant whom Isaiah predicted. The words 'Listen to him' come from Deuteronomy, and are spoken of the coming prophet. So the vision on the mountain-top reveals that the love of Jesus is the love of God, and that Jesus is going to suffer for those he loves. We have a God who loves us so much that he shares our suffering! But God's too great for our words: we don't know what 'God' means so we can't know what 'Son of God' means. We can only wonder at Jesus, and listen to him, and imitate his love. Thank God for your 'mountain-top' moments of inspiration, but much of the time being a Christian is sheer hard slog. The glory's in the love and the self-sacrifice.

## Applying it to you

Jesus became what we are, so that we might become what he is. A process of metamorphosis is going on in your life. You are turning into a servant of God and a child of God. Listen to the voice from heaven. God's saying of you: '*You* are my beloved daughter – or son – with you I am well pleased.' And those who've died have now been transfigured into people far more wonderful than they were on earth. One day we shall join them, metamorphosed into that state, which we have no words to describe except the language of symbol and imagination.

### All-age worship

*Read, tell or draw the story of 'The Very Hungry Caterpillar', who turned into a butterfly.*

### Suggested hymns

*From glory to glory advancing; God has spoken to his people; Thou, whose almighty word; 'Tis good, Lord, to be here.*

# Sunday next before Lent

*Second Service*   **Elijah** Ps. 84 How lovely is your dwelling;
Ecclus. 48:1–10 Elijah's work; *or* 2 Kings 2:1–12 Elijah ascends to
heaven; Matt. 17:9–23 (*or* 1–23) Jesus speaks of Elijah

> *'[Jesus said,] "Elijah is indeed coming and will restore all things;*
> *but I tell you that Elijah has already come, and they did not recog-*
> *nize him, but they did to him whatever they pleased."' Matthew*
> *17:11–12*

## The greatest of the prophets

The story of Elijah, the greatest of the prophets, in the First and
Second Books of Kings, is full of drama. He kept suddenly appearing, unannounced, and challenging the authority of King Ahab and
his wife Jezebel. He came from the desert region east of the River
Jordan, where the religion of Jehovah had started, and was still
observed with the rigorous moral challenge of the desert nomads.
Jezebel, however, came from Tyre, a Mediterranean port city,
and brought with her the worship of the Phoenician Baal. We are
brought up today to be tolerant of other religions, but the fertility
religions of the Middle East were another matter altogether. The
worship of Baal involved temple prostitutes, orgies, and sometimes
human sacrifice. It taught that the authority of the king and the
royal family were essential to the fertility of the land. Everybody
knew that fertility was essential to survival. If a man's fields didn't
produce crops, nor his sheep produce lambs, nor his wife produce
babies, then sooner or later he'd be dead of starvation. That's what
made these appalling religions so attractive. Even those who'd been
brought up in the religion of Jehovah were tempted to join in the
orgies for Baal, 'to be on the safe side'.

## Challenging corruption

In his great contest with the prophets of Baal on Mount Carmel,
Elijah asserted that Jehovah is the source of light and health, but he
demands complete loyalty. The royal court was corrupt; Jehovah
demands honesty. So Elijah was the scourge of those in authority,
and a teacher of strict morality. He left no writings, but his disciples
told his story. He didn't die a natural death, they said, but ascended
alive into heaven, in a chariot of fire. Soon, a belief grew up that

one day he'd return from heaven, and once again rid society of corruption and dishonesty. In this way he'd prepare the world for the coming of the Messiah. Three and a half centuries later, the prophet Malachi wrote:

> Lo, I will send you the prophet Elijah before the great and terrible day of the LORD comes. He will turn the hearts of parents to their children and the hearts of children to their parents, so that I will not come and strike the land with a curse.

## John the Baptist

It was natural, then, that when John the Baptist appeared out of the desert as suddenly as Elijah had, saying that he was to 'prepare the way of the Lord', many people assumed that John was Elijah, come back from heaven to earth. He denied it, but he did what Elijah had done. John, too, challenged immorality among the people and corruption in their leaders. But instead of triumphantly sweeping the earth clean, John suffered for his boldness, was imprisoned and eventually beheaded. The people had expected a returned Elijah wielding power; John's power was the power of weakness and the witness of suffering; so they turned their backs on him. Jesus said, 'Elijah is indeed coming and will restore all things; but I tell you that Elijah has already come, and they did not recognize him, but they did to him whatever they pleased.'

## Jesus and John

It was the same with Jesus. The people had expected a military Messiah who would drive out the Romans and give power back to Israel. Jesus taught that the only way to power is the way of the cross; the only true authority is what comes from sacrificing yourself for others.

## What is your calling?

The desire for power is natural in all human beings. We wish we had the power to put right what's wrong in our own lives, and in the world around us. But we must be very careful what sort of power we seek, and what means we use to obtain it. If it's the power of King Ahab and Queen Jezebel, obtained by corruption and immorality, then we need an Elijah to rebuke us. What is your calling? Some of us are called to be prophets, to rebuke wickedness in high places. We mustn't be surprised if we suffer for it. If you aren't called to be a prophet, you must at all costs support those who are, in a non-violent campaign to bring our nation back to the road of morality under God.

## Suggested hymns

*On Jordan's bank the Baptist's cry; Take up thy cross, the Saviour said; The great forerunner of the morn; 'Tis good, Lord, to be here.*

---

### LENT

Lent is observed in the forty days leading up to Holy Week. The figure forty is based on the forty days that Jesus fasted in the wilderness after his baptism, before he began his ministry. It is calculated either by omitting the Sundays, when the Lenten discipline is relaxed, or by finishing on Palm Sunday. In the early Church, candidates for baptism at Easter prepared for it by forty days of learning and fasting, and soon the rest of the congregation wanted to join with them. Instead of doing without food, today Christians 'give up something for Lent'. This is a good lesson in self-control, but mustn't lead to self-righteousness. More important is to train oneself to do something good in Lent: to read the Bible, spend more time in prayer, attend extra services or a study group, or do something to help others. Like Advent, Lent is a penitential season, so altar frontals and vestments are purple, or unbleached linen representing sackcloth (except that the Fourth Sunday in Lent may be rose), and 'Glory to God in the highest' is often omitted. It is good to examine our lives, accept responsibility for our sins, and confess them to God. Sermons in Lent are often linked together on a common theme; a series on the Sermon on the Mount or the Ten Commandments can help with self-examination, or sermons on aspects of Christian living can lead to practical action. There are some fine Lenten hymns, but they can be too gloomy unless mixed with others on lighter but relevant themes.

# Ash Wednesday  6 February
## Broken Hearts and Smiling Faces

Joel 2:1–2, 12–17 Rend your hearts; *or* Isa. 58:1–12 Care for the needy; Ps. 51:1–18 Cleanse me from my sin; 2 Cor. 5:20b—6:10 Suffering of an Apostle; Matt. 6:1–6, 16–21 Secret fasting; *or* John 8:1–11 Adultery and forgiveness

> *'Yet even now, says the LORD, return to me with all your heart, with fasting, with weeping, and with mourning; rend your hearts and not your clothing. Return to the LORD, your God, for he is gracious and merciful, slow to anger, and abounding in steadfast love, and relents from punishing.' Joel 2:12–13*

### Broken hearts

*[handwritten: W ~ 26/2/09 story]*

The prophet Joel tells us to rend our hearts and not our clothing. Jesus tells us not to let anyone know that we're fasting. So a preacher chose as the title of his sermon 'Broken hearts and smiling faces'. It stirred up a hornets' nest, though it was a good thing eventually. So many from the congregation came and told the preacher that this was the story of their lives: 'Broken hearts and smiling faces'. He was glad they had the confidence to tell him their hearts were broken, and admired their courage in putting a brave face on it. It's fashionable in counselling and psychotherapy these days to say that people need to 'get in touch with their feelings'. Certainly it's good to know what your feelings are, and it's dangerous to repress them. But it's also dangerous to express them inappropriately. It's good to tell a priest about your feelings, in the confidence of the confessional. Or, if that's too formal for you, to go up to your minister and say, 'May I tell you something in confidence?' Tell the minister that your heart's broken; but it's dangerous to tell everyone else. Keeping a stiff upper lip in public is admirable, provided there's some way of letting go in private: broken hearts and smiling faces.

### Fasting

Lent's a good time to deal with our broken hearts, by disciplining ourselves in private. Originally this took the form of fasting, to express our penitence for sins. Commemorating the forty days that Jesus fasted in the wilderness, Christians used to fast from

Ash Wednesday to Good Friday, not including Sundays. There are different ways of fasting. Unless you went into training first, total abstinence from food for forty days would kill you. Even a few hours without water is dangerous. But some people find it helpful to fast in daylight. More often, Christians like to give up something for Lent – something they find it hard to do without. Why do we do this? I want to suggest four reasons.

## Humility

The first is to practise humility. Jesus says showing off is wrong – you get your reward on earth, if you think that admiration by others is a reward, but none in heaven. But if you can fast in private, without letting anyone know about it, you can train yourself to keep quiet about your virtues all the time.

## Fitness

The second reason is to train your body. Our bodies need to be fit if we're to live a life of service to others. If you need to give up smoking, Lent's a good time to do it, because if you pray about it regularly, God will give you the will-power you need. If you need to lose weight, a Lenten fast's a good way, provided you don't put it all back on again as soon as Easter comes. We don't do these things as a bribe for God; God will give us his blessing because he loves us, there's no need to twist his arm. St Paul writes about training the body as an athlete goes into training. We do it for our own sake, so that we can be helpful to others without always grumbling about our health.

## Repentance

Third, we fast as a sign of repentance. The Bible talks about repenting in dust and ashes. Wearing a cross of ashes on our forehead shows that we accept responsibility for the bad things we've done. But the important thing is the mental attitude: rend your heart, not your garments. It's probably best to wash the ashes off before strangers can see them.

## Prayer

The remaining reason for fasting is to help us to pray. Self-indulgence is a hindrance to prayer – on a full stomach you're more likely to sleep than to pray. Abstaining from material things may help us to concentrate on spiritual matters. But Jesus tells us that prayer should normally be as relaxed and natural as a private conversation with our heavenly Dad. If you need to abstain from indulgence to concentrate your mind, do so. But don't claim any merit for it, and don't tell anyone what you're doing. It's between you and God. Broken hearts and smiling faces.

### Suggested hymns

*Dear Lord and Father of mankind; Forty days and forty nights; Jesu, lover of my soul; Lord, teach us how to pray aright.*

## First Sunday of Lent   10 February
### *Principal Service*   Temptation
Gen. 2:15–17; 3:1–7 The fall; Ps. 32 Happy are those who know God's forgiveness; Rom. 5:12–19 Christ's obedience cancels Adam's disobedience; Matt. 4:1–11 The temptation of Christ

*'Then Jesus was led up by the Spirit into the wilderness to be tempted.' Matthew 4:1*

### Temptation

A class of schoolboys was asked to give the meaning of the word 'temptation'. One boy came up with what he hoped would be a very useful definition: 'Temptation is when I do something wrong, but it's not my fault, because the devil made me do it.' A good try! Some people use the idea of the devil to evade taking personal responsibility for their actions. No, temptation's when I want to do something which I know is wrong. It's very hard to resist, because it comes from desires within us. So there are two parts of us at war with each other: the desire to do wrong, and the conscience which holds us back. These ideas are out of fashion in that part of modem psychology which believes you should never repress your desires, always do what you want. But reflection shows that many of the things we want to do, actually hurt ourselves and hurt other people.

## Just say no

For instance, young people are tempted to experiment with drugs. Often it comes from peer pressure: 'Everybody's doing it,' says the drugs-pusher. It's a very difficult pressure to resist. So the anti-drugs posters teach them: 'Just Say No'. The proprietor of a guest house on one of the Greek islands confided in a visitor that as soon as he had cash, he gambled it away. There's an organization called Gamblers Anonymous, which works on the same successful twelve-step principles as Alcoholics Anonymous. But there wasn't a branch on the island, so all the visitor could advise him was, 'Just say no.' Here's another 'light-bulb joke': how many counsellors does it take to change a light bulb? Only one, but the light bulb must really want to change! So the first step in resisting temptation is to recognize you have a problem, and really want to do something about it.

## Lead us not

Some people puzzle about the phrase in the Lord's Prayer, 'Lead us not into temptation'. Why would God do that? It helps if you insert a comma, 'Lead us, comma, not into temptation'. God wouldn't deliberately cause us to be tempted. God's job is to lead us, if not away from, at least through temptation. Our job is to avoid 'occasions of sin' as far as we can. We can't expect God to do that for us.

## Testing

The word usually translated as temptation has another meaning: it could be translated as 'testing'. The Bible promises us that if we pray for God's grace, he'll give us the strength to come through difficult times. In that sense the temptation of Jesus was a necessary part of his training. He was completely human, 'tempted in all things like as we are'. That means he must sometimes have wanted to do things that are wrong. There's nothing to be ashamed of in being tempted, it's the price of being human – what's wrong is giving in to temptation.

71

## The devil

Jesus must have told his disciples the story of his temptation in the wilderness himself. The devil, he said, tempted him to gain power over the people by wrong means. He was tempted to feed them, force them or fascinate them. Jesus wanted to control the people, for their good, but he knew it wouldn't work except by means of love: they must really want to change. So he rejected the devil's way, and chose the way of the cross. Yet the temptation to choose the easy way must have returned to him daily.

## Training

Lent's useful, because it trains us to resist temptation. If you learn to 'just say no' to little things like chocolates, you'll have more self-confidence, or rather God-confidence: confidence in God's grace to see you through the hard tests. Like the temptations to pride and hatred. Temptation's our own desire to choose any way rather than the way of love.

## Your most difficult temptation

When we're tempted to criticize other people, we should always make sure we do it in such a way as to build up their self-confidence, not knock it down: 'I believe you have it in you to do better than that.' Which temptation do you find it hardest to resist? When you pray 'Lead us not into temptation', maybe what you should be guarding against is the temptation of the acid tongue and the cutting remark. Then Lent's a good time to practise resisting the desire we all have to do that, and learn to make other people feel loved and lovable instead.

## *All-age worship*

*Make a series of 'Just say no' posters about resisting different temptations.*

## *Suggested hymns*

*Father, hear the prayer we offer; Forty days and forty nights; Lead us, heavenly Father, lead us; Through the night of doubt and sorrow.*

# First Sunday of Lent
## *Second Service*   A Lost Coin

Ps. 50:1–15 A sacrifice of thanksgiving; Deut. 6:4–9, 16–25
Keeping God's commandments; Luke 15:1–10 Lost sheep, lost coin

> *'[Jesus said to his disciples,] "What woman having ten silver coins,*
> *if she loses one of them, does not light a lamp, sweep the house,*
> *and search carefully until she finds it? When she has found it, she*
> *calls together her friends and neighbours, saying, 'Rejoice with*
> *me, for I have found the coin that I had lost.'"'* Luke 15:8–9

## Dowry

The composer Beethoven, who was not noted for his sense of humour, wrote a furious *Rondo a capriccio*. Whether the nickname, 'Rage over a lost penny', is by Beethoven or somebody else is uncertain. It's particularly apt, because the music really does convey a sense of a lot of fuss over something unimportant. But in the parable that Jesus told, about a lost coin, the loss was not trivial. When a Jewish woman married, in Jesus's time, she was given a dowry in the form of ten silver coins, which she wore on her forehead on a band. It was very easy for a husband to stand up in the presence of witnesses and divorce his wife, even for burning his lunch, which would leave her penniless except for the ten coins on her forehead. In those days, it's said, only ten per cent of the population lived to over forty-five. So even if she wasn't divorced, she was very likely to become a widow. Then those ten coins became vital to her survival – without them she'd starve. So if one was lost, it was a very serious matter. When Jesus told the parable of the Lost Coin, his audience will have understood at once that the small coin, which might seem quite unimportant to other people, was vitally important to the woman who'd lost it. She'd sweep every corner of her room till she found it. Then she'd run to tell the neighbours, so that they could share her joy because what had been lost was now found.

## Relative importance

Like the parables either side of it, it's a story of the importance to some people of what may seem relatively unimportant to others. The parable itself gets a bit lost, because it's sandwiched between the much better known parables of the Lost Sheep and the Lost

Son, or Prodigal Son as it's usually called. What's the value of one lost sheep, compared with the ninety-nine who were safe? But the shepherd went to look for his sheep because he loved it. What's the importance of a wastrel who comes home begging? Yet the father loved the prodigal because he was his son. The sheep, the son, the coin might seem unimportant to other people. But to those who'd lost them, they were the most important things in the world.

## Sinners and Gentiles

Jesus told all three parables to teach a single lesson: that people who seem unimportant to others are precious to God. The so-called 'sinners' of his time were quite ordinary people. But they couldn't manage to fit in the detailed demands of the Old Testament law with their busy life in the commercial world, so they were outcast by respectable society. Never mind that, said Jesus; they're precious to God, and I've come to save them. The non-Jews, the Gentiles, were regarded as beneath contempt by the law-abiding Pharisees, but Jesus may have been hinting that nobody's irredeemably lost to God. God's too big to be confined within the narrow confines of your respectable prejudices.

## You and me

Unless we're hopelessly conceited and over-confident, we all have moments of self-doubt. Never mind, said Jesus, you're precious to God, and I've come to save you. You're as precious to God as the one lost sheep is to the shepherd, as the one lost coin is to the widow, as the one lost son is to his loving father. Don't despair! I've come to earth to search for you. You may be lost now, but I'll stop at nothing to find you. Jesus is saying that to you, not the person in the pew behind. Well, yes, he's saying it to them too. You're all precious to God. Hold your head up high: you're loved. Jesus loves you.

## Precious to us

If Jesus loves everybody, then we've got to love everybody, if we're to be able to receive his love. Even those whom it's difficult to love. That means you've got to love the black sheep in your family, the unmarried mother who lives down the street, the asylum-seeker. The down-and-out, the bag-lady, the drop-out, the junkie. They're precious to God, as precious as the lost coin was to the poor widow; Jesus came to earth to look for them. If they're that important to Jesus, we who claim to be followers of Jesus can't ignore them. They must be precious to us too.

## Suggested hymns

*All praise to thee, for thou, O king divine; Amazing grace; And can it be that I should gain?; Lord of all, to whom alone.*

## Second Sunday of Lent   17 February

*Principal Service*   **Born Again** Gen. 12:1–4a Abram begins his journey of faith; Ps. 121 I lift my eyes to the hills; Rom. 4:1–5, 13–17 Abraham was justified by faith; John 3:1–17 Born again

> *'Jesus answered [Nicodemus,] "Very truly, I tell you, no one can see the kingdom of God without being born anew."' John 3:3 [The reading in the margin]*

## Symptoms

Listen to these four symptoms:

One:   he's sometimes depressed, and often very tense and stressed.

Two:   when he can't have his own way he becomes angry.

Three: he's afraid of those around him, and imagines they're conspiring against him.

Four:  with those who tell him they love him he's frequently very difficult, as if he were trying to test whether they mean what they say.

## Schizophrenia

As you may have guessed, this isn't a particular man who's being described. But the description exactly fits a lot of men, and women too. The frightening thing is that it can apply to some extent to each one of us: listen while I list the four points again, and ask yourself whether you can recognize yourself in the description? [*Read the first paragraph again.*] Taken to its extreme it's a description of

75

someone with a psychological disorder. Some psychiatrists describe it as schizophrenia; others prefer not to label it. 'Schizophrenia' is an inability to connect your emotions with your reason. We can't judge people with schizophrenia, because we all suffer from these symptoms to some extent, and with acute cases they can't help it. Pity those who hear voices in their heads telling them what to do. A long course of 'listening therapy' can help; most doctors have only time to prescribe medicine to counteract the depression. When patients need the medicine most, they often stop taking it. The only thing that can help such people is to offer them unconditional love.

## Unconditional love

A psychiatrist wrote, after a gruelling session with a person suffering from schizophrenia: 'He tried so hard to provoke me into saying that I didn't love him, that I thought the only thing that would satisfy him would be if he could kill me, and still hear me say that I loved him.' That's just what Jesus did; as the soldiers drove in the nails, he cried out: 'Father, forgive them; for they do not know what they are doing.' He didn't just mean the soldiers; he meant each one of us. We don't realize how our sin hurts Jesus. A parent who loves their child can be incredibly hurt by the child's disobedience, more than the child ever realizes. Jesus shows us on the cross that he loves us no matter what we do to him. It's the answer to all the problems we listed at the beginning. The trouble is that so few of us have ever experienced it, so we're not good at offering it; there's a very profound saying to the effect that, 'As I am loved, so will I love.'

So when someone is depressed or angry, all we can do is point to the cross and say, 'There's one person who loves you.'

## God's love

The Bible says that what we see on the cross is God's love:

'God so loved the world that he gave his only Son, so that everyone who believes in him may not perish but may have eternal life.'

This is the heart of the gospel. God loves us. When we suffer, God suffers. When we disobey, God's loving heart is deeply wounded. Jesus said, 'The Father and I are one.' In some way God was suffering on the cross, and we can be sure that God's not far away when we suffer; God's down here, suffering with us.

## A fresh start

The old Pharisee, Nicodemus, was shocked when Jesus said, 'No one can see the kingdom of God without being born anew.' He knew perfectly well that Jesus didn't mean re-entering the womb; he was creating a diversion to evade the uncomfortable idea of making a fresh start in life, at his age. He thought he deserved God's love, because he was descended from Abraham, and obeyed the law of Moses. Jesus challenged him to begin again, not depending on race, or anything he'd done, but only on God's unconditional love. God's promises to Abraham, as Paul points out, were not because he deserved them, but because he trusted.

## The cure

Perhaps the reason so many people have problems of depression and anger is because they're unwilling to accept God's unconditional love. You see, it means a complete reassessment of the selfish basis on which we live our lives. I pray to God that you, my friends, have accepted God's unconditional love, and are no longer trying to deserve it by your efforts. Then you have been truly born again; but it's not something we can boast or feel superior about, because it is all the result of God's love.

## *All-age worship*

*Write a love-letter from God to the world.*

## *Suggested hymns*

*God forgave my sin in Jesus' name; Jesu, lover of my soul; To God be the glory; When I survey the wondrous cross.*

## Second Sunday of Lent
### Second Service    Confronting the Darkness
Ps. 135 God is good; Num. 21:4–9 The bronze serpent; Luke
14:27–33 Counting the cost

> 'The LORD said to Moses, "Make a poisonous serpent, and set it
> on a pole; and everyone who is bitten shall look at it and live."'
> Numbers 21:8

### The snake

Poisonous snakes are one of the greatest hazards of walking
through the desert. So it's hardly surprising that the Israelites, on
their journey from Egypt after the Exodus, were losing many of
their number to snake bites. There were no anti-venom serums in
those days. So what did Moses do? He made a bronze snake and
put it on a pole. All that those who'd been bitten had to do was to
look at it, then they wouldn't die. I imagine that doesn't mean they
were to give it a casual glance; they had to face up to it, stare at it,
and contemplate it, wouldn't you think? How they were cured we
can't guess, though I'm sure God arranged it. The really amazing
thing was that the healing only happened when they faced up to
what had hurt them. Now the snake was a symbol of evil; we think
of the snake which tempted Eve in the Garden of Eden. The book
of the Revelation to John talks about 'that ancient serpent who is
called the Devil, and Satan'. But it was also a symbol of healing:
this survives today in the medical profession's symbol of the two
entwined snakes, called the *caduceus*. We can apply this story to
our own lives by saying that only if we confront the reality of evil
shall we find healing.

### Confronting evil

What do I mean by confronting evil? Well, there's a tendency today
to gloss over the word 'evil'. In the musical *West Side Story* the
naughty boys of the street gangs call, 'Hey, Officer Krupke', and
then make a series of excuses for their bad behaviour. It's caused by
heredity or environment: 'I'm depraved on account I'm deprived',
or 'I've got a social disease.' It's good to understand and sympathize
with the causes which make people do evil things; but we can't help
them unless we face up to the fact that what they do is evil. The

holocaust was evil; terrorism is evil; racism is evil; violence is evil; and no amount of explanation of the underlying causes helps us to overcome the evil. The world is a dark and evil place: we must look it full in the face, and resist the evil before it can do any more harm.

## The darkness in ourselves

But then, the evil isn't only in other people. We each of us have a dark side to our nature, which we prefer to keep hidden. Temptation only works because part of me, at least, actually wants to do the thing which I find so tempting. Then, when I've done it, I want to lie and cheat, so that I can wriggle out of admitting that what I've done was wrong. We have to confront the darkness in ourselves before we can overcome it.

## Confronting death

Then, the serpent's also a symbol of healing. Somebody who refuses to go to the doctor no matter how sick they are is beyond the reach of medical help. Like the Israelites staring at the bronze snake, we have to recognize the reality of the sickness in our body, and especially its causes, before we can be healed. If it's too late for healing, then we need to face up to the certainty that every one of us will die some day. Robert Browning wrote a verse about facing death bravely eyeball-to-eyeball:

> I was ever a fighter, so one fight more,
> The best and the last!
> I would hate that death bandaged my eyes, and forbore,
> And bade me creep past.
> No! let me taste the whole of it, fare like my peers
> The heroes of old,
> Bear the brunt, in a minute pay glad life's arrears
> Of pain, darkness and cold.

Some patients refuse to talk about death. OK, if that's their way of dealing with it. But many Christians would say, I'd rather know what the probability is of my dying soon, so that I can prepare myself for death, if necessary. A paper delivered to a conference of doctors, about preparing their patients for death, was called 'Confronting the darkness together'. For the Christian, the pain associated with dying is dark and evil, but death itself is bright, because

79

it's the gateway to the kingdom of light. The only way into that kingdom is by confronting the darkness. Look the bronze snake in the eyes; then the serpent of evil can't hurt you.

## Suggested hymns

*Bread of heaven, on thee we feed; I, the Lord of sea and sky; Lead, kindly light, amid th'encircling gloom; Lord, it belongs not to my care.*

## Third Sunday of Lent   24 February
*Principal Service*   **Living Water** Ex. 17:1–7 Water from the rock; Ps. 95 Testing God; Rom. 5:1–11 Reconciliation to God; John 4:5–42 The Samaritan woman at the well

> *'Jesus answered [the Samaritan woman,] "If you knew the gift of God, and who it is that is saying to you, 'Give me a drink,' you would have asked him, and he would have given you living water."' John 4:10*

### Needing water

In the 1958 western film *The Big Country*, the plot centres on the feuding between two families for control of a water source, without which their cattle would die of thirst. The need for water in a dry land is desperate. Stagnant water's no use; it must be fresh, running, healthy and refreshing. Jacob the nomad found a well near Samaria, north of Jerusalem, and it was named after him. Hundreds of years later, people from the area around still came there for water, for their flocks and themselves. Jesus stopped there, and got into conversation with a local woman.

### Exclusion

Women were second-class citizens in those days. The fact that Jesus was seen speaking to a woman, on her own with nobody around to chaperone her, was deeply shocking. That was the first surprising thing. The next was that she was foreign. The Jews believed that the Samaritans were of mixed race, even though they'd lived in the same country with them for generations. Worse still, they had a different religion. Not very different: they accepted the first five books of the Old Testament, but they worshipped in a different temple. Jesus may have been making a joke about this when he told the woman, 'You have had five husbands, and the one you have now is not your husband.' But it was true as well: she was a multiple divorcee, and was now living with a man she wasn't married to. Yet Jesus was talking to her! She was despised because she was a woman; excluded because she was a Samaritan; outcast because her life was disreputable. Yet Jesus treated her politely and with respect. What a man!

## Living water

They were talking about water. Jesus asked the woman for a drink; she was surprised, because Jews don't share things with Samaritans: neither cups nor conversation. He replied that he could give her 'living water'. This was the Hebrew phrase for fresh, running, drinkable water, and at first that's what the woman thought Jesus meant. But he was shifting the emphasis of the words to the sense of 'life-giving water'. But then, God's 'life-giving' too; many of the psalms call him 'the living God'. God's as essential to our survival as fresh water is. It's a cruel fact that hundreds of the world's population die daily because of the lack of fresh drinking water. Isn't it also a tragedy that the beautiful personalities of so many people wither and die because they're without God, the life-giving God?

## Water of the Spirit

To the Samaritan woman, Jesus said that 'God is spirit, and those who worship him must worship in spirit and truth.' True worship is when we stop looking at the surface meaning of life, and go beneath to its spiritual depths. True worship is when we let God's Holy Spirit take control of us, and speak to God in the way that the Holy Spirit within us leads us to. It's good to have a shape and dignity to our worship, but there must also be an element of spontaneity – worship with a smile.

## White for the harvest

The disciples had gone off to find food. When they came back, they offered Jesus bread, and missed the point when he offered them spiritual nourishment. It was still four months until harvest-time, what did he mean when he said the fields were white for the harvest? Then they looked up towards the hill-village where the Samaritan woman had gone to fetch her friends. The road was covered with people, wearing the white clothing of the Middle East, and all eager to meet Jesus. Surely we, too, need to get out of our stick-in-the-mud ways, drink deep of the life-giving Spirit which Jesus offers us, worship God in spirit and truth, and share this bubbling-up spring of joy with others who've not yet found God. We don't have to press it on unwilling recipients; many people hunger and thirst for spiritual joy, but they haven't yet realized that it's Jesus who can give them 'a spring of water gushing up to eternal life'. Have you? If so, are you willing to share it by your friendship with the most unlikely and excluded people, just because they're spiritually needy?

## All-age worship

*Find out as much as you can about people who lack fresh water, and make a poster about charities that help them.*

## Suggested hymns

*God forgave my sin in Jesus' name; Glorious things of thee are spoken; I heard the voice of Jesus say; Peace is flowing like a river.*

# Third Sunday of Lent
*Second Service*   **The Armour of God** Ps. 40 Deliver me; Josh. 1:1–9 Be courageous; Eph. 6:10–20 The armour of God; *Gospel at Holy Communion*: John 2:13–22 Cleansing the Temple

> *'Therefore take up the whole armour of God, so that you may be able to withstand on that evil day, and having done everything, to stand firm.' Ephesians 6:13*

## A defence strategy

There's no end to the arguments about a national defence strategy. What about a strategy to defend the individual Christian against spiritual attacks? I mean, the attacks of temptation to do wrong, to drop away from church attendance, to stop believing, to go along with the crowd. Fortunately, St Paul gives us a Christian spiritual defence strategy in his letter to the Ephesians.

## Paul the prisoner

When he wrote this letter, Paul was a prisoner. He'd endured many physical hardships in his life, from shipwreck to stoning, but with stoic fortitude he'd come through them and kept going. He knew that the attacks on his faith were far more dangerous. Now, nearing the end of a long and arduous ministry, he was probably a prisoner in Rome, waiting for his case to be heard by the Emperor Nero himself. He was under house arrest; some say he was chained to a Roman soldier at all times; others imagine that he was free as long as he didn't leave the house, but there was always a Roman soldier in full Roman armour on guard over him. In either case he had plenty of opportunity to study the armour, and perhaps to discuss with the soldiers what each piece was for and how it kept them safe. So he used the Roman armour to explain to the Christians in far-away Ephesus what their spiritual defence strategy should be.

## God's armour

But there was another thought at the back of the Apostle's mind. In the book of the prophet Isaiah there's an imaginative description of the armour which God wears when he goes into battle against the evil in the world: 'He put on righteousness like a breastplate, and a helmet of salvation on his head; he put on garments of vengeance for clothing, and wrapped himself in fury as in a mantle.' Perhaps it was this which gave Paul the prisoner the idea of identifying each piece of the armour with a spiritual grace. Let's go through them one by one:

*'Stand therefore, and fasten the belt of truth around your waist,'*
If you're to stand firm against temptation, the first thing you must do is make sure you are utterly true in what you think, say or do, so that nobody can throw against you the accusation of being a deceitful liar.

*'and put on the breastplate of righteousness.'*
Righteous behaviour is the other prerequisite. Without it you are always vulnerable to attack from those who whisper, 'Well, you compromised in the past, why not compromise now?'

*'As shoes for your feet put on whatever will make you ready to proclaim the gospel of peace.'*
This seems a puzzling sentence, until you remember that Isaiah wrote of the dust kicked up by the feet of the messenger who brought the news of the returning exiles: 'How beautiful upon the mountains are the feet of the messenger who announces peace, who brings good news, who announces salvation, who says to Zion, "Your God reigns."' We must be ready to proclaim anytime and anywhere that Jesus brings us salvation from the grip of sin and the terror of death.

*'With all of these, take the shield of faith, with which you will be able to quench all the flaming arrows of the evil one.'*
Roman soldiers feared most the ancient equivalent of the Molotov cocktail: an arrow with a rag tied to it, dipped in oil and set alight as it's shot from the bow. The devil, says St Paul, has just as deadly weapons for setting ablaze our plans and hopes; the only defence is a strong faith in God and his power to save – trust him!

*'Take the helmet of salvation'*
The Roman helmet carried a plume, showing which legion the soldier was proud to belong to; we should wear with pride our status as forgiven sinners.

*'and the sword of the Spirit, which is the word of God.'*
St Paul is shown in stained-glass windows holding a sword and an open Bible. God's power is available to us through his Holy Spirit at work within us, and a thorough knowledge of his promises in the Bible. Notice that this is the only offensive weapon in the list: if we're to attack unbelief and wrong belief, it can only be verbally, and must be based on the Bible.

## Prayer

Finally, Paul emphasizes the need for prayer. We shall never defend ourselves against temptation and mockery unless we're in daily contact with our loving heavenly Father.

## *Suggested hymns*

*Be thou my vision, O Lord of my heart; Oft in danger, oft in woe; Soldiers of Christ, arise; Stand up, stand up for Jesus.*

**MOTHERING SUNDAY**

Mothering Sunday is celebrated in the UK on the Fourth Sunday in Lent; Christians in the USA celebrate Mother's Day on the second Sunday in May. 'Mid-Lent Sunday' has for long been a time for a relaxation of the Lenten fast. Domestic servants and apprentices were allowed the day off, and gathered flowers from the hedgerows on their way home to give to their mothers. The readings for the Principal Service are concerned with the family, but instead of a sermon for the Second Service this book provides a special sermon for Mothering Sunday. If there is a special service, young people can make flowers into posies, or draw pictures of flowers on greetings cards. These can be blessed with words such as the following, then given out at the peace, or at the end of the service, for those present to give to their mothers, or put in a suitable place in memory of her, saying, 'Thank you, mother, for all you have done for me.'

O God, bless these flowers, bless us, and bless our mothers. May the flowers remind us how much our mothers have done for us; may they remind our mothers that we love them; and may they remind us all that God cares for us better than any mother ever could. **Amen.**

# Fourth Sunday of Lent  2 March

(For Mothering Sunday, see the Second Service. If the Principal Service readings have been displaced by Mothering Sunday provisions, they may be used for the Second Service.)

## *Principal Service*  **The Light of the World**

1 Sam. 16:1–13 Samuel anoints David as king; Ps. 23 The Lord is my shepherd; Eph. 5:8–14 Live as children of light; John 9:1–41 The light of the world

*'[Jesus said,] "As long as I am in the world, I am the light of the world."' John 9:5*

## Darkness

Sometimes we're really floundering. We don't understand what's happening in our lives. We can't see what we should do to sort out the problems. Everything seems dark. Then suddenly a flash of understanding dawns on us. 'I've got it,' we cry. 'Now I can see!' Our friends ask us, 'Have you seen the light yet?' 'Yes! Now everything's clear to me,' we want to answer. Seeing the light's a metaphor for understanding the truth, and seeing our way clear before us. Jesus said, 'I am the light of the world.'

## Revealing evil

Of course, light's not always welcome. If you're doing something bad, you can hide in the dark. Then if a bright light's shone on you, everyone can see how bad you are. When Jesus healed the man who was born blind, the Pharisees didn't want to believe that Jesus had done it. They refused to see the truth when it was staring them in the face. Jesus teased them that they were the ones who were really blind; in the words of Dean Swift, 'There's none so blind as them that will not see.' The Pharisees weren't wicked people, but they were selfish and self-centred. So they refused to see Jesus's example of unselfishness. They shrank from him, like creepy-crawlies wriggling into a dark corner away from the light of a torch. We think of Holman Hunt's famous painting *The Light of the World*, with Jesus holding a lantern, knocking on the door and asking to be admitted to our lives.

## Revealing truth

Sometimes, when we were children, we used to wake up in the middle of the night convinced that there was a monster in our bedroom. We'd cry out for Mummy, and she brought a nightlight into the room, so that we could see it wasn't a monster at all, only a funny-shaped piece of furniture! Light reveals the truth, and drives away fear. People often get it complexly wrong about what's important in life, and shrink from God's love because of nameless fears. Jesus said, 'I am the light of the world' – he reveals the truth about God, and banishes fear.

## Guidance

Jesus knew that he was fulfilling the prophecy of Isaiah that God's Servant would be 'a light to the nations'. 'The people who dwelt in darkness have seen a great light.' The nations of the world lack guidance; Jesus shone out like a lighthouse in a storm, pointing out our course into the safe harbour. 'Your word is a lantern for my feet,' sang the Psalmist: no more stumbling in the dark, Jesus has shown us the way to go. People still do evil things, but the world is a very different place from what it was before Jesus brought the light of love and forgiveness; some people are moving towards the light, and at least we know what we should be aiming for.

## Gives hope

Light gives us hope. When people are depressed, we say 'Cheer up, there's light at the end of the tunnel.' Mind you, cynics say that the light at the end of the tunnel is the light of a train coming straight at you! Then there's another joke about the sign hanging in an office reading, 'As an economy measure, the light at the end of the tunnel will be turned off until further notice!' But not for the Christian: we have hope, because we have Jesus, the light of the world.

## You are the light

Jesus didn't only say, 'I am the light of the world'; he also turned to his disciples and said, 'You are the light of the world.' It's our job to do what Jesus did. At the end of *The Merchant of Venice*, Portia says,

> How far that little candle throws his beams!
> So shines a good deed in a naughty world.

Her friend objects,

> When the moon shone, we did not see the candle,

so Portia explains,

> So doth the greater glory dim the less.

By our goodness, we have to show up evil for what it is; by our understanding of God's love, we must reveal the truth about the world to those who haven't yet seen the light; by our example, we are to be a beacon guiding others towards heaven; by our joy, Jesus calls us to give hope to the hopeless. Maybe you feel your little light isn't bright enough to have much effect on the world, but if we all reflect the light of Jesus in our lives, the total illumination will be dazzling.

### Suggested hymns

*Amazing grace; And can it be?; Lord, the light of your love is shining (Shine, Jesus, shine); Thou, whose almighty word.*

## Mothering Sunday  2 March
## Jesus was Obedient

(*The Christian Year, Calendar, Lectionary and Collects* gives two Old and New Testament readings, Psalms and Gospels for Mothering Sunday, either of which may be used in any year. *The Canterbury Preacher's Companion* will set the first of each for year B and the second for year C, and offer a new set of readings for Year A.)
Tob. 4:1–5 Honour your mother; *or* Prov. 31:10–31 A good wife; Ps. 113 The joyous mother of children; Eph. 5:21; 6:1–4 Mutual submission of parents and children; Luke 2:41–52 Jesus at twelve

> *'[Jesus] went down with [his parents] and came to Nazareth, and was obedient to them.' Luke 2:51*

### Mothering Sunday

In the middle of the season called Lent, there's a pause, called mid-Lent or Refreshment Sunday. In days gone by, young domestic servants and apprentices, who lived where they worked, were allowed to go home today to visit their parents. On the way they'd pick a bunch of wild flowers from the roadside (not allowed today!). They gave them to their mothers, as a way of saying, 'Thank you for all you've done for me.' This was called 'Going a-mothering', and Mid-Lent Sunday was named 'Mothering Sunday'.

### Jesus at twelve

When Jewish boys were twelve years old they performed a ceremony, now known as bar mitzvah. They recited words from the Bible that they'd learnt by heart. After that they were regarded as adults. Then they went home and worked with their father at his business. Jesus was taken to the Temple in Jerusalem when he was twelve. But he'd learnt his Bible so well that he got into discussions with the Bible experts in the Temple. They were astonished to find that he knew more about God than any of them! The days sped by, and he forgot that his parents were setting off towards their home in Nazareth. A day later when they found that he was missing, they dropped everything to go back for him. His reply was a half-joking reference to his new status as a grown-up: 'Didn't you understand that now I must be joining my father in his business?' Only he didn't mean the carpentry business run by Joseph; he meant God his heavenly Father, whose business is helping people to love God, and to love their neighbours. Now was the time for Jesus to join his heavenly father in his work of spreading the good news of love.

## Jesus's mother Mary

But Jesus loved his parents. The time would come later when, in her love for her son, Mary tried to stop him doing God's work. Then, in his love for his mother, Jesus would have to stand up to her. Meanwhile, he went back with his parents to Nazareth and 'was obedient to them'. Although Jesus wanted to get on with God's business of loving the whole world, he started off by loving his parents and doing what they told him to. He must have been a very remarkable son to love his parents so much. And they must have been very remarkable parents, to earn such love from their child. What a family! If only we were all like that!

## Mutual submission

St Paul, not many years later, was writing a letter to the church in Ephesus. They wanted to know how they should live, so that everybody'd know they were Christians. He wrote to the children in the church, telling them to obey their parents: 'Children, it's your Christian duty to obey your parents.' But then he wrote something which wasn't often heard in his day: 'Parents, don't treat your children in such a way as to make them angry. Instead, bring them up with Christian discipline and instruction.' What's new in the Bible is that it points out that there are duties on both sides. But if you love each other, it doesn't feel like a duty; it's a pleasure. We like to find out what our parents, or our children, want us to do for them. We like to do it for them, as a way of showing how much we love them. 'Mutual submission', St Paul called it. When you realize how much your mother loves you, nothing's too much to do for her, to show how much you love her. When you realize how much Jesus loves you, nothing's too much to do for him, either.

## All-age worship

*Flowers can be blessed, then given out at the end of the service; see the note above.*

## Suggested hymns

*All things bright and beautiful; For the beauty of the earth; Jesus, good above all other; Lord of all hopefulness.*

## Fifth Sunday of Lent  9 March
*Principal Service*  **Dry Bones** Ezek. 37:1–14 The valley of dry bones; Ps. 130 Out of the depths; Rom. 8:6–11 The Spirit gives life; John 11:1–45 The resurrection of Lazarus

> '[The LORD] said to me, "Prophesy to these bones, and say to them: O dry bones, hear the word of the LORD."' Ezekiel 37:4

## Long readings

The readings today are very long, and are a surprising choice for Passion Sunday. They're all about the resurrection, and you would expect to hear them at Easter. Ezekiel has a vision of dead bones brought back to life. St Paul declares that the Holy Spirit gives us new life. The Gospel tells of the resurrection of Jesus. What have they got to do with the way of the cross?

## Dry bones

Mind you, Ezekiel doesn't mean what you think he means. He was writing at a time when the Jews had been defeated, and taken into exile in Babylon. Their kings and leaders had been killed, there was no national life, the nation was dead, and the structure of society was just a skeleton of its former self. Ezekiel asks, 'Can these dry bones live?' He means, 'Can the nation be reinvigorated?' He gets the answer, 'With God's power, yes!' Remember that the same word means 'breath', 'wind' and 'Spirit' in the Bible languages. There's the sound of a wind, God's Spirit is breathed into the dry bones like God breathing into Adam at the creation. Then, as it's described in the American spiritual:

> The foot bone's connected to the ankle bone... [and so on] ...
> Oh hear the word of the Lord!

But this promise is all about national resurrection, and the inner renewal of the community. We need to remember that one aspect of resurrection is something that we don't have to wait for till we die. Resurrection happens here and now in the inner rebirth of individuals and communities, when we allow the Holy Spirit to move among us.

## The Spirit gives life

St Paul declares that here and now, the Spirit of God sets up home in our hearts. Some people say that the eighth chapter of his letter to the Romans is 'The Gospel according to Paul': 'If Christ is in you, though the body is dead because of sin, the Spirit is life because of righteousness.' 'Righteousness' here doesn't mean good behaviour. It means that in spite of our bad behaviour, God's declared us 'not guilty'. You must never write off any person or nation as hopeless; God can give them new life and new hope, through his Holy Spirit.

## Resuscitation

Some Jews took the promise of resurrection literally. By Jesus's time, the Pharisees – but not the Sadducees – believed that, at the end of the age, the Messiah would come. He would drive out the Roman army, and there would be a resuscitation of dead Jews to live again in the promised land. St Paul was a Pharisee, and originally that's what he believed. But gradually he changed his ideas, and developed a more spiritual understanding of life after death: 'Flesh and blood cannot inherit the kingdom of God,' he wrote to the Corinthians.

## Lazarus

Yet Jesus himself had already contradicted the Pharisee's notions. Lazarus and his family were probably Pharisees. When Jesus said to Martha, 'Your brother will rise again,' she answered, 'I know that he'll rise again at the resurrection on the last day' – but what help's that to me now? Jesus answered, 'I am the Resurrection, and the Life.' You don't have to wait, you can experience new life now. To convince them, he raised Lazarus from the dead, with a physical body. When Jesus himself rose from the dead, his resurrection body was partly physical, partly spiritual. So far as we know, nobody else has returned physically to earth. Why not? Because Jesus has something better in store, those were demonstrations. He wanted us to understand that we can begin to experience heaven here and now, if we have faith.

## Passiontide

But these readings come in Passiontide, when we're thinking about the death of Jesus, to remind us that death leads to new life. 'Lent' is an Old English word meaning 'spring'. Spring's full of signs of new life and growth after winter's death: the young animals and birds, the fresh green growth of the plants. I've saved my joke until the end of the sermon today. A preacher told his congregation, 'Every blade of grass is a sermon.' Next day a parishioner saw him mowing his lawn. 'That's right, Preacher,' the man said, 'cut your sermons short!' I think I'd better end there!

## All-age worship

*Gather signs of new life at springtime.*

## Suggested hymns

*Breathe on me, breath of God; Sometimes a light surprises; Spirit of holiness; Wind, wind, blow on me.*

# Fifth Sunday of Lent
## *Second Service*   Joy Comes in the Morning
Ps. 30 Mourning turned to dancing; Lam. 3:19–33 New every
morning; Matt. 20:17–34 Jesus predicts death and resurrection

*'Heaviness may endure for a night, but joy comes in the morning.'*
*Psalm 30:5* (Common Worship)

### Darkest before dawn

Those who've been recently bereaved often feel as though a great
darkness has closed over them. It may seem as though their grief
will never go away. Yet the proverb has it that the darkest time is
just before dawn. The poet William Cowper wrote,

> The darkest day
> (Live till tomorrow) will have passed away.

Of course you never forget the one who's died; you wouldn't want
to. The pain of loss continues, but when you believe that we shall
meet again the other side of death, we learn to live with the temporary separation. We may even be able to accept that those who've
died would want us to pick up the pieces and rebuild our lives for
their sake. They'd want us to be happy – even joyful, so far as we
can. As the Psalmist wrote:

> Heaviness may endure for a night,
> but joy comes in the morning.

### Enduring loss

This applies to all experiences of sadness and loss, great or small.
We have to learn to bear them bravely and patiently, to accept
them as a hard lesson we must learn. If we do, we discover again
that night always comes to an end sometime. 'Rosy-fingered dawn'
is bound to come eventually. God promises that if we pray, he'll
either heal our pain, or at least give us strength to bear it.

### Preparing the disciples

Jesus tried to prepare his disciples for the inevitable grief that was
coming to them at his crucifixion.

While Jesus was going up to Jerusalem, he took the twelve

disciples aside by themselves, and said to them on the way, 'See, we are going up to Jerusalem, and the Son of Man will be handed over to the chief priests and scribes, and they will condemn him to death; then they will hand him over to the Gentiles to be mocked and flogged and crucified; and on the third day he will be raised.'

He promised them resurrection. How could they believe it? Death seemed to them, as it does to us, like a disaster. But they'd never be able to bear their grief unless he taught them to believe that the night doesn't last for ever. Death is followed by new life.

## What is death?

That, surely, gives the dread face of death a different complexion. If death is the way to eternal life, it becomes a sign of joy, not a cause of endless grief. The death of Jesus opened for us the gate of heaven. Our own death is the way to resurrection. The experience of suffering bravely borne is the school in which we learn to trust in God's love. The death of those we love is a temporary separation, leading to togetherness in eternity. The psalm opens:

> I will exalt you, O LORD, because you have raised me up ...
> You brought me up, O LORD, from the dead;
> You restored me to life from among those who go down to
>     the Pit.

What, then, is death? Nothing but the gateway to life.

## The only entrance

Imagine, then, a royal palace, and you're standing outside, hungry in the freezing night. Inside, you know, there's light and warmth, food and drink and jollity. You have a good look round and find there's only one entrance. It looks pretty forbidding: oak doors, iron bars. But it's the only way in. Your heart's in your mouth, but wouldn't you dare it none the less? If it's the only entrance, you'd brave the dark passageway for the sake of the light at the end of it. Heaven's the name of that palace. There's only one entrance, and that's the gate of death. The other side of the gateway, Jesus is waiting to welcome us. Until he's ready for us, we'll wait patiently in the dark, and put up with any pain he calls us to bear for his sake, so that he'll be able to say, 'Well done, good and faithful servant, come in and share your master's joy!'

## Learning the lesson

During Holy Week and Easter, let's learn this one lesson: heaven's like a palace with a single doorway. The only entrance to heaven is through the gate of death. We must bear our suffering and grief bravely, for the sake of the joy that's coming to us hereafter. The psalm concludes:

> You have turned my mourning into dancing;
> You have put off my sackcloth and girded me with gladness;
> Therefore my heart sings to you without ceasing;
> O Lord my God, I will give you thanks for ever.

To which we can only add, 'Amen'.

## Suggested hymns

*Jesus put this song into our hearts; O love that wilt not let me go; The Church's one foundation; Through the night of doubt and sorrow.*

---

**HOLY WEEK**

The final week of Jesus' life on earth is celebrated from Palm Sunday to Easter Eve. Long readings of the Passion Narrative are set at all the services. Palm Sunday is often marked with a procession of palms, Maundy Thursday by the washing of feet, Good Friday by the veneration of the cross, and Easter Eve by a vigil with the lighting of the new fire. An informal Passover supper to commemorate the Last Supper can be held on any day but is especially suitable for Maundy Thursday. A series of sermons on the Passion, or on the seven words of Christ from the cross, can be preached throughout Holy Week, or to mark the Three Hours on Good Friday. Most of the sermons provided in this book for specific days in Holy Week could be used on other days instead.

---

## Palm Sunday   16 March

*Principal Service*   **A King on a Donkey** Isa. 50:4–9a God's suffering servant; Ps. 31:9–16 Assurance in suffering; Phil. 2:5–11 Jesus' obedience unto death; Matt. 26:14—27:66 The Last Supper to the burial; *or* Matt. 27:11–54 The trial to the death on the cross

> *'Tell the daughter of Zion, Look, your king is coming to you, humble, and mounted on a donkey, and on a colt, the foal of a donkey.' Matthew 21:5*

### A king on a donkey

A king on a donkey? Ridiculous! But Jesus was preparing his disciples to discover even more paradoxical things. During the Oberammergau Passion play, half the village came on stage waving palm branches. The audience was so close that everyone felt they were part of the crowd – the same crowd which later shouted 'crucify!'

### Antisemitism

So everyone was forced to ask themselves, if I'd actually been among the crowd in Jerusalem, would I have done anything different from what they did? Could I have resisted the crowd hysteria? That raises another question: who's to blame for the death of Jesus? This was a burning issue in Oberammergau, because the script of the play has often been accused of antisemitism. None of those taking part in the play today were adults at the time of Hitler, but they have to admit that their forebears did cruel things to the Jews. So they've changed the script in many places to show that Jesus was a Jew, and that not all the Jewish leaders were opposed to Jesus. The crucifixion was the result of a dispute between Jews; it was not a case of Jews versus Christians. But it's almost impossible to reassure Jews that most Christians no longer blame them for the death of Jesus.

### Blood

The script now misses out the words said by the crowd in Matthew's Gospel: 'His blood be on us and on our children.' Christians in the past have interpreted those words as an acceptance of Jewish guilt. But Matthew was a Jew. For Pontius Pilate, blood was guilt, and he tried in vain to wash his hands clean. For Jews, blood is a symbol of redemption, as when the blood of a sacrificial animal was sprinkled on the guilty. If the blood of Jesus brings salvation, then every Christian would want to pray that his blood may be on all of us.

## Universal guilt

The Bible teaches universal guilt, and universal forgiveness. If I'd been in the crowd that bayed for Jesus's blood, I should have done the same as they did. I share the guilt of Christ's death, and of many other wicked things the human race has done. If I want to share the blessings of being human, I must share the responsibility it brings.

## Scapegoats

The trouble is, we always want to find a scapegoat to blame for what goes wrong. When things go wrong at home, we blame our spouse or our parents. When things go wrong at work, we blame the boss or the odd-one-out. When things go wrong in the nation, we blame the government, forgetting that we elected them. When things go wrong in the world, politicians blame our enemies. The media spend most of their time looking for scapegoats; that's why people read and view the news so avidly. It saves us from having to take responsibility ourselves. But if we evade our own responsibility, we also miss out on the forgiveness that follows repentance. People don't like goodness, it shows up their own wickedness. So they make the good person the scapegoat. 'Twas ever thus. What was different about Jesus, was that the scapegoat is God – a 'scape-God'. St Paul writes about a God who was willing to empty himself, take the form of a suffering servant, and ride triumphantly to his death on a stupid donkey.

## Why?

If God is love, why does he allow suffering? Perhaps, because he loves us enough to leave us free to disobey him. God knows we always look for a scapegoat to blame, but God's willing to be the scapegoat himself. It's all too easy to cause others to suffer, and then blame God for allowing it!

## Paradox

The deaths of many innocent people have been reported in the past year. Who's to blame? All of us. All of us, because we're part of the human race, and we didn't speak out against the injustices which caused these tragedies. But as soon as you confess your share in the guilt, you're forgiven. The real paradox of Holy Week isn't just a Prince of Peace on a donkey. It's a God who empties himself of his power, comes down and shares our suffering, and allows himself to be made a scapegoat. Then God takes away our sin, forgives us for what we've done to him, and invites us to share eternal life with him. My God!

## All-age worship

*Process together round the church during the final hymn holding palm crosses. Bless them saying:*

The Lord be with you.
**And also with you.**

Let us give thanks to the Lord our God.
**It is right to give thanks and praise.**

It is right to praise you, Almighty God, for the acts of love by which you have redeemed us through your Son Jesus Christ our Lord. On this day he entered the holy city of Jerusalem in triumph, and was proclaimed as King of kings by those who spread their garments and branches of palm along his way. Let these branches be for us signs of his victory, and grant that we who bear them in his name may ever hail him as our King, and follow him in the way that leads to eternal life; who lives and reigns in glory with you and the Holy Spirit, now and for ever. **Amen.**

Blessed is he who comes in the name of the Lord.
**Hosanna in the highest.**

Let us go forth in peace.
**In the name of Christ. Amen.**
(*United States Book of Common Prayer 1979*)

## Suggested hymns

*All glory, laud and honour; My song is love unknown; Ride on, ride on in majesty; There is a green hill far away.*

# Palm Sunday

*Second Service* **Hosanna**

Ps. 80 Come to save us; Isa. 5:1–7 The song of the vineyard;
Matt. 21:33–46 Parable of the wicked tenants

*'Stir up your might, and come to save us!' Psalm 80:2*

## Welcome

If ever a Jew should call on you and you want to make him or her
feel at home, you should learn two Hebrew words which mean
'welcome'. They're pronounced *Ba-rook ha-bah*. In fact, since we
all became honorary Jews when we were baptized into Christ, perhaps we should say welcome to our fellow Christians in Hebrew:
*Ba-rook ha-bah*. It means, literally, 'Blessed is the one who comes.'
Now where have we heard those words before?

## Triumphal entry

Of course! It's what the crowd shouted out when they welcomed
Jesus to Jerusalem. Jesus was riding on a donkey, and

> A very large crowd spread their cloaks on the road, and others
> cut branches from the trees and spread them on the road. The
> crowds that went ahead of him and that followed were shouting,
> 'Hosanna to the Son of David! Blessed is the one who comes in
> the name of the Lord! Hosanna in the highest heaven!'

We usually call this the 'triumphal entry'. A schoolboy was once
asked what Jesus was riding on at the triumphal entry – this is
a true story. He didn't know the answer, so he made an inspired
guess: 'Perhaps he was riding on ... a Triumph motor-bike?'

## Psalms

The crowd at the triumphal entry were using the usual words for
welcome. But they made two important additions. The first was a
quotation from Psalm 118:

> Blessed is the one who comes in the name of the LORD.
> We bless you from the house of the LORD.

This was a psalm which was sung as pilgrims arrived at the Temple in Jerusalem. They stood outside the gates of the Temple and asked for admission. The priests from inside gave them a welcome. Jesus, like pilgrims before him, was coming 'in the name of the Lord' – to do the Lord's business – and as the Lord's representative. The people of Jerusalem welcomed him – on Palm Sunday. A few days later it was a different story.

## Hosanna

Wrapped around this welcome were two sentences beginning *Hosan-na*. This is another Hebrew word, which you know already. It means 'Save us now', and it too is in Psalm 118:

> Come, O LORD, and save us, we pray,
> Come, LORD, send us now prosperity.

There are similar words also in Psalm 80 which is set for this service:

> Stir up your might, and come to save us!

The Jews in the Temple wanted to be saved from their enemies. When we use the word Hosanna, we want God to save us from the guilt and power of sin and the fear of death. And we don't want God to save us at any old time in the future: 'Save us *now*,' we cry: Hosan-*na*.

## Benedictus

These, then, are the words with which the crowd welcomed Jesus on his triumphal entry to Jerusalem on the first Palm Sunday: 'Save us now, Son of David; welcome in God's name; sing "save us now" in the heights of heaven.' Many Christians use them every time they have a Holy Communion service, or Eucharist, or Mass, or Lord's Supper. They are known as the *Hosanna* and the *Benedictus*, that being the Latin word for 'Blessed'. Bach, Haydn and Mozart are among the many great composers who have set beautiful and haunting music to those words. When we say or sing them in the context of a service of worship, we're welcoming Jesus to be present with us as we pray. Especially in the sacrament; we may not be able to explain it in words, but we feel in our hearts that Jesus is close to us as we eat the bread and drink the wine, and we want to welcome him. 'Blessed is he who comes in the name of the Lord,' we cry; 'Save us now.' We ask Jesus to make a triumphal entry into our hearts and lay claim to them for himself.

## Holy Week

Palm Sunday, then, is the ideal preparation for Holy Week. We welcome Jesus as our king, the Son of David. We welcome him into our church and into our hearts, and ask him to rule there. We remember that our worship is only one tiny strand in the worship which is going on all the time throughout the earth and in the highest heavens. We promise to stay beside him as he endures all the grief and suffering of Holy Week, for we know that it's *now* that he's going to save us. Then we share with him in the joy of the resurrection, when he gives us eternal life. *Ba-rook ha-bah*, blessed is he who comes – welcome, Jesus! 'Hosanna' – save us now!

### Suggested hymns

*Give me joy in my heart, keep me praising; Hosanna, hosanna, hosanna in the highest (Tuttle); Ride on, ride on in majesty; You are the King of glory.*

## First Three Days in Holy Week    17–19 March
## A Grain of Wheat

*(Following are the Tuesday readings but this sermon may be used on any day this week)*
Isa. 49.1–7 The servant a light to the nations; Ps. 71.1–14 Rescue me from the wicked; 1 Cor. 1.18–31 The cross, the power and wisdom of God; John 12.20–36 Death of a seed, resurrection of a great harvest

> *'Jesus answered them, "The hour has come for the Son of Man to be glorified. Very truly, I tell you, unless a grain of wheat falls into the earth and dies, it remains just a single grain; but if it dies, it bears much fruit."' John 12:23–24*

### 'Better the devil you know'

'Better the devil you know than the devil you don't,' we say. And so we're frightened of change. Sometimes the future opens a door to us, but because we're not quite sure what's on the other side, we're reluctant to step through it. Yes, all right, sometimes the future *is* worse than the present, but often it's better, much better. Many people believe in Murphy's Law, as they call it, which says 'If things *can* go wrong, they will'! But we believe in God's law. If God calls us into an uncertain future, we can be sure that he'll be with us, and will bring everything out all right at the end. Only, you have to let go of the present if you're going to be able to move forward. That cosy, familiar, present tense, where you're familiar with your surroundings and only have to follow well-worn paths and habitual patterns – it's got to go, if you're to have any future. For individuals as well as nations, clinging to a glorious past can prevent you taking the steps in the present which are necessary to ensure glorious years to come. The present holds the seeds of the future. And the seed must die, in order for it to rise again.

## The seed must die

Jesus pictures a farmer with a supply of seed-corn, which has to be planted to grow into next year's harvest. They're very beautiful seeds, and they look very splendid in the farmer's basket. But they mustn't stay there. The seed must be planted. But once out of the cosy security of the farmer's basket and into the moist earth, they soon stop being seeds. The hard outer layers which have held and protected the germ at the centre begin to disintegrate. They turn into something else, something which is very necessary to nourish the growing germ. Of course the seed doesn't literally 'die', it's very much alive, we mustn't take the parable too literally. But change has begun, and once change has started, it's unstoppable.

## The death of Jesus

Jesus told this mini-parable after some Greeks had been brought to see him by Philip and Andrew. Jesus said, 'The hour has come for the Son of Man to be glorified.' It had become clear that his followers wouldn't only be Jews in future. What was later called Christianity wouldn't be a small Jewish sect but a worldwide religion. But for this to happen, the seed must die. Jesus himself couldn't go on as he had been. Now he must be 'lifted up' on the cross, so that he could draw the whole world to himself. He could no longer just teach a small group of disciples; now he had to go public, and for that to happen would certainly involve crucifixion. But crucifixion, he knew, would be followed by resurrection. When Jesus rose up from the tomb, it was like a seed which has been buried in the ground, and apparently dead, suddenly bursting forth with shoots of new life. There'll be a great harvest of new believers; today there are two billion, in every nation on earth. But there can be no harvest without the 'death' of the seed. Jesus knew that he'd be crucified, but he knew it was worth it, because only so could he save the world.

## Dying to self

What was wrong with the seed which hadn't yet been planted was that it remained just a single grain, all wrapped up in itself and with no thought of anything outside its cosy environment. It's obvious that Jesus isn't talking about seeds at this point or even about himself any more, but about you and me. We must be willing to sacrifice our time, our money, our cosy comfortable never-changing rut, so that we can devote everything to serving God and other people. Just as Jesus did. George Macdonald, the novelist, prayed:

> Lord, teach us to understand that your Son died to save us, not from suffering, but from ourselves; not from injustice, far less from justice, but from being unjust. He died that we might live – but live as he lives, by dying as he died, who died to himself.

### Suggested hymns

*Broken for me, broken for you; Lift high the cross, the love of Christ proclaim; O Jesus, I have promised; Take up your cross, the Saviour said.*

## Maundy Thursday  20 March
## Passover

Ex. 12:1–4 [5–10] 11–14 The Passover; Ps. 116:1, 10–17 The cup of salvation; 1 Cor. 11:23–26 The Last Supper; John 13:1–17, 31b–35 Foot-washing

*'This day shall be a day of remembrance for you. You shall celebrate it as a festival to the Lord; throughout your generations you shall observe it as a perpetual ordinance.' Exodus 12:14*

## The first Passover

Many tribes celebrate annual ceremonies, commemorating events in the past which have made them what they are. Keeping these events green in the memory gives the people their identity. For the people of Israel, it was the Exodus of their ancestors from Egypt which they celebrated in the annual ceremonies of the Passover. Not only had it changed a disheartened scattering of slaves into a people under God; it had taught them that the Lord is a God who saves. They had no time to allow the bread to rise, so they ate unleavened bread. They wore their outdoor clothes, ready to travel. Each family sacrificed a lamb to the God who saves, and ate it. They put the blood of the lamb in a T-shaped cross on the doorposts of their house, so that the angel of death who had been sent to kill the firstborn would recognize that this was an Israelite dwelling, and pass over the house without harming those within. Then, next morning, they crossed the Red Sea and began their journey to the promised land. God told Moses that this ceremony was to be repeated every year, in remembrance of how God had saved them.

## Seder meal

To this day, observant Jews celebrate the Passover every year on the first full moon after the spring equinox. The traditional order of the ceremony's called the Seder, from the Hebrew word for 'order'. Four cups of wine are passed round so that all can drink from them. The first is called the cup of freedom, remembering that God had set the Israelites free from slavery. This is followed by the washing of the feet of the guests. Then they eat green herbs, symbolizing the new life that comes at springtime; but dipped in salt water, reminding them that new life can't come without tears. Three pieces of unleavened bread, 'the bread of affliction', today called 'matzos', are produced; the middle one's broken and half's wrapped in a napkin and hidden. A child asks the head of the family why this night's different from all other nights. He answers, explaining the symbolism of Passover. Bitter herbs, usually horseradish, are eaten to remind them of the bitterness of slavery, with a sweet paste called 'haroset', symbolizing the clay from which their ancestors were told to make 'bricks without straw'. The second cup's drunk, 'the Cup of the Plagues', and then the Passover meal's eaten. After supper, the hidden bread's found and eaten; the Cup of Blessing's drunk; and the fourth cup, called the Cup of Elijah. The door's always left open to welcome any stranger who calls; if Elijah has come when nobody was looking, they'll know because he'll have drunk from this cup. That means that the Messiah will come this year. Finally, a group of psalms is sung, called the 'Hallel', from the Hebrew word for 'praise'.

## The Last Supper

The four Gospels and St Paul all tell us that the Last Supper which Jesus ate with his disciples was a Passover meal, though he may possibly have anticipated the usual day by twenty-four hours. Jesus washed his disciples' feet, the task of the lowliest slave, to teach them humility. During the supper he explained that his life was being offered as a sacrifice, like that of the Passover lamb. He broke the hidden piece of bread, and startled them by saying, 'This is my body, broken for you; do this in remembrance of me.' After supper, as he passed round the Cup of Blessing he said, 'This is my blood of the covenant.' 'After they had sung a hymn', he led them out to Gethsemane. He took the traditional Passover ceremonies and imbued them with new meaning.

## The Eucharist

So every time we celebrate the Holy Communion, Eucharist or Mass, we're obeying God's command to celebrate the Passover in remembrance of a God who saves; and we're also obeying Jesus's command to do this in remembrance of him. We thank God for our freedom from slavery to the guilt and power of sin, and the fear of death, brought to us by the sacrifice of Jesus, the Lamb of God who takes away the sin of the world. New life is brought to us by the bread and wine, remembering that resurrection comes after the tears of suffering. Understanding the historic symbolism underlying all our actions, and thanksgiving for what God has done to save us, helps to form us into the people of God.

### Suggested hymns

*An Upper Room did our Lord prepare; Broken for me, broken for you; This is the night, dear friends, the night for weeping; Now, my tongue, the mystery telling.*

## Good Friday  21 March
### Seven Words

Isa. 52:13—53:12 The suffering servant; Ps. 22 Why have you forsaken me?; Heb. 10:16–25; *or* Heb. 4:14–16 Jesus the priest; John 18:1—19:42 The blood of the covenant

*'It is finished.' John 19.30*

## Famous last words

There's a widespread belief that the last words somebody says before they die sum up the total experience of their life. It isn't always true, but when it is, they are often quoted as 'famous last words'. As Shakespeare said, 'The tongues of dying men enforce attention like deep harmony.' According to the four Gospels, Jesus spoke several times when he was being crucified. Considering the pain involved, it's amazing that he was able to speak at all. If you add all the four Gospels together, we have seven famous last words of Jesus on the record; there may well have been more. They are called the 'Seven Words from the Cross'; and each one tells us something about how we should live, and hope to die.

The first was spoken, according to Luke, while the soldiers were nailing Jesus to the cross. 'Then Jesus said, "Father, forgive them; for they do not know what they are doing."' It was not only the soldiers, each one of us often does things which hurt Jesus. But he forgives us; bringing forgiveness was the purpose of his life and death.

To the penitent thief, Jesus said, 'Truly I tell you, today you will be with me in Paradise.' Here was forgiveness at its most demanding; Jesus forgives someone who may well have been a murderer, but who, at the last minute, showed a flash of faith. Jesus encouraged him with the promise of eternal life.

According to John, when Jesus saw his mother and the disciple whom he loved standing beside her, he said to his mother, 'Woman, here is your son.' Then he said to the disciple, 'Here is your mother.' 'And from that hour the disciple took her into his own home.' At times of intense pain, most of us are only capable of thinking of ourselves; Jesus was unselfishly caring for his mother and his best friend.

St Mark writes, 'At three o'clock Jesus cried out with a loud voice, *"Eloi, Eloi, lema sabachthani?"* which means, "My God, my

God, why have you forsaken me?" ' Matthew has the same thing in slightly different words. Jesus entered fully into our human experience, even to the extent of feeling as though God had deserted him. Yet the words were a quotation from Psalm 22, which ends on a joyful note. It's as though he had to work bravely through his despair in order to return to hope.

'After this,' writes St John, 'when Jesus knew that all was now finished, he said (in order to fulfil the Scripture), "I am thirsty." ' Psalm 69 includes the words, 'When I was thirsty, they gave me vinegar to drink.' Jesus, who was fully human, was dehydrated after three hours in the heat of the noonday sun. But he was also fully divine, and he thirsted to obey the will of his Father.

'When Jesus had received the wine, he said, "It is finished." ' This is a cry of triumph; Jesus seized victory from the jaws of defeat. 'Love's redeeming work is done.'

'Then Jesus,' concludes St Luke, 'crying with a loud voice, said, "Father, into your hands I commend my spirit." Having said this, he breathed his last.' This is a quotation from Psalm 31, and may well have been the prayer of faith which Jesus, in common with many other people, used to say just before he went to sleep each night.

## Seven words, seven virtues

Seven famous last words from the cross. Each of them reveals a particular virtue which we can imitate. The first, his forgiveness of sinners. Then his encouragement of the hopeless. Third his compassion for others, his mother and his friend. Fourth, his courage; and fifth, his obedience to his Father. 'It is finished' reveals his ability to recognize that submission is often the greatest triumph. Seventh and last is his trust in his Father. Could you live like that? Could you die like that? Of course not. But we can try.

## *All-age worship*

*Make a poster advising young people how to deal with bullies.*

## *Suggested hymns*

*Ah, holy Jesu, how hast thou offended?; Love's redeeming work is done; O come and mourn with me a while; Were you there when they crucified my Lord?*

## EASTER

The forty days of Easter, up to Ascension Day, are a season of joyful celebration. We celebrate the Resurrection of Jesus from the dead, and are filled with hope as inheritors of eternal life. The altar frontals and vestments are white, or gold on Easter Day, and the wonderful Easter hymns resound with alleluias. If the 'Gloria in excelsis' has been omitted in Lent, it is sung again for the first time at the Easter vigil. At the vigil, the Easter candle may be lit; it then burns at all services during the season, and at baptisms in the rest of the year. At the vigil, or some other service, there may be a renewal of Baptism promises. There may be an Easter garden with a model of the empty tomb. Eastertide sermons expound our reasons for believing that Jesus is alive, and for hoping for an eternal future for ourselves.

## Easter Vigil  22–23 March
## Women See Jesus

*(A minimum of three Old Testament readings should be chosen. The reading from Ex. 14 should always be used.)*

Gen. 1:1—2:4a Creation, Ps. 136:1–9, 23–26 Thank the Lord who delivered us; Gen. 7:1–5, 11–18; 8:6–18; 9:8–13 Noah, Ps. 46 Our refuge and strength; Gen. 22:1–18 Sacrifice of Isaac, Ps. 16 The path of life; Ex. 14:10–31; 15:20–21 The Exodus, *Canticle*: Ex. 15:1b–13, 17–18 The song of Moses; Isa. 55:1–11 Come to the waters, *Canticle*: Isa. 12:2–6 Great in your midst; Bar. 3:9–15, 32—4:4 God gives the light of wisdom *or* Prov. 8:1–8, 19–21; 9:4b–6 Wisdom, Ps. 19 The heavens declare God's glory; Ezek. 36:24–28 I will sprinkle clean water on you, Ps. 42 and 43 Faith and hope; Ezek. 37:1–14 The valley of dry bones, Ps. 143 A prayer for deliverance; Zeph. 3:14–20 I will bring you home, Ps. 98 Salvation and Justice; Rom. 6:3–11 Baptism, death and resurrection, Ps. 114 The Exodus; Matt. 28:1–10 The women see Jesus

*'Suddenly Jesus met [the women] and said, "Greetings!" And they*

*came to him, took hold of his feet, and worshipped him. Then Jesus said to them, "Do not be afraid; go and tell my brothers to go to Galilee; there they will see me."' Matthew 28:9–10*

### *Vive la différence*

It's been known for a long time in genetics that females have two X chromosomes on their genome, and males have an X and a Y. Recently it's been discovered that there are significant differences between the X chromosomes in men and women. It's difficult to analyse the implications of this without sounding sexist. There are too many exceptions to allow us to be specific about the differences between men and women. Neither can we be sure whether they're due to nurture or nature. In general, however, many women are drawn more to communication and caring skills, whereas men are more aggressive and mechanically minded. Wait! I know this isn't true in every individual, and people can train themselves to perform tasks well to which they're not instinctively drawn. Certainly Christians can't approve of any form of discrimination based on presumed differences between the sexes. Perhaps we should learn to enjoy and value what makes us different. There is a story about a Frenchman who heard a lecturer saying that between men and women there is only a very little difference. He exclaimed, '*Vive la différence!*'

### Women at the tomb

Maybe this explains why Jesus appeared first to the women after his resurrection. The Bible, although written in a patriarchal age, makes it quite clear that Jesus treated women with courtesy and respect. Anointing a body after it had been buried was women's work, and because of the Sabbath they hadn't been able to do it until sunrise on the Sunday morning. So they were the first to arrive at the tomb – but I'm sure if Jesus had wanted to appear first to the men among his disciples, he could have arranged it. Yet he chose the women to see him first. Why?

### Communication

Possibly it was because they were more sensitive to the spiritual aspects of life. Still today there are more women in church than men in many countries. More likely Jesus chose them because of their communication skills. Many men, for whatever reason, find it hard to talk about their emotions. Those who saw Jesus were told to go and tell others what they'd seen. They were sent to communicate the facts to others. Perhaps Jesus thought the women would be particularly good at this. It took the men a little longer before they found the words to express their faith. Yet none of us can escape the challenge; if we believe that something significant happened in this night, we must be prepared to communicate it to others. Many of our friends are longing to believe that there is life after death. Jesus himself said that even if somebody did return from the grave, nobody would believe him. But if you've read the story in the Bible, and felt at times that Jesus was close to you when you prayed, your friends will believe you because they know you. If they regard you as a generally trustworthy person, they'll know you haven't made it up. You don't need to ram it down their throats; but sooner or later there may come an opportunity quietly to drop into the conversation your belief in an afterlife, based on your experience that Jesus hears our prayers.

## Witnesses

The choice of women to be witnesses to the resurrection of Jesus is even more surprising when we remember that in those days women weren't even allowed to give evidence in court. Some say this was because they were regarded as untrustworthy. I think it's more likely to be because in those days the men thought they could tell their womenfolk what to say. For whatever reason, however, Jesus appeared first to Mary Magdalene and the other Mary, telling them not to be afraid, but to go and tell his brothers that they had seen him. Whether you have two X chromosomes or an X and a Y, you can train yourself to communicate what's important to you. And the resurrection of Jesus, in fulfilment of prophecy, is important to each one of us, because it's our guarantee that after we ourselves have died, we shall be raised to eternal life with Jesus in heaven. Jesus loves each of us equally; each of us is unique; in heaven we shall be able to enjoy what makes us different from anyone else: 'Vive la différence.'

## *Suggested hymns*

*Alleluia, alleluia, give thanks to the risen Lord; Christ is alive! Let Christians sing; Christ the Lord is risen again; Good Joseph had a garden.*

# Easter Day   23 March
## *Principal Service*   The Probability of Resurrection

Acts 10:34–43 Peter and other witnesses to the resurrection; *or* Jer. 31:1–6 An everlasting Love; Ps. 118:1–2, 14–24 I shall not die but live; Col. 3:1–4 Resurrection with Christ; *or* Acts 10:34–43 Peter and other witnesses to the resurrection; John 20:1–18 Magdalene at the tomb; *or* Matt. 28:1–10 The women see Jesus

*'[Peter said to the Gentiles,] "We are witnesses to all that he did both in Judea and in Jerusalem. They put him to death by hanging him on a tree; but God raised him on the third day and allowed him to appear, not to all the people but to us who were chosen by God as witnesses, and who ate and drank with him after he rose from the dead." '* Acts 10:39–41

## Witnesses

The Roman centurion, Cornelius, and his friends, were Gentiles, not Jews; they didn't know the prophecies in Scripture of the coming of the Messiah, his death and resurrection. But they were interested; Cornelius had prayed, and was told to send for a Jew called Peter who would tell them what they wanted to know. Roman soldiers liked everything to be cut and dried with military precision. Perhaps Cornelius hoped that Peter would prove to him that there was something to hope for after death. But Peter proved nothing. Instead, he said he was a witness – witnessing that Jesus was alive. Cornelius knew all about the Roman system of law, which they were very proud of. It's the basis of our legal system today. Witnesses were called to give evidence. They had to be eyewitnesses, reporting on what they'd seen for themselves; hearsay evidence, reporting what somebody else told you, won't do. Very seldom can a court prove what happened; they often have to rely on the balance of probabilities. Is it overwhelmingly more probable that witnesses are telling the truth than that they're lying? Peter said that he'd been chosen by God as a witness, and that he'd eaten and drunk with Jesus after he rose from the dead.

## Proof

In fact there are very few things in life that we can prove. Scientific 'laws', as we call them, are nothing of the kind. When we did A, then B happened, says the scientist. Therefore, if we do A again, it's extremely probable that B will happen again. Probable – but she can't prove it. It's probable that electric currents are caused by the movement of electrons; it's probable that one species evolves into another. It's probable that greenhouse gases cause global warming; it's probable that smoking causes cancer. You'd be a fool if you went against all the weight of probability and disbelieved these things. But they're probability, not proof. We learn to live without requiring absolute proof of everything.

## Probability

The theory of probability is perfectly simple: there's six sides to the dice; so the chance of a six (or any other number) coming up's one in six. If there's two dice, the chance of any combination of numbers is six times six, equals 36. So if you've thrown two double-sixes one after the other, the chances of getting another double-six the next time you throw is still one in 36, or just under 3 per cent. If five hundred witnesses give evidence that something happened, it's just possible that they're all mistaken, but the probability is extremely low. You'd be a fool to base your life on a refusal to accept anything less than absolute proof.

## Faith

So why doesn't God prove that there's life after death? Because that would take away our free will. God doesn't want to bludgeon us into belief; he wants it to be our choice, based on the balance of probabilities. God wants our freely given love. But it would be madness to refuse. So Peter said, 'God raised [Jesus] on the third day and allowed him to appear, not to all the people but to us who were chosen by God as witnesses.' If Jesus had appeared to all the people in Jerusalem, it would have forced them to believe, and that's not faith. But there are witnesses, starting with Mary Magdalene, then Peter, then over five hundred people at once. Since then, millions of people have testified that Jesus gives them strength when they pray to him. He couldn't do that if he was dead. All these witnesses don't constitute a proof of the resurrection, but they add up to a very strong probability. A very strong probability that Jesus is alive is all you need, before you put your faith in him, and praise him, obey him and hope to live with him for ever.

## All-age worship

*Throw dice to learn about multiplying probabilities. Assume the probability that a stranger is lying is about 50 per cent. What's the probability that 500 people who report that Jesus is alive are all lying? 50 per cent × 50 per cent ... 500 times over!*

## Suggested hymns

*Blest be the everlasting Lord; God sent his Son, they called him Jesus; Thine be the glory; This joyful Eastertide.*

# Easter Day
## Second Service   Love is Strong as Death
Morning Ps. 114 The Exodus, 117 God's love for all nations; Evening Ps. 105 The Exodus, *or* 66:1–11 God holds our souls in life; S. of Sol. 3:2–5; 8:6–7 Love is strong as death; John 20:11–18 *if not read at the Principal Service* Mary Magdalene; *or* Rev. 1:12–18 I was dead and am alive

> *'Love is strong as death, passion fierce as the grave. Its flashes are flashes of fire, a raging flame. Many waters cannot quench love, neither can floods drown it.' Song of Solomon 8:6–7*

## Song of Solomon

The Song of Solomon, in the Bible, is one of the world's greatest love-songs. It's in dramatic form, with the alternating voices of the Lover, called Solomon; the Beloved, who is 'dark but lovely'; their friends; and the Women of Jerusalem. It's full of unforgettable phrases, and celebrates the power of human love. That's a surprising thing to find in the Bible, which is sometimes wrongly portrayed as being opposed to sex. It's probably there because it's often been read as an allegory of the love between God and his people.

113

## Human love

Human love is how we learn about God's love. Of course, sexual attraction can be explained in terms of hormones and genes, but that's only part of the story. Anyone who's ever been in love knows that. And most of those who've never experienced the full intensity of human passion have known, from the love they give to their close family and friends, and receive from them in return, what a powerful force for change love can be. A cynical novelist wrote, 'There is no reciprocity in love. Men love women, women love children, and children love hamsters.' Thank God that's not entirely true! Even if it were, as Tennyson wrote,

> 'Tis better to have loved and lost
> Than never to have loved at all.

Knowing you're loved is the most wonderful experience in the world. And when you're loved, far beyond what you deserve, by that wonderful person to whom you've offered the love of your own heart, it's totally amazing. The Song of Solomon puts it perfectly:

> Love is strong as death,
>     passion fierce as the grave.
> Its flashes are flashes of fire,
>     a raging flame.
> Many waters cannot quench love,
>     neither can floods drown it.
> If one offered for love all the wealth of his house,
>     it would be utterly scorned.

So what does that tell us of God's love for us?

## God's love

First it tells us that God protects us and provides for us as any human lover would for their beloved. Second, that he longs for us to love him in return. God suffers heartbreak when we don't love him. Did you realize that's how God feels about you? Isn't it amazing? We can't withhold our love any longer. Love like that of God for us deserves the gift of our whole heart and life in return. And like true love between humans, the love that God feels for us, and that we feel for God, grows deeper as the years go by. God never wants it to end.

## Strong as death

But earthly love affairs do come to an end, when one or other of the lovers dies. What about God's love for us? Do you imagine God would go to all the trouble of creating us, revealing his love to us, winning and wooing us until we fall in love with God in return, only to see the whole romance crumble into dust when we die? Surely not! 'Love is strong as death.' God wants to love us for ever and ever, so God will raise us from death to eternal life. That's what Easter's about. God sent his Son to die for us and rise again, to drive away any shreds of doubt lingering in our minds that God would ever let a little thing like the death of the body interrupt his endless love for you and for me.

## Hope

Easter brings hope, too, to lovers who've been bereaved. To be parted from the one you love, when they die, turns romance into tragedy. Yet God promises that we shall meet again. Dante Gabriel Rossetti imagined his beloved in heaven praying that they may be reunited:

> The blessed damozel leaned out
> From the gold bar of Heaven ...
> 'I wish that he were come to me,
> For he will come,' she said.
> 'Have I not prayed in heaven? – on earth,
> Lord, Lord, has he not prayed?
> Are not two prayers a perfect strength?
> And shall I feel afraid?'

And the reason for this hope is that God loves us even more strongly than we love each other. 'Love is strong as death, passion fierce as the grave.' Happy Easter!

## Suggested hymns

*Hark, my soul, it is the Lord; King of glory, King of peace; Love's redeeming work is done; My God, I love thee – not because.*

## Second Sunday of Easter (or Eve of the Annunciation;
see p. 307) 30 March

*Principal Service* **Truth** Ex. 14:10–31; 15:20–21 The Exodus
(*if used, the reading from Acts must be used as the second
reading*); or Acts 2:14a, 22–32 Peter and other witnesses to the
resurrection; Ps. 16 You show me the path of life; 1 Peter 1:3–9
Hope from the resurrection; John 20:19–31 Thomas's doubt and
faith

> *'Jesus said to [Thomas,] "Have you believed because you have
> seen me? Blessed are those who have not seen and yet have come
> to believe."' John 20:29*

### Differing witnesses

Try asking two football fans to describe a match they both attended.
Each will have seen, and remembered, what was important to them.
Other happenings, which they thought were less important, they'll
have forgotten about altogether. Maybe they'll swear they never
happened, simply because they hardly noticed them. It's the same
with witnesses in court. They're all sworn to tell the truth, the whole
truth and nothing but the truth; yet the accounts of the same event
given by different witnesses often differ radically. If they didn't,
we'd suspect collusion. So the fact that there are four different accounts of the resurrection in the four Gospels shouldn't surprise
us. They're all true, but different witnesses remembered different
aspects of the truth. Questions: were there two angels or only one?
How many women? Who was the first to see Jesus? Answer: we
don't know. And it doesn't matter. If the accounts were tidy and
consistent you'd think someone had made it all up.

### Startling

What the witnesses to the resurrection of Jesus had seen was so
completely unexpected that their main emotions, at first, were not
joy, but surprise, fear and doubt. Truth, if it's really true, is often
startling. New truth can be very unsettling. The rejoicing comes
later. Looking back, all you can remember at first is confusion and
conflicting accounts. Everyone was caught off-guard; they needed
time to adjust to a new view of the world. So death, they marvelled,
is not a tragedy, but the beginning of glory! My defeat, because I

stuck to my principles, is my victory. Power to do amazing things can be given to the powerless. The love of God doesn't have to be earned: it's a free gift. Those are very startling new ideas, quite different to what they'd thought before. Quite different, in fact, to what most people think still. But the disciples were ordinary human beings like you and me. On Easter morning, they struggled to understand. Resurrection's an idea that takes a bit of getting used to.

## What is truth?

'What is truth?' asked jesting Pilate. Jesus said, 'I am truth.' Just because Jesus is so unlike anything we've ever experienced before, doubters like Pilate can't even recognize truth when he's standing in front of them. Doubting Thomas, later, surrendered his doubts when confronted with the evidence. He thought it was incredible that Jesus was alive – incredible, but true. So he believed the incredible. What is truth, indeed? Is truth limited to the things we can understand? Is it limited to things we can measure and express in scientific formulae? Or is there a truth bigger than human reason? Is there a truth that goes beyond what we're able to grasp? Is there a reality more real than the stark finality of death?

## Yes

Yes, there is a truth which soars far above the down-to-earth truths we've met so far. The truth of the resurrection; the truth of Jesus; the truth of God. That's why we're here in church. Because Jesus is alive and well, and living in our hearts. Contrary to our expectations; contrary to common sense if you like. But we know it's true, because we've prayed to him, and then our lives have been transformed. The love of God's stronger than death. If that isn't true, I don't know what is.

## Togetherness

Yet the big truths are bigger than we can handle on our own; that's why we come together to proclaim with one voice, 'Christ is risen.' 'He is risen indeed – in truth.' We need each other, to deal with a truth as big as that. We need to help each other get used to the startling and the unexpected. The American poet, Emily Dickinson, wrote:

Truth must dazzle gradually, or every man be blind.

The thing about the big truths, however, is that when we've grasped them, we can all agree on them, never mind the details. Ask two people who went to the football match, 'Who won?' 'We won,' they'll cry together. And that's what happened that first Easter. We all won. That's true, without a doubt.

## All-age worship

*Ask two people to go out of the room, then return one at a time to describe something they both saw on TV, or on the way to church. Which are the unimportant details, and which are the big truths?*

## Suggested hymns

*Alleluia! (3) O sons and daughters, let us sing; Good Christians all, rejoice and sing; Thine be the glory, risen, conquering Son; Thou art the way: by thee alone.*

# Second Sunday of Easter
## *Second Service*   Why Stop There?

Ps. 30:1–5 You restored me to life; Dan. 6:1–23 *or* 6:6–23 The lions' den; Mark 15:46—16:8 They were afraid

> *'So they went out and fled from the tomb, for terror and amazement had seized them; and they said nothing to anyone, for they were afraid.' Mark 16:8*

## Why stop there?

In most modern Bibles, St Mark's Gospel ends at chapter 16, verse 8, with the words 'They said nothing to anyone, for they were afraid.' Why stop there? It's an oddly negative note to finish on. Quite early on, some people thought Mark wrote more words which have been lost. Two attempts were made to replace the supposed 'lost ending of Mark'. In my Bible, there's a few lines headed, 'The Shorter Ending of Mark', ending on a triumphant note about eternal salvation. Then verses 9 to 20 are headed 'The Longer Ending of Mark'. Both endings are good stuff; but today, most scholars think they're not by St Mark. So why stop there? Why did St Mark end at that point?

## Stumpy-fingers

Some people think he can't have meant to end with the words, 'They were afraid.' Maybe Mark wrote some more in his original, but, before any copies had been made, the end of the scroll got torn off in some accident and was never replaced. There's even a story that Mark's nickname was 'Stumpy-fingers'. That wasn't because he worked in a butcher's shop, it's claimed: it's because the end of his Gospel was chopped off by accident. No, I don't believe it either, but it's a curious story. The other one is that Mark was called away when he reached that point, and never returned – maybe he was martyred before he'd finished writing. Not very likely, I'd say.

## The beginning of a new chapter

Perhaps we'd better consider again whether John Mark really did mean to end there. St Luke, after all, went on to write a sequel to his Gospel, which we call 'The Acts of the Apostles'. The sequel describes the growth of the Christian Church, once the disciples at last realized that Jesus really was alive. Perhaps Mark, too, intended to write a sequel, and knew that the real turning point between the two, was to end Part One with the disciples afraid, and begin Part Two as they begin to grow in confidence through the power of the Spirit. Did Mark write a sequel which has been lost, or did he never get around to it? Of course, we simply don't know. But the fact that St Mark's Gospel ends where it does shows up very clearly that the resurrection of Jesus meant the closing of the old history books, where everyone is full of fear, and the beginning of a new chapter.

## In our lives

A new chapter in our own lives, too. Nobody hears the story of the death and resurrection of Jesus read out in church, then goes out of the church unchanged by it. The old unchanged you, filled with terror and amazement, belongs to the old book, which is closed now. The new you begins a new chapter when you walk out of this church. The resurrection of Jesus means a change in you. If you let him, he'll fill you with joy, and with the Holy Spirit. Jesus will give you the power to bear witness to those around you – by your changed life – that something's happened to you because you've been to church, that you couldn't have done for yourself. You'll have a new confidence that you can do anything, and speak to anybody, because the power of the risen Christ is within you. You'll be able to stand up for what's right, and overcome the evil in the world, through the power of the Holy Spirit.

## The real world

There's an artist's colony in the USA, where the painters and writers and musicians can concentrate on their creations because all is peace. On an arch as they come in they see the word 'Welcome'. But as they go out again, they see, written on the inside of the same arch, 'To the Real World'. Perhaps it should be written on the inside of our church doors, for people to read as they go out. For the real world is where our Christianity has to be put into practice. We couldn't possibly do that on our own. But if we let the resurrection of Jesus change us, and the love of Jesus flow through us, we can stand that world on its head. You come into church, and hear the story of the resurrection of Jesus read to you. Why stop there? If the resurrection means anything to you, you'll go out into the real world, as those first disciples did, and raise the whole world to new life in Jesus.

### Suggested hymns

*Alleluia! Alleluia! Hearts to heaven and voices raise; A brighter dawn is breaking; Christ for the world we sing; Light's glittering morn bedecks the sky.*

## Third Sunday of Easter   6 April
*Principal Service*   **Emmaus**
Zeph. 3:14–20 The Lord is in your midst (*if used, the reading from Acts must be used as the second reading*); or Acts 2:14a, 36–41 The response to Peter's preaching; Ps. 116:1–3, 10–17 The cup of salvation; 1 Peter 1:17–23 Born anew through the resurrection; Luke 24:13–35 The road to Emmaus

> *'Then they told what had happened on the road, and how he had been made known to them in the breaking of the bread.'*
> *Luke 24:35*

## Emmaus

Two disciples were walking along the road to Emmaus. They met Jesus, who'd been crucified and was now alive again. But they didn't recognize him. Seven things had to happen to them before they could be convinced. The same pieces of evidence can convince us, too.

## Tomb

First, there's the evidence of the empty tomb. The women, then the men who followed them, had to admit that the tomb where Jesus had been buried was indeed empty. There was no body there.

## Visions

The second piece of evidence is the vision of angels. When people die they sometimes appear to those they love, to reassure the bereaved that everything's all right with the one who's died. If visions can be caused by dead people, why shouldn't they be caused by God himself, to persuade us that he loves us, and has wonderful things in store for us in the afterlife?

## Scripture

The third testimony to the resurrection is the Old Testament Scripture. There are passages like Ezekiel's vision of the valley of dry bones coming back to life, or Hosea's words 'On the third day he will raise me up,' or the Psalm which says,

> You will not leave my soul in hell,
> nor allow your holy one to see corruption.

## Communion

Then there's the breaking of bread. The evidence for the resurrection is not something you look for on your own; it's a corporate experience which you find when you gather together with others for fellowship and worship: the Holy Communion. Other people, too, have the feeling that Jesus is really present with us when we break bread together. Other people, too, find themselves transformed by this sacrament, so that we can go out to do God's work in the power of the Holy Spirit. These things couldn't happen if Jesus were dead.

## Revelation

The disciples at Emmaus didn't recognize Jesus until God opened their eyes. The history of religion isn't the story of the human race searching for God; it's the story of God, the Good Shepherd, searching for us, his lost sheep.

## Emotion

The disciples at Emmaus asked each other, 'Weren't our hearts burning within us?' They'd obviously been in the grip of powerful emotion. You can't rely on emotion alone, but our feelings can confirm a truth which reason alone wouldn't be able to arrive at.

## Six pointers

So we have the following evidence for believing that Jesus is alive, and that we shall live again after we die:

- the empty tomb
- the vision of angels
- the predictions of the Old Testament
- the breaking of the bread
- the opening of our eyes in answer to prayer
- and the evidence of our own emotions.

In the light of all this it's just possible that the disciples were mistaken, and Jesus isn't alive. But that's extremely unlikely, and grows more unlikely with each new piece of evidence. No sensible person chooses the least probable explanation of something, over the glaringly obvious one!

## Eyewitness

Our last piece of evidence is the eyewitness of those who actually saw Jesus alive. St Paul tells us that there were more than five hundred of them. Now it's just possible that all of them were victims of self-delusion caused by wishful thinking. But if that were true, ask yourself why, when they were ostracized by their friends, thrown out of the synagogues, put on trial by the Roman governors, flogged, thrown to the lions, and crucified, they didn't own up? Wouldn't they have cried out, 'No, don't kill me, I admit I was lying. The tomb wasn't empty, Jesus isn't alive!' But that's not what they said. Instead they endured hardships to travel round the world to tell as many people as they could that Jesus is alive. That surely ought to be enough to convince us, today, of the truth of the resurrection. But then, if it's true that by putting our trust in Jesus we can live with him for ever in a heaven too wonderful to describe, where we shall meet after we die with all those we love who've died already, that's very good news. Too good to keep to ourselves. So if you're convinced by these seven evidences for the resurrection, then you'll want to tell your friends how happy it makes you to believe in Jesus.

### All-age worship

*Tell in your own words what the two disciples from Emmaus told the others.*

### Suggested hymns

*Abide with me, fast falls the eventide; Break thou the bread of life, dear Lord, to me; The Lord is risen indeed; We have a gospel to proclaim.*

## Third Sunday of Easter
### *Second Service*   You are God's Temple

Ps. 48 In the midst of your Temple; Hag. 1:13—2:9 Rebuilding the Temple; 1 Cor. 3:10–17 You are God's Temple; *Gospel at Holy Communion* John 2:13–22 Cleansing the Temple

> '*Do you not know that you are God's temple and that God's Spirit dwells in you?*' *1 Corinthians 3:16*

### Three little pigs

29
ww 14 09

Once upon a time there were three little pigs. When they left home their Mummy told them, 'To get on in life, always use the best method. And look out for the big, bad wolf.' They went off singing

'Who's afraid of the big bad wolf? ... Not me! Not me! Not me!' The first little pig built his house out of straw, because that was the easiest method and needed little effort. The second little pig built his house out of sticks, because that was the quickest method and left him time to play. The third little pig built his house out of bricks. It took him longer, but he knew that was the best method. Then the big, bad wolf came by. He said to the first little pig, 'Let me in, let me in, little pig, or I'll HUFF and I'll PUFF and I'll blow your house in.' 'Not me,' cried the first little pig, 'not by the hair on my chinny chin chin!' So the big, bad wolf ... Well, you know the rest. Only be careful, if you're telling the story to children, that you don't miss out the gory endings of the first two pigs and the wolf himself, because you think they're unsuitable for children. Children probably know the whole story by heart much better than you do, and they'll never forgive you if you change even one little word!

## Divisions

Psychologists tell us this story is popular because it teaches children to prefer long-term satisfaction over short-term pleasures. So if your teenagers seem to be only interested in short-term pleasure, it's all your fault, because you never told them the story of the three little pigs when they were younger! But if the message of the story is simply, 'Be careful how you build,' that's one which St Paul would have understood. He was writing to the young and inexperienced church members in the sea-port of Corinth. He'd been told that they were splitting into cliques and factions, a sure sign of immaturity in the Church! Some claimed to be followers of Apollos, a wise and philosophical Christian preacher from Alexandria. Some said they belonged to St Peter's party. Others said, 'Never mind the rest, Paul is best.' St Paul was not flattered. To him, divisions in the Church were the worst possible news, because they threatened its very survival. So he uses a picture very like the story of the three little pigs. Remember there were no church buildings in those days, Christians met in private houses. When Paul talks of building up the Church he means developing its community life.

## Building materials

First Paul talks about foundations. Your community is not founded on Paul, he says, nor is it founded on Apollos. There's only one foundation that's strong enough to withstand the storms: the

Church must be built on the foundation of Jesus Christ. What the Apostles have to do is to build on top of that foundation, using the best possible materials. Build your community life on the foundation of your shared faith in Jesus, and don't skimp on the time and effort it needs to make a real fellowship. Give to God the best of yourself, then nobody need be afraid of the big bad wolf.

## Temple

So, because St Paul's been writing about the church fellowship as if it were a building, and because God is found in the community life of the Church, he says, 'you are the Temple of God'. Where should you go to look for God? Some go on long pilgrimages, some climb high mountains, some seek a distant guru. And all the time God's right there, in your own heart. God's Holy Spirit dwells in the heart of every Christian, and especially in the companionship which grows up when Christians meet together to worship God and to love their neighbours. Even in a struggling, small congregation, God's there in the midst of them. God loves each congregation of Christians, because he's made his home there. St Peter writes, in one of his letters, that the church fellowship is a living Temple, and each individual Christian's a living stone in that Temple. Not an easy picture to visualize, but you realize the implication: you are bricks in the wall of God's house, and if even one brick is missing, the wall could tumble down. Make sure you're in church next Sunday. Or else the big bad wolf might HUFF and he'd PUFF and ... well, I leave the rest to your imagination.

## *Suggested hymns*

*Blessed city, heavenly Salem; Christ is our corner-stone; Glorious things of thee are spoken; Ye that know the Lord is gracious.*

## Fourth Sunday of Easter   13 April
*Principal Service*   **The Good Shepherd**

Gen. 7 Noah goes into the ark (*if used, the reading from Acts must be used as the second reading*); or Acts 2:42–47 Life in the early Church; Ps. 23 The Lord is my Shepherd; 1 Peter 2:19–25 Christ the Shepherd of your souls; John 10:1–10 I am the Good Shepherd

> '[Jesus said,] "I am the good shepherd. The good shepherd lays down his life for the sheep."' John 10:11

### Psalm 23

Psalm 23 is everybody's favourite. David, the shepherd boy who'd become king of Israel, wrote it from his own experience. Facing the problems of keeping a nation together and travelling in the right direction, he came to see that it was not that different from his task when shepherding a flock of sheep. In fact all forms of human leadership, from the leadership of a nation to the care of a family, have similarities to the life of the shepherd. There's the question of defending from harm those whom you lead; pointing them towards where their needs will be met; and bringing back those who go astray. This leads David on to the realization that the Lord God cares for the king in the same way as the king cares for the nation: like a shepherd: 'The Lord is my Shepherd.'

### Shepherds today

Even if you've no personal experience of shepherding today, you may have watched the sheepdog trials on television, or on your way down a country road you've stopped to marvel at the skill with which a couple of shepherds with their dogs drive their flock from one field into another. Some of them use tractors in this country, but they still have to spend nights in the fields in the lambing season, and it's hard work. In many of the hilly countries around the Mediterranean, you can still see an individual shepherd, or a shepherd boy, leading a flock from the front, and spending all day long with them, and probably the nights too. The sheep recognize the shepherd's voice; the shepherds know each sheep by name, and are prepared to risk their lives for their flock.

## God, our Shepherd

So King David says that God will defend us – 'your rod and your staff' – just as a shepherd cares for his flock. God will supply our needs – 'lead me to green pastures'; guide our lives into 'paths of righteousness'; and bring us home to heaven at the last – 'I will dwell in the house of the Lord for ever'. The same words translated as 'the valley of deep shadow' could also mean 'the shadow of death', and King David surely made a deliberate pun. On the treacherous limestone hills of Judea, slashed by ravines or *wadis*, for a sheep or a shepherd to slip on the loose rocks could mean certain death, or to be attacked in the 'hills of the robbers' by the marauding bands of sheep-stealers would put a shepherd's life at risk. David the shepherd boy, and David the king, knew what fear of death was. But he was convinced that God was with him, and when at last David had to go through the valley of the shadow of death, God would see him through and into the sunshine at the other end.

## The Good Shepherd

So when Jesus said 'I am the Good Shepherd', he was claiming to be the Son of David, and the rightful king of Israel. But also, he was claiming to be Son of God. 'I am' is the name of the Lord God, and the prophet Ezekiel had said that God was the Shepherd of Israel. Jesus is our shepherd, our guide, our companion, our defender, our provider. He goes in front of us, to show us how to live. He gently prods us until we do what he wants us to, and live as he would have us live.

## The gate

Jesus said, 'I am the gate.' Shepherds used to lie down across the entrance to the sheepfold, to defend the sheep against robbers, and to let the sheep go out and come in again at the right times. Your going out and coming in must be through Jesus, and it will be, if you begin and end each day with prayer, then live each day in following his example and rejoicing in his company. And when you're afraid, or when death approaches, remember that Christ the Good Shepherd is with you. So if we follow Jesus, he'll lead us through the valley of death, into the green pastures of heaven, home where we belong.

## All-age worship

*Make model sheep from wool or curled paper. Model, or draw, the dark valley, the still waters, and the green pastures. Draw Jesus, the Good Shepherd, with a lamb across his shoulders.*

## Suggested hymns

*Lord, it belongs not to my care; Loving shepherd of thy sheep; The Lord's my shepherd; Thine for ever, God of love.*

# Fourth Sunday of Easter
## *Second Service* Jew and Gentile United

Ps. 29:1–10 God in the storm; Ezra 3:1–13 Foundations of the Temple; Eph. 2:11–22 Jew and Gentile united; *Gospel at Holy Communion*: Luke 19:37–48 Cleansing the Temple

> *'[Christ] has abolished the law with its commandments and ordinances, that he might create in himself one new humanity in place of the two, thus making peace, and might reconcile both groups to God in one body through the cross, thus putting to death that hostility through it.' Ephesians 2:15*

## Racial tension

Think of the worst examples you know of racial tension and tribal hatred in the world today. None of them is anything like as bad as the mutual hatred and loathing between Jew and non-Jew in St Paul's day. Sometimes it spilled over into violence; most of the time they quietly despised and detested each other. In the Temple in Jerusalem there was a wall between the Court of Israel and the Court of the Gentiles, with stone plaques every few yards, threatening death to any non-Jew who passed beyond the wall into the section of the Temple reserved for the Chosen People – that's how serious it was.

## Christ breaks down the barrier

So the Christians in Ephesus must have been astonished when they read St Paul's letter:

[Christ has created] in himself one new humanity in place of the two, thus making peace, [to] reconcile both groups to God in one body through the cross, thus putting to death that hostility through it.

Jews and non-Jews united into one body! Absurd, ridiculous, impossible! Yet that's what Jesus has done, says Paul. Jesus has broken down the dividing wall in the Temple, which separates Jews from non-Jews. The barriers are broken, the wall's come down, we're all one in Christ. If it works, thought his readers, that'll be one of the most amazing developments in the history of the world. Well, for a while it did work; Jewish Christians and Gentile Christians worshipped together in the same church; and it was almost entirely due to Paul. He had to overcome a lot of prejudice. You could read almost all of his letters as a passionate plea for unity between Gentile Christians and Jewish Christians. He wasn't writing theology, he was pleading with his fellow Jews, and the Gentiles, to whom he'd been sent, to love each other.

## In context

This puts a lot of what Paul writes into context. Jews thought the only way to become a member of the people of God was to obey every law in the Hebrew Scriptures. If these Gentile dogs want to share in the promises God had made to his chosen people, they must be made to obey every one of those laws and live exactly as if they were Jews. 'No,' shouts Paul, 'no, no, no, no, *no!*' If you want to be one with Jesus, you must be one in heart with every other believer, no matter what background they come from. You can't lead your heavenly Father into a corner and keep him to yourselves: you must share everything. You must accept the Gentile Christians exactly as they are, without demanding that they change into imitation Jews. '[Jesus] has abolished the law with its commandments and ordinances, that he might create in himself one new humanity in place of the two, thus making peace.' This doesn't mean, of course, that the Ten Commandments can be forgotten. The great achievement of the Jews was to show that God cares about the way we treat each other. Morality matters, but you mustn't make it a ticket to church membership, still less a ticket to heaven. We're justified by faith, not by the works of the law.

## Other divisions

Then most of the Jewish Christians perished in the destruction of Jerusalem, and what was left was an almost entirely Gentile church. But although the problem of Jewish Christians and Gentile Christians is no longer at the top of our agenda, the words of St Paul are still crucially important. Because the truth is, we go on making divisions. We divide the one Church up into little ghettoes, with different races not speaking to each other, different languages not listening to each other, different cultures thinking theirs is the only way to worship God. Different denominations un-church each other, saying, 'You're not a real Christian, because you don't believe the same things that I believe.' Christians drive other Christians from the Church because 'their way of life doesn't match up to *our* moral code'. If only we'd listen to St Paul today, what would he be saying about our intolerance?

> [Christ] has abolished the law with its commandments and ordinances, that he might create in himself one new humanity in place of the two, thus making peace, and might reconcile both groups to God in one body through the cross, thus putting to death that hostility through it.

### Suggested hymns

*Christ is the world's light, he and none other; In Christ there is no east or west; O thou who at thy Eucharist didst pray; Thy hand, O God, has guided.*

## Fifth Sunday of Easter   20 April
### Principal Service   The Way, the Truth and the Life
Gen. 8:1–19 Noah comes out of the ark (*if used, the reading from Acts must be used as the second reading*); *or* Acts 7:55–60 The death and faith of Stephen; Ps. 31:1–5, 15–16 Deliver me; 1 Peter 2:2–10 Living stones in God's Temple; John 14:1–14 The way, truth and life

> *'Jesus said to [Thomas,] "I am the way, and the truth, and the life. No one comes to the Father except through me."' John 14:6*

## Exclusive?

There's an anonymous verse which satirizes the superior attitudes of some Christians:

> We are God's chosen few,
> All others will be damned;
> There is no place in heaven for you –
> We can't have heaven crammed.

Some Christians are certainly exclusive, but does the gospel of Jesus paint such a narrow vision of heaven as that?

## Trust?

Well, Jesus met his friends in the upper room for the Last Supper. He told them he was going to die, and found them puzzled and frightened. There were more words in that long conversation than are recorded in the Bible. We can imagine Jesus asking them, 'Do you trust me?' Their experience led them to answer: 'A man like you would never lie, far less deliberately mislead his friends.' Next, asks Jesus, do you believe that the God I've been telling you about would lie? The answer doesn't need to be spoken: Jesus described a Father whose Son takes after him; God would no more lie than Jesus would. So, said Jesus, believe what I say about life after death: 'In my Father's house ...'. So death's like going home, where we find ourselves once more among the people we love.

## Room for all?

But who's in heaven? Jesus said: 'In my Father's house are many mansions.' The Roman roads in Jesus's time had an inn, called a *mansio*, at the end of each day's journey. So heaven's like a huge pilgrims' hotel, and there's a room reserved with your name on the door. In heaven there'll be room for all, even forgiven sinners like me and you. Jesus has gone to prepare a place there for us: he's going to take us to be with him there. In heaven we'll all be with Jesus, who loves us, and he'll have all the time in the world to show us around.

## The life?

But poor old doubting Thomas asked the unspoken question which they must all have been thinking: 'Where *is* heaven? What's the *way* to get there?' To which Jesus replied: 'I am the way, the truth and the life.' What did he mean? Let's start at the end: 'I am the life.' What is eternal life? We can't describe it – all our words have been formed for talking about time – but we can make comparisons. If you say to a child, it's wonderful to get out of the traffic and drive your car down an open road, they won't understand, because they've never experienced those sensations. But ask them what it's like to take your tricycle out in the garden, and they'll know what you're talking about. Then say, driving a car in the country's like that only more so, and they'll understand! Jesus had shown his disciples what real life's like: it's life lived with love, joy and creativity. Well, eternal life's like that, only more so! I am the life, he said. That's the truth.

## The truth?

Yet so many people claim to tell us the truth, which of them do we believe? Jesus said, 'I am the truth.' Not 'I tell the truth', because truth that can be told is made up of words, and words never get to grips with reality. The truth's a person, true to himself, true to his principles, true to his friends – and the truth about eternal life is that such a man would never let mere death interrupt his love for us.

## The way?

So if that's the truth about heaven, how do we get there? 'I am the way,' said Jesus. You get to heaven, not by following a set of rules, but by following a person. Play the game of 'Follow my leader' with Jesus: aim to live his sort of life, a life of unselfish love and self-sacrifice, and no matter how many times you slip, he'll see that you get to your destination in the end. 'I am the way, the truth and the life.'

So heaven's not reserved for those who feel superior for keeping the rules, but for those who know they're forgiven sinners, who could never earn a place in heaven by doing good, but who accept God's gift of love. Yes, heaven *will* be crammed, full of the most unlikely people. But there's always room for one more!

## All-age worship

*Write in your most beautiful lettering: 'I am the way, the truth and the life.'*

## Suggested hymns

*Come, my way, my truth, my life; There's a wideness in God's mercy; Thine for ever, God of love; Thou art the way, by thee alone.*

# Fifth Sunday of Easter
## Second Service   The New Jerusalem

Ps. 147:1–12 God heals the broken-hearted; Zech. 4:1–10 Not by might nor by power but by my spirit; Rev. 21:1–14 The new Jerusalem; *Gospel at Holy Communion*: Luke 2:25–32 [33–38] Simeon's song

> *'I saw the holy city, the new Jerusalem, coming down out of heaven from God, prepared as a bride adorned for her husband.'*
> Revelation 21:2

## The new city

Pilgrims visiting the Holy Land say it's somewhat disconcerting to come to a signpost pointing to 'Jerusalem – the new city'. Those familiar with the book of the Revelation to John may begin to think that the future which he predicted has suddenly come to pass, and the new Jerusalem has already come 'down out of heaven from God'. Of course, the signposts are there to distinguish the newer part of Israel's capital from the Old City, occupied mostly by Arabs. First-time visitors then have to confront the problem that the reality of Jerusalem may fall well below the idealized picture that they may have based on picture-books they read in Sunday school. Jerusalem today is full of shabby buildings, tawdry decorations, soldiers in uniform, racial tensions and fear. But then so it was in the time of Jesus, and until we realize this we may completely misunderstand what he said and did.

## The ideal

It's good to have an ideal of anything at the back of your mind, provided you don't ever expect to find the ideal in this life. The Greek philosopher Plato liked to imagine another world full of ideals; the ideal prototypes of every category of imperfect object which exists in the real world. Sometimes this ideal world was called heaven; whether the philosophers believed that it really existed is a hard question to answer. But the thought of an ideal heaven inspired many Jewish writers to a new type of literature. They would write about visions of this ideal world – 'I saw the heavens open' was a common phrase to begin with. This enabled them to discuss how God wanted the world to be, and how different this was from the reality. It was a very useful means for critical remarks on the society of their day, especially if they were under the thumb of an occupying power who wouldn't have a clue what the writers were on about, even if they could read their books. There are several accounts of visions of this type in the Old and New Testaments, and a lot more in other Jewish literature at the time. The technical term is 'apocalyptic literature'. The danger is that today's readers may misunderstand them through not recognizing the convention that it was an ideal world which was being described. On some cars in the USA you'll see a warning that the car may suddenly have no driver if God snatches them up to heaven. If they want to be equally literal about the new Jerusalem coming down from heaven, fifteen hundred miles square, they should put up signs warning you to 'Mind your head'!

## Poetry

What is sad about these literal interpretations of the Bible is that they spoil our appreciation of the poetry. John's description of the ideal Jerusalem has inspired some wonderful songs, from Dante's *Paradise*, through St Bernard's 'Jerusalem the Golden', and the North American spiritual 'I'm going to walk in Jerusalem just like John', to the Victorian ballad by Frederick Weatherly:

> And once again the scene was chang'd,
> New earth there seem'd to be,
> I saw the Holy City
> Beside the tideless sea;
> The light of God was on its streets,
> The gates were open wide,

And all who would might enter,
And no one was denied.
No need of moon or stars by night,
Or sun to shine by day,
It was the new Jerusalem,
That would not pass away.

## Heaven

For it's not on earth that we shall find the ideal Jerusalem, either now or sometime in the future. St John's revelation was a vision of heaven. We must struggle to bring our society as close as we can to God's kingdom 'on earth, as it is in heaven', even if we never fully succeed. This will involve us in care for the poor and the powerless, in healing the sick and the sad, and sharing in the struggle for peace and justice throughout the earth. Surely the vision of a city means that this is something we do together with other people, not just in the privacy of our own prayers. If we work at this, we shall look forward to our reward in the heavenly city, in another world of eternity, outside of space and time. Poetry like that of St John is the only way to think about this ultimate reality, and the only way to inspire us to make this present world as near the ideal as we can.

### Suggested hymns

*City of God, how broad and far; Jerusalem the Golden; Light's abode, celestial Salem; Where cross the crowded ways of life.*

## Sixth Sunday of Easter (Rogation Sunday) 27 April
*Principal Service* **Not Orphans**
Gen. 8:20—9:17 God's covenant with Noah (*if used, the reading from Acts must be used as the second reading*); or Acts 17:22–31 Paul witnesses to the resurrection in Athens; Ps. 66:7–18 God brought us out; 1 Peter 3:13–22 Christ preached to the spirits in prison; John 14:15–21 The promise of the Holy Spirit, the Advocate

*'Jesus said to his disciples, "I will not leave you orphaned; I am coming to you." ' John 14:18*

135

## Orphans

Our hearts go out to children whose parents have died. Tragically, it happens too often that first one and then the other parent dies, or they may die together in an accident. If the children are lucky, some close relative will take them into their home, and care for them tenderly while they try to come to terms with their loss. In days gone by, orphanages in this country used to be rather awful places; nowadays, if there are no suitable relatives, a child may be taken into care while the local authority appeals for families to adopt or foster children in need. In the developed world there's an increasing problem where parents die of drug abuse; in Africa there are millions of AIDS orphans whom nobody cares for, unless some charity comes forward to do their best for them. Although most adoptive parents show wonderfully sacrificial love to their adopted children, nothing, it seems, can quite take the place of the natural parents.

## Not orphans

Jesus realized that the disciples felt alone and abandoned, as if they had suddenly become orphans. They'd enjoyed a close relationship with Jesus as he travelled with them and taught them; it was like one big happy family. Then their friend Jesus was arrested and executed, all in the space of less than twenty-four hours. To their astonishment and relief, Jesus came back to them, risen from the dead. But he said it was only a temporary arrangement – forty days, as it turned out, before he left them again and ascended into heaven. After that, it looked as though they'd have to spend the rest of their lives feeling bereaved. What a terrible future! But no, said Jesus, 'I will not leave you orphaned.'

## 'I will come'

How they must have hung on his next words. What arrangements was he going to make for his orphaned children? Who'll adopt grown men and women? But no, Jesus promised that he himself will look after those who love him: 'I will not leave you orphaned; I am coming to you.' How could this be, when Jesus was taken out of their sight? They were being forced to re-examine what they meant by somebody being present. It's not only in science fiction that you have invisible men. Every time you say your prayers, you're proclaiming that you believe that Jesus is present, even though you can't see him.

## Paul in Athens

The Pharisees had a very literal belief in resurrection. They thought that good people who'd died would one day come back to earth in the flesh – resuscitation, in fact. Paul the Pharisee realized this wasn't so when the risen Christ appeared to him on the road to Damascus, and then vanished again. He realized he'd have to find some new words, when he found himself preaching to a crowd of philosophers in Athens. Paul told the Athenians, 'God doesn't live in man-made temples' – a pretty provocative thing to say when you're standing in front of the Parthenon and all the other temples on the Acropolis. He wanted them to understand that God's always present, even when you can't see him.

## The Advocate

So how do we know that Jesus is invisibly with us here and now? Because we can feel his power! When we pray to Jesus for strength to serve him, he gives us his Holy Spirit to fill our hearts. Then anything God wants us to do, we can do, not through own power, but through the power of God dwelling within us. When the power of the Holy Spirit is with us, said Jesus, then Jesus himself is with us: 'On that day you will know that I am in my Father, and you in me, and I in you.'

So cheer up. We're not orphans at all; our Father's with us, all the time, even though we can't see him. All we have to do is pray, and be willing to obey his commandment to love our neighbours as ourselves, and then Jesus will be with us always, to the end of the world.

## *All-age worship*

*Find out all you can about an orphanage in the developing world. Write to the children there to tell them they're not forgotten, and pray for them.*

## *Suggested hymns*

*Alleluia, sing to Jesus; Be still, for the presence [or Spirit] of the Lord; Our blest Redeemer, ere he breathed; O thou who camest from above.*

137

# Sixth Sunday of Easter
*Second Service*  **The River of Life**
Ps. 87 Glorious things, 36:5–10 The fountain of life; Zech. 8:1–13
The faithful city; Rev. 21:22—22:5 The river of life; *Gospel at Holy Communion* John: 21:1–14 The lakeside

> *'The angel showed me the river of the water of life, bright as crystal, flowing from the throne of God and of the Lamb through the middle of the street of the city. On either side of the river is the tree of life with its twelve kinds of fruit, producing its fruit each month; and the leaves of the tree are for the healing of the nations.' Revelation 22:1–2*

## Water!

The city of Jerusalem today stands on a dry, arid hilltop – it was the same in Jesus's time. There was one natural spring, called Gihon, from which ran a streamlet call the Kidron. There were a few wells, and that was the total water supply. Until Pontius Pilate built an aqueduct, traces of which can still be seen to the south of the city. So when John the Divine described the heavenly Jerusalem as having a river flowing through the middle of the streets it was a startling image. A bit like Bourton-on-the-Water in the Cotswolds, or Hobson's Conduit in Cambridge. The earthly Jerusalem was desperate for water. The heavenly, ideal Jerusalem's full of the water of life.

## Tree of life

On both banks of the river of life, wrote St John, grows the tree of life. Now the tree of life was one of the two trees in the Garden of Eden, in the story of Adam and Eve; the other was the tree of the knowledge of good and evil. The human race was intended to live in harmony with each other, with the world of nature, and with God. In the story, human beings seek to experience evil, and in so doing they disobey God. In this way they forfeit the immortality for which God had intended them. This happened as soon as *Homo sapiens* evolved the power of choice; it's still happening today. The story of Adam and Eve is your story and mine: the disaster which comes from wrong choices and turning our backs on God.

## A better plan

But all is not lost. God has a better plan. The tree of life's still waiting for us in the ideal world of the heavenly Jerusalem. All we have to do, to regain immortality, is to obey God once again. But how are we to do that? 'For the good that I would I do not: but the evil which I would not, that I do,' wrote St Paul. Until Jesus came along and rescued us. The death of Jesus on the cross was the supreme act of obedience to his Father. God wanted to show us what obedience is like. In Jesus we see the best and kindest person that ever lived, sticking to his principles to the end, and accepting the consequences. He could so easily have escaped death, by lying or betraying. But obedience to God often leads to persecution, and sometimes to an unjust slaying or judicial murder. Gethsemane shows us it wasn't easy for Jesus; but he stuck to his guns and obeyed. Now all we have to do, is to join ourselves to Jesus in love and faith, and his obedience becomes our obedience. An old Easter song describes Adam's disobedience paradoxically like this:

O happy fault, O necessary sin of Adam,
which gained for us so great a Redeemer.

## Healing of the nations

If we pray, Jesus gives us immortality and new life. His resurrection becomes our resurrection; his new life becomes our new life; his power to resist temptation becomes our power; his love becomes our love. The fruit of the spirit, love, joy, peace and so on, are available to us, because they grow on the branches of the tree of life which Jesus has won for us. Then we can take the new life which Jesus gives us and offer it to those around us. The people of the world are as desperate for new life as the people of Jerusalem were desperate for water. Most of the time, all they've ever known is bitterness, hatred, war and death. But 'the leaves of the tree are for the healing of the nations'. Just think how our warring world would be transformed, if we could carry to its inhabitants the leaves from the tree of life. Living in harmony with each other, with the world of nature, and with God as he intended. Then physical death would be followed by immortality for all, as God had planned. What powerful medicine that is, the medicine of life! It's available to you, if you love Jesus; you can share it with all the nations of the world, if you love them.

*A city radiant as a bride; For the healing of the nations; Glorious things of thee are spoken; There in God's garden stands the tree of wisdom.*

## Ascension Day   1 May
## The Right-hand Man

Acts 1:1–11 The Ascension (*must be used as either the first or second reading*); or Dan. 7:9–14 The Son of Man; Ps. 47 God has gone up, *or* Ps. 93 The Lord is king; Eph. 1:15–23 Christ is seated beside God; Luke 24:44–53 The Ascension message for all nations

> 'God put this power to work in Christ when he raised him from the dead and seated him at his right hand in the heavenly places, far above all rule and authority and power and dominion, and above every name that is named, not only in this age but also in the age to come.' Ephesians 1:20–21

### A childish mistake

Children have very matter-of-fact minds. Coming out of church, a child remarked, 'God must have terrible pins and needles.' Puzzled, the astonished parents asked, 'Pins and needles? What on earth makes you say that?' 'Well, because every Sunday in church we say that Jesus is sitting on God's right hand.' Slowly it dawned on the parents that the child had misunderstood the words by taking them literally.

### Poetic image

The poetic image which lies behind the phrase we repeat so glibly in the Creed is that of a king's throne room. Beside the big throne for the king himself, there might be other thrones for his advisers, or for people whom the king wanted to honour. Or he might even have a long bench-like throne where he could invite others to sit on the throne with him. The place of honour, in a throne room or at a feast, was always on the right-hand side of the king. Perhaps that's why we talk about somebody's 'right-hand man'. Symbolically, we're saying that Jesus was raised to the position of honour; he was God's right-hand man.

## A friend at court

This is important to us, first because it means we've got what they call 'a friend at court'. If you were a humble subject hoping for some honour or preferment from the king, it would help if you knew somebody who had the king's ear. Well, if you think of heaven as God's royal court, there's no doubt that Jesus is very close to God. And Jesus is our friend; he said so. Now God's 'more ready to hear than we to pray'; you don't have to twist God's arm to make him give you good things. But it gives us confidence in God's providence if we think of Jesus sitting next to his Father and carrying our individual needs and wishes direct to the highest authority.

## Next after God

Second, the Ascension's important because it means there's nobody more important than Jesus. We say this, but we don't always show it by our actions. We may pay more attention to the words of some great teacher than we do to the words of Jesus. We may put more effort into action on behalf of the programme of some great politician than we do for Jesus's programme for the world. We may spend more time worshipping some so-called celebrity than we do in worshipping Jesus. All these are wrong, because God has raised Jesus to the position of highest authority in the universe, and even the greatest human beings on earth, even the angels, rank below him.

## Human nature exalted

Third, the Ascension's important because Jesus has raised our human nature to glory. We often behave as though human beings were the most important creatures in the universe; we destroy our environment and drive other species into extinction. No other species has done as much harm to the earth as *Homo sapiens* has, in the very brief period of time that we've lived on the planet. No other creature has disobeyed the creator as we have. We're a natural disaster walking on two legs. Yet Jesus was incarnate into a human body; he became a human being, and remained a human being when he was exalted into heaven. So human nature, with all its failings, was raised to God's right hand on high. Weak fallible human beings like you and me are capable of occupying the spiritual realm. The old theologians used to call this salvation by divinization or deification: Jesus became what we are in order that we might become what he is. We were made in the image of God, but by our sin we had debased God's coinage; Jesus has minted it afresh, with the image of God stamped clear on human nature again. He has gone before us as the pioneer and representative of the human race, to sit on the throne with God. Jesus has shown what we could become. If we worship him, he'll make us fit to live in the presence of God through all eternity.

### Suggested hymns

*Crown him with many crowns; Hail the day that sees him rise, Alleluia; From glory to glory advancing; Sing alleluia forth ye saints on high.*

## Seventh Sunday of Easter
(Sunday after Ascension Day)   4 May
*Principal Service*   **The Spread of the Church**
Ezek. 36:24–28 I will put my Spirit in you (*if used, the reading from Acts must be used as the second reading*); Acts 1:6–14 The Ascension; Ps. 68:1–10, 32–35 Let God arise; 1 Peter 4:12–14; 5:6–11 Share Christ's suffering and his glory; John 17:1–11 Father, glorify your Son

> '[Jesus said to his disciples,] "You will receive power when the Holy Spirit has come upon you; and you will be my witnesses in Jerusalem, in all Judea and Samaria, and to the ends of the earth."' Acts 1:8

### Luke's reason for writing

What we call the 'Acts of the Apostles' and the third of the four Gospels both begin with a dedication to somebody called Theophilus, so they're obviously written by the same person; probably by the Apostle Paul's private travelling physician, Doctor Luke. In the Gospel, Luke tells us of the life of Jesus; in Acts he tells us about the growth of the Christian Church in the Roman Empire. Picture, if you will, Doctor Luke at the end of a busy day, settling down at his writing desk with some sheets of papyrus and a quill pen, to scratch out in Greek the story, as far as he'd been able to research it, of Jesus and the Church. Perhaps 'His Excellency, Theophilus' was a Greek who was thinking about becoming a Christian. One theory holds that he was the judge at the trial of St Paul, though opinions differ on this. Luke knew it had to be a two-volume work: Part 1, 'The Gospel', about Jesus; and Part 2, 'The Acts' about the Church. The link which holds the two together is the ascension of Jesus into heaven, which comes at the end of the Gospel, and is described again at the beginning of the Acts.

## Ascension

If you like, you can think of the ascension as a simple description of the disciples watching Jesus going up into the sky. Or, if you prefer, you can view it as a vision, in which they realized that Jesus would be no longer visible to them on earth because he'd passed into a higher level of existence. Whichever approach you choose, the important thing is that phase 1 was coming to an end, and phase 2 was about to begin. The time in which they could touch Jesus and hear his voice was over. No more asking him questions; by now they should have understood what he wanted them to do. Now they had to get on and do it. They had to be his witnesses, and carry the good news with them wherever they went. At the end of St Luke's Gospel Jesus told them:

'repentance and forgiveness of sins is to be proclaimed ... to all nations, beginning from Jerusalem. You are witnesses of these things. And see, I am sending upon you what my Father promised; so stay here in the city until you have been clothed with power from on high.'

And at the beginning of Acts, Jesus said to his disciples,

'You will receive power when the Holy Spirit has come upon you; and you will be my witnesses in Jerusalem, in all Judea and Samaria, and to the ends of the earth.'

## A job to do

Jesus gave his disciples a job to do. He's given exactly the same job to me, and to you; we have to carry on the good work which

143

the Apostles began, of spreading the good news of repentance and forgiveness of sins. Maybe our way of doing it will be different from theirs. You probably won't be called to go to another country where none of the people have ever heard of Jesus – there aren't too many of those left. But plenty of the people you meet every day know very little about Jesus. Do they know that the things they feel guilty about can be forgiven by Jesus, and then forgotten? Do they know they can make a completely new start in life – that's what 'repentance' means – confident that they're important to God and God loves them? And if *you* don't tell them, who will? Sure, you've got to be tactful and wait for the right moment. But you, too, are a witness.

## The Spirit

That sounds a pretty impossible task. And so it is, if you try to do it on your own. But Jesus promises you 'power from on high' to enable you to speak out when the time's right. 'You will receive power when the Holy Spirit has come upon you', he promised. But you'll have to wait till next Sunday, Whitsunday, to hear what Doctor Luke had to say about the Holy Spirit.

### All-age worship

*List the kinds of people who would be helped if they could find forgiveness and a fresh start in life.*

### Suggested hymns

*Christ triumphant, ever reigning; Crown him with many crowns; Jesus is Lord! Creation's voice proclaims it; We have a gospel to proclaim.*

# The Seventh Sunday of Easter
(Sunday after Ascension Day)
*Second Service* **God Has Gone Up** Ps. 47 God has gone up; 2 Sam. 23:1–5 The Spirit of the Lord speaks through David; Eph. 1:15–23 Seated at the right hand of God; *Gospel at Holy Communion*: Mark 16:14–20 The Ascension of Jesus

> *'God has gone up with a merry noise, the Lord with the sound of the trumpet.' Psalm 47:5* (Common Worship)

## A merry noise

Lovers of cathedral music may perhaps have heard a choir sing a marvellous anthem by William Croft, to the words 'God is gone up with a merry noise, and the Lord with the sound of the trumpet'. A good choir can make the polyphonic interplay of the voices repeating those words, one vocal part after another, sound like a chorus of angels' trumpets welcoming Jesus at his ascension back to his throne in heaven. So the music sets the tone of celebration which is appropriate for Ascensiontide, for this is Jesus's coronation day. Jesus has always been king, but only after he had been to earth, died and risen again was he given his heavenly crown. But what do the words 'God is gone up' actually mean?

## Jerusalem festival

Psalm 47 was probably written for a festival in Jerusalem. The city of Jerusalem stands on the ridge of limestone hills which form the spine of the Holy Land, between the Mediterranean and the Jordan Valley. To get to Jerusalem from almost anywhere else you have to go up. Probably in the early days they would carry the Ark of the Covenant – the box containing the stone tablets of the Ten Commandments – on shoulder poles up to the Jerusalem Temple in a procession at festival time. The Ark was a symbol of God's presence among them, and the priests blew ram's horns; so God really did go up with the sound of the trumpet. It must have been a very merry noise!

## Ascension

The Christian liturgy applies these words to the Ascension of Jesus into heaven. Jesus was the Son of God, so of course they're appropriate. But what do we mean when we talk of going *up* to heaven? What do we mean by heaven? Yuri Gagarin, the first astronaut to fly through space, reportedly said something like, 'I've been up to heaven and I didn't see God there.' Which illustrates how ridiculous it is to think of heaven as being a place located somewhere vertically above us.

## Upwards

But then we use the idea of upwards in many metaphors which have nothing to do with location in space:

- A child in the junior school is considered old enough to join the upper school.
- An MP in the House of Commons is given a peerage and joins the upper house.
- A legal argument is settled by the High Court.
- An employee in a lowly job, who does it well, is promoted to a higher position in the firm.
- Rocket science requires the knowledge of higher mathematics.
- Or an army officer may do his job so badly that he's 'kicked upstairs' to a higher rank where he can do less harm – no, that's a myth, it never happens. Does it?

Longfellow wrote a famous poem, 'Excelsior', which begins:

> The shades of night were falling fast,
> As through an Alpine village past,
> A youth, who bore, 'mid snow and ice,
> A banner with the strange device,
> *Excelsior!*

'*Excelsior*' means 'higher'; a vulgar parody of the poem replaces it with the word 'Up'ards!' But Longfellow meant to symbolize the human aspiration for things that are better and more noble in life. We should always aspire to the highest things in life: truth, beauty, honesty, kindness and love. We call these things higher because they are morally and spiritually better than those that are low. And because higher and more lasting pleasure comes from them than from the sensual gratification of our lower appetites. Onwards and upwards should be our motto; nothing but the highest personal standards are good enough for servants of God most high.

146

## Heaven

So heaven's not vertically up, it's morally and spiritually better. It's a better place than earth. Jesus was exalted to the highest position of authority to be crowned after his resurrection. When we die, we pass into a higher dimension. Perhaps, when we get there, we shall find that to mark our arrival, like that of Bunyan's Pilgrim, 'the trumpets sounded for him on the other side'. Then I hope also that my relations will rejoice at my funeral – not because they've got rid of me at last, but thanking God for the good life he's given me. Then you and I, too, can hope at last to go 'up with a merry noise'.

### Suggested hymns

*Alleluia, sing to Jesus; Lord, enthroned in heavenly splendour; Our eyes have seen the glory; The head that once was crowned with thorns.*

## Day of Pentecost (Whit Sunday) 11 May
*Principal Service*   **Tongues**

(*The reading from Acts must be used as either the first or second reading.*)
Acts 2:1–21 The day of Pentecost; *or* Num. 11:24–30 The elders receive the Spirit; Ps. 104:26–36, 37b The Spirit in creation; 1 Cor. 12:3b–13 Different gifts, one Spirit; John 20:19–23 Jesus breathes the Holy Spirit; *or* John 7:37–39 Living water of the Spirit

'*There are varieties of gifts, but the same Spirit.*' 1 Corinthians 12:4

### The Holy Bird

A missionary was talking to an enquirer about the Holy Spirit, and used the Greek word *Paraclete*, usually translated as 'Comforter' or 'Advocate'. The enquirer misunderstood him. 'First you tell me God appeared as a dove,' he said, 'then I see there's a brass eagle at the front of your church; and now you tell me God's a parakeet! Holy Father I understand, Holy Son I understand, but Holy Bird I can't understand.'

## The Holy Spirit

The Holy Spirit's a difficult idea to grasp. But the Holy Spirit's not a theory; the Holy Spirit's an experience. St Paul tells us to look at what the Holy Spirit has done in our own lives. If you talk to some people about what it means to be a Christian, the excitement comes bubbling out of them. 'When I realized I was a Christian,' they say, 'I found I could do things which I never thought I could: I could keep my temper, stop drinking when I've had enough, stop arguing with my family, tell a friend about Jesus, give a talk to a group of people, and I could pray. Before, I couldn't do any of these things.'

## God working through people

We can all do these things, and many even more wonderful things, not through our own power, but through God's power. If you want a short simple definition, memorize this phrase: 'The Holy Spirit is God working through people.' The experience of the first converts was this: God was using ordinary people to change the world. This gave them enormous self-confidence, or, rather, 'God-confidence'.

## Prayer in the Spirit

They found, and people still find today, that they could pray. Hear one Christian, just like you, describe it: 'I used to kneel by my bed and wonder what words to use. Then I discovered that Jesus is my friend, and now my conversation with him just comes tumbling out of my mouth.' In fact, when you open yourself to the Holy Spirit, sometimes the words come so fast they all run together, and looking back you can't remember what you said, only that God was in you, praying through you. St Paul wrote: 'The Spirit prays within us with yearnings too deep for words.'

## Tongues

When this happened, at first, the early Christians thought it was a foreign tongue. Like when Peter spoke on the day of Pentecost and everybody understood him. That hasn't happened very often since. Then they thought it might be the language or tongue that angels speak. So they called this experience of the Holy Spirit speaking through their mouths, 'speaking in tongues'. You'll find this mentioned in the Bible, and may puzzle what it means. Ecstatic utterance, or 'holy babbling', still happens, when people are praying on their own, or together with others. For those who are blessed with the gift of praying in tongues, it gives God-confidence: if God can speak through me like that, he could do through me anything he wants.

## Tolerance

Speaking in tongues is a gift of the Holy Spirit. St Paul wrote: 'I thank God that I speak in tongues more than all of you.' But many Christians didn't have this gift; they had others instead. So he wrote: 'There are varieties of gifts, but the same Spirit.' Yet some of the Christians in Corinth started to say that their particular gift was the best; anyone who couldn't do what they did wasn't a real Christian. That's a cruel thing to say to anyone. St Paul told the Corinthians that without love, which binds Christians together in tolerance, 'though I speak with the tongues of men or of angels, I am an empty gong', all noise and no content. The gift of tongues is being used today, in the Pentecostal and Charismatic churches, but also by many individuals in their private prayers. If you have it, thank God; if you haven't, don't worry. Love and tolerance are far more important. But remember that the Holy Spirit is there for you: open your heart to God, let him take control, and there's no limit to what God can do through you. Yes, even you.

### All-age worship

*Ask God to help you to pray. Then write down the words you would like to say to God, and read them out loud.*

### Suggested hymns

*Come down, O Love divine; Gracious Spirit, Holy Ghost; Spirit of holiness, wisdom and faithfulness; Spirit of the living God, fall afresh on me.*

# Day of Pentecost
## *Second Service*   Fulfilment of Prophecy

Morning Ps. 87 As they dance; Evening Ps. 67 God bless us, 133
Anointing; Joel 2:21–32 I will pour out my spirit; Acts 2:14–21
[22–38] Fulfilment of prophecy; *Gospel at Holy Communion*:
Luke 24:44–53 Power from on high

> *'Indeed, these are not drunk, as you suppose, for it is only nine o'clock in the morning. No, this is what was spoken through the prophet Joel: "In the last days it will be, God declares, that I will pour out my Spirit upon all flesh."'* Acts 2:15–17a

## What happened to Peter?

What happened to St Peter and the rest? What came over them? At first the crowd thought they were all drunk. They must have been behaving in a very peculiar way. Then Peter stood up and said that something had happened to them that was far more powerful than alcohol; they were fulfilling prophecy. Perhaps there was a bit of nervous giggling at first. What on earth was Peter talking about? Was he joking? Then as Peter went on quoting from the Hebrew Scriptures, the crowd sobered up and all went quiet.

> 'In the last days it will be, God declares, that I will pour out my Spirit upon all flesh, and your sons and your daughters shall prophesy, and your young men shall see visions, and your old men shall dream dreams. Even upon my slaves, both men and women, in those days I will pour out my Spirit; and they shall prophesy.'

What the crowd had seen happen before their very eyes, said Peter, was the fulfilment of this prophecy.

## What did Joel mean?

Those words were quoted from the prophet Joel. He was one of the last of the Jewish prophets, speaking after the Jewish refugees had returned from their deportation to Babylon. Prophecy was pretty rare in those days; perhaps it had never been common, just a few gifted individuals. In the early days there had been groups of them attached to various sanctuaries. Maybe the prophets occasionally foretold the future. Usually they just spoke out on behalf of God, to tell the people what God thought of how they were behaving here and now: 'Thus saith the Lord' – the prophets can't have been popular, but they were respected. 'But in the last days', prophesied Joel, *everyone* will prophesy. When Peter quoted these words and applied them to what had just happened, the crowd realized that the 'last days' had already come. No more waiting; God wasn't hanging about, he'd already come to earth. Later, they put it this way: first God the Father had come to earth in the person of God the Son; now they were both coming in the person of God the Holy Spirit. The last days were here and now. Now everyone will prophesy.

## What's that to do with me?

But, you may well ask, what's that got to do with me? Well, the answer is, *you're* going to become a prophet. Hold on a moment, you say, I didn't sign up to be a prophet, I don't want people thinking *I'm* drunk! No, of course not, my dears. But God will speak through you, even you, if you let him. When you first realize that God can speak through you it's a pretty staggering experience, a bit like being drunk. Not with wine, but with spirit – the Spirit of God. But it soon settles down. God may not want you to foretell the future.

## Speaking for God

No, you'll be not so much *foretelling* the future, as *forth-telling* what God has to say about the present. God does have an opinion, on everything that happens. If you read your Bible carefully, you'll know what God thought about things that happened in the past, so you can easily work out what he thinks about what people are doing here and now. Where God wants society to care more for the underprivileged, you've got to speak up for God. You may do it in conversations with your friends, or letters to the newspaper, or organizing petitions, or by going into politics. Some years ago the yearbook of the USPG missionary society defined their policy as a *holistic* mission which helps people

- to grow spiritually,
- to thrive physically,
- and to have a voice in an unjust world.

Perhaps that's what God's calling you to do, as his prophet, speaking up for God's point of view. God wants you to help people

- to grow spiritually,
- to thrive physically,
- and to have a voice in an unjust world.

## The power to do it

Don't worry. As St Peter said, we all have the power to speak for God, as Joel foretold: young and old, men and women, slaves and free, God's poured his Spirit on you, in fulfilment of the prophecy. Each one of us has the power to be a spokesperson for God, calling for unselfishness and care for the needy.

## Suggested hymns

*Breathe on me, breath of God; Come down, O love divine; God's Spirit is in my heart; O thou, who camest from above.*

## Trinity Sunday  18 May
*Principal Service*  **A Road Map**
Isa. 40:12–17, 27–31 The greatness of God; Ps. 8 Stewardship of nature; 2 Cor. 13:11–13 God, Jesus and the Holy Spirit; Matt. 28:16–20 Baptism in the name of the Trinity

> *'Jesus came and said to them, "All authority in heaven and on earth has been given to me. Go therefore and make disciples of all nations, baptizing them in the name of the Father and of the Son and of the Holy Spirit."' Matthew 28:18–19*

## A road map

A student, training for ordination to the ministry of the church, was allowed to preach his first practice sermon in a tiny church tucked away in the Oxfordshire countryside. His misfortune was that this was to be on Trinity Sunday. So the student thought about the language we use – Father, Son and Holy Spirit, three Persons in one God. What inadequate words to describe the majesty of God, he thought. God's far too big to be contained in tiny, nit-picking phrases like that. God's bigger than the universe he created, so no doctrine formed out of mere words can even begin to describe the nature of God. The student seized his pen and began to write his sermon notes. 'God has no more resemblance to the doctrine of the Trinity', he wrote, 'than a ... hilly landscape has to a road map.' He completed the notes, and set off to find the church where he was going to preach. Unfortunately, he arrived after the service had started, having got thoroughly lost while looking for the church, because he hadn't got a road map!

## A salutary lesson

The student had learnt a very salutary lesson. However inadequate a road map may be in describing the full reality, we do actually need a road map. However insufficient the doctrine of the Trinity may be at describing the majesty of God, we do actually need that form of words. Without it, we may easily lose our way when trying to talk about God.

## Baptism in the name of the Trinity

Jesus told his disciples to baptize their new converts 'in the name of the Father and of the Son and of the Holy Spirit'. There are many other places in the gospel where Jesus speaks about his Father, and his Spirit, and he said 'I and my Father are one'. Because of this, many churches allow anyone who's been 'baptized in the name of the Trinity', to receive the Holy Communion. The insistence on the trinitarian nature of the baptism is not to set up verbal hurdles for people to jump, but to emphasize that the nature of the God we believe in is like that of a loving family. A Trinity in Unity.

## Monotheism

You see, there are many sorts of unity. There's the one-ness of the man who goes off alone for a week's hunting in the woods, and never speaks to another living soul. Enjoyable for those who have that sort of temperament, but it doesn't do any good to anybody else. Or there's the one-ness of a large family, who've learnt not only to tolerate each other's quirky characteristics, but to enjoy the fact that no two of them are the same. Therefore they're happy to welcome even quite eccentric visitors to their home, because they're already quite used to the variety of human nature. I think the second sort of one-ness is a much better picture for imagining God than the first. It's a unity of love, Father, Son and Holy Spirit living together, each with their own job to do, but with only one plan, one purpose, one will, one aim. That aim is to draw the whole human race into their family of love, so that we can all enjoy each other in our exciting diversity, in the great dance of love that we call the Kingdom of heaven.

## Theology

That sort of language might not satisfy the theologians, I don't know. But it seems to me to express the loving wonder of what St Paul meant when he wished his friends: 'The grace of the Lord Jesus Christ, the love of God, and the communion of the Holy Spirit be with you all.' The idea of God as a family, with an open welcome, expresses some of the loving generosity of Jesus when he said: 'Go therefore and make disciples of all nations, baptizing them in the name of the Father and of the Son and of the Holy Spirit.' And although it may not quite convey the loving majesty of Jesus when he said: 'All authority in heaven and on earth has been given to me', yet at least it gives us a sort of road map, which points us in the right direction to glimpse the indescribable greatness of God.

### All-age worship

*Discuss how families can settle their arguments.*

### Suggested hymns

*Father of heaven, whose love profound; Firmly I believe and truly; Holy holy, holy holy, holy holy, Lord God almighty; Meekness and majesty.*

## Trinity Sunday

*(For Corpus Christi, the Thursday after Trinity Sunday, see page 324.)*

**Second Service   Awe** Ps. 93 God's majesty, 150 Praise God in his sanctuary; Isa. 6:1–8 Holy, holy, holy; John 16:5–15 The Father, Jesus and the Advocate

> *'One called to another and said: "Holy, holy, holy is the Lord of hosts; the whole earth is full of his glory." ' Isaiah 6:3*

### John Wayne

When they were filming the biblical epic *The Greatest Story Ever Told*, John Wayne, hero of so many western movies, played the centurion at the crucifixion. At the first take, he's supposed to have said his one and only line in a totally flat, emotionless tone of voice: 'Truly-this-man-was-the-son-of-God.' 'No, no, John,' protested the director, 'say it with *awe, A W E awe!*' In the second take, the great actor used the exclamation spelt AW, saying, 'Aw, truly-this-man-was-the-son-of-God.'

## Awe

What is awe, spelt A W E? The dictionary definition is 'dread mingled with veneration, as of the Divine Being'; 'solemn and reverential wonder, tinged with latent fear, inspired by what is sublime and majestic in nature'. This may have been the first feeling of religious emotion that human beings ever knew. A man came to a gnarled and knotted tree in a clearing, and realized it was very, very old – far older than he was, or any of his relatives. He stood still, transfixed with awe at the unimaginable length of time, and the brevity of his own life in comparison. He called it a holy place. Or he climbed to the top of a mountain, and gasped when he saw another valley beyond the one he lived in, and another, and another. He sat down, wondering at the wideness of the world, and how little of it he knew. These feelings of awe continue today. Most people, the first time they look through a telescope, are overcome by the vastness of space, the whirling galaxies millions of light-years away, how many stars there are, and how tiny we are. The only possible reaction is to keep a respectful silence. Awe before nature is the beginning of sensing the holiness of God, the 'fascinating and frightening mystery'.

## God

God made the universe, so God's far greater than the universe; greater than we can even begin to imagine. This sense of awe before God's majesty runs right through the Bible. When Isaiah received his call to be a prophet, he *saw* the invisible God high and lifted up, and heard the seraphim singing the praise of the Trinity: 'Holy, holy, holy is the LORD of hosts; the whole earth is full of his glory.' Then Isaiah said, 'Woe is me! I am lost, for I am a man of unclean lips, and I live among a people of unclean lips; yet my eyes have seen the King, the LORD of hosts!'

## The holiness of love

Isaiah discovered that the holiness of God is a moral holiness. Many tribes believed in the ritual purity of their temple, and that nothing unclean or ritually defiled must be taken in. But Isaiah's awe-struck reaction was to be ashamed of his words: 'I am a man of unclean lips, and I live among a people of unclean lips.' It was what he and his people had *said* that made them unworthy to come into the presence of the Holy One: their words of hatred, their words of pride, their gossip about their neighbours, and the lack of charity with which they judged them. That's what makes us unholy, that's why we're all unholy, why none of us is worthy to come into the presence of God as we are. We've all spoken words lacking in love. And what should make us stand in dread and fascination before almighty God, is not just his greatness, but the incredible greatness of his love. How can unloving and unlovely human beings dare to come into the presence of high-voltage love like that? We should be burnt to a cinder. 'It is a terrible thing to fall into the presence of the living God.' What frightens us is the holiness of love. That's what truly calls forth our awe.

## The solution

There is, however, a solution to this dilemma. God sends a red-hot coal from his altar and sears away the sin from our lips, cauterizing them with his burning love. The love of Jesus on the cross, the flame of the Holy Spirit. Now we're pure enough to approach God, and hear the One-in-three saying,

> 'Whom shall *I* send, and who will go for *us*?'
> 'You must be holy, because I am holy.'

Now that our lips have been cleansed by the holiness of God's love, we're fit to answer: 'Here am I. Send me.' All the words of hatred are burnt away, so that we can carry God's messages of love to his children whom he loves, that we may all become holy in love. What an awe-inspiring idea!

### Suggested hymns

*Bright the vision that delighted; Holy, holy, holy, Lord God al-mighty; I, the Lord of sea and sky; Majesty, worship his majesty.*

## First Sunday after Trinity (Proper 3)   25 May
*Principal Service*   **Love Your Enemies**
Lev. 19:1–2, 9–18 Love your neighbour; Ps. 119:33–40 Trust in God's word; 1 Cor. 3:10–11, 16–23 Building God's Temple; Matt. 5:38–48 Love your enemies

> *'You have heard that it was said, "You shall love your neighbour and hate your enemy." But I say to you, Love your enemies.'*
> *Matthew 5:43–44*

### Oberammergau

In the German town of Oberammergau, a Passion play's produced every ten years. After the powerful depiction of the crucifixion in the theatre, a united service is held in the little Lutheran church nearby. One day, during the production in the year 2000, an elderly Englishman was seen coming out of the church in tears. When the chaplain asked him why, he replied it was because it was the first time he'd ever said the 'Our Father' together with a German, kneeling side by side. During the war, he'd been taught to hate all Germans because they were the enemy. Now he'd understood that every German, whether they'd fought in the war or not, is his brother or sister, children of the same heavenly Father. He knew at last what Jesus meant by 'Love your enemies'.

## What enemies do

The difficulty, of course, is that we have to hate what our enemies do, while loving them as people. Hate the sin and love the sinner. For those who are pacifists, this involves submitting to the worst your enemies can do to you without using violence to resist. For others, it'll be a question of defending your friends and family while using minimum force. And when anyone does something bad, it doesn't mean leaving them unpunished, or they'll never learn to be good. But it does mean punishing them, not in order to get revenge, but in such a way as to build up their character, because you love them. Compare the relationship of parent and child: you'll use gentle discipline to help your child towards personal growth, and you'll tell your child that no matter how you hate what they do, you'll always love your children.

## Personal relationships

For this command to love our enemies isn't only about international relations, war and peace; it's also about personal relationships. It's about how you treat the person who's done you a really bad turn, or been cruel to you. No revenge, says Jesus; learn to love them instead. Now, this would be impossible if it was a matter of how you feel about them. Your feelings aren't under your control to that extent. It would even be wrong to like someone who does evil. One sort of love comes from your feelings, and you can't help loving those who love you. But loving your enemies is an act of the will. However much you hate what they do, you decide to treat them in a kind, compassionate and caring way, to do what's in their long-term best interests. You make up your mind to behave towards them in a loving way.

## Christians only

This decision that 'I *will* love my enemy' is only possible if you're a Christian. Christians know that we've made ourselves God's enemies by our sin and disobedience. Yet even so, Jesus laid down his life for us, the just for the unjust. In gratitude for that, we must love those whom Jesus loves, and Jesus loves everybody. It's only possible if you open your heart to Jesus and let him come in, and then Jesus will love your enemies *through you*, no matter what your feelings are. Loving enemies is a job for which only Christians need apply.

## To be like God

The reason why Christians will want to love their enemies, is because it makes us like God. God doesn't make sure that the life-giving rain only falls on the crops in the fields of good people, leaving the bad people's fields dry and parched. Though you perhaps know the little parody of Jesus's words which runs:

> The rain it raineth every day
> upon the just and unjust feller,
> but chiefly on the just, because
> the unjust has the just's umbrella!

But God's love is universal, undiscriminating, even for his enemies. God made us to be like him. So God will give us the grace to love even our enemies, like God does. Where do you start? By kneeling down and praying for them, even praying with them if it's possible. Say the 'Our Father' for them. Nobody can hate someone whom they've just declared to be their brother or sister.

## *All-age worship*

*Write on a piece of paper the names of people you find it hard to love. Don't show anybody, but fold it and take it to a safe place where you can make a cross inscribed 'Jesus loved me when I was his enemy.' Then burn the paper at the foot of the cross.*

## *Suggested hymns*

*For the healing of the nations; It is a thing most wonderful; Make me a channel of your peace; There is a green hill far away.*

# First Sunday after Trinity
*Second Service*   **Judgement and Restoration**

Ps. 18: 1–20 *or* 18:21–30 The Lord my shield; Amos 9:5–15 Sieving and building; Eph. 6:1–20 The armour of God; *Gospel at Holy Communion*: Mark 2:1–12 A paralysed man healed

> *'The eyes of the Lord God are upon the sinful kingdom, and I will destroy it from the face of the earth – except that I will not utterly destroy the house of Jacob, says the Lord.'* Amos 9:8

## Si monumentum requiris, circumspice

Over the north door of St Paul's in London there's a famous plaque commemorating the man who designed the cathedral, Sir Christopher Wren. The dedication simply consists of four words of Latin, which, translated into English, mean, 'If you require a monument, look around you.' No further tribute to the architect was necessary: the cathedral which he'd built was sufficient evidence of his genius. Yet even the finest building begins with a building-site. And what a mess they are! Perhaps old buildings are being demolished because they're no longer suitable. There are bricks and stones to stumble over, and seemingly meaningless trenches to fall into, and to the ignorant visitor it seems impossible that this chaos could ever turn into a fine edifice. Somewhere there's a huge pile of sand. These days it comes in huge sacks, ready-to-use. Not so long ago, however, there was a big wire sieve and a man with a shovel would throw the sand, which had come straight from the quarry, through the sieve. The fine sand would pass through, and the pebbles would be stopped by the mesh. In ancient times a small sieve was held in the hands, and shaken about so that the sand fell through.

## Work in progress

In the Old Testament, the prophet Amos describes the universe as a building site. He was a poet, and wasn't stupid enough to imagine that God literally laid the foundation of the vault of the skies on the earth, and built his upper rooms above them. But it's an imagination-boggling metaphor. If you want a monument to God's activity, look around you. Yet Amos makes a very profound point: human souls and human society are an integral part of God's plan for the universe. And God hasn't finished that part of his construction yet. It is work in progress. Some people put a paper on their bedroom doors, or over the place where they work, which reads: 'Be patient with me, God hasn't finished with me yet.' It gives us some comfort to know that, in spite of our failings, God's still at work on us, trying to turn us, if we'll let him, into the sort of people he wants us to be.

## Society

Human society's made up of imperfect and unfinished individuals, so it's no wonder that our national life sometimes resembles a building site. There's a lot wrong with it, but there's hope that one day it'll emerge as a fine structure. But in this stage of God's work, God requires the willing co-operation of individual people. He needs people who are willing to be changed themselves, and to work with God in changing the world into the sort of place God designed it to be.

## Nations

First of all God chose a nation, the Israelites, saved them from their slavery in Egypt, and took them to the promised land. He did this to show them they were nothing in themselves, but totally dependent on God. Yet they began to think they'd been given the land because they were better than their neighbours. So God tells them that he's also saved the Ethiopians, the Philistines and the Syrians, the enemies of the Israelites, who all had a part in God's design for the world. God will demolish anything on the building site which isn't good enough for him to use – including, if necessary, the Israelite kingdom. But he'll sift the individuals, like a builder sieving the stones from the sand, selecting those who'll be useful to him in building the kingdom of God. 'For lo, I will command, and shake the house of Israel ... as one shakes with a sieve.'

We're all of us being judged, all the time, to see whether we're pliable enough to be of any use to God. Then God can start building, but the kingdom of God's still 'work in progress'. We've all got a different task to do in working towards God's final design. Are you willing to make changes in your life, to become more loving and more imaginative, so that you'll be a useful tool in God's hand? We're all needed. Then we can look around, and praise God the builder, and take a pride in our part in the work. 'If you require a monument, look around you.'

*God is working his purpose out; Thy kingdom come, O God; Will you come and follow me?; Ye who know the Lord is gracious.*

## Second Sunday after Trinity (Proper 4)    1 June
*Principal Service*    **Excitement**

(*Continuous*): Gen. 6:9–22; 7:24; 8:14–19 Noah; Ps. 46 Our refuge and strength, be still and know; *or* (*Related*): Deut. 11:18–21, 26–28 Choose blessing; Ps. 31:1–5, 19–24 Providence; Rom. 1:16–17; 3:22b–28 [29–31] Justified by grace through faith; Matt. 7:21–29 The house on the rock

> *'[Jesus said,] "Everyone then who hears these words of mine and acts on them will be like a wise man who built his house on rock. The rain fell, the floods came, and the winds blew and beat on that house, but it did not fall, because it had been founded on rock."' Matthew 7:24–25*

### Sundays after Trinity

A poem by John Meade Falkner called 'Sundays after Trinity' begins like this:

> We have done with dogma and divinity,
> Easter and Whitsun past,
> The long, long Sundays after Trinity
> Are with us at last;
> The passionless Sundays after Trinity,
> Neither feast-day not fast.

At this time of year, we long to be rid of excitement and have a peaceful summer. Churches which have coloured hangings and vestments change them to green for the Sundays after Trinity, for green's the colour of growing things, plants and trees. So this is supposed to be a period of slow but steady spiritual growth, when we reflect on what we learnt at Christmas and Easter, and how we can put it into practice by living a kind and compassionate life.

## No peaceful life

Unfortunately, if you long for a peaceful life, free of interruptions and excitements, I'm sorry to tell you that in the real world there's no such thing. There's said to be an old Chinese curse, where you wish your enemy, 'May you live in *interesting* times!' Unfortunately, all times are interesting, and the ups and downs of world events are bound to impinge on all of us eventually.

## Built on the rock

Jesus told a story of two houses, one with firm foundations, built on the rock, and one with no foundations at all, just resting on the sand. Children learn an action song:

> The wise man built his house on the rock, (3)
> And the rain came tumbling down.
> And the rain came down and the floods came up, (3)
> And the house on the rock stood firm.
> The foolish man built his house on the sand, (3)
> And the rain came tumbling down.
> And the rain came down and the floods came up, (3)
> And the house on the sand fell CRASH!

We all need firm foundations to our lives, to withstand the storms of life which come our way. The only way is to found our lives on the teaching of Jesus.

## Living dangerously

Some people like living dangerously. They go in for hazardous sports – mountain climbing, parachuting or white-water rafting. Yet even these have rules, and people are careful to abide by the safety procedures. The rules for coping with the risks of everyday life are to hear the words of Jesus and to obey them.

## Obedience

William Barclay, in *The Daily Study Bible,* tells the story of a group of sailors whose officer suddenly shouted 'Lie down!' What he could see, but they couldn't, was that a steel cable had snapped. If they hadn't obeyed instantly, their heads would all have been cut off by the cable. Our obedience to the words of Jesus must be as instant and unquestioning as that.

## Risking all

Living the Christian life means risking all for God. There's an exhilaration which comes from not knowing where we shall go or what may happen to us if we're faithful to Christ. Yet God's taken a risk, too, in giving us free will, for even God doesn't know whether we shall misuse our freedom. Canon Vanstone wrote a book called *Love's Endeavour, Love's Expense,* about the risks God takes in creating us. The author starts with the image of a potter shaping a vase, holding his breath in case the vase is misshapen, willing it to 'come out right'. Being a parent's a bit like that, he says: watching your children learn from their mistakes, teaching them the rules that at least mitigate the disasters, but knowing that they'll never grow up if you forbid them to take risks. Then God our Father must feel the same, as he watches us misusing the freedom he's given us. There's no way he can prevent us hurting ourselves without taking away our free will. So God bites his fingers and holds his breath as he watches to see whether we shall resist the temptation to go wrong. When the peaceful Sundays after Trinity are over, and the storms begin again, God will make sure that in the end we're safe, so long as we build our lives on the firm foundation of hearing and obeying the teaching of Jesus.

### All-age worship

*Learn the actions for the song. Make cardboard houses on rock and sand foundations.*

### Suggested hymns

*Affirm anew the threefold name; City of God, how broad and far; How sweet the name of Jesus sounds; Morning glory, starlit sky.*

## Second Sunday after Trinity
*Second Service*  **Ruth**  Ps. 33 The word of the Lord; Ruth 2:1–20a Ruth meets Boaz; Luke 8:4–15 The parable of the sower

*'Boaz took Ruth and she became his wife. When they came together, the Lord made her conceive, and she bore a son ... They named him Obed; he became the father of Jesse, the father of David.' Ruth 4:13, 17*

## A romantic novel

In the Old Testament you'll find one of the oldest and most beautiful examples of what's now called the Romantic Novel. Like many historical fictions it's based on real people and actual events, written up to make a gripping tear-jerker. The name of the book is Ruth.

## The story so far

It's a story about events in the past. Ruth wasn't Jewish; she came from Moab, in the mountains south-east of the Dead Sea. Her mother-in-law, Naomi, was a Jew who'd emigrated to Moab with her sons, one of whom married a local girl, Ruth. But Ruth's married happiness was short-lived, for not long after the wedding day her new Jewish husband died. What could she do now? Her own people regarded her mixed marriage with distaste, and she'd never find another husband in those parts. So, to escape starvation, she decided to accompany her mother-in-law who was returning to Israel, a distant land which Ruth had never seen. Ruth said a lovely thing to Naomi:

> 'Where you go, I will go; where you lodge, I will lodge; your people shall be my people, and your God my God. Where you die, I will die – there will I be buried ... [not even death will part] me from you!'

They travelled back to Bethlehem, a town whose name makes Christians and Jews alike prick up their ears, and there the local landowner was a man called Boaz. Ruth was a foreigner, an alien, an immigrant; she knew no local people, little of their language, and nothing of their customs. But Naomi had explained to her daughter-in-law a very practical Jewish custom. If a Jewish man died, his widow wasn't left to fend for herself, but the dead man's brother took her into his home, married her, and she bore children to him who were counted as the dead man's children, and would support her in her old age. Now Boaz wasn't a brother to Ruth's late husband, but he *was* next-of-kin. The next part of the story's very delicately told. Naomi tells Ruth to glean the ears of wheat left behind by the reapers, and Boaz notices this beautiful foreigner. Keats suggested that the song of the nightingale was

> Perhaps the self-same song that found a path
> Through the sad heart of Ruth, when, sick for home,
> She stood in tears amid the alien corn.

Anyway, that night Boaz wakes up to find Ruth lying at his feet. 'He said, "Who are you?" And she answered, "I am Ruth, your servant; spread your cloak over your servant, for you are next-of-kin."' He draws his cloak over her; suffice it to say that he goes to court to affirm his right, as next-of-kin to her late husband, to marry the beautiful widow.

## Anti-racist

So the story had a happy ending. But actually it's an anti-racist novel, and the sting's in the tail, where it mentions King David – until Jesus, the greatest of the kings of Israel. The final words of the book of Ruth are: 'Boaz took Ruth and she became his wife. When they came together, the LORD made her conceive, and she bore a son. They named him Obed; he became the father of Jesse, the father of David.' So the novel was written after David became king, and some think even five hundred years later, at the time when Ezra was telling every Jewish man who'd married a foreigner to divorce his foreign wife, to avoid the abomination of miscegenation, and mixed-race children diluting the purity of the race. 'Hang on a minute,' the anonymous author of this political novel's saying, 'even the great King David had a "filthy foreign woman", as you call them, as his great-grandmother!'

## Aliens

So this nice mushy romantic story turns out to be very controversial, today, just as when it was written. The Chief Rabbi recently pointed out that the Hebrew Scriptures in as many as thirty-six places tells us to love 'the alien'. We don't call them that today, as the word has come to apply to extra-terrestrials! We call them foreigners. Immigrants. Asylum-seekers. If they have a darker skin than ours, we have some even ruder words. The Bible says we have a duty to respect them and care for their needs. Jesus was the 'Son of David', so Ruth was Jesus's ancestor. Ruth the Moabitess, the foreign wife. Surely that lays a duty on every Christian to respect every foreigner as if they were our own family?

## *Suggested hymns*

*Brother, sister, let me serve you; Christ is the world's true light; In Christ there is no east or west; We are marching in the light of God (Siyahamba).*

## Third Sunday after Trinity (Proper 5)   8 June
*Principal Service*   **Healing through Peace**

(*Continuous*): Gen. 12:1–9 Abram sets out in faith; Ps. 33:1–12 The Word in creation; *or* (*Related*): Hos. 5:15—6:6 Return to the Lord; Ps. 50:7–15 A sacrifice of thanksgiving; Rom. 4:13–25 Abraham's faith, not works of the law; Matt. 9:9–13, 18–26 Healing, forgiveness and faith

> '*Jesus turned, and seeing her he said, "Take heart, daughter; your faith has made you well." And instantly the woman was made well.*' *Matthew 9:22*

### Miracles

Do you believe in miracles? We read in the Gospels that Jesus healed many sick people, and that appears to be a miracle, though the word miracle appears in none of the Gospels. Most people think a miracle is something which goes against the laws of science. But many scientists and medical people have no problem with the healings in the Bible.

### Science

Science consists in analysing events, and predicting what'll happen if they're repeated under controlled conditions. In that sense it's very like the Christian faith: we look at the evidence, guess at an explanation, and then perform an experiment to see whether the explanation is true. Only, in the case of Christianity, the experiment involves giving your whole life to God. But in this sense, medicine, while it depends on observation and experiment, is not an exact science, because the same set of circumstances are never repeated in two patients. All a doctor can say is that, if nothing unexpected happens, there's a statistical probability whether a patient will be healed or not. But the presence of Jesus, God incarnate, was a very unforeseen circumstance, and no scientist would dare to predict what could or could not happen in that case.

### Hindrances and helps

What's more, God's put into our bodies a wonderful and complex mechanism for self-healing. Very often what the doctor does is to create the right circumstances to enable the body to heal itself. Among the chief hindrances to this process are the stresses and tensions which are set up in the mind. The body affects the mind, but the mind also affects the body. It's well known that stress can cause cancer, and can aggravate many other illnesses. Many of the cases of paralysis that Jesus healed, and maybe also those of blindness, may have been psychosomatic, when the mind caused the body to show symptoms which saved it from having to face the causes of stress. So if Jesus could bring peace to troubled minds, it could easily have been the means of healing.

## Forgiveness

Jesus said to the woman with a haemorrhage, in today's Gospel reading, 'Your sins are forgiven, your faith has saved you.' That must have surprised her; it wasn't what she'd been asking for. Many people believed then in a judgemental God, who punishes us and rejects us because of the things we've done. Many people today still think of God like that. Jesus taught them about a loving Father, who's only waiting for us to turn to him, so that he can welcome us back to his heart. Faith in a God like that will remove stress and give a deep inner peace.

## Peace and healing

In some cases peace will give physical healing; it did with this woman. This is still true today. People who pray with somebody who's sick, or, failing that, pray for them in their absence, have always found that to surround somebody with love brings deep peace of mind, and sometimes physical healing. Sometimes, but not always. Nearly everyone has seen some miraculous answers to prayer, and the healing of people who nobody had expected would get better. God always answers prayer, but not always in the way and at the time that we want him to. Often in a better way than we had expected. Sometimes, instead of taking away the pain, God gives us the patience and the grace to endure it. Finally, death is surely the ultimate healing, when all tears are wiped from our eyes, and sufferers are at peace in eternity with our loving heavenly Father. It may not be the form of healing we'd asked for, but often we can see in retrospect that eternal rest is a better outcome than the one we'd wanted. God's will for us is peace, and with his peace he gives us his healing. The peace which comes to us when we pray is the real miracle. The healing which often follows is quite natural. I began by asking whether you believe in miracles. One of those fridge-magnet things has the words, 'I don't just believe in miracles – I depend on them!' I pray that you, too, may know God's peace in your hearts.

## All-age worship

*Relax, one after the other, each leg and arm, your neck and your face, then your mind. Ask God to take away your pain and stress.*

## Suggested hymns

*Be still, for the presence (Spirit) of the Lord; Lord of all, to whom alone; Peace, perfect peace; Thine arm, O Lord, in days of old.*

# Third Sunday after Trinity
## *Second Service* Friends

Ps. [39 Prayer for wisdom] 41 My friend; 1 Sam. 18:1–16 Saul, Jonathan and David; Luke 8:41–56 Jairus' daughter and the sick woman

> *'Jonathan made a covenant with David, because he loved him as his own soul.' 1 Samuel 18:3*

## Saul and David

King Saul liked the young shepherd-boy named David. When Saul had one of his increasingly frequent fits of incipient madness, he sent for David to play soothingly to him on the harp. David, for his part, seems to have liked and admired King Saul. But the friendship went sour, and soon Saul threw his spear at David, and hunted him across country trying to kill him. David, however, remembered how deep their friendship had been, to begin with. Today we'd probably have warned him, 'With friends like that, who needs enemies?' David wrote a psalm about false friends, which was later applied to Judas Iscariot, whom Jesus befriended with such fatal consequences:

> Yea, mine own familiar friend, in whom I trusted,
> which did eat of my bread,
> hath lifted up his heel against me.

Times of difficulty show up who are your true friends; when you're in trouble, false friends vanish as quickly as do the morning mists when the day gets hot.

## David and Jonathan

King Saul had a son called Jonathan. Between David and Jonathan there sprang up a very deep and true friendship. Jonathan swore an oath of never-ending friendship with David, 'because he loved him as his own soul'. When Saul threatened to kill David, Jonathan saved David's life, at some risk to his own. David never forgot his friendship with Jonathan or Saul, and when they were both killed in battle David composed an unforgettable lament for them; for his friend who'd been a faithful friend, and his friend who'd become his enemy:

> Saul and Jonathan, beloved and lovely!
> In life and in death they were not divided ...
> I am distressed for you, my brother Jonathan;
> greatly beloved were you to me;
> your love to me was wonderful, passing the love of women.

## Dangers in friendship

These days, some people might raise an eyebrow at such language used between men. Same-sex friendships are under suspicion. Freudians would have us believe that there's a sexual element in every friendship, however small and subconscious, but that's no reason why we should be afraid of making close friends of either gender. It's a question of how we handle our friendships. In most cultures, friends will want to show their friendship by giving each other a hug, at least. What else they do is entirely their own business, and no concern of snoopy neighbours. But there are dangers in even the most innocent friendship. If it becomes passionate, the friends may become so engrossed in each other that they forget about their other friends altogether. This can happen in a marriage between two people who are deeply in love, and while it's understandable, it's not healthy. If God comes into our relationships, we shan't forget to be kind and companionable to the people around us.

## Blessings of friendship

But while remembering the dangers, let's thank God for the blessing of friendship. Friends are what make life enjoyable; the friendless person's a sad sack. But friendship, like marriage, needs working at. Ralph Waldo Emerson wrote 'A friend may well be reckoned the masterpiece of nature', and, 'The only way to have a friend is to be one.' There's a verse in the book of Proverbs:

> Some friends play at friendship,
> but a true friend sticks closer than one's nearest kin.

or you may know it better in the Authorized Version: 'There is a friend that sticketh closer than a brother.' If you find such a friend, count yourself richly blessed.

## Aelred of Rievaulx

So how do we balance the blessing of friendship with its dangers? St Aelred lived in the twelfth century; priests were allowed to marry in those days, and he was the son of a Saxon priest in Hexham. Monks, of course, were committed to celibacy, and Aelred went on to become the Abbott of the Cistercian Abbey of Rievaulx – now one of the many beautiful ruined monasteries in Yorkshire. He worried about how he was to handle the deep and sometimes passionate friendships between the men in the community he was responsible for. Aelred wrote a book on friendship, in which he recommended his monks to learn from their friendships, and use them to inspire a deep and personal friendship with Jesus. Jesus said, 'You are my friends if you do what I command you.' Friendship with Jesus is the best friendship of all. It's a friendship which is really worth working at.

## Suggested hymns

*Bind us together, Lord; Blest be the tie that binds; He wants (lacks) not friends that hath thy love; What a friend we have in Jesus.*

## Fourth Sunday after Trinity (Proper 6)   15 June
*Principal Service*   **Proclaiming God**
(*Continuous*): Gen. 18:1–15 [21:1–7] Abraham entertains the
strangers; Ps. 116:1, 10–17 Thanks; *or* (*Related*): Ex. 19:2–8a
A kingdom of priests; Ps. 100 Worship in the Temple; Rom. 5:1–8
While we were sinners; Matt. 9:35—10:8 [9–23] Witness to the
kingdom

> *'[Jesus said,] "As you go, proclaim the good news, 'The kingdom*
> *of heaven has come near.'" ' Matthew 10:7*

### Monkeys

If an infinite number of monkeys banged at random on the keys
of an infinite number of typewriters for an infinite length of time,
what's the probability that they would accidentally type the complete works of Shakespeare? The answer, because of what math-
ematicians mean by infinity, is that the probability also is infinite
– in other words, it's absolutely certain to happen eventually! But
of course, infinity doesn't exist in the real world, and we all know
that it could never really happen in a month of Sundays. Anyone
who insisted that it's already happened would be called a fool for
choosing the least likely alternative.

### Existence of God

Yet atheists do this all the time. Someone who insists that 'there is
no God' has to explain how the universe came to be so complex,
beautiful and efficient. They usually answer that it happened purely
by chance, evolving by a serious of random mutations. But it would
need an infinite number of mutations and an infinite length of time
for nature to throw up something like the human mind, purely by
accident. It's about as likely as a roomful of monkeys typing a play
by Shakespeare. Christians say that throughout the whole process,
God must have been at work. To say otherwise is to choose the
least likely explanation.

### Proofs

This is one of the classic arguments for the existence of God, the
'argument from design'. It isn't a proof that God exists; none of

them is. God doesn't want to clobber us over the head by proving that he exists; he prefers to allow space for faith to respond to love. But did this wonderful world happen by accident, or because God caused it to? In each argument, to say that it was accidental, because there is no God, is to choose the least likely option. To choose the atheist's explanation in the face of *all* these arguments is the height of folly.

## Arguments

Jesus tells us to proclaim the good news that God's kingdom's come near. But first we must proclaim that God exists. So you need to have at least heard of the classic arguments for the existence of God.

- We've already mentioned the *argument from design.*
- Then there's the *argument from purpose*: there seems to be a slow but steady progress in the universe and in human society towards a goal which God's already decided on.
- The *moral argument* points out that almost every human being distinguishes between right and wrong, yet if there's no God what's wrong with being utterly selfish? Dostoevsky wrote, 'If God is dead, everything is permitted.'
- The *human arguments* are a group of dilemmas based on the nature of human beings: it's hard to see how beings capable of rational thought could have evolved by accidental chance from an unthinking universe. Many of the world's cleverest and best people have believed in God; is it likely that they were all deluded? If so, how could they have achieved the good they've done?
- Then there's the *aesthetic argument*: how could the world be full of beauty, how could human beings appreciate beauty and create beauty, unless the universe were created by an artist?
- The *argument from scripture* and the *argument from prophecy* ask where so much great literature came from if not from God's revelation of himself.
- The *argument from miracle* depends on the fact that so many things happen in the universe that we can't explain by reason alone.
- The *ontological argument* says that everything exists because something else existed first; if God didn't exist, nothing else would exist.

## Good news

These aren't proofs; nobody can prove that God exists or that God doesn't exist. But each argument, separately, shows that it's easier to explain the facts on the assumption that there is a God than if there's not. Cumulatively, they add up to an overwhelming probability that God does exist. What they can't tell you is what God's like. Only Jesus can do that, with his talk of a loving and forgiving Father. If he's right, then the existence of God is really good news, which we should share boldly with the doubters. It's not unreasonable nonsense, it's not out-of-date and old-fashioned. In the life of Jesus, God came very close to us. So we should boldly 'proclaim the good news, "The kingdom of heaven has come near."' Anything else would be 'a load of monkeys'.

### All-age worship

*Discuss the possibility of a computer being able to programme another computer to be cleverer than the first one is.*

### Suggested hymns

*Lord of beauty, thine the splendour; Morning has broken; O Lord my God, when I in awesome wonder; The spacious firmament on high.*

## Fourth Sunday after Trinity
### *Second Service*   **Altar Bread**
Ps. [42 Like a deer] 43 The altar of God; 1 Sam. 21:1–15 Altar bread; Luke 11:14–28 The return of the demon

> 'That I may go to the altar of God, to the God of my joy and gladness: and on the lyre I will give thanks to you, O God my God.' *Psalm 43:4* (Common Worship)

### Nob

Young David was running away from King Saul, who threatened to kill him. He was hungry and had no food with him. He came to a town, east of Jerusalem, with the delightful name of Nob, and entered the local temple there. The priest, Ahimelech, said he had no ordinary bread to give him, only the consecrated bread. It seems there was an old tradition of sacrificing bread to the Lord in the temple, alongside the animal sacrifices. Only the priests were supposed to eat this bread, but Ahimelech agreed to let David have it, and David was nourished in the Temple. It's a curious story, and Jesus made use of it to justify his breaking the Sabbath law. He said:

> 'Have you not read what David did when he and his companions were hungry? He entered the house of God and ate the bread of the Presence, which it was not lawful for him or his companions to eat, but only for the priests ... But if you had known what this means, "I desire mercy and not sacrifice," you would not have condemned the guiltless. For the Son of Man is lord of the sabbath.'

## Spiritual food

Both David and Jesus broke the law because they were in need of material food. Both of them knew that it symbolized spiritual nourishment. In Psalm 43, the singer realizes that it's in God's house that he'll find food for the soul:

> That I may go to the altar of God,
> to the God of my joy and gladness:
> and on the lyre I will give thanks to you,
> O God my God.

Psalms 42 and 43 are really one psalm, the song of someone in sadness and despair, with a repeated refrain running through both of them:

> Why are you cast down, O my soul,
> and why are you disquieted within me?
> Hope in God;
> for I shall again praise him, my help and my God.

## Understanding

People sometimes say they've stopped going to church because they don't understand the services. Often what they mean is that they don't understand life: they don't understand why unbelievers become rich and good people suffer. You'll never find the answers to those questions by staying away; the answers are discovered as you wrestle with God in prayer, and give thanks to him for the good things he's given you. Like doubting Thomas, who found no answers while he hugged his doubts to himself, you only begin to see the meaning of life when you meet with others. The writer of Psalm 73 wrestled with the same problem, as to why wicked people prosper, and he wrote:

> Then thought I to understand this,
> but it was too hard for me,
> until I entered the sanctuary of God.

## The Living Bread

It's in church that we find nourishment for soul and mind, to strengthen us for the journey of life. Jesus said: 'I am the living bread that came down from heaven. Whoever eats of this bread will live forever; and the bread that I will give for the life of the world is my flesh.' We come to church to meet Jesus, and he feeds us here. In church, Jesus helps us to grow towards Christian maturity; we grow in understanding, and we grow in our relationship with God. Just as physical bread helps the body to grow strong, so the worship of the church strengthens our faith.

## Consecrated bread

David ate consecrated bread in the temple at Nob, which strengthened him for his journey. In the Church, too, we have consecrated bread, the bread of the Holy Communion, Eucharist, Mass, Lord's Supper, call it what you will. We may not understand how attendance at this sacrament gives us spiritual strength, but it's a fact of experience that it does. So if ever you're puzzled, depressed or angry with God, don't think you can solve it by staying away. How can God strengthen you then?

> Why are you cast down, O my soul,
> and why are you disquieted within me?
> Hope in God; for I shall again praise him,
> my help and my God …
> That I may go to the altar of God,
> to the God of my joy and gladness:
> and on the lyre I will give thanks to you,
> O God my God.

## Suggested hymns

*As pants the hart; How lovely is your dwelling place; I am the bread of life; O food to pilgrims given.*

## Fifth Sunday after Trinity (Proper 7)   22 June
*Principal Service*   **God Cares for Sparrows**

(*Continuous*): Gen. 21:8–21 Hagar; Ps. 86:1–10, 16–17 All nations; or (*Related*): Jer. 20:7–13 Jeremiah's prayer; Ps. 69:8–11 [12–17] 18–20 Zeal for the Temple; Rom. 6:1b–11 Dead to sin and alive to God; Matt. 10:24–39 His eye on the sparrow

> '[Jesus said to his disciples,] "Are not two sparrows sold for a penny? Yet not one of them will fall to the ground apart from your Father ... So do not be afraid; you are of more value than many sparrows."' Matthew 10:29, 31

### 'His eye is on the sparrow'

In 1905, an American woman called Mrs Civilla Martin became friends with a Mr and Mrs Doolittle in Elmira, New York. Mrs Doolittle had been bedridden for twenty years; her husband set off to work each day in a wheelchair. When the Martins asked them how their faith in God kept them so cheerful, Mrs Doolittle replied, 'His eye is on the sparrow, and I know he watches me.' Mrs Martin immediately wrote a hymn with these words as the refrain, and it's been popular ever since:

> Why should I feel discouraged, why should the shadows come,
> Why should my heart be lonely, and long for heaven and home,
> When Jesus is my portion? My constant friend is he:
> His eye is on the sparrow, and I know he watches me.
> > *I sing because I'm happy,*
> > *I sing because I'm free,*
> > *For his eye is on the sparrow,*
> > *And I know he watches me.*

### Jesus on sparrows

Jesus probably chose to speak about sparrows because they were the commonest wild birds in the Holy Land. In Britain, also, they used to be, but their numbers have declined recently. The cheeky way that sparrows peck up seeds in gardens or streets led to Londoners calling themselves 'Cockney sparrows'. Yet the lives of sparrows are short, and to suggest that the creator of the universe cares about each individual sparrow which falls dead to the ground was an astonishing claim to make. But we're used nowadays to the thought of super-computers which can hold billions and squillions of facts in their memory at one time. Whatever picture we have in our minds of the awesome greatness of God, surely he can do the same and more so. Therefore, as Jesus said, if God can care for each unthinking sparrow, how much more will he care for you! You're the creatures he's made able to think and reason, to be aware of God's love for you, and respond by loving God in return. Surely God will care, then, about even the most trivial things that happen to you, and nothing's too unimportant to ask him about in your prayers.

## Suffering

That isn't to say that he keeps you from suffering, any more than he stops the sparrow falling to the ground. He didn't lift Mrs Doolittle from her bed or Mr Doolittle from his wheelchair. But Jesus, on the cross, shows us that Almighty God cares so much about our suffering that he comes down to earth and suffers with us. It's knowing that, which helps suffering Christians keep cheerful: God cares about suffering sparrows, and God cares about suffering people.

## Persecution

Jesus uses this comparison in the context of a warning to his followers that they'll be persecuted. Roman Emperors could, and did, take the lives of Christians who refused to deny their faith, and Christians were very frightened of the Emperor. But all the Emperor could do was kill their body, predicted Jesus; he couldn't touch their immortal soul. Whereas if they escaped from the Emperor by saying that they didn't believe in a loving God, then they'd be liable to the judgement of God, who's much more powerful than the Emperor. It was not the Emperor they should fear, said Jesus, but God, who could judge them for being faithless.

## Faithful

Yet for Christians who *are* faithful, it's not God the Judge we're dealing with, but the loving God who cares even for the sparrows. We're unlikely to risk our lives for our faith these days. But if we admit to being a Christian, we may risk mockery by our friends, we may risk our job or our promotion, we may risk being written off by our relations as old-fashioned and irrelevant. And we shall very likely have to endure physical suffering, great or small, at some time in our lives. But be steadfast, hold on to your faith, proclaim it boldly, and Jesus will be with you in your suffering. Then store these words in your memory for when you feel low:

> *I sing because I'm happy,*
> *I sing because I'm free,*
> *For his eye is on the sparrow,*
> *And I know he watches me.*

### All-age worship

*Learn the names of some common garden birds. What can we do to protect them?*

### Suggested hymns

*All things bright and beautiful; I, the Lord of sea and sky; Like a mighty river flowing; Seek ye first the kingdom of God.* See www.cyberhymnal.org/htm/h/i/hiseyeis.htm

## Fifth Sunday after Trinity
*Second Service*   **War and Peace**
Ps. 46 God makes wars cease [48 Walk about Zion]; 1 Sam. 24:1–17 David spares Saul; Luke 14:12–24 Dinner guests

> '[God] makes wars to cease in all the world.' Psalm 46:9 (Common Worship)

## Vietnam

In 1968 an American colonel, serving in Vietnam, remarked to his pastor, 'Chaplain, we read Psalm 46 in church this morning, with

179

the words, "God makes wars to cease in all the world." Well, in this part of the world, he's not doing real well at it right now!' Yet a few years later, the Vietnam War did come to an end. Who can say whether or not God was involved in the process that brought it to a conclusion?

## The Old Testament

So what's God's record of peace-making? When that psalm was written, many people firmly believed that it was God's will that they should kill their enemies and seize their lands. You'll find many traces of this in the Old Testament, which creates a problem for those who think the whole Bible was dictated by God verbatim. Did God really tell Joshua to kill all the inhabitants of Jericho when the walls fell down? Did God really want King Saul to slay all the Amalekites, and for the prophet Samuel to hew their king, Agag, in pieces before the Lord? And so on, with many other seemingly God-inspired slaughters in the pages of Scripture. If that's what the Old Testament God wants, then he's not the sort of God I could worship. It's much more likely that these bloodthirsty people had misunderstood the will of God. God *was* making wars to cease, but it's a process, not an instantaneous change.

## Role-models

The Old Testament isn't all wrong. It's vitally important, because from its pages we learn that there's one God, who cares deeply about how we treat each other, and when we get ourselves into a mess, steps in to save us from it. Without the Old Testament, we shouldn't be able to understand what Jesus said about God, or what Jesus did to save us from our sins. But the Old Testament's not about perfect people – far from it. A novelist recently complained that the pictures in her Sunday school Bible made all the men look like heroes. Yet they weren't: even good King David had a rival murdered, so that David could sleep with the murdered man's wife. It'd be a big mistake to take the Bible characters as role-models; usually they're quite the opposite. But that's why it's such an encouraging book. If God could get his will done by working through imperfect people like them, he might even be able to work through you and me. If God could gradually get his desire for peace through to a violent society like that, he might be able to make it heard today.

## Jesus

Jesus didn't criticize the Old Testament. But he did criticize the way some people interpreted it. He went behind the words to the principles that lay behind them.

'You have heard that it was said, "An eye for an eye and a tooth for a tooth." 'But I say to you, Do not resist an evildoer ... You have heard that it was said, "You shall love your neighbour and hate your enemy." But I say to you, Love your enemies ... so that you may be children of your Father in heaven.'

## 2000 years

So why have there been so many wars since Jesus said that? Many of these wars have been waged in the name of religion, and opponents of Christianity often blame us for that. But irreligious people often choose to fight and merely use religion as an excuse, a peg to hang their guns from. And remember that two atheists, Joseph Stalin and Mao-tse-Tung, *each* caused the deaths of more people than all the religious wars of the past two thousand years. Probably if you calculated what proportion of the world's population died each year during the inter-tribal conflicts of the past, and set that against the worldwide casualty figures in the twenty-first century, you'd have to say that the teachings of Jesus have had an effect, though there's a long way to go before they're universally accepted.

## Peacemakers

In the Old Testament reading at this service, David had his persecutor King Saul at his mercy, but refused to kill him. That's how God makes wars to cease, when he persuades rivals not to retaliate. That's why God depends on you to be his peacemakers. It's only when you learn to not even think about seeking revenge on those who've hurt us – to set an example to others and to teach them to seek the way of reconciliation – that God will be able to make wars to cease in all the world. Through you. There's no other way.

## *Suggested hymns*

*For the healing of the nations; God is our strength and refuge; Make me a channel of your peace; O God of earth and altar.*

## Sixth Sunday after Trinity (Proper 8)
### (SS Peter and Paul)  29 June
*Principal Service*  **A Cup of Water**
(*Continuous*): Gen. 22:1–14 The sacrifice of Isaac; Ps. 13 How
long? or (*Related*): Jer. 28:5–9 True prophecy; Ps. 89:1–4, 15–18
Covenant with David; Rom. 6:12–23 Freed from sin;
Matt. 10:40–42 A cup of cold water

> '[Jesus said to his disciples,] "Whoever welcomes a prophet in the
> name of a prophet will receive a prophet's reward … and who-
> ever gives even a cup of cold water to one of these little ones in
> the name of a disciple – truly I tell you, none of these will lose their
> reward."' Matthew 10:41–42

### Don't shoot the messenger

When the Athenian army was wiped out in Sicily, the messenger
who brought the bad news back to Athens was condemned to be
fastened to a wheel and racked for a long time, according to Plu-
tarch. Possibly based on this story, the modern popular saying is,
'Don't shoot the messenger who brings you bad news.' It's quite
obvious that if something unpleasant's happened, it's not the messenger's fault. We ought to be grateful to messengers, even those
who bring a bad report; much more do we owe our gratitude to
someone who brings good news. If a messenger comes from a friend
of ours, to bring us greetings, we slap him on the back, sit him down
with a drink, and rhapsodize that 'Any friend of old so-and-so's a
friend of mine.' We treat with great kindness anyone who acts as
representative of someone we admire, almost as if the messenger
were the very one he's representing.

### Messengers of Jesus

Jesus sent the Twelve out on a mission as his representatives, saying, 'Whoever welcomes you welcomes me, and whoever welcomes
me welcomes the one who sent me.' In other words, if you give a
welcome to the messengers of Jesus, you're showing your love to
God. The next bit's a bit confusing in the NRSV translation, which
has kept the same literal translation as the Authorized Version. 'In
the name of a prophet' is an idiom in the language Jesus spoke for

'in the character of', or 'because you are a prophet'. If you praise a preacher, it's not just because he or she speaks well, it's because he or she is a messenger of Jesus. 'Prophets' in the New Testament usually means 'preachers' – occasionally they foretell the future, but mostly they proclaim what God thinks about the present. Preachers will be rewarded in heaven for what they've done, says Jesus. But so will people who couldn't preach to save their lives, but who've been kind to the preacher because preachers speak to us for Jesus, as his representatives. Any kindness shown to Christians because you respect them for what they are, will bring you a reward in heaven. Even a cup of cold water on a hot day.

## Orders of ministry

The words used in the Gospels for Christian ministers are not the words we normally choose. We don't usually call our preachers prophets, but that's what they are. The Twelve are simply called 'the Twelve' in this passage, though in other places they're called 'Apostles', which simply means missionaries. People in our church who are not in the ordained ministry we call 'lay people' – Jesus calls them 'disciples', which means 'learners' or 'students'. Or he calls you 'one of these little ones of mine' – my children. Isn't that nice? Apostles, prophets and disciples. There's a similar list of church officials in First Corinthians: 'God has appointed in the church first apostles, second prophets, third teachers ...'. Why not priests?

## A kingdom of priests

Actually there's no mention of Christian priests in the New Testament. Jewish priests, Christian bishops, deacons, elders, yes, but only Jesus is referred to as our great high priest. What St Peter *does* say is that the whole Church acts as a priest: 'Like living stones, let yourselves be built into a spiritual house, to be a holy priesthood, to offer spiritual sacrifices acceptable to God through Jesus Christ.' Our job as a community is to offer the world to God in prayer and Eucharist, and to offer God to the world in our words and in loving service to our neighbours. This is not quite the same as 'the priesthood of all believers', a Reformation idea which could easily mean everyone their own priest and no need for ministers. But if the whole Church has a priestly role, then that priesthood is focused in its leaders. It's right to call your ministers priests, because they lead you in your priesthood; and as they care for you, and you care

for them, don't forget that even a cup of water offered to a fellow
Christian earns you a reward in heaven.

### All-age worship

*Arrange to offer everyone in church a cup of cold water at the end
of the service.*

### Suggested hymns

*Forth in the name of Christ we go; O thou who camest from above;
Stand up and bless the Lord; Where cross the crowded ways of
life.*

## SS Peter and Paul, Apostles   29 June
*(or may be transferred to 30 June)*
**My Chains Fell Off** Zech. 4:1–6a, 10b–14 Two anointed ones;
Ps. 125 Stand fast for ever; Acts 12:1–11 Peter released from
Prison (*if the Acts reading is used instead of the Old Testament
reading, the New Testament reading is* 2 Tim. 4:6–8, 17–18 Poured
out); Matt. 16:13–19 Peter recognizes the Messiah;
**or for Peter alone** Ezek. 3:22–27 Preaching to his own; Ps.
125; Acts 12:1–11 (*if the Acts reading is used instead of the Old
Testament reading, the New Testament reading is* 1 Peter 2:19–25
Suffering for God); Matt. 16:13–19.

 'Then Peter came to himself and said, "Now I am sure that the
 Lord has sent his angel and rescued me."' Acts 12:11

### Amazement

Have you ever been so astonished at something wonderful that was
happening to you, that you felt as though you were in a daze? The
Psalmist put it like this:

> When the Lord restored the fortunes of Zion,
> then were we like those who dream.

Peter must have felt like that when the angel set him free from
prison. It's a marvellously vivid story, and must have come from

Peter's own mouth, because there were no other witnesses. There's a lovely touch at the end where it says, 'Peter came to himself.' If he came to himself, who or where was he before? Obviously on another planet! He'd been in a daze, unable to believe his luck. He didn't believe it was true, until he was safely out in the street, and the angel had gone away. Poor Peter! But at least he'd at last learnt humility, and didn't claim any credit for himself: 'The Lord sent his angel and rescued me', he said.

## What happened?

What happened? There's no way of knowing; we've only Peter's own account to go on, and he was in a daze. The word 'angel' could mean a human messenger, someone in authority, one of the jailers perhaps; or someone who'd got hold of a key and 'sprang' the prisoners when the guards were asleep. But I think it's more likely to have been a miracle, and miracles by definition are inexplicable.

## Thank God

But thank God, Peter was released. He went on to become the leader of all the Jewish Christians living outside Palestine, and according to tradition to become the first Bishop of Rome, or Pope. Herod had already killed James, one of the sons of Zebedee. If Peter had been killed too at that moment, the infant Church would have found it even harder to survive. Peter thanked God for his rescue. It's all very well to know intellectually that God's a god who saves; who brought the Israelites through the Red Sea, and who, through the cross of Jesus, saves us all from sin and death. But it's not until something happens to you personally that you really believe it. Then the knowledge makes what's called the longest journey in the world, from the head to the heart. This had probably happened to Peter already; has it happened to you? Do you know in your heart that 'The Lord has ... rescued me'?

## The Wesleys

The two Wesley brothers knew it. They were the founders of the movement which later became the Methodist Church. John Wesley came to personal faith when he felt his 'heart strangely warmed' at the age of thirty-five; Charles had experienced conversion three days earlier. Both felt this as a great release, and both wrote many hundreds of hymns. One of Charles Wesley's most-loved hymns was based on St Peter's release from prison, together with the similar experience which St Paul had when he was released from prison in Philippi during an earthquake. The hymn begins with the same sense of amazement that we spoke of earlier: 'And *can it be* ... that *I* ... should gain an interest in my Saviour's name?' What, me? Saved, set free and taken to heaven? Incredible!

> Died he for *me*, who caused His pain –
> For me, who him to death pursued?
> *Amazing love!* How can it be,
> That *thou*, my *God*, shouldst die for *me*?

## My chains fell off

And then in the fourth verse comes the comparison to St Peter and St Paul:

> Long my imprisoned spirit lay,
> Fast bound in sin and nature's night;
> Thine eye diffused a quickening ray –
> I woke, the dungeon flamed with light;
> My chains fell off, my heart was free,
> I rose, went forth, and followed Thee.
> My chains fell off, my heart was free,
> I rose, went forth, and followed Thee.

Can *you* say, from the heart, as both Peter and Paul did, that you *know* you've been set free from the guilt and power of sin, and the fear of death?

## Suggested hymns

*And can it be that I should gain; 'Thou art the Christ, O Lord'; 'Tis good, Lord, to be here; We sing the glorious conquest.*

## Seventh Sunday after Trinity (Proper 9)  6 July
*Principal Service*  **Some People are Never Satisfied**
(*Continuous*): Gen. 24:34–38, 42–49, 58–67 Rebecca betrothed; Ps. 45:10–17 A royal wedding; *or Canticle*: S. of Sol. 2:8–13, Love and springtime; *or* (*Related*): Zech. 9:9–12 Rejoice; Ps. 145:8–14

186

God's kingdom and love; Rom. 7:15–25a Judgement and the law
of God; Matt. 11:16–19, 25–30 John the Baptist

*'To what will I compare this generation? It is like children sitting
in the marketplaces and calling to one another, "We played the
flute for you, and you did not dance; we wailed, and you did not
mourn." '* Matthew 11:16–17

## Stories

'Yesterday', wailed the tour guide, 'all the passengers were complaining that the weather was too cold. Now they say it's too hot.
Some people are never satisfied!' An imaginary situation, but that's
an expression in common use. Jesus described another imaginary
situation, of some children playing games in the marketplace. One
lot are playing at weddings. They've got some flutes, and they're
playing wedding music – dance music. The rest of the children are
looking on, but they won't join in – dancing's the last thing they
want to do. Another group start playing funerals. An odd choice,
but children do strange things sometimes. They start weeping and
wailing, like at a funeral, and invite the rest to do the same. But nobody wants to share in a gloomy game like that. Nobody wants to
join in, at weddings or funerals. Some people are never satisfied.

## The application

When Jesus told this parable, people probably laughed, as they usually did at his stories. 'Children!' they chuckled. 'Never satisfied;
complaining that their playmates are too happy or too gloomy!
Daft kids!' Then they felt uncomfortable, because, as with many
of Jesus's stories, they realized the joke was on them. They'd been
criticizing Jesus for being too happy, and condemning John the
Baptist for being too gloomy. Jesus's satirical shaft had struck its
target: some people are never satisfied!

## John the Baptist

John the Baptist told the people that being religious and respectable wasn't good enough. He called them to repent of their sins
– they didn't think they'd committed any – and start living in a
more actively loving way. That's never a popular message; people
don't like sermons which make them think twice about their way

of life. So they changed the subject, and ridiculed John for being too judgemental.

## Jesus

Jesus was the opposite. He was always going to parties with disreputable folk, people who were immoral and might even have been traitors. Not the sort that respectable people would want to be seen with. And Jesus seemed to enjoy the revelry, so they said he was a 'glutton and a wine-bibber'; not to mince words, a greedy drunkard. It wasn't true, of course, but 'any stick will do to beat a dog'. What they really didn't like, however, was that Jesus didn't seem to condemn the sinners that he ate and drank with. Instead of telling them that they were beyond the pale and beyond hope of salvation, he had a quite different message. He spoke of a God who forgives sinners, goes after the one lost sheep with love and brings it home, then rejoices over one sinner who trusts completely in God's mercy, more than over ninety-nine self-righteous folk who imagine they've done nothing to repent of. You see the similarity to the parable of the children? John's condemnation was like a funeral, Jesus's forgiveness was more wedding-like. Neither John nor Jesus would do. Some people are never satisfied.

## World-affirming

We call these two approaches to faith 'world-affirming' and 'world-denying'. They both have a place in Christianity. The world-denying Christians are those who feel the world's a terrible place, everybody's far too self-indulgent, and they give up things for Lent to show God how sorry they are. They spend hours in prayer, and they're the salt of the earth. But they make others feel uncomfortable, so the others write them off as Puritan killjoys. The world-affirming Christians, on the other hand, are much more relaxed. They thank God for the beauty of his creation, and for the delights of good living. They talk a lot about love, and not much about sin. The crowd refuses to take them seriously: 'Far too lazy, they don't practise what they preach.' There may be some truth in the criticism, but you can't have it both ways. You can't reject Christianity one day because you think it's too strict, and the next because it's too lax. The fact is, everyone has to strike their own balance between being world-affirming and world-denying, and be tolerant of those who choose a different approach. But some people are never satisfied, and they'll make any criticism which helps them avoid facing the challenge of faith for themselves.

## All-age worship

*Act as children playing at weddings and funerals, and a third group rejecting them both.*

## Suggested hymns

*Fairest Lord Jesus; Great is thy faithfulness; Just as I am, without one plea; On Jordan's bank the Baptist's cry.*

# Seventh Sunday after Trinity
## Second Service    In God We Trust

Ps. 56 In God I trust [57 Steadfast love]; 2 Sam. 2:1–11; 3:1 David anointed king; Luke 18:31—19:10 Jericho

> 'In God, whose word I praise, in the Lord, whose word I praise, in God I trust; I am not afraid. What can a mere mortal do to me?' Psalm 56:10–11

### In God we trust

Some American coins have the words 'In God we trust' inscribed on them. Jokey shopkeepers put up a sign behind the till, reading, 'In God we trust. All others pay cash!' It's rather sad that they don't feel they can give anybody credit. But it's probably wise; they've had their fingers burned by bad debts, and they know better now. It emphasizes even more strongly that God's the exception. God's completely trustworthy.

### Psalms

The words on the coin are a quotation from Psalm 56: 'In God I trust.' The Psalmist is being persecuted: 'My enemies trample on me all day long.' He has wept over his predicament, and asks God to put his tears in a bottle, so that the depth of his grief can be measured. None of his neighbours has proved trustworthy. But still in his despair he holds onto one thing: 'In God I trust.'

## King David

The heading to the psalm says that it was written by David when the Philistines seized him in Gath, the city which Goliath came from. The headings were written a long time after the psalms were, but, if that's true, it was before David became king, and when he was running away from King Saul, who wanted to kill him. Later, after King Saul had been killed in battle by the Philistines, David wrote a lament for the death of Saul and his son Jonathan: 'Tell it not in Gath ...'. Then the tribe of Judah anointed David to be their king, at the city of Hebron. He had a long struggle ahead of him, beginning with the capture of Jerusalem. The other eleven tribes were not yet united to Judah, and David had to win their loyalty. The descendants of Saul fought against him; even his own sons fought among themselves and against their father. Many of his friends proved untrustworthy. But still he insists, twice in that psalm, 'In God I trust.'

## Jesus

In the Gospel, Jesus passes through Jericho on his way up to Jerusalem. He warns his disciples that he'll be crucified there, after one of his closest friends proves untrustworthy and betrays him. The other disciples don't understand, but Jesus goes ahead. His agony in the Garden of Gethsemane shows us how much Jesus dreaded the ordeal he'd have to undergo. But he trusted his heavenly Father, and didn't flinch.

## Bartimaeus

On the outskirts of Jericho they met a blind beggar. St Luke's Gospel doesn't name him, but Mark tells us the beggar's name was Bartimaeus, 'blind Bartimaeus'. Although he couldn't see Jesus, he'd heard about him, and he knew that Jesus had a reputation as a healer. So he shouted out, begging for help. Jesus asked him what he wanted, and he said, 'Lord, let me see again.' That was an amazing step of faith. Jesus's reputation might have been quite false, he might have been a charlatan, and not a real healer at all. Or perhaps he only healed rich people, not penniless beggars. But Jesus came as God's representative, and blind Bartimaeus trusted in God. So he asked for his sight back, and he got it. Jesus said, 'Your faith has saved you!' Trust in God, and heaven knows what might happen to you.

## Zacchaeus

They made their way through the streets of Jericho, with Barti-maeus, who once was blind and now could see, jumping up and down behind them praising God, and they bumped into a tax collector called Zacchaeus. Well, they didn't actually bump into him, because he was up above them in the branches of a fig tree. Everybody hated Zacchaeus, so he didn't think Jesus would be interested in him, but he wanted to at least see the Master. Then Jesus invited himself to supper at Zacchaeus's house. Anybody else who did that would have been turned away with a flea in their ear. But Jesus was different. Somehow Zacchaeus trusted him. The evening finished with Zacchaeus giving away all his ill-gotten gains.

## In you, God trusts

You see what can happen when you trust in God? Your whole life gets turned around, and God helps you through situations you could never have got through on your own. Try it, as a matter of daily policy. Remember, God trusts in you. And a good thing too, because if we had to pay cash to get into heaven, none of us could afford it! It's by God's grace, through our faith in him, that we're saved. Trust him!

## Suggested hymns

*All my hope in God is founded; Amazing grace – how sweet the sound; Put thou thy trust in God; When we walk with the Lord.*

## Eighth Sunday after Trinity (Proper 10)  13 July
*Principal Service*  **The Sower**
(*Continuous*): Gen. 25:19–34 Esau sells his birthright; Ps. 119:105–112 Your word a lamp; *or* (*Related*): Isa. 55:10–13 God's word brings joy; Ps. 65:[1–7] 8–13 Joy of harvest; Rom. 8:1–11 Flesh, law and Spirit; Matt. 13:1–9, 18–23 Parable of the sower

> '[Jesus] told them many things in parables, saying: "Listen! A sower went out to sow."' Matthew 13:3

## Why bother?

'Why bother? What's the use?' Sometimes we're tempted to give up when we seem to be getting nowhere. But you may be succeeding in areas you hadn't even noticed. The disciples who tried to spread the message of Jesus must often have felt that their preaching was completely futile. The purpose of the parable of the Sower is to say, 'Don't give up. If only one person heard the message, their life may have been changed by what you said.'

## Sowing

Maybe there was a farmer at work close to where Jesus was sitting, and Jesus pointed to what he was doing. The usual way of sowing seed in those days was for a peasant to carry a bag or basket of seed with him, perhaps of wheat, and throw it out a handful at a time in a wide arc as he walked through his field – sowing 'broadcast', they called it. Some of the seed may not have germinated – it depended on the type of soil. Other seeds sprouted all right, but the young plants never grew to maturity. But some of the seed grew into plants with large ears of wheat grain. There'd be some for next year's seed corn, some to bake into bread for the farmer and his family, and some to sell in the market to pay for the other necessities of life. Some of the seed was wasted, and that was a shame; but enough grew to fruition to make the farmer's work worthwhile.

## The path

In St Luke's Gospel, the parable's explained like this: 'The seed is the word of God.' Each type of soil symbolizes different types of listener. We should ask ourselves, 'Am I like that?' The first type's the hard trodden soil of the path beside the field. No seed can sink into such a surface; it just sits on top until the birds come along and eat it. This soil is like people with shut minds. 'I know what I think,' they say, 'don't confuse me with new ideas.' So they never hear the news that God loves them, because they're unwilling to change.

## Rocky ground

When we hear the phrase 'rocky ground', we think of soil full of stones. But that's not what the parable means. On the limestone hills of the Holy Land, you often find a layer of bedrock so close to the surface that there's only a thin layer of soil over it. The rock holds the heat of the sun, so the seeds germinate quickly. Yet the soil holds no moisture, so the plants are rootless, and wither almost as soon as they come up. This represents the shallow people who're always full of enthusiasm for the latest new craze; they're briefly religious; but they've got no stickability, and soon move on to something else.

## Thorns

'Thorns' stands for distractions. People with too many interests, people who want to make loads of money, are just too busy to listen to Jesus.

## Good soil

But, thank God, there's *some* good soil, where the seed grows into a healthy plant, and produces ears heavy with thirty, sixty or a hundred grains on them. Now a harvest like that would be a miracle. But one new convert can tell ten friends what's so exciting about Jesus Christ, and if each of them tells ten others, you've got a hundred new Christians. In no time flat. It's not impossible. Are you a listener with a shut mind, a shallow soul, or a life full of distractions, or all of the above? Or are you the good soil, one who believes, and tells others? Be careful how you hear. 'Let anyone with ears, listen.'

## Don't despair

Farmers should certainly examine their methods, avoid their mistakes and build on their successes. So should everyone else. But don't despair, whether you're a teacher with an unresponsive class, or a doctor whose patients never listen to your advice, or a parent whose children always do the opposite of what you tell them. Or even a preacher. Ninety-nine out of a hundred words you say may have absolutely no effect. But the hundredth! That may have results which make all the apparently wasted effort worthwhile. Listen carefully when you're listening, and talk patiently when you're talking; remember what Jesus said about the soil and the sower.

## All-age worship

*Plant seeds, in good or bad soil. What does this tell us about listening to Christian teaching?*

## Suggested hymns

*God, whose farm is all creation; Forth in thy name, O Lord, I go; Lord, thy word abideth; Rise and hear, the Lord is speaking.*


# Eighth Sunday after Trinity
## *Second service* The Time of Visitation
Ps. 60 Prayer for victory [63 The king rejoices]; 2 Sam. 7:18–29 David's prayer; Luke 19:41—20:8 The time of visitation

> *'[Jesus wept over Jerusalem saying,] "you did not recognize the time of your visitation from God."' Luke 19:44*

## Hometown

In these days of mobile populations, some people don't feel that they belong anywhere. But if you're lucky, there's somewhere which you can call home, no matter how far you wander away from it. When you go back there, it's 'The Return of the Native'. When you hear people speaking in the familiar accent, you think, 'I've come home!' It may be a 'Dirty Old Town' yet you love it because it's yours. Or it may have some monuments, buildings and views which are quite beautiful; and have an added significance for you, because they've been the background to your hopes and dreams.

## Jerusalem

Jesus felt like that about Jerusalem. He'd been there as a pilgrim three times a year since he was born. Jerusalem was the centre of his world. The prophet Isaiah had predicted that the whole world would come to Jerusalem to learn about God; he wrote:

> Many peoples shall come and say, 'Come, let us go up to the mountain of the LORD, to the house of the God of Jacob; that he may teach us his ways and that we may walk in his paths.' For

out of Zion shall go forth instruction, and the word of the LORD from Jerusalem.

The Temple contained what was called 'the Court of the Gentiles', where foreigners could bring their requests before the Jewish God, who answers everyone's prayers.

## The Temple

The Temple in Jerusalem was breathtakingly beautiful, its huge white stones rising up on the hilltop like a fairytale palace. David wasn't allowed to build the Temple, because he was an adulterer – that was left to his son Solomon. But David prayed that God would bless his descendants, as they established the worship of the true God there in Jerusalem. That blessing had descended to Jesus the Messiah, the Son of David. Yet corruption among the temple officials was a risk, as in any other institution, so Malachi warned:

> The Lord whom you seek will suddenly come to his temple ... But who can endure the day of his coming, and who can stand when he appears? ... he will purify the descendants of Levi and refine them like gold and silver, until they present offerings to the LORD in righteousness ... Then I will draw near to you for judgement; I will be swift to bear witness against the sorcerers, against the adulterers, against those who swear falsely, against those who oppress the hired workers in their wages, the widow and the orphan, against those who thrust aside the alien, and do not fear me, says the LORD of hosts.

## Visitation

It was a frightening prospect: that one day, God himself would come to his own city, to his own Temple, and judge his own people. That would be no friendly visit to God's hometown; that would be a visitation. The dictionary defines a visitation as 'a formal or official visit by a superior, an examination by authority'. The coming of Jesus to Jerusalem was a visitation by God. When the Messiah came, the people of Jerusalem should have given him a warm welcome. Instead, Jesus was rejected. Did he like what he saw? No, the Court of the Gentiles was full of money-changers. God's Temple failed its Ofsted – they didn't even know they'd been inspected. So Jesus wept over Jerusalem saying, 'You didn't recognize the time of your visitation from God.' Then he went into the Court of the Gentiles and drove out all the money-changers who were preventing non-Jews from praying there.

## Continuous assessment

When is the day of visitation for you and me? When should we expect 'a formal or official visit by a superior, an examination by authority'? Jesus said that nobody knows when judgement's coming. But God is judging us every minute of our lives, with a sort of continuous assessment. We can't see him, but he watches us to see whether we resist temptation; whether we're compassionate to the poor; whether we're kind to our families; whether we remember to thank him when things go well. God's quick to notice 'the adulterers, those who tell lies, who pay the workers less than a fair wage, who neglect the needy and the foreigners'. Each of those moments is a time of visitation. Don't worry about it, God isn't trying to catch us out, and if we slip up, he'll forgive us. But if you totally ignore the presence of God in our midst, then Jesus will weep over you, as he did over Jerusalem. And, Jesus wept, you don't want that, do you?

### Suggested hymns

*Love divine, all loves excelling; Mine eyes have seen the glory of the coming of the Lord; O God of earth and altar; Spirit divine, attend our prayers.*

# Ninth Sunday after Trinity (Proper 11)  20 July
## *Principal Service*  Weeds
(*Continuous*): Gen. 28:10–19a Jacob's ladder; Ps. 139:1–11, 23–24 Ascension into heaven; *or* (*Related*): Wisd. 12:13, 16–19 Righteousness and love; *or* Isa. 44:6–8 Witnesses to the one God; Ps. 86:11–17 God's grace; Rom. 8:12–25 Children of God; Matt. 13:24–30, 36–43 Parable of the weeds: God's justice and patience

> '[Jesus] put before them another parable: "The kingdom of heaven may be compared to someone who sowed good seed in his field."' *Matthew 13:24*

## Weeds

Weeding! It's a never-ending battle. If you're a gardener you weed a bed, or if you're a farmer you weed a field, and within a week there's more weeds than before you started. It's been said that a weed is only a flower in the wrong place. But if you're growing plants for food, it's not as simple as that. There's a particularly pernicious weed called 'darnel'. In its early stages it looks just like a young shoot of wheat. You can't tell them apart until the seed heads appear: the seed of the darnel is a grey colour. But by that time the roots of the wheat and the roots of the darnel are all intertwined. You couldn't pull up the darnel without pulling up the wheat with it. Remember, in Bible times they had no machines and no weed-killers. What can the farmer do? Well, he should wait until harvest-time, then, after the field's been reaped, he can separate the wheat from the darnel. He better had, because darnel's poisonous.

## Parables

Jesus told a parable about the wheat and the weeds. The central point of the parable is this: don't be too quick to condemn other people. You can't separate them, any more than you can separate wheat from darnel in the early stages. The parable begins with the words: 'The kingdom of heaven may be compared to someone ...' Jews were careful not to break the commandment by taking God's name in vain. So where other people would have said, 'The kingdom of God', Matthew writes 'The kingdom of heaven'. This isn't a story about heaven, though, it's a story about God, and his way of being a king. So let's rephrase it like this: 'God's reign in the world is like what happens when a farmer sows good wheat, and it comes up mixed with poisonous weeds.'

## Sin

'The field is the world,' said Jesus. God created the world, and sowed it thickly with human souls. The seed is good, Jesus added; human beings are naturally good. But at some point things started going wrong. You and I, whom God created to be his agents in doing good, began doing bad things, hurting other people and being selfish. 'All have sinned,' says the Bible, only we don't like to admit it. Before long the roots of good and evil are all intertwined in our souls. You can't divide the world into white hats and black hats, like a western movie; there are no perfectly good people or perfectly bad people; only people, each of whom is a mixture, with goodness and badness battling it out in our souls. 'If only God would destroy all the evil in the world,' we moan. Only he can't, because then he'd have to destroy every one of us. Not until we die can you separate the good and evil in our souls: you can't separate the wheat and the weeds until the harvest-time. I certainly hope that God will sort us out when we die; I don't want to go on living with the dark side of me into eternity.

## Judging

If that's so, then you can't condemn other people. You don't know what a struggle they're having with the sin in their souls; and none of us can cast the first stone. Lots of people lump others into groups: 'The trouble with all those ... [English, or whoever we feel like criticizing at the time] ... is that they're all alike.' Which is patently untrue. We get periodic attacks of self-righteousness, and want to purify our community: drive all the foreigners out of our nation, or drive all the sinners out of the church. Don't be too hasty, says Jesus. Only God can judge, and he waits until people die before judging them. A child's parents, or teachers, say, 'What a bad child you are', and deprive the child of all hope of becoming better. All right, say you don't like some of the things that other people do, but never write anyone off as a hopeless case. The fault-line between good and evil runs through the middle of every human soul, yours and mine as well as the mad and the bad. Judge yourself, but don't judge other people – leave that to God.

### All-age worship

*Try weeding. How can you decide what is a weed and what isn't?*

### Suggested hymns

*Alleluia! Alleluia! Hearts to heaven and voices raise; Come, ye thankful people come; Happy are they, they that love God; Make me a channel of your peace.*

# Ninth Sunday after Trinity
## *Second service*   The Judgement of Solomon

Ps. 67 Let the peoples praise you [70 God is great]; 1 Kings
2:10–12; 3:16–28 The judgement of Solomon; Acts 4:1–22 Judged
by the Council; *Gospel at Holy Communion*: Mark 6.30–34, 53–56
Feeding and healing

> *'All Israel heard of the judgement that the king had rendered; and
> they stood in awe of the king, because they perceived that the
> wisdom of God was in him, to execute justice.' 1 Kings 3:28*

## A judge

In Gilbert and Sullivan's *Trial by Jury*, the judge sings:

> For I am a judge,
> and a good judge too.

Gilbert the satirist is suggesting that not only is the judge proficient
in administering the law, but also at judging what's in his own best
interests. Those who live in a country where the judiciary is honest
and incorruptible have a lot to thank God for. We all benefit from
the rule of law, when it's administered fairly and above board. Jesus
warns us against judging others, in the sense of making personal
moral condemnations. This doesn't mean, however, that we have no
need of judges – they administer the legal system which protects us
all from burglary, violence and murder. The judge's job's to advise
the jury; they must decide whether the accused has been proved to
be guilty beyond all reasonable doubt. Then the judge decides the
sentence. We'd all live in fear if there were no judges.

## Peter and John

We've two stories of judgement in the Bible readings at this service; they're both rather odd, but they're rattling good yarns! In
the New Testament, Peter and John were arrested in the Temple
in Jerusalem, for preaching about the resurrection. Peter took the
opportunity to make his defence before the whole ruling Council
of the Jewish nation, and to proclaim the good news of salvation.
The Council wanted to find them guilty of the capital offence of
blasphemy; they knew perfectly well that there was no evidence,

but that hadn't stopped them before. Yet they realized they could never get away with it this time, because public opinion was against them. 'They said, "What will we do with them? For it is obvious to all who live in Jerusalem that a notable sign has been done through them; we cannot deny it."' The council tried to shut them up, but Peter and John refused to keep quiet. Their wise answer has been the defence of everybody since then who's been ordered to do something immoral: 'Whether it is right in God's sight to listen to you rather than to God, you must judge.' Justice was done, and justice was seen to be done when they were released, and the attempt of their judges to play fast and loose with the law was defeated.

## The judgement of Solomon

The Old Testament tells us of the judgement of Solomon. When he succeeded his father David to the throne of Israel, he prayed to God asking for wisdom, and the wisdom of Solomon became famous. One example is given. Solomon had to judge between two prostitutes who lived together in the same house. Each had a baby, three days apart. One of the babies died, and the women argued about whose the baby was who was still alive. So they brought their case to the king to be settled. What all this says about the tolerance of their society is fascinating, but that's not the point. Solomon knew there was no convincing evidence, so he tested them by threatening to kill the surviving bairn and cut it in two. He was wise enough to know that the real mother would never allow this, and so he could discern the truth. It wasn't normal legal procedure, but it showed great wisdom and understanding of human nature. Solomon was a judge, and a wise judge too.

## Wisdom

Everybody should pray for wisdom. No matter how well judges know the law, they'll never be able to achieve justice in their courts unless they know how people's minds work. No amount of book-learning will do you any good in life, if you don't have the wisdom to understand other people. You may have all the facts at your fingertips, or know how to look them up on the internet, but facts won't lead you to the truth until you've learnt how to apply them. Wisdom enabled Peter and John to defy the unjust judges; wisdom helped the just judge Solomon to apply justice in a difficult case. In any situation, from knowing how to bring up children to how to answer your employer, no amount of knowledge is any substitute for wisdom. Ask God for wisdom, like Solomon did, reverently and trustingly. Then of truth you'll be a judge, and a good judge too.

## Suggested hymns

*Immortal, invisible, God only wise; Judge eternal, throned in splendour; My God, how wonderful thou art; Teach me, my God and King.*

## Tenth Sunday after Trinity (Proper 12)   27 July
*Principal Service*   **The Pearl of Great Price**
(*Continuous*): Gen. 29:15–28 Jacob loves Rachel; Ps. 105:1–11, 45b Authority and thanksgiving; *or* Ps. 128 Family and possessions; *or* (*Related*): 1 Kings 3:5–12 Solomon's prayer for wisdom; Ps. 119:129–136 God's word is light; Rom. 8:26–39 All things work together for good; Matt. 13:31–33, 44–52 Parables of the kingdom

> '[Jesus said,] "The kingdom of heaven is like a merchant in search of fine pearls; on finding one pearl of great value, he went and sold all that he had and bought it."' *Matthew 13:45–46*

## Pearls

Pearls are very beautiful things. A perfect sphere of purest white, or sometimes pink or occasionally black, cloudily reflective with a multitude of subtle shades known as 'orient', a pearl is one of the loveliest things on earth. As you know, a natural pearl is formed when a piece of sand falls into the open shell of the oyster. To avoid irritation, the oyster slowly covers the gritty fragment with concentric layers of smooth and translucent nacre or 'mother-of-pearl'. If it's less than perfectly spherical or the purity of the colour is marred, it's much less valuable. The value comes from rarity, and from the labour of the pearl fishers, who often have to dive to great depths to bring up the oysters, only a few of which will contain a pearl. Cleopatra dissolved pearls in wine and drank it as an ostentatious display of wealth. In the Bible, Job compares the value of the wisdom that comes from God to the most expensive things he knows:

> No mention shall be made of coral or of crystal;
> the price of wisdom is above pearls.

So pearls were bought, and sold on at a profit, by greedy merchants, until they could find a king or a princess who was willing to pay a worthy price for a perfect pearl. Jesus told a parable about a pearl-merchant who dreamt of owning a pearl of great price; when he came across one, he had no hesitation in selling off everything that he owned so that he'd have enough money to buy his life's dream, an absolutely perfect pearl.

## Beauty of the kingdom

Jesus said we should desire the kingdom of God as much as that merchant desired the pearl. No sacrifice is too great to make, so that we may obtain the kingdom of God; the kingdom of God should be the number-one priority in our whole life. God's the king wherever people obey him. In comparing the kingdom to a pearl, Jesus is saying that the kingdom is beautiful. You might not think it, to look at the gloomy and forbidding Puritans who are nagged by 'the haunting fear that someone, somewhere may be happy'. But if you're one of the blessed ones who's in love, or have ever been in love, you know that love is beautiful, precious and wonderful, above anything else on earth. Well, the kingdom of God's being in love with God, and knowing that God loves you.

## Other beauty

The kingdom of God's the pearl of great price. Many other things in life are precious and lovely. Art and music, fine clothes and good food, foreign travel, a comfortable home and a desirable motor car, controlling a large organization, providing for your children – these are all good things and worthy ambitions. God's pleased when we have them. But they're not as important as the kingdom of God. They're like grade-two pearls, compared to a really magnificent top-of-the-range specimen. The kingdom of God must always take priority. A poem with the title 'God First' hung over a child's bed. When the child grew up, those words reminded her always that however important other things might seem, serving God must always take first place.

## Sacrifice all

A proverb quoted by Voltaire runs: 'The best is the enemy of the good.' In other words, to achieve the best in life, you'll often have to reject other things which are quite good, but not so important. If a couple have found true love, they'll gladly sacrifice trivial pleasures for the joy of being together. John Dryden, in his play *All for Love*, wrote:

> Errors, like straws, upon the surface flow;
> He who would search for pearls must dive below.

To find love and meaning in your life, you must go below the surface to find the kingdom of God. When you've found it, be ready to sacrifice anything, however good and important, to make God the ruler of your life. The pearl of great price takes priority over lesser goods, and whatever you've sacrificed, you'll get back in other ways. Jesus said: 'Seek ye first the kingdom of God, and all these things shall be added unto you.'

### All-age worship

*Play at being pearl-merchants, selling everything to buy the most precious pearl, using beads and Monopoly® money.*

### Suggested hymns

*Be thou my vision, O Lord of my heart; God of grace and God of glory; Jesu, priceless treasure; Seek ye first the kingdom of God.*

# Tenth Sunday after Trinity
## *Second Service*  **Peter and Rhoda**
Ps. 75 God executes judgement [76 Judge of the earth]; 1 Kings 6:11–14, 23–38 Solomon builds the Temple; Acts 12:1–17 Peter and Rhoda; *Gospel at Holy Communion*: John 6:1–21 Feeding five thousand, walking on water

*'When [Peter] knocked at the outer gate, a maid named Rhoda came to answer.' Acts 12:13*

## Peter in prison

St Peter was arrested by King Herod and thrown into prison. During the night, an angel came and released him: his chains fell off; the angel led him out of the prison and then disappeared. Peter went to the place where he knew all the other Christians would be praying together. This was at a place which the Acts of the Apostles refers to as John Mark's mother's house. John Mark, the nephew of Barnabas, was probably the one who wrote the Gospel of Mark. His mother must have been a widow, otherwise it would have been called Mark's father's house. It's probably where the Last Supper was held, and where the Spirit came down at Pentecost. When Peter reached this house, there occurred an amusing incident, which has no real relevance to the story, but vividly shows that these were real events.

## Rhoda

Mark and his mother had a housemaid called Rhoda. All the Christians were praying, maybe in the upper room, when there came a knock on the door. So as not to interrupt their prayers, Rhoda was sent to find out who was disturbing them in the middle of the night. She looked through the door-grille and saw it was Peter. She was so astonished, she forgot to unlock the door! She left poor Peter standing there outside and rushed back up to tell the others. Whatever must he have felt like? The Prince of the Apostles, left to kick his heels on the doorstep while a mere serving wench ran off to ask advice. Fortunately he didn't take umbrage, and when he was eventually let in, he didn't mention Rhoda's stupid mistake, but told the rest how he'd been freed, and went off to hide, so that they shouldn't get arrested when the soldiers came for him in the morning.

## Humility

What, then, did Rhoda feel like?

> She ran in and announced that Peter was standing at the gate. They said to her, 'You are out of your mind!' But she insisted that it was so. They said, 'It is his angel.' Meanwhile Peter continued knocking; and when they opened the gate, they saw him and were amazed.

And then, I expect, they all had a good laugh at Rhoda's expense.

'What a stupid thing to do! Fancy leaving the leader of the Twelve, called by Jesus the foundation-stone of the church, standing outside the room where the church was meeting! Idiot! Why didn't you think to let him in?' Well, when people are laughing at you, there's only one thing to do, and that's to laugh with them. It's no use being uptight, and resenting the fact that you're being laughed at. If Rhoda had done that, her relationship with the other Christians would have been stiff and awkward for ever after. She'd probably have lost her job. But if she had a good laugh with them about how stupid she'd been, they probably wiped the laughter-tears out of their eyes, and loved her for being so honest. Neither Peter nor Rhoda could afford to ride a high horse. I feel sure the reason this funny story's told in the Bible is because both of them were big enough people to be humble.

## Stupidity

The fact is, though we like to pretend to be wise, we all do stupid things from time to time. The German philosopher Wittgenstein wrote: 'No one did anything great who did not do something ridiculous.' That's a great comfort to those of us who do ridiculous things every day – it means that maybe we've also done a few things that, in the eyes of God at least, are great! The Bible tells you clearly what you should do if you're a sinner: you should repent, confess it, and accept God's forgiveness. But stupidity isn't sin; you didn't deliberately choose to do something wrong, and if you wail, 'But I didn't think ...' other people will only say, 'Well, you should have done.' Which isn't much comfort when you've already lost all your self-esteem. No, the only thing is to laugh at yourself, and remember that God loves fools, too. St Paul wrote to the Corinthians: 'We are fools for the sake of Christ!'

The great Apostle Peter and the lowly servant-girl Rhoda both learnt from this trivial incident that dignity's not improved by standing on it, but everyone respects those who have the grace to be humble and laugh at themselves. God loves us all, even the stupid and the ridiculous; but it's harder to accept God's love if you're proud and haughty.

### Suggested hymns

*Amazing grace, how sweet the sound; And can it be that I should gain?; Immortal, invisible, God only wise; Just as I am, without one plea.*

## Eleventh Sunday after Trinity (Proper 13)   3 August
*Principal Service*   **Feeding the Hungry**

(*Continuous*): Gen. 32:22–31 Wrestling Jacob; Ps. 17:1–7, 16
Guidance and righteousness; *or* (*Related*): Isa. 55:1–5 Come to me;
Ps. 145:8–9, 15–22 Providence and prayer; Rom. 9:1–5 Christians
and Jews; Matt. 14:13–21 Feeding the five thousand

> '*When [Jesus] went ashore, he saw a great crowd; and he had compassion for them.*' *Matthew 14:14*

### Poverty

It's quite common for somebody from our country to make their first ever visit to the Third World, on their way to a beach holiday for instance, and come home severely traumatized. It's one thing to read about world poverty, but it's quite different to see with your own eyes a starving child with a swollen belly, or an old man dying on the roadside. The world's population is roughly six billion. Consider these figures:

- Half the world – nearly 3 billion people – live on less than two dollars (or just over one pound) a day; 1.3 billion live on less than half that amount.
- Half the world's children live in poverty.
- 790 million people are chronically under-nourished.
- 20 per cent of the world population – all of us who live in the developed nations – consume 86 per cent of the world's goods; and our average income is 74 times that of the poorest 20 per cent.
- 1 child dies every 2 seconds of poverty.
- 1.3 billion people have no access to clean water; 3 billion have no access to sanitation; 2 billion have no electricity.
- 12 per cent of the world's population uses 85 per cent of its drinking water.
- Nearly 1 billion people entered the twenty-first century unable to read a book or sign their names.
- Less than 1 per cent of what the world spends on weapons could put every child in the world in school.

## Compassion

According to the Gospel, Jesus saw a crowd of five thousand people who'd had nothing to eat all day, and he felt compassion towards them. He took practical action, with the help of others, to feed them. The story raises the question whether you believe in miracles, but I want you to concentrate, for now, on the compassion of Jesus for the hungry. He put himself in their shoes. Carpenters were less wealthy than fishermen or land-owning peasant farmers. Part of what was involved in becoming human was that Jesus could imagine what it was like to be the poorest of the poor. So his message to the world is that *God cares*. He concentrated his time and his attention on the needy; can we, who follow him, do any less?

## Today

There's always been poverty, and it's been made a little less acute by the work of compassionate Christians. But we've also made it worse, by introducing medicines which mean that fewer children need die, without giving them the means to earn enough to feed themselves. The world's population has mushroomed, and there's plenty of food to feed them all, but it's not fairly distributed.

## Emergencies

So famine emergencies arise, and we're generous at giving to appeals for relief. But it's only temporary, because we haven't put in the infrastructure and the transport vehicles to distribute the food quickly to those who need it, and we haven't trained the local officials and the local NGOs to cope with a crisis.

## Aid

Then we give government money as aid, which is a tiny percentage of our taxes. But much of it's absorbed by corrupt and inefficient governments, and debt repayments. The most effective aid goes into providing medicines and clean water, yet we don't help the developing nations to pay their medical staff enough. So as soon as they're trained, the doctors and nurses from the Third World want to come to this country because the pay's so much better.

## Debt relief

The richer nations have resolved to reduce the problem of Third-World debt; we shall be judged by the results.

## Fair trade

But the most effective thing we can do is to encourage fair trade. I don't just mean buying food that's labelled 'fairly traded' in the supermarkets, though that helps. It means persuading the politicians that we ourselves are willing to make sacrifices. Let them know we're willing to pay higher prices for the food and goods in the shops, so as to cut the subsidies. Then we shan't dump cheap goods in the poorer countries, bankrupting their own producers, and we shall allow them to gain a fair price by selling their produce here.

## For Christ's sake

Giving to emergency appeals, pressing for increasing aid in food, water and medicines, debt relief and fairer trading practices – we can all play our part. When Jesus saw that the multitude were hungry, he had compassion on them. I appeal to you, *for Christ's sake*, to do the same.

## *All-age worship*

*Draw posters appealing for emergency relief, food aid, water, medicines, debt relief and fair trade for the poorer nations.*

## *Suggested hymns*

*For the fruits of his creation; For the healing of the nations; O God of earth and altar; Where cross the crowded ways of life.*

# Eleventh Sunday after Trinity
## *Second service*   The Queen of Sheba
Ps. 80 The Vine; 1 Kings 10:1–13 The Queen of Sheba; Acts 13:1–13 Paul and Barnabas in Cyprus; *Gospel at Holy Communion*: John 6:24–35 I am the bread

'When the queen of Sheba had observed all the wisdom of Solomon, the house that he had built, the food of his table, the seating of his officials, and the attendance of his servants, their clothing, his valets, and his burnt offerings that he offered at the house of the LORD, there was no more spirit in her.' 1 Kings 10:4–5

## Handel

Everybody knows 'The Arrival of the Queen of Sheba', from Handel's oratorio *Solomon*, with its falling sequences of notes: 'DUM-de-de-dee, DUM-de-de-dee, DUM-de-de-dee, DUM-de-de-dee ...' and so on. Yet very few people could tell you where Sheba was. We're not quite certain, beyond the fact that it was in Arabia, but it was probably in the south, somewhere near the Yemen. Recent archaeological discoveries have shown that this area was occupied centuries before Solomon's time. Later it became very rich through the export of frankincense. So it's quite possible that the Queen of Sheba was an historical person, though, curiously enough, frankincense isn't mentioned among the gifts that she brought to the King. But it's very likely that an historical incident's been written up into a purple passage glorifying King Solomon and his riches.

## The managing director

King Solomon was a successful managing director. His court was like a big business organization, and the MD kept it all running smoothly because his eye was on everything. The Queen admired 'the house that he had built, the food of his table, the seating of his officials, and the attendance of his servants, their clothing, his valets, and his burnt offerings that he offered at the house of the LORD'. It takes a lot of skill to organize all of those things. He must have won the trust and admiration of all those under him. Organizational skill's what makes the composer of a symphony more honourable than someone who produces a charming miniature. To bring the different themes, developments and recapitulations, the fast movements and the slow movement, and all the different instruments together into a unified whole requires genius. A Jewish author was asked recently how he responded to the Roman Catholic emphasis in Elgar's *The Dream of Gerontius*. His reply was that great art makes faith universal. Solomon's organizational skills – what the Bible calls his 'wisdom' – won the admiration of the Queen of

Sheba. Whether she shared Solomon's faith in the one God who organizes the whole world into a universal work of art is doubtful; but her awe was a sign that she could understand the underlying motives which drove him.

## Thanksgiving for riches

Solomon's central priority was the worship of Almighty God. The Queen admired the sacrifices which Solomon offered in the Temple which he'd built in Jerusalem. The danger of riches is that they can make you self-indulgent. You've heard of the rich man who was described as 'a self-made man who worshipped his creator'. Solomon could easily have been spoilt by his great wealth; the Bible suggests that towards the end of his life he was. But at this stage he acknowledged that his wealth came from God, and he thanked God for it. If only rich people today would thank God regularly, who's the source of their wealth, they might be more generous with it.

## The end of unity

After the Israelites settled in the Holy Land, they remained an assortment of scattered tribes under various so-called 'judges'. King Saul was king of a few tribes only, David was the first to bring all the tribes together under one king, and under Solomon that unity flourished. But when he died it all fell apart; the Northern Kingdom, called Israel, separated itself from the Southern Kingdom of Judah. The vine which God had planted split in two, and Solomon was remembered nostalgically as the last king of the 'United Kingdom of the Twelve Tribes', as you might say.

## Hope for unity and prosperity for all

Telling the story of the Queen of Sheba was a way of reminding the divided kingdoms of the golden days gone by. It kept alive the hope that sometime the glory days might return, the nation be reunited, and the wealth of Solomon enjoyed by all. A nation can only prosper economically if it's united in a single loyalty and with a common set of ideals. Maybe the Church in our land will only prosper spiritually and attract new members when it remembers the ideal of unity with a common goal in sacrifice to God. Then visitors may feel that 'there is no spirit in them', when they see the spiritual riches of the reunited Church.

**Suggested hymns**

*From the eastern mountains; Hail to the Lord's anointed; In Christ there is no east or west; O worship the Lord in the beauty of holiness.*

## Twelfth Sunday after Trinity (Proper 14)
10 August
*Principal Service*   **He Came to Them**

(*Continuous*): Gen. 37:1–4, 12–28 Joseph and his family; Ps. 105:1–6, 16–22, 45b Joseph in authority; *or* (*Related*): 1 Kings 19:9–18 A still small voice; Ps. 85:8–13 Love, works, peace, faith; Rom. 10:5–15 Justification by faith, not by works; Matt. 14:22–33 Walking on water

> *'Early in the morning [Jesus] came walking toward them on the sea.' Matthew 14:25*

### Walking on water

The story of Jesus walking on the water used to be told boastfully by Christians: 'You see what Jesus can do? Won't you follow a man who can work miracles like that?' The 'argument from miracles' is not so persuasive these days, as more and more people doubt whether miracles ever happened. Science is much better at predicting what will probably happen than at saying for certain that something can't happen. Yet there's no need to make it difficult for these sceptics to become followers of Jesus by insisting that anything happened contrary to the laws of nature. It could be that the Greek words simply mean that Jesus came striding through the surf where Lake Galilee is very shallow. Or maybe a vision of Jesus that the disciples saw *after* the resurrection has been misplaced. You're free to believe in the miracle or not, as you please. But to use it as an argument that Jesus was the Son of God only invites ridicule these days. We may pity the sceptics for their lack of poetry, but it's no use arguing with them.

### Jesus comes to us

So what other useful message can we draw from this story? I think it's that Jesus didn't desert his disciples in their hour of need. He came to them as they struggled with the waves. They could see him coming. Lucky them. We today need faith that Jesus comes to us, even though we can't see him. When we're struggling with ourselves; when we're struggling with circumstances; when we're struggling with temptation; when we're struggling with sorrow; when we're struggling with decisions, Jesus comes to us.

## Struggling with ourselves

How often we struggle with ourselves! Half of me wants to do one thing and half of me wants another; I have, for the time being, a sort of split personality. But if I call to Jesus in my prayers, he'll come to me, heal me and quieten the storm.

## Struggling with circumstances

Sometimes we struggle with circumstances. Not enough money to meet our needs; not enough time to do what we have to do; not enough power to change things for the better; not enough security to free us from worry; not enough friends to support us and encourage us. Cry out to Jesus in your prayers, and he'll come to you, be your friend and help you to cope with your circumstances.

## Struggling with temptation

Daily we have to struggle with temptation. There's not one of the Ten Commandments that we aren't tempted to break in some way at some time in our lives. Jesus said in the Sermon on the Mount: 'You have heard that it was said to those of ancient times, "You shall not murder" ... but I say to you that if you are angry with a brother or sister, you will be liable to judgement.' Anger's as bad as murder, says Jesus. Maybe you can resist the temptation to break the commandments of Moses, but can you obey the commands of Jesus without a struggle? Cry out to him when you're tempted, and he'll come to you, help you to manage your anger and show you that your heavenly reward's much more precious than the temptation that attracts you.

## Struggling with sorrow

Many people struggle with sorrow. The death of a loved one, the break-up of a relationship, failure to achieve one's ambitions, all leave us feeling baffled and alone. Then we cry out to Jesus, and he comes to us with the comfort of God's unconditional love and the promise of eternal life.

## Struggling with decisions

Circumstances; temptation; sorrow; and finally, when we're struggling with decisions, Jesus comes to us. So many difficult decisions have to be made; often we're choosing the lesser of two evils, and it's a real struggle to make up our mind. But when the wind's fierce and the waves are high, we've no need to struggle alone. Jesus comes to us through all the stormy times of life, with his hand stretched out to save us, and with his calm, clear voice calling, 'Cheer up, it's me; don't be afraid.' We may not see him, but Jesus is there, whenever we need him, whenever we call out to him.

### All-age worship

*Draw the disciples in the boat in the storm, Jesus in the distance, and write a prayer calling Jesus to come to you when life is hard.*

### Suggested hymns

*Dear Lord and Father of mankind; Eternal Father, strong to save; Have faith in God, my heart; In heavenly love abiding.*

## Twelfth Sunday after Trinity
### Second Service   Division or Unity?
Ps. 86 Show me a sign; 1 Kings 11:41—12:20 Two kingdoms; Acts 14:8–20 Paul and Barnabas mistaken for gods; *Gospel at Holy Communion*: John 6.35, 41–51 The one who is from God

*'To your tents, O Israel!' 1 Kings 12:16*

## Federations

Federations are fragile. Separate states become joined by a treaty, but there are always tensions. The United States of America, soon after its founding, was split in two by the Civil War and, although the rift was healed, resentments still smoulder in the South. In the last century there were attempts at federal government in Singapore and Malaysia, and in Central Africa between the two Rhodesias and Nyasaland, neither of which lasted long. In the Balkans, the coalescence of states and their subsequent division on ethnic lines are notorious. The European Union has struggled to discover a degree of economic co-operation without surrendering too much national independence. You can probably think of many other examples of the fragility of federal government. And yet, if it's to the mutual benefit of both parties, it ought to be possible to make it work.

## Two kingdoms

The problem goes back to Bible times. According to the Old Testament, each of the twelve tribes was ruled from time to time by one of the so-called 'judges', though today we'd call them 'warlords'. Saul and David ruled the tribes of Judah and Benjamin around Jerusalem in the south, and gradually built an alliance with the ten northern tribes of Israel. In King David's time the tribes were a loose federation bound together by a covenant. But it was King Solomon who really united all twelve tribes into a single monarchy. Then, after Solomon's death, the united kingdom of Israel and Judah split apart again. His heir, Rehoboam, imposed too heavy an economic burden, so the ten northern tribes rebelled. Under Jeroboam, who was not a descendant of David, they set up the northern kingdom – called 'Israel'.

When all Israel [the northern tribes] saw that the king [Rehoboam] would not listen to them, the people answered the king, 'What share do we have in David? We have no inheritance in the son of Jesse. To your tents, O Israel! Look now to your own house, O David.' So Israel went away to their tents.

Rehoboam was left with only the two southern tribes, thereafter called the kingdom of Judah. The attempt at federation was short-lived. Four hundred years later when the remnant of Judah returned from exile in Babylon, they were reunited with what was left of Israel. Most of the books of the Old Testament were re-edited at this period, emphasizing the need for national unity, with one God, one set of Scriptures, only one sanctuary in Jerusalem, and a new king who'd be a descendant of David.

## Why is unity important?

Why's unity so important? Why's it so difficult to sustain? The answer to those questions will affect our thinking, not only about international federations, but also about the unity of the Church. When the great European empires broke up at the time of the Renaissance it was because of the difficulty of imposing central control. With the fragmentation of the Holy Roman Empire into a multitude of independent nation states went the splitting of the Roman Catholic Church into different national churches. But the nations gradually realized that to remain in a state of war with each other was a waste of money and lives. So they formed alliances and drew up trading treaties. Those who dreamed of a united Europe quoted the economic benefits if trade barriers were broken down; those who dreamed of the United Nations hoped that wars would cease when there was an international forum in which to discuss differences. Neither dream's been fully realized, because people are terrified of giving up their independence and their local traditions. A way must be found whereby people on both sides of a conflict realize that their demands can never be fully met, but that by co-operation between former enemies, compromises can be reached which leave each group, if anything, more proud of their own traditions.

## Church unity

There's a temptation in the Church also, when disputes break out, for one or both sides to cry, 'To your tents, O Israel!' But division's not the will of God; Jesus prayed that we might all be one. Yet the search for church unity's as difficult as the attempt to build inter-national federations. Again, we have to realize that the demand that everyone should do things our way can never be realized; but that we can still enjoy our local traditions when we form federa-tions with our former enemies. Local federations may fall short of the total unity which God wills, and because of human selfishness they're fragile. But they're a step in the right direction.

## Suggested hymns

*In Christ there is no east or west; Jesus put this song into our hearts; Lord of lords and King eternal; O thou, who at thy Eucharist didst pray.*

215

# Thirteenth Sunday after Trinity (Proper 15)
## 17 August
### *Principal Service*  **Puppy dogs**

(*Continuous*): Gen. 45:1–15 Joseph and his family; Ps. 133 Victory; or (*Related*): Isa. 56:1, 6–8 A house of prayer for all nations; Ps. 67 Let all the peoples praise you; Rom. 11:1–2a, 29–32 God and Israel; Matt. 15:[10–20] 21–28 Crumbs from the table

> *'Even the dogs eat the crumbs that fall from their masters' table.'*
> Matthew 15:27

## Dogs

Dog-lovers take note: not everyone's a dog-lover. You think that a dog is man's best friend, a loyal companion. A young puppy dog is something for children to play with and to cuddle. But not everyone agrees with you. In poor countries, packs of wild and mangey pi-dogs attack and bite anyone who threatens their lair or their food. Dogs are useful scavengers for removing carcasses, but such dogs can spread infection. So in the Bible the word 'dog' is used as an insult. The children of Israel, as Jews called themselves, hated non-Jews, so they referred to them as 'Gentile dogs'. It reminds you of the way some of us Christians speak about the Jews. Such racial abuse is intolerable, no matter who says it and about whom.

## Jesus and Gentiles

So it's surprising to read that Jesus said to a Gentile woman who'd asked him for help, 'It's not fair to take the children's food and throw it to the dogs.' Was Jesus being racist? I'm sure he wasn't, so let's look at the context. Jesus was born a Jew. He came to save the whole world, but he had to begin with those who understood what salvation meant. The Jews had read in their Scriptures about a God who saves, who'd saved them from Egypt and from Babylon – they could understand that Jesus had come to save. So it was to the Jews that he explained that if we accept his love, he can save us from sin and death. He told his disciples that there just wasn't time at that stage to go any further: 'Go nowhere among the Gentiles ... but go rather to the lost sheep of the house of Israel.' It's a question of priorities: you have to start somewhere, and you mustn't spread your efforts too thinly. After he'd risen again from the dead, then they could take the good news to the whole world. In the meanwhile, talk of a Gentile mission was a distraction. Jesus had come into Gentile territory because the hostile pressures on him were too great in Israel. When this unknown foreign woman came yapping at his heels, his initial reaction was to ignore her. But he wouldn't send her away as the disciples wanted; instead he turned and tested her – teased her, if you like. Was she capable of understanding what salvation means?

## Puppy dogs

Now there's a very important point that doesn't come out in most English translations. Jesus didn't speak the insulting word used for the pariah dogs of the streets; instead he used a diminutive, something like 'puppy dogs'. So the humorous expression on his face may have softened the impact of what he asked: 'Is it right to share the children's bread with the puppy dogs?' Well, of course it is, if the children don't starve. The foreign woman's witty response showed she'd understood the point: 'Even the puppy dogs can lick up the scraps which the children toss to them!' Even we foreigners, we so-called 'Gentile dogs', can benefit from the salvation which begins with the children of Israel.

## The foreign woman

Let's focus on this anonymous foreigner. Can we learn from her example? She was humble, she was witty, she was persistent. She loved her sick daughter, and nothing would stop her begging for help, even from the strange Jewish preacher. But she was open to new ideas and ready to learn. She knew what most Jews thought of her, but she discovered at least one Jew who was willing to help her. She understood Jesus's point about priorities, but trusted him to make an exception in her case. She soon realized that he was more than a quack wonder-worker; she knelt down before him and called him Lord. Anyone who can recognize God in the preacher from Nazareth is capable of understanding what salvation means. So her faith was rewarded, and she was given what she asked for: her sick daughter was restored to health. What a woman! If we have faith like hers, and worship Jesus as she did, we shall be saved, too. There may have to be temporary restrictions on what's currently possible – not all sick daughters can be saved in this life, though eternity's open to all. In the long term, God wants everyone, of every race, to know the joy of his saving love.

## All-age worship

*Draw the puppy dogs eating the scraps which the children give them. Write underneath: 'Children love puppies. Parents love children. God loves everyone.'*

## Suggested hymns

*Happy are they, they that love God; Jesus shall reign where'er the sun; My God, and is thy table spread?; One more step along the road I go.*

# Thirteenth Sunday after Trinity
## *Second Service*   The Death of Children

Ps. 90 Our everlasting refuge; 2 Kings 4:1–37 Widow's jar, widow's dead son; Acts 16:1–15 Come over and help us; *Gospel at Holy Communion*: John 6.51–58 Eating flesh and drinking blood

*'[Elisha] got down, walked once to and fro in the room, then got up again and bent over him; the child sneezed seven times, and the child opened his eyes.' 2 Kings 4:35*

### Archbishop Benson

Edward White Benson was Archbishop of Canterbury from 1883 to 1896. When his young son Martin died, he wrote this beautiful prayer:

O God, to me who am left to mourn his departure, grant that I may not sorrow as one without hope for my beloved who sleeps in you; but, as always remembering his courage, and the love that united us on earth, I may begin again with new courage to serve you more fervently who are the only source of true love and true fortitude; that when I have passed a few more days in this valley of tears and this shadow of death, supported by your rod and staff, I may see him face to face, in those pastures and beside those waters of comfort where I believe he already walks with you. O Shepherd of the sheep, have pity on this darkened soul of mine.

## Elijah and Elisha

The death of a child is always painful. There are two pairs of stories in the Old Testament, very like each other. In 1 Kings 17 the prophet Elijah is sent to a widow in Zarephath, who feeds him during a famine, when he makes sure that her jar of oil never runs dry – the 'widow's cruse'. Then the widow's son dies, and Elijah brings him to life again. In 2 Kings 4, Elijah's successor Elisha provided a jar of oil for a widow which never ran dry. Immediately after that, the story's told of Elisha's visit to an old man and his wife at their home in Shunem; and how in answer to Elisha's prayers God gave them a son. Some years later the child died, and Elijah brought him back to life. Most people think these stories were passed down by word of mouth. But the same stories may have got attached to the names of two different prophets, and the editors who first wrote them down were far too respectful of the tradition to cut out either version. But who knows? It could be just coincidence.

## The death of children

So what do these strange stories tell us about the death of children? What comfort would Archbishop Benson have found in them? Well, first of all it doesn't sound as though the children were really dead; they may have been in a cataleptic trance or something. Miracles do happen, so we can't be sure. But it would be cruel to give the parents of a dead child, or a sick child near to death, false hopes. God sends a miracle when he decides in his wisdom that the child would be happier on earth than in heaven, and that's not very often. We mustn't try to twist God's arm; Jesus was tempted to ask God for a miracle by throwing himself off the top of the Temple in Jerusalem, and demanding that angels should save him. He replied, 'You mustn't put the Lord your God to the test.' It takes bereaved parents some time before they can really believe the tragedy has actually occurred. One day, they think, I'll wake up from this terrible nightmare. But eventually they have to accept what's happened, and even if they know they'll never come to terms with their loss, at least they gradually come to terms with the fact that there will always be this great hole in their hearts. It's the slow healing of the bereaved that's the real miracle. For the rest of us, who don't know what to say to bereaved parents, the best policy is probably just to say nothing. Give them a hug if it's appropriate, and sit with them in silence for as long as they ask you to. And leave a cooked meal anonymously on their doorstep if they don't feel like cooking.

## Resurrection

Then we must be prepared, whenever bereaved people feel ready to ask, to answer their questions humbly about what we believe. These are stories of resurrection, after all. Christians believe that God has a better resurrection in store for our loved ones even than that which Elijah and Elisha gave to the dead children. *They* only came back to life on earth; *we* shall be restored to life in heaven, where we shall meet again with those who've gone there before us. What a grand family reunion that will be when, as Archbishop Benson wrote, we see each other again 'face to face'.

### Suggested hymns

*From thee all skill and science flow; Immortal love, for ever full; O love, that will not let me go; There's a song for all the children.*

## Fourteenth Sunday after Trinity (Proper 16) (St Bartholomew the Apostle)  24 August
*Principal Service*  **Thinkers or Doers?**
(*Continuous*): Ex. 1:8—2:10 Moses in the bulrushes; Ps. 124 Salvation and providence; or (*Related*): Isa. 51:1–6 The servant, a light to the peoples; Ps. 138 Temple and prayer; Rom. 12:1–8 Be transformed by the Holy Spirit; Matt. 16:13–20 Peter recognizes the Messiah

> '*When Jesus came into the district of Caesarea Philippi, he asked his disciples, "Who do people say that the Son of Man is?"* '
> Matthew 16:13

### Action man

When 'Action Man' came into the toyshops, millions of little boys now imagined themselves as the new action hero, leaping between blazing buildings. As we progress towards equality, I imagine that girls, too, now look forward to the time when they can be as active in doing good and saving others as their brothers. So a generation of 'action heroes' have flung themselves across our cinema screens, and the cult of the 'action movie' has spawned sequel after sequel. It makes you exhausted just to think about it!

## Thinkers

Thinking's not something you usually associate with an action hero. Some of the actors who took these parts were mocked as being not particularly bright; and some of them have surprised us since then by revealing hidden depths. And remember, some of the characters they played were written as though they were distinguished academics as well as athletic achievers. So I wonder, can thinking and doing go together? They need to, for if you don't stop first to think out the consequences, before taking vigorous or violent action, you can do a lot of damage, to yourself and to other people. So we should also give equal honour to the great thinkers – the philosophers, scientists and poets. The thinkers give us insights into what's right and what's possible; and then the doers can put the thinkers' ideas into practice. Thank God for the thinkers *and* the doers.

## Prophets

The thinkers in the Bible were the prophets and the wise men. They spoke on behalf of God – 'thus says the Lord' – and showed us how God views the world. Then they told us what to do about it, to make the world more like the place that God wants it to be. Or more often the prophets left us to work it out for ourselves. Jesus was a prophet; he was known as 'the prophet from Nazareth'. When he asked his disciples, 'who do people say that I am?' they answered that most people thought of him as a prophet: 'Some say John the Baptist, but others Elijah, and still others Jeremiah or one of the prophets.' Did the people imagine that Jesus was one of the prophets of old come back to life, by some process of reincarnation? If so, they were wrong. But maybe they thought he was just fulfilling the same purpose in God's plan that the prophets had done: to think on behalf of the people, and to speak on behalf of God. To that extent, they were absolutely right. Jesus was the greatest thinker there's ever been.

## Messiah

But Jesus wasn't only a thinker, he was a doer as well. St Peter was the first to realize this; he blurted out, 'You're the Messiah!' The Messiah was the long-expected King, the Superman who would change history. Jesus emphatically did change history. Maybe not in the way Peter expected, by throwing the Romans out of the Holy Land. Jesus changed history by confronting the cruellest enemy the human race has ever had cause to fear, and the name of that enemy is 'death'. Jesus faced death head on, by dying on the cross, and he conquered it, by rising to life again on the third day. Jesus was the greatest action hero. He didn't just come to earth to teach us a new philosophy; he came down to save us.

## Thinkers and doers

Peter the fisherman was a man of action, but he wasn't much of a thinker. Usually he worked on hunches. When he tried to think, he usually got it all wrong; and he was a dreadful coward when the servant-girl asked him if he knew Jesus. But later, when Peter went to Rome, he wrote some wise advice in what we call the First Letter of Peter, and he faced death with courage, demanding to be crucified upside down. If even Peter learnt to be both a thinker and a doer, there's hope for you and me. We need to apply all our brain-power to thinking what God wants us to do to change things for the better. Then we must go out boldly and do it, for Jesus's sake. Jesus can make us strong; his Holy Spirit can make us the action heroes we've always dreamt of becoming.

## All-age worship

*With the Action Man toy, show how he can only be strong when a human being bigger than himself moves him. Where do human beings get their strength from?*

## Suggested hymns

*Fight the good fight; I danced in the morning; I want to walk with Jesus Christ; Lord of all hopefulness.*

# St Bartholomew the Apostle   24 August
## (or may be transferred to 25 August)
## Signs and Wonders

Isa. 43:8–13 My witnesses; Ps. 145:1–7 Speak of your wondrous acts; Acts 5:12–16 The Apostles heal (*if the Acts reading is used instead of the Old Testament reading, the New Testament reading is* 1 Cor. 4:9–15 The shame of the Apostles); Luke 22:24–30 Judging the twelve tribes

> *'Now many signs and wonders were done among the people through the apostles.'* Acts 5:12

### The age of miracles

There's a proverb which says, 'The age of miracles is past.' The reference books tell you this was first said by people in the sixteenth century. They were wrong. But first you must ask, what do you mean by a miracle? Miracles are things to wonder at – things which make us admire God. Most of the miracles in the Bible are healing miracles, and modern medical people, aware of the power of mind over body, have no problem is accepting these. The writers of the Bible didn't think they 'went against the laws of nature', because they didn't know any laws of nature; but they'd have been surprised if there were no miracles, because miracles show that God's at work. The author of the Letter to the Hebrews put it like this: 'God added his testimony by signs and wonders and various miracles, and by gifts of the Holy Spirit, distributed according to his will.' For modern scientists, laws are a statement of the probability of certain consequences following certain causes in controlled and repeatable conditions. But scientists don't take into account the activity of God, which isn't a factor mere humans can predict.

### Healing

St Bartholomew was one of the twelve disciples, who carried on the work of Jesus after he died. That included preaching and also healing. Healing is making a sick person whole and healthy; restoring them to physical and mental health. The Bible's quite clear that cures can be brought about by herbs and medicines, and by unbelievers, but that God's the ultimate source of all healing. Jesus healed the sick, and instructed his followers to do the same. St Luke was a physician, who used prayer and medicines alongside each other. St Paul wrote that healing's one of the gifts of the Spirit. St James describes the use of prayer, and anointing with oil, in healing the sick. Christians have always been active in the physical care of the sick. Hospitals began in monasteries – the word hospital means 'a place for guests' – and medical missionaries carried healing around the world. But Christians also carry on the work of healing in the ministry of prayer. People pray for a sick person, in church, in a prayer group or on their own. Or they may gather round the sickbed and pray using the Holy Communion, anointing with oil and the laying on of hands.

## Answers to prayer

The whole ministry of healing is incarnational and sacramental. Healing uses material things like medicines, and the body's built-in power of healing itself, for spiritual purposes. We pray that God in his mercy will answer our prayers in the way he sees to be best for us. Answers to prayer for healing may sometimes involve a miracle, and when we pray, we should always have faith that God can do things which the doctors wouldn't have thought possible. But God doesn't often do miracles, because he'd rather that his world worked according to regular laws of cause and effect. The wisdom of the doctors, the effectiveness of the medicines and the self-healing powers in the body are all the work of God the Creator, and that in itself's a sort of miracle. Also, the effects of surrounding a sick person with prayer and love are unimaginable. Sometimes, however, our prayer for healing seems to be unanswered. What's happening then is that God's giving the sick person the grace to endure their suffering bravely. Eventually God gives the best healing of all, when he leads us through death and resurrection to a better life, free from all pain.

## Bartholomew

When St Bartholomew was martyred, he was buried on an island on the River Tiber in Rome where there was an old pagan healing centre, and the Christians took over its work. Then churches associated with hospitals were named after him, such as 'St Bart's' in London. Following the example of St Bartholomew and the other Apostles, all Christians are used by God in the healing ministry, combining physical means with prayer. The results God gives will be 'signs and wonders', pointing to the power of God, and making people wonder at God's love. 'Many signs and wonders were done among the people through the apostles ... A great number of people would gather ... bringing the sick and those tormented by unclean spirits, and they were all cured.'

## Suggested hymns

*At even, ere the sun was set; From thee all skill and science flow; Immortal love, for ever full; Peter and John went to pray.*

## Fifteenth Sunday after Trinity (Proper 17)
## 31 August
*Principal Service*   **Take Up Your Cross**
(*Continuous*): Ex. 3:1–15 The burning bush; Ps. 105:1–6, 23–26, 45b Moses; or (*Related*): Jer. 15:15–21 Jeremiah's call; Ps. 26:1–8 Temple thanksgiving; Rom. 12:9–21 Love in action; Matt. 16:21–28 Take up your cross

> *'Jesus told his disciples, "If any want to become my followers, let them deny themselves and take up their cross and follow me."'*
> Matthew 16:24

### Judas the Galilean

Around AD 6, a Jew called Judas (a common enough name) led a revolt against the Roman occupying army. He gained popular support because he protested against the taxes they imposed. He's mentioned by the Jewish historian Josephus and in the Acts of the Apostles. He was defeated, of course, and he and many of his followers were killed. Crucifixion was the usual Roman punishment for rebels. Nailing criminals to two pieces of wood in the shape of a cross was probably invented by the Persians; Alexander the Great had two thousand inhabitants of Tyre crucified, and all the slaves who rebelled under Spartacus were crucified on the roadside along the Appian Way. So the followers of Judas the Galilean were probably hanged on crosses lining all the roads in the province of Galilee. The custom was for them to carry the cross-beam of the cross on their backs through the streets. This added to the deterrent effect of their shame. When they were dead, their bodies were left hanging there for the dogs and vultures.

## Jesus knew

This must have been when Jesus of Nazareth was a young lad; he knew all about what crucifixion meant. So did all the people who heard him. When the word went round that he might be the Messiah, it was obvious how the Romans would deal with him if they got enough evidence. So he probably knew full well that, one day, he'd be carrying his own cross through the streets of Jerusalem on his way to execution.

## Take up your cross

So what did his hearers think when they heard him say, 'If any want to become my followers, let them deny themselves and take up their cross and follow me'? Words can't describe the gasp of horror. Me, be crucified? My God, anything but that! Of course only a few of his disciples were literally killed on a cross. So we take the words metaphorically, to describe sacrificial living. 'Self-denial' doesn't mean just giving up chocolates for Lent. It means denying your very self. Saying to God, 'What I want doesn't matter. Your will be done.' The 'I' crossed out. Even speaking metaphorically, that's an enormous challenge. Perhaps Jesus needed to create the initial gasp of horror so that people now, as then, would be shocked – shocked into realizing what it means to be a disciple of Christ.

## Sacrificial living

But what does sacrificial living actually imply? What's the real cost of discipleship? Well, let's listen to what St Paul said to the Christians in Rome. And let's apply it literally to ourselves. Of course the deeper meaning of the words goes beyond the literal meaning into a whole new approach to a life of sacrificial love. But the initial shock of applying Paul's words literally to yourself helps us understand how demanding it is to be a Christian. Listen carefully:

Show genuine love; hate everything that's evil, hold tight to all
  that's good;
love one another with mutual affection;
be rivals only over how much respect you can show each other.

Don't lag behind the others; shine with the Holy Spirit; be
slaves of God.
Be joyful with hope, suffer without grumbling, persevere in
prayer.
Give money for those who are needy; be hospitable to
foreigners.
Pray for those who make your life difficult; pray for them, don't
curse them.
Be joyful with those who are happy, weep with those who weep.
Live in harmony with one another;
don't be snobbish, but mix with rich and poor alike.
Don't claim to be cleverer than you are.
Don't pay evil back with evil,
but concentrate on what everyone regards as praiseworthy.
If possible, if it depends on you, live at peace with everyone.
My friends, never take revenge; leave punishment to God.
No, 'if your enemies are hungry, feed them;
if they're thirsty, give them something to drink;
In this way you'll make them burn with shame.'
Don't be defeated by evil, but defeat evil with goodness.

## Grace

It's pretty challenging, isn't it? Fortunately we don't have to do it
on our own; Jesus gives us the grace of the Holy Spirit. If the Spirit
is working within us, we shall be changed till we become more like
Jesus, who said, 'If you want to become my follower, cross out all
selfishness, shoulder your cross, and follow me.'

## All-age worship

*Play follow-my-leader. If Jesus was at the front of the line, what
would you do to follow his example?*

## Suggested hymns

*I want to walk with Jesus Christ; Take up your cross, the Saviour
said; Lord, for the years your love has kept and guided; Will you
come and follow me?*

# The Fifteenth Sunday after Trinity
*Second Service*  **Speak, for I Am with You**

Ps. 105:1–15 Mindful of his covenant; 2 Kings 6:24–25; 7:3–20
The siege of Samaria; Acts 18:1–16 Paul in Corinth; *Gospel at Holy Communion*: Mark 7:1–8, 14–15, 21–23 Tradition

> *'Do not be afraid, but speak and do not be silent; for I am with you ... for there are many in this city who are my people.' Acts 18:9–10*

## Corinth

Corinth was a bustling seaport on the narrow strip of land that joins the mainland of Greece to the enormous peninsula known as the Peloponnese. Corinth had all the vices that are found where sailors come ashore; it was famous for slaves, prostitutes and arguments. It had no time for a little Jewish tent-maker called Paul, who wanted to tell them about another Jew called Jesus. Things looked pretty hopeless for him.

## Friends and enemies

Paul made many friends in Corinth, and many enemies. He stayed with a Jewish husband-and-wife team of tent-makers called Aquila and Priscilla. Paul sat cross-legged in their shop and gossiped the gospel to the customers as he plied his needle. He preached in the Jewish synagogue, and got thrown out. Depressed by the attacks of his enemies and the resistance of materialistic Corinth to any talk of spiritual things, he went to bed miserable. Then in the night he had a dream. He saw Jesus, who told him to cheer up: 'Don't be afraid, but speak out and don't stay silent; for I, Jesus, am with you, and ... there are many in this city who are my people.'

## Sharing good news

Well, Jesus was right. There were many in Corinth who belonged to Jesus, though they didn't know it yet. The church grew there until there were several different congregations in different parts of the city. Eventually it was one of the biggest churches in the country, and the good news about Jesus fanned out from there to build growing congregations all over southern Greece. This wouldn't have happened if Paul had given up when things were hard. But he himself wrote that the story of Jesus was like a fire blazing up in his heart. He just had to share it. He couldn't help it. You can't keep good news bottled up inside you.

## The siege of Samaria

There's a perfect illustration of this in the Old Testament story of the siege of Samaria. All the people were trapped inside the city, while the army of the king of Syria was camped round it, waiting for them to starve. The only people who weren't inside the city were four men, and they weren't allowed in because they were lepers. They squatted outside the city gate, starving like everyone else. Eventually they said to one another, 'If we sit here, we die. If we go to the Syrian army camp, they might feed us, in which case we live a bit longer; or they might kill us, in which case we die a little sooner. Might as well take a chance.' So they hobbled up to the Syrian camp and found it empty – all the soldiers had done a bunk the previous evening when they heard of an Egyptian army coming to attack them. The people inside Samaria didn't know this, but the four lepers found food aplenty in the abandoned camp, and started to gorge themselves. But soon they realized they'd have to go back to the city and tell the others. You can't keep good news bottled up inside you.

## Don't be afraid

You and I have some good news. It's the good news that God loves us, and that Jesus died and rose again to save us from sin and death. You can't keep good news like that to yourself, any more than the four lepers could have kept the good news of free food a secret from those who didn't know about it. There are many ways of sharing good news. God may be calling you to study until you can proclaim it from the pulpit. Or you may be called to gossip the gospel with your family, friends and workmates. Or you may be one who proclaims God's love by showing love for your family and friends, your neighbours and people who are needy, until they can see the love of God shining out of you. Whichever way God calls you to, don't hold back because you think the task's impossible. Jesus says to you, as he said to the Apostle Paul, 'Don't be afraid: speak out and don't remain silent; for I, Jesus, am with you, and no one will harm you, for there are many people in this place who are my people' – though they may not realize it until you tell them that Jesus loves them.

## Suggested hymns

*Do not be afraid, for I have redeemed you; Fight the good fight with all thy might; One shall tell another, and he shall tell his friends; Through all the changing scenes of life.*

## The Sixteenth Sunday after Trinity (Proper 18)
## 7 September
*Principal Service*   **Christ Among Us**
(*Continuous*): Ex. 12:1–14 The Passover; Ps. 149 Praise and judgement; *or* (*Related*): Ezek. 33:7–11 Turn back from evil; Ps. 119:33–40 Law and repentance; Rom. 13:8–14 Love fulfils the law; Matt. 18:15–20 Where two or three agree

> '[Jesus said,] "Where two or three are gathered in my name, I am there among them."' *Matthew 18:20*

## A joke?

A comedian was quoted in the newspapers recently for making a so-called 'joke'. He was reported to have said, 'When I was a child I had a friend who was always with me. Then I grew up and stopped going to church.' That's a joke? Instead of being funny, most Christians would say it was unutterably sad. We must feel profoundly sorry for him. Many quite young children do have this very deep faith in the presence of Jesus their friend. Quite young children can understand that Jesus is invisibly present with them, even though they can't see him. Then this childlike faith often grows into a mature, adult relationship with our Saviour. The comedian may have got an easy laugh with his unintelligent joke. But he's condemned himself to a lifetime of loneliness by rejecting the friendship of Jesus. Jesus himself said, 'Where two or three are gathered in my name, I am there among them.'

## Together with friends

Two or three people gather in the name of Jesus, when a handful of Christian friends meet to pray together, or to talk about what their faith means to them, and plan what they should do about it, or to study the Bible. Do you ever do this? Do you go to weekday Bible study meetings? When you're discussing the problems of the world with your Christian friends, do you ever pray together? When there's a family crisis, or somebody you know is quite sick, do you share it with Jesus? Remember his promise, as you meet with other Christians, that he's right there in the middle of the group, listening to you. Close your eyes and feel his presence. Jesus is together with you among your friends.

## Together in church

Jesus is present with you also when you worship him in the church building. Whether it's a tiny handful of people in a struggling congregation, or an encouraging celebration by a large and successful church, Jesus is there in the midst. It's very easy to go through the whole ritual of a service of Christian worship as a matter of form, without ever remembering that Jesus is alive and it's to him that your worship is addressed. Jesus isn't far away, he's close to each one of us. Jesus wants you to have a good sing in church. Do remember, however, that you're doing it for him, and take a moment to offer your talents and your enjoyment of the music to Jesus. With our butterfly minds fluttering from subject to subject, nobody can be consciously thinking of Jesus every second. Jesus knows that, and forgives us. But do try to develop a habit of coming back to him. Think of Jesus in the midst of us in church, as often as you can.

## Together when we pray

Jesus is close to you, also, when you pray at home. He told us to go into our bedroom, shut the door and talk to our heavenly Father. Jesus is no less present when we pray alone, than when we pray with friends or in church. Often we have the warm certainty in our hearts that Jesus is there with us as we pray, and listening to every word we say. But our feelings aren't totally under our control, and at other times prayer feels cold and emotionless. Don't be put off by that. We *know*, with our minds, that Jesus is there, loving us, whether we feel it or not, because that's what he's promised. Private prayer and public worship aren't alternatives. Prayer trains us to worship, and worship trains us to pray.

## Together when alone

By public worship, small groups and private prayer, we become increasingly aware of the presence of Jesus with us at all times. Then we need never be lonely. The simple childlike faith that I have an invisible friend can carry over into adulthood without any intellectual dishonesty. The Beatles sang a song about 'Eleanor Rigby' asking where all the lonely people come from. Perhaps a lot of today's loneliness comes from forgetting the promise of Jesus of his invisible presence at all times: 'Where two or three are gathered in my name, I am there among them.'

### All-age worship

*Play at putting on a blindfold. Do your friends stop being there with you when you can't see them? Talk to Jesus.*

### Suggested hymns

*Be still, for the presence of the Lord; Jesus, where'er thy people meet; The king is among us; What a friend we have in Jesus.*

## The Sixteenth Sunday after Trinity
### Second Service    Superstition

Ps. 108 Steadfast love [115 Not to us]; Ezek. 12:21—13:16 False prophets; Acts 19:1–20 Magic; *Gospel at Holy Communion*: Mark 7:24–37 Crumbs from the table

> *'A number of those who practised magic collected their books and burned them publicly ... So the word of the Lord grew mightily and prevailed.'* Acts 19:19–20

## Placebo

One of the prayers in the Latin office of Vespers begins 'Placebo Domino', meaning 'I shall please the Lord.' In the old days, when a patient visited a doctor, although there was nothing wrong with them that any medicine could cure, the doctor used to write on the prescription one word: 'Placebo'. Then the pharmacist knew that the patient was to be given a bottle of something which would have no physical effect; however, it would make the patient feel better, simply because they believed it would. Nowadays a placebo is defined as 'a medicine given to humour or gratify a patient', and the 'placebo effect' is 'a beneficial effect of a placebo, ascribed to the patient's belief in its efficacy'. Is this wrong? Reports appear from time to time protesting that various forms of 'alternative' medicine 'are no better than placebos'. But you could argue that a placebo makes you feel better, and feeling better makes you get better – it's the power of mind over body. The danger lies, reply the practitioners of scientific medicine, when people turn to placebos and reject the help which scientific treatment could give them. The argument remains unsettled, but Christians have an interest in it. Praying for people who are sick, in many cases, releases the natural powers of self-healing which God has put into our bodies, and speeds up the cure. Yet self-proclaimed faith healers can occasionally harm their patients by discouraging them from using scientific medicine. And this harms the reputation of Christianity, by making it appear unscientific. There's no simple answer to this dilemma.

## False prophets

A similar dilemma faced Ezekiel and other Old Testament prophets, when confronted with false prophets. The false prophets had been saying 'Peace', when there was no peace. So God condemns those who 'have prophesied falsehood and lying divination'. But how do you tell the difference between false prophets and true prophets? The only help the Bible gives is to warn us that the predictions of the false prophets won't come true. But you could wait a long time before you find out whose predictions are fulfilled, and whose are not.

## Magic

St Paul had the same problem in the New Testament, in dealing with magicians. Paul worked miracles of healing, and the seven sons of Sceva tried to do the same in the name of Jesus. How were the people of Ephesus to distinguish between Christian healing and magic? Fortunately for Paul's reputation, his opponents failed. Magic was discredited, and 'A number of those who practised magic collected their books and burned them publicly ... So the word of the Lord grew mightily and prevailed.'

## Faith and reason

The first point to hold onto is that faith goes beyond reason, but faith isn't contrary to reason. That means that Christian prayer can do some things which science can't do. Yet Christianity doesn't demand that you should believe anything unreasonable. Nor should you refuse the help which science can give us in living our lives. Prayer and medicine have to work hand in hand.

## Superstition

Yet an awful lot of superstition gathers around Christianity. The way many people regard Christian worship and Christian sacraments is pretty close to magic. Much of it does no harm at all – we have no wish to attack the faith of simple people. So we can't make up our minds whether to condemn superstition which passes itself off as religion, or not. Yet lucky charms and fortune-telling, if they take the place of genuine religion, can do harm. For it means that anyone with a scientific education, or who has benefited from the discoveries of science, may be tempted to dismiss the Christian faith as mere superstition. This in turn may make it harder for Christians to accept the help that science offers. Superstition needs handling with kid gloves on. If people believe strongly in something which I believe to be untrue, it may do them good because of the placebo effect. Alternatively, they may be depriving themselves of a relationship with the loving and living God, by putting something else in its place, which is very sad. We mustn't attack superstition; all we can do is offer our own love and God's love, and a better system of beliefs. Edmund Burke said 'religion, not atheism, is the true remedy for superstition'.

## *Suggested hymns*

*Firmly I believe and truly; God moves in a mysterious way; Jesus the Lord said, I am the bread; O for a closer walk with God.*

## Seventeenth Sunday after Trinity (Proper 19)
## (Holy Cross Day)  14 September
*Principal Service*  **Forgiveness**

(*Continuous*): Ex. 14:19–31 The Exodus; Ps. 114 The Exodus; *or Canticle*: Ex. 15:1b–11, 20–21 The Exodus; *or* (*Related*): Gen. 50:15–21 God turns evil to good; Ps. 103:[1–7] 8–13 God's love and fatherhood; Rom. 14:1–12 Tolerance and justice; Matt. 18:21–35 Forgiveness seventy times seven

> '[Peter asked Jesus,] "Lord, if another member of the church sins against me, how often should I forgive? As many as seven times?" Jesus said to him, "Not seven times, but, I tell you, seventy-seven times."' Matthew 18:21–22

### Television debate

A televised debate was discussing forgiveness. Various people, who'd suffered grievous hurts at the hands of others, were asked if they could contemplate forgiving those who'd offended them. A man whose child had been killed in a terrorist incident confessed that for the first time since it happened, he'd been made really angry by the suggestion that he should forgive the villains who'd done it. Others sympathized with this, because none of the terrorists had shown any repentance for what they did; it's almost impossible, they agreed, to forgive someone who has no regrets for what they've done. But another man, whose son had been killed by a drunk driver, reported how the police told him that the driver, who himself had a son of the same age, had gone to pieces with remorse. Eventually the parents wrote a letter for the driver to show to the judge, which was summed up in three words: 'We forgive you.'

### Reasons for forgiveness

One good result of their actions was that the tabloid newspapers discussed the Christian doctrine of forgiveness on their front pages, though most of them thought that drunk drivers should never be forgiven. But the reasons the parents wrote as they did were complex. First it was for the sake of the driver's family: if he'd been sent to prison, his wife and children would have found it hard to make ends meet, and his family might have been broken up. After seeing the letter, the judge decided to give the driver a large fine and ban him from driving – but no prison sentence. Yet the main reason the parents had felt bound to offer forgiveness was for their own sakes. They'd seen people making a public career, to put it bluntly, out of their refusal to forgive somebody, and they'd no wish to consume the rest of their own lives by nourishing a grudge. Third, they were Christians. How could they say the Lord's Prayer, they asked, with its request that God should forgive us as we forgive those who sin against us, if they refused forgiveness to another human being?

## What is forgiveness?

The reason why so many people find forgiveness difficult is that they don't understand what forgiveness means. They imagine, quite wrongly, that 'I forgive you' means, 'There, there, just forget about it, what you've done doesn't really matter.' Of course it matters! If you've killed my child, it matters all the world to me, and I shall never forget. But after the case was over, the father and the driver met outside the court, put their arms round each other, and sobbed on each other's shoulders. Gradually the father learnt that there's just one thing that matters more than remembering the wrong that somebody's done. And that's changing the relationship between two people who *had* hated each other, into an acceptance that we're all sinners, in our different ways, and we desperately need to find a way to live together in the same, imperfect, world.

## Seventy times seven

Peter asked Jesus about the limits of forgiveness. If one of my friends hurts me, he asked, how many times must I forgive him? Twice? Three times? As many as seven times? Jesus replied, Not seven times – seventy-seven times! Can you just imagine it? Poor Peter, trying to keep a score of how many times he's been offended: '69, 70, 71 ... Bother, I've lost count. Start again: 1, 2, 3 ... !' Peter realized that anyone who tries to keep a score of grudges only makes a fool of themselves.

## Thank God

Thank God that God doesn't keep a score of how many times we hurt him. When God says to you 'I forgive you', he doesn't mean, 'There, there, just forget about it, what you've done doesn't really matter.' Our sins matter a lot to God, and forgiveness is costly. But our relationship with him matters even more; he wants it to be a relationship of acceptance and love. That's why God forgives us. That's why we *must* forgive our neighbours, no matter how hard it seems.

## All-age worship

*List the ways in which people have hurt you in the past week. Then list the ways you've hurt God. Put the lists in a metal bowl, or another safe place, and burn them.*

## Suggested hymns

*Forgive our sins as we forgive; Make me a channel of your peace; O the deep, deep love of Jesus; Rock of ages.*

# Holy Cross Day   14 September
## (*or may be transferred to 15 September*)
## Obedient to Death on the Cross
Num. 21:4–9 The bronze serpent; Ps. 22:23–28 All the earth shall turn to the Lord; Phil. 2:6–11 Obedient to death on the cross; John 3:13–17 God so loved the world

*'Being found in human form he humbled himself and became obedient to the point of death – even death on a cross.' Philippians 2:8*

## Obedience

Soldiers in the army are supposed to show absolute and unquestioning obedience, to their superior officers. This is essential, for if a platoon's in a dangerous situation, there's no time to have a debate about how to escape: those in charge have to make up their minds quickly on a plan of action, and everybody else has to do what they're told, or they'll all end up dead. Nevertheless, there are some commands which most people would refuse to obey, unless for a very good reason. If the commanding officer orders you to walk into a hail of bullets, it's hard to imagine any circumstances where such a command would be justified. The charge of the Light

Brigade was heroic, but the order was a bad one, and their deaths did nobody any good. On the other hand, the order to blow up the bridge on the River Kwai, though it was unpopular, may have saved hundreds of lives in the long run. Those who died carrying out the order were martyrs for a cause.

## Incarnation

St Paul wrote a letter to the Christians in Philippi, which was a Roman colony. Most of the inhabitants were ex-soldiers, or the children or grandchildren of soldiers who'd fought in the Battle of Philippi following the assassination of Julius Caesar. They knew all about obedience. So the Apostle tried to paint a picture of what Jesus did for us, using the metaphor of soldierly obedience to his heavenly Father. It's a difficult picture to paint, because we're not quite sure what words to use for the relationship between God the Father and Jesus his Son. St Paul said, 'God was in Christ, reconciling the world to himself', so in some ways they were one and the same God. On the other hand, the story of Jesus wrestling with his conscience in the Garden of Gethsemane shows that obedience wasn't easy for him. Then we find it hard to visualize the glory of heaven which Jesus enjoyed with his Father before he came to earth as a baby in Bethlehem. So the first step was for Jesus to obey his Father's command to leave behind him the splendour of eternity, empty himself of his omnipotence and his omniscience, and become an ordinary, weak and powerless human baby.

## Obedience to death

But that wasn't all; there was worse to come. His Father ordered Jesus to die; Jesus was obedient unto death, writes St Paul. There's the crunch point; that's where most of us would rebel, when somebody, anybody, ordered us to die. Yet Jesus was 'obedient to the point of death ...' and here Paul pauses to let the sheer horror of what he's going to say next sink in: 'obedient to the point of death – *even death on a cross*'. The most painful death that's ever been invented, and Jesus was commanded to submit to it willingly.

## Holy Cross Day

So, just in case the awfulness of the cross hasn't sunk in on Good Friday, the Church has set aside another day, the fourteenth of

September, to be called 'Holy Cross Day'. Now we can meditate on just how great was the self-sacrifice of Jesus when he freely chose to obey his Father's order to die. Through that sacrifice, Jesus won the forgiveness of sins for you and for me, and the promise of eternal life for us all. It was no cheap salvation, when he had to obey his Father's command to come to earth and to die. We should be very grateful that Jesus was obedient in the one case in which an order to lay down your life is recognized by every soldier to be justified: when, by your sacrifice, you're able to save the lives of your friends.

## Our obedience

If that was how Jesus obeyed his Father, you and I should be willing to obey God like that. We shan't necessarily be called on to lay down our lives, but we shall certainly be commanded to sacrifice our selfish wish to have everything our own way. When next you catch yourself grumbling about how unfair life is, and how much inconvenience and discomfort you have to put up with, remember the good soldier, who obeys without questioning; and Jesus who followed his Father's command to leave heaven behind, come to earth, and was 'obedient to the point of death – *even death on a cross*'.

### Suggested hymns

*Faithful cross, above all other* (part of *Sing, my tongue, the glorious battle*); *Such love*; *Were you there when they crucified my Lord?*; *When I survey the wondrous cross*.

## Eighteenth Sunday after Trinity (Proper 20)
## (St Matthew, Apostle and Evangelist) 21 September
*Principal Service* **Labourers in the Vineyard**
(*Continuous*): Ex. 16:2–15 Manna; Ps. 105:1–6, 37–45 Manna; *or* (*Related*): Jonah 3:10—4:11 Anger, love and prayer; Ps. 145:1–8 God's love; Phil. 1:21–30 Death and suffering; Matt. 20:1–16 Vineyard labourers

'Are you envious because I am generous?' Matthew 20:15

## Omnicompetent

Isn't it infuriating when you meet somebody who's good at everything? You know, your schoolfriend who's best at sports and comes top in all the exams. The woman who's beautiful, popular and wise. The 'Renaissance man' who's a well-read expert in several different subjects. Or the surgeon, who plays a musical instrument in an orchestra for relaxation. These multi-talented, omni-competent people make us feel so humiliated! Why do some people have *all* the gifts? We have to struggle ever so hard not to be jealous. Now, if you can laugh at yourself, the battle's half won; you've recognized jealousy as a temptation and are trying to resist it. Your friends will reassure you that you've many talents of your own. But when you find somebody who excels at something that you're only average at, it's a real struggle to stop the little green-eyed monster of envy sneaking into your heart.

## Labourers in the vineyard

Jesus told a story about envy. Society was changing in his day. The peasant farmers, each tilling his own small plot of land, had been bought out by the big landowners, who employed hired hands to work in the fields. But there wasn't enough work to go round, and the workers had to face the new threat of unemployment. Jesus told us to picture a landowner hiring labourers to pick the grapes in his vineyard. At daybreak he employed a few workers and promised them a full day's wage at the going rate. But there weren't enough of them to finish the job, so mid-morning and again in the middle of the afternoon he hired some more. At sunset he paid them all the same: a full day's wage. Those who'd been employed at daybreak, and had 'born the burden and heat of the day', were horrified to see that the workers who were hired mid-afternoon were paid the same as them, even though they'd only worked a few hours. But the landowner retorted that nobody had any cause for complaint. 'It's my money, so I can do what I like with it,' he said. 'I've given you what I agreed, a generous day's wage. What's it got to do with you what I pay to anybody else?' And then the landowner made his parting shot. 'Are you envious because I'm generous?' he asked, and sent them away with a flea in their ear.

## 'Are you envious because I'm generous?'

'Are you envious because I'm generous?' The people who listened to Jesus's parable must have recognized that there was nothing unjust in the treatment of the men who'd worked all day: they'd got what they signed on for. The reason we all wince when we hear the story, is because we often grumble to God in similar words to the ones they used to their boss. 'Dear God, it's so unfair. Some of my schoolfriends are minor celebrities, my son earns more than I do, and young Johnny-come-lately there who joined the organization after I did's been promoted to a position of responsibility already over my head. It's just not right!' And God wants to say to us, when he can get a word in edgeways, 'Now just calm down! When did I ever promise you a bed of roses? I only promised you your daily bread, so why are you grumbling because you haven't any cake? Cake wasn't in the contract; on the days you do have it, just learn to be thankful. Or are you envious because I'm generous?'

## When others prosper

So when we see other people do well we should rejoice with them, and thank God for the talents and openings he's given them. Then we should also thank God for the quite different talents and opportunities *we've* received. The greatest gift of all is God's love, and he showers that generously on everybody, although nobody truly deserves it. God doesn't love people more because they're cleverer than you, or more good-looking. God loves you because you're you, and because you're his child. He's pleased, of course, if you're grateful for the gifts you have and try to use them to serve him. We've all received from God far more than we deserve. Even if you'll never be a captain of industry, a celebrity, a top professor, a brain-surgeon or an Olympic athlete, learn to thank God for the gifts he's already given you.

## *All-age worship*

*Make a list of the things you've learnt to do in the past few years. Turn it into a prayer of thanks to God for the talents he's given you.*

*Father, hear the prayer we offer; From heaven you came (The Servant King); Great is thy faithfulness, O God my Father; Take my life, and let it be.*

## St Matthew, Apostle and Evangelist 21 September
## (or may be transferred to 22 September)
## The Open Statement of the Truth

Prov. 3:13–18 Wisdom more precious than jewels; Ps. 119:65–72 Better than gold; 2 Cor. 4:1–6 The open statement of the truth; Matt. 9:9–13 The call of Matthew

> 'By the open statement of the truth we commend ourselves to the conscience of everyone in the sight of God.' 2 Corinthians 4:2

### Would you believe?

A long time ago there was a comedy series on American television, so I'm told, which gave a new phrase to the English language. The comic character was in trouble for causing a disaster by his carelessness, and tried increasingly fantastic explanations. Something like, 'Why haven't I brought back the hamburger you gave me the money to buy? Would you believe that a hurricane blew it out of my hand and into the river? No, you don't believe me? Well, would you believe that a giant bird flew down and snatched it away? You can't believe that either? Would you believe that a flying saucer full of little green men demanded to take it to their leader?' And so on. Hence, 'Would you believe …' has become the phrase with which you introduce an improbable statement that you don't really expect anyone to believe in a month of Sundays. It's much simpler to tell the plain, unvarnished truth and have done with it.

### Gospel truth

St Matthew, whom we commemorate today, wanted people to believe him. He wrote the Gospel which bears his name because he wanted people who read it to believe in Jesus. But it's a pretty improbable story that he has to tell. Would you believe in a God who, from love for the human race, becomes one of us, is born in a stable, mixes with simple fishermen, is killed on a cross, and rises to life again on the third day? Who's going to believe a story like that? Well, only those who accept that the gospel-writers were at all times telling the plain unvarnished truth – the 'gospel truth'.

## Myths and legends

So it was vital that the gospel-writers shouldn't tell stories which were merely myths and legends. Now myths and legends have their place. There are truths you can convey through a story which no amount of cold facts will make people understand. And some of the miracles which Matthew recounts are hard for scientifically educated people today to grasp. But Matthew must have believed that they were true. His readers must have been prepared to accept that a God-become-man would behave in some unexpected ways. It was no use Matthew playing fast and loose with the truth, however. As that other Apostle, St Paul, put it, 'By the open statement of the truth we commend ourselves to the conscience of everyone in the sight of God.' There's an old saying, 'Great is truth, and it will prevail.'

## Dodgy arguments

There's still a temptation for us today to use dodgy arguments when we're talking about Christianity. You won't persuade anybody to accept an argument simply by saying 'That's our tradition' if your tradition is contrary to Scripture. It's no use quoting Scripture if your way of interpreting Scripture is unreasonable. Scripture, tradition and reason have been called the three-legged stool: rest your beliefs on all three and they'll rest secure; pull any one away, Scripture, tradition or reason, and everything will fall to the ground.

## Defending the faith

Any one of us can be called on at some time to defend our faith in Jesus – to 'give a reason for the hope that is in us', as St Peter put it. If somebody asks you why you believe, or why you go to church, you must give an answer out of your own experience. It's no use trying to make up an answer, or muddying the water by using dodgy arguments. If you don't know how to put it into words, say so. Don't suggest that the enquirer is dishonest or unintelligent; treat them with respect. Don't get trapped into defending some superstitious nonsense which is nowhere to be found in the Bible, or a literalist interpretation of Bible history. But have confidence in what you say. If a spiritual message really does come from the Bible, and you've found the promises that God makes in the Bible come true in your experience, then it's the gospel truth. Nobody need be ashamed of believing in this. And anyone with an open mind can be trusted to accept it, if by the open statement of the truth you commend yourself to the conscience of everyone in the sight of God. That's what Matthew did, and people believe him; you can expect them to believe you, too. 'Great is the truth, and it will prevail.'

### Suggested hymns

*Come sing, ye choirs exultant; Disposer supreme, and Judge of the earth; He sat to watch o'er customs paid; Thou art the Way, by thee alone.*

# Nineteenth Sunday after Trinity (Proper 21)
## 28 September (Eve of Michaelmas, see page 345.)
*Principal Service*   **Two Sons**
(*Continuous*): Ex. 17:1–7 Water from the rock; Ps. 78:1–4, 12–16 Water from the rock; *or* (*Related*): Ezek. 18:1–4, 25–32 Individual responsibility; Ps. 25:1–8 Teach me your ways; Phil. 2:1–13 The mind of Christ; Matt. 21:23–32 The Baptist's authority

*'Which of the two did the will of his father?' Matthew 21:31*

### Two sons

It's not easy being a parent. Most parents try to play fair and treat their children equally. But what if the children don't play fair? It's easier to like a child who's easy-going and cheerful. Easier than with one who's surly. Fiction's full of stories about siblings who look alike, but inside they're as different as chalk from cheese. There are plenty of families like that in real life, too. Jesus told a story about a father who owned a vineyard. There are jobs in agriculture that just won't wait, and one day he asked both his two sons to go and work in the vineyard. One son was Mr Cheerful. He smiled and he nodded, and he said, 'Yes Dad, of course I'll do it for you.'

His father liked him for his willingness. But on his way to the family vineyard he met a few friends, and before long he'd completely forgotten about his promise. The other son was the sour-faced one. 'Why should I?' he spat out. 'It's my life, and I'll do what I like with my time. I'm not having anyone giving me orders, even if you are my father.' But then he went outside, and he thought what a fool he'd been. If the work in the vineyard didn't keep up with the seasons the vintage would fail, and then they'd all be poor. One day he and his brother would inherit the vineyard between them, and it'd be worthless if they didn't look after it. His father wasn't such a bad old stick anyway. So without telling anybody, he went and did the work that needed doing. When his Dad found out, he was delighted, and quite forgot how surly this son had been earlier in the day. Like many of Jesus's parables, the story of the two sons ends with a question: 'Which of the two did the will of his father?' It's not a difficult question to answer. So however even-handed the father tried to be, he couldn't help liking the son who promised nothing but got the job done. As for the lad who made big promises then didn't keep them, I expect his father still loved him. But it'd be a struggle to trust him ever again.

## Pharisees

Jesus told this story when some Pharisees challenged him about what authority he had to preach and to undermine their interpretation of Scripture. He compared his authority to that of John the Baptist, who'd been welcomed by the ordinary folk. The Pharisees were very religious people. They really tried to keep the laws of Moses in every detail. As Jesus said, they gave a tithe or a tenth of even the smallest crops to the Temple, but they neglected the weightier matters of the law. The law told them to tithe, certainly, but it also told them to love their neighbour, and I doubt if the Pharisees even knew what love means. They were like the smiling son in the story, full of promises to do what God commanded them, but, in terms of making the world a better place, actually they achieved nothing at all. Many of the ordinary people, who made no pretence of being religious, and didn't claim to be particularly good, were much more loving than the Pharisees. So 'which of the two did the will of his Father?' Pretty obvious, really. The ordinary people did much more good in the world than the religious people, because they were much more open and loving.

## God's will

God's like that father. Of course he likes people who promise to obey him. But it's not much use if you don't keep your promises. Fine words butter no parsnips. God wants his children to put their promises into practice. You promise that you're going to be a good Christian, but actually, most weeks something else gets in the way, and you don't go to church very often. Or you come to church and you promise to love God with all your heart and mind and soul and strength, and your neighbour as yourself. Then you're not very nice to your family, and there are needy people in the next street that you haven't even taken the trouble to find out about. Now what are your promises worth? Ask yourself which of the two sons in the parable you are most like. Then try to obey God in action as well as in words.

### All-age worship

*Role-play a drama about children who make promises but don't keep them.*

### Suggested hymns

*O for a heart to praise my God; O Jesus, I have promised; Rejoice, the Lord is king; Tell out, my soul.*

## Nineteenth Sunday after Trinity
### Second Service    Factions
Ps. [120 Lying lips, 123 As a handmaid] 124 The Lord on our side; Ezek. 37:15–28 Reuniting the nation; 1 John 2:22–29 Abide in him; *Gospel at Holy Communion*: Mark 9:38–50 Those not against are for

> *'If the Lord had not been on our side …'* Psalm 124:1

## There is no uniquely righteous nation

'There is no uniquely righteous nation.' The phrase comes from a report of the Bishops of the Church of England. They could equally as well have said, there's no entirely righteous nation. Every state makes mistakes. We all do things which, looked back on, can be seen to be unwise. The truly great nations are the ones that can admit it and apologize. Tragically, it's sometimes when a nation's really trying to do the right thing that it makes its biggest blunders. Human beings are seldom self-critical. They set off in one direction like a charging rhinoceros and nothing can divert them. Worse still is when an individual or a nation brings in religion to support their sense of rightness. When they say, 'We did what God wanted us to do. Anyone who speaks against our policies is speaking against God.' That's the last line of defence for the immoral hypocrite. And it's very, very dangerous talk.

## Self-defence

So what about the psalm which sings:

> If the Lord had not been our side,
> when enemies rose up against us;
> Then they would have swallowed us alive.

Is it ever justified to say that God's on our side, particularly in a war? Probably not; God grieves for those who are killed and injured on both sides, and God's on the side of justice. If a small and weak nation's being unjustifiably attacked by stronger neighbours, they may be right to defend themselves. They're right to thank God that they managed to repel the invaders, which they couldn't have done without God's help. But that's a very different thing from claiming that your nation is uniquely righteous, and God is against your enemies. When *both* sides claim to have God with them, you wonder what sort of God they're worshipping. The French philosopher Voltaire cynically wrote, 'God is not on the side of the big battalions, but on the side of those who shoot best.'

## Israel and Judah

It's not only warring nations that claim a monopoly on God. It happens when there are factions within a nation. The twelve tribes of Israel were fairly united under King David and King Solomon, but after that they split into two rival kingdoms, ten tribes in the north calling themselves Ephraim or Israel, and the two southern tribes calling themselves Judah. The two kingdoms were bitter rivals; they fought each other from time to time; each of them thought God was on their side. Then the northern tribes were defeated and exiled to

Assyria; later the southern tribes were exiled to Babylon. Some of the people, at least, must have been left behind; eventually most of the exiles returned. Ezekiel was a prophet during the exile, who looked forward to the task of rebuilding the nation after the return. Which he knew would be impossible if they remained divided into two factions. So in a wonderful piece of prophetic symbolism, he took two sticks, wrote on one the name of the former southern kingdom, and wrote the name of the northern tribes on the other; then he joined them together in his hand so that they appeared to have become one stick. Everybody who saw him knew that reconciling the quarrelling factions was the only way to unite the nation; indeed, without unity the nation couldn't survive.

## Factions

So we've seen the danger of claiming that God's on your side in international affairs, and in civil war. Isn't this also true in all factional disputes? There's nothing wrong with the weak defending themselves against the strong, and the poor struggling against oppression by the rich: God wants justice to be done. But to claim that God is on the side of capitalism, or socialism, or democracy, or Christianity, or Protestantism, or your political party, or your faction in the party, or in the union, or in your workplace, or in the family ... Well, the list's endless of the factions that claim to know which way God would vote. Of course we can never know that. We should argue for the truth but try to avoid forming factions, having the grace to admit that those that are not against us may be for us. We can all try to be right and loving as often as we can, and to admit our mistakes. We must thank God when we win our struggles, but care for the losers, for God's sake. Nobody's got God in their pocket; God loves everyone.

## Suggested hymns

*Judge eternal, throned in splendour; Lord, while for all mankind we pray; O God of earth and altar; Rejoice, O Land, in God thy might.*

# Twentieth Sunday after Trinity (Proper 22)
## 5 October
## (Alternatively the Dedication Festival)
*Principal Service*   **Wicked Tenants**
(*Continuous*): Ex. 20:1–4, 7–9, 12–20 The Ten Commandments; Ps. 19 The heavens declare the glory of God; *or* (*Related*): Isa. 5:1–7 Song of the vine; Ps. 80:9–17 The vine; Phil. 3:4b–14 Persevere; Matt. 21:33–46 The vine

> '[Jesus said,] "There was a landowner who planted a vineyard ... Then he leased it to tenants."' *Matthew 21:33*

## The grapevine

'I heard it on the grapevine.' How often have you heard that said by somebody who wants to pass on a piece of information, but doesn't want to tell you from whom they heard it? Sometimes, but not always, the information's malicious gossip, which has been passed from person to person to make trouble. Nobody wants their name associated with that sort of thing, so they pretend they're passing on what they heard on 'the grapevine'. The responsible, Christian thing to do when you hear gossip like that is to make up your mind not to tell anyone else. That way, you won't bear any share of the responsibility for destroying somebody else's reputation. If you find out that the allegation's not true, of course, you should publish the correction as widely as you can.

## Networking

The grapevine's not always malicious, though. Just think of somebody saying, 'I heard on the grapevine that it's your birthday, so I've brought you a present.' In fact some people are praised for their skill at 'networking'. This is nothing to do with the internet; it means building up a network of contacts, friends who'll share important information with you, and pass on things you want to be circulated. Friends whom you can call on when you're in a fix to help you out of it, on the understanding that you'll do the same for them if asked. People get promotions if they're good at networking, because it means they can use the grapevine in a responsible way.

## Israel

The people of Israel must have been good at networking. One of the Bible's favourite metaphors for describing the Chosen People was as a grapevine. Isaiah sang the Song of the Vine:

> My beloved had a vineyard
> On a very fertile hill ...
> He expected it to yield grapes,
> But it yielded wild grapes ...
> For the vineyard of the LORD of hosts
> Is the house of Israel.

Psalm 80 uses the same image:

> You brought a vine out of Egypt,
> You drove out the nations and planted it ...
> Why then have you broken down its wall
> So that all who pass by pluck off its grapes?

It's no use having a business where everybody's fantastic at networking, if there's no product coming out of the factory gates. In that case you need to examine the quality of the management.

## Leaders

So it was with Israel. The leaders were inward-looking, feathering their own nest, looking after number one, and forgetting what the nation was there for. As far as Jesus was concerned the Chosen People had been chosen for service, not for privilege. It wouldn't work if God revealed himself to the whole world all at once; so he chose one poor nation to learn about him and pass the message on. Only they weren't doing it. So he compared the leaders to wicked tenants, who didn't actually own the vine, but were ignoring their responsibilities while they were temporarily in charge. The tenants had killed the messengers sent from the owner, even finally killing the owner's son. It's not too difficult to see that by the owner he meant God, and by the son he meant himself. Then, said Jesus, 'The kingdom of God will be taken away from you and given to a people that produces the fruits of the kingdom.'

## Christians

Whom did Jesus mean that the kingdom would be given to? Perhaps he meant a new leadership in Israel. Perhaps he meant non-Jews, the Gentiles, nations who would learn to pass on the concept of a loving God, a God who requires love between his children. Perhaps Jesus was deliberately hinting at the growth of the Christian Church throughout the world. If so, that gives us a great privilege, but it also calls us to deeper commitment to service. Christians claim to have been grafted into God's Chosen People. And it's not only the leaders who are responsible. Every Christian's part of the grapevine; we're all entrusted with responsible networking. Do you use your key position as one of the strands in God's grapevine to pass on gossip? Or do you communicate the good news to people who may not realize that God loves them?

### All-age worship

*Play 'Chinese whispers'. Refuse to pass on critical comments, but replace them with messages about God's love.*

### Suggested hymns

*I am the vine, you are the branches; I danced in the morning; My song is love unknown; We hail thy presence glorious; We have a gospel to proclaim.*

## Twentieth Sunday after Trinity
### Second Service   Walking the Walk

Ps. 136 God's love lasts for ever; Prov. 2:1–11 Search for wisdom; 1 John 2:1–17 Walk the way he walked; *Gospel at Holy Communion*: Mark 10.2–16 Divorce

> *'Whoever says, "I abide in him," ought to walk just as he walked.'* 1 John 2:6

### Follow-my-leader

What a ridiculous dance the conga is! I wonder who first thought up the idea of a line of supposedly grown-up people coiling round a dance floor one behind the other, doing strange things. About the only thing that can be said in its favour is that it's not as stupid as the hokey-cokey. I ask you: 'You put your right arm in, you put your right arm out, in out, in out, you shake it all about.' What idiots we must look! Yet we enjoy these, and other 'novelty dances', which are invented from time to time, because they're based on the children's game of follow-my-leader. Follow-my-leader's quite educational, because children learn to control their movements by copying the movements of the person in charge. Follow-my-leader's a good recipe for learning, from the apprentice learning his trade by watching and imitating the master craftsman, to the Christian learning to live the Christian life by copying the life of Jesus. Follow-my-leader – it says it all.

## Walk the way he walked

The First Letter of St John says we must be imitators of Christ. Jesus is the leader we must follow. St John keeps returning to the same themes over and over again. But if you look more closely, each time a phrase comes back, new light's thrown on it, so that eventually you come to a deeper understanding. One of those repeated themes is love. God loves us, because God is love. The love of God was shown in the life of Jesus. Jesus lives in us, and we live in him. Jesus gives us a new commandment, to love one another. We must love one another in the same way that Jesus loves us. We must be imitators of his love.

> Whoever says, 'I have come to know him,' but does not obey his commandments, is a liar, and in such a person the truth does not exist ... but whoever obeys his word, truly in this person the love of God has reached perfection. By this we may be sure that we are in him.

Then comes this phrase which illustrates what it means to love other people in the way that Jesus did: 'Whoever says, "I abide in him," ought to walk just as he walked.' 'Walk just as he walked.' That particular image doesn't come anywhere else in the letter, and it's written so briefly you might miss it if you're not paying attention. But it casts new light on the theme of what it means to love, by picturing the Christian life as a game of follow-my-leader. Think about it. Jesus's life was a life of self-sacrificing love and service to others. We must imitate him, by living a life which is filled with self-sacrificing love and service to others. We must 'walk just as he walked'. Follow-my-leader.

## 'Won't you walk this way?'

Unfortunately, the serious recommendation to followers of Jesus to 'Walk the way he walked' will conjure up another ridiculous image to anyone with a wicked sense of humour. There's a sight-gag which goes back at least to the Marx Brothers films, and probably further. A customer goes into a department store and asks to be shown a particular line of merchandise. 'Certainly,' replies the salesman, 'won't you walk this way?' He turns round and moves off with what comedians from a later era would call one of Monty Python's 'Ministry for Silly Walks'. So the customer follows behind, taking the instruction literally, and copying the salesman's every movement.

## Talk the talk and walk the walk

'Won't you walk this way?' Yet even this piece of visual humour casts new light on what it means to follow Jesus. We have to be prepared to make fools of ourselves, if need be, in our discipleship; become 'fools for Christ', if that's what he requires. There's no room for pomposity, or false modesty, in the Christian life; we have to take the imitation of Christ to any extreme he asks of us. We can't be half-hearted in the practice of love. 'Whoever says, "I abide in him," ought to walk just as he walked.' To those sham-Christians who talk a lot about what they believe, but don't put their words into action, St John would say, 'We've heard you can talk the talk, now let's see whether you can walk the walk!' Listen, he's asking you, 'We've heard *you* can talk the talk, now let's see whether *you* can walk the walk!'

## Suggested hymns

*I want to walk with Jesus Christ; O for a closer walk with God; Thou art the way, by thee alone; We are walking (Siyahamba)*

## Twenty-first Sunday after Trinity (Proper 23)
## 12 October
*Principal Service*   **Ready for the Party**
(*Continuous*): Ex. 32:1–14 The golden calf; Ps. 106:1–6, 19–23
The golden calf; *or (Related)*: Isa. 25:1–9 A refuge for the needy;
Ps. 23 The Lord's my Shepherd; Phil. 4:1–9 Rejoice in the Lord;
Matt. 22:1–14 The wedding banquet

> '*Go out into the highways and hedges, and compel them to come in.*' *Luke 14:23*

### Ready for the party

Some people receive lots of invitations, some receive none. If you're never invited to anything, you think nobody's interested in you. If you receive many invitations, the most insulting thing you can do is forget you've accepted one, and arrange to do something else at the same time. Maybe it was only forgetfulness, but the person who sent you the invitation will take it as a personal insult. So the best thing you can do is make a note of every invitation in your diary, clear the evening of every other engagement, get ready for the party, put on your best clothes, and turn up with a smile on your face. That shows you were honoured by the invitation, and it honours the person who invited you.

### The wedding reception

Jesus told a story about a party, the host and the guests. It was a wedding reception – a very important one, because the host was a king. He'd sent out ever so many invitations to all sorts of important people. The custom in those days was to send a reminder on the actual day of the party. But in this story, they all began to make excuses. Excuses, excuses. Some of them were quite good excuses, but if they'd wanted to please the king, they'd have found a way round the obstacles. St Luke's Gospel lists some of the excuses:

- 'I've bought a field' – or as we might say today, 'I've moved into a new home.'
- 'I've bought five yoke of oxen, and I go to examine them' – today it would be a new car, 'and I'm taking it for a trial run'.
- And finally in that phrase so often quoted by husbands who think

they're hen-pecked, 'I have married a wife, and therefore I cannot come!' – though actually the Jewish law laid down very humanely that newlyweds should be allowed a whole year free of other engagements, so as to get to know each other.

## The B-team

The king took these excuses as a calculated insult. So if the top people, the good and the great, wouldn't come to his party, he decided to invite the B-team. He sent invites to everyone whose address he knew, and most of them were honoured and came to the party, but there was still room for more. So he sent his servants to round up those of no fixed abode, the homeless and the tramps: 'Go out into the highways and hedges, and compel them to come in.'

## The message

What was Jesus trying to teach us in this story? 'The kingdom of God's like a party,' he said. Heaven's an endless celebration to which everybody's invited. In the Church, here and now, we're enjoying a sort of trial run for heaven. It's a party. Nobody's turned away because they're not good enough, either from the Church or from heaven. Even the needy and the outcast are given a welcome. Isaiah said God is

> a refuge for the poor,
> a refuge for the needy in their distress,
> a shelter from the storm and a shade from the heat.

The invitation's free, but you have to be willing to accept. No excuses are accepted. Property, travel and family are all of them important. But nothing's more important than accepting God's invitation to join his Church and his kingdom. If you haven't committed yourself yet to making God the king of your life, what's your excuse? Are the other things really more important than God, or are you insulting him by turning down his invitation?

## The party clothes

Then St Matthew seems to spoil it all by suggesting that, yes, there are some conditions after all. One of the guests didn't have on the right party clothes, and he was thrown out. Perhaps this is an entirely different story, nothing to do with the other one. Perhaps the party clothes were issued to the guests free of charge when they arrived. The book of Revelation says that 'the fine clothes are the good deeds of God's people'. So perhaps there's something we need to do to get ready for the heavenly party. The invitation's free, without conditions; but we have to respond to it by living a life of love and kindness, to show how important it is that we've been invited by the king to his party.

### All-age worship

*Write invitations from God to his heavenly party, to 'the snobbish people', 'the money-grubbing people', etc. Write on the bottom of each their excuses for not coming. Write one to yourself with, 'No excuses.' Reply, 'I gladly accept.'*

### Suggested hymns

*Faithful Shepherd, feed me; Jerusalem the golden; Light's abode, celestial Salem; We come as guests invited.*

## Twenty-first Sunday after Trinity
*Second Service*   **Children of God**
Ps. 139:1–18 God's omniscience; Prov. 3:1–18 God disciplines his children; 1 John 3:1–15 Children of God; *Gospel at Holy Communion*: Mark 10:17–31 Camels and needles

> *'See what love the Father has given us, that we should be called children of God, and that is what we are.'* 1 John 3:1

### In Mother's lap

You've seen the expression on the face of a sleeping baby, haven't you? A well-fed baby fast asleep in Mother's lap. Although the child can't express feelings in words, the smiling face tells you about complete contentment and well-being, compounded with utter trust in Mother's ability to care for her child, and her will to do so. Later, the child's expression may tell you something else: that baby's experiencing a touch of wind! Yet with minor discomforts or major ailments, Mother can be relied on to do her best to make the trouble go away.

## Good parenting

The relationship between children and parents is a very special one. If they're good children and good parents, their life together is full of happiness and discovery. But no children are perfect, and neither are parents. If you had a mostly happy upbringing, thank God for it. Though it's amazing how many children survive a quite disastrous childhood, and grow into good and loving people. Yet whatever your childish years were like, everyone can at least imagine what an ideal relationship between parents and children should be.

## Children of God

Hang on to that idea of good parenting, and look again at the first letter of St John, which was read earlier:

> See what love the Father has given us, that we should be called children of God; and that is what we are ... Beloved, we are God's children now; what we will be has not yet been revealed. What we do know is this: when he is revealed, we will be like him, for we will see him as he is. And all who have this hope in him purify themselves, just as he is pure.

That's you he's talking about. You are children of God. We sometimes become over-familiar with that idea, and forget what an amazing thought it is. Your relationship with God is like that of a child with a perfect parent. You owe your existence to God – he created the world and the human race and your parents, so you are his child in that sense. But he has also provided you with food, clothing, housing, family and friends, and the knowledge that he loves you. Who could ask for anything more? And if discomfort comes, or even major suffering, you can trust God to do all he can to make it go away.

## Your part

So that's the relationship from God's side: you're God's child, and he loves you better than any parent ever could. What's your part in this relationship? Surely, to be as good a child of God as you possibly can, to bring a smile of pleasure and pride to God's parental face! That's why St John writes, 'All who have this hope in him purify themselves, just as he is pure.' God is pure love through and through; God cares for his children, and sacrifices his own interests

257

for the sake of his children, as any good parent would. The least we can do is try to grow up to be like our heavenly Father. We can try to love God, and to love our neighbours as ourselves, for God is the best of all possible role-models. Of course we can never be perfect like God, but we can aim for perfection. Then God accepts the will for the deed, and if you slip up sometimes – and who doesn't? – God forgives you and helps you get started again on the path of behaving like your heavenly Father.

## Heaven our family home

Earth is a schoolroom for the children of God. The real adult life, when we become grown-ups in our relationship with God, is when we die and go to heaven.

Beloved, we are God's children now; what we will be has not yet been revealed. What we do know is this: when he is revealed, we will be like him, for we will see him as he is.

Sometimes people tell us off for never having grown up. It's a just accusation if they mean that we haven't yet learnt a sense of responsibility and to be mature in our relationships with others. But there's something to be said for enjoying the world and its beauty, and trusting God to care for us, in a child-like way because we're children of God. Particularly if we know that at the end of this life, we shall go to heaven, our family home, to be with our Father, and the other members of his family, cosy and happy for evermore.

## Suggested hymns

*Children of the heavenly King; Dear Lord and Father of mankind; Father of heaven, whose love profound; It is a thing most wonderful.*

## Twenty-second Sunday after Trinity (Proper 24)
### 19 October
*Principal Service*   **Caesar and God**
(*Continuous*): Ex. 33:12–23 Moses sees God's back; Ps. 99 Moses' Prayer; or (*Related*): Isa. 45:1–7 God uses Cyrus; Ps. 96:1–9 [10–13] Creation; 1 Thess. 1:1–10 Thanks for the Church; Matt. 22:15–22 Give back to Caesar

*'Give back to Caesar what belongs to Caesar, and give back to God what belongs to God.' Matthew 22:21*

## Death and taxes

There are only two things which are certain in this life, they say: death and taxes. Those are the two things which people dread most, and resent most when they come to them. Yet it's no use fighting them; perhaps we need a more Christian attitude to both tax and death. Well, we know what the Christian attitude to death is: it's the gateway to eternal life, when we shall meet again the loving Saviour whom we've served and obeyed all our life. Or should have done, if only we'd thought about him more often. So what's the Christian attitude to taxation?

## The question about tax

That very question was put to Jesus. 'Is it lawful to pay taxes to Caesar, or not?' The Pharisees who put it were thinking of the Jewish law. Is it compatible, they meant, with the law of Moses, which demands exclusive obedience to the Lord, to pay money to the Roman emperors – who were all known as Caesar? Wasn't that disloyalty to the one true God? Worse still, the Roman money, which they used to pay the tax, had the emperor's head on it – a graven image, idolatry! It was a trick question. If Jesus spoke in favour of paying tax, he'd seem to demote God, and he'd lose the support of the unwilling tax-payers. If Jesus came out against tax, he'd call down the wrath of the Roman Empire on his own head. It was a lose–lose situation.

## Jesus's answer about tax

So first, Jesus called for a visual-aid – the silver tribute-money coin which was used to pay the Roman taxes. On the obverse it carried the image of the reigning emperor at the time the coin was minted. Then, around the edge of the head there were some words, including the emperor's name. Now ask yourself this: what do *you* put *your* name on? The obvious answer is, things that belong to me: my clothes, my tools, my books – things I might lend somebody, but I want to have them back. So, why does the emperor put his name on the coin? Obviously, because it belongs to him; he's lent it to us and he wants it back. This wasn't just a trick answer. The

Romans had spent a lot of money on the Jews. They'd given them an international system of coinage; freedom from attacks by their neighbours; an administration and a legal system which were on the whole fair; and the excellent Roman roads and shipping routes which enabled them to export and import and do business all over the empire. Much of their wealth literally belonged to Rome; what right had they to grumble if they were asked for some of it back in taxes, as repayment of the loan? The emperor's put his name on the coin, which is his property. So, said Jesus, 'give back to the emperor what belongs to the emperor'.

## The image of God

Jesus goes further. The coin bears the image of the emperor. What, then, is made in the image of God? Why, we are! God said, 'Let us make human beings in our own image.' We humans resemble God – not in our appearance, because God has no body – but in our unique ability to choose and to love. Therefore, as the coin belongs to the state which issued it, so we belong totally to God who made us and whose image we bear – we're God's property. You can't split the world into two parts, the spiritual part which belongs to God and the material part which belongs to the state. Caesar, too, bears the image of God, so he belongs to God and everything that belongs to Caesar belongs to God also. We have to use our money responsibly, for God's sake, because it's God's money, temporarily on loan to us. Jesus's answer's as important for us as it was for the Pharisees: when you pay taxes, you're only repaying to the state what belongs to the state. When God asks for the obedience of your body, and the use of some of your possessions, in service to the state and to your needy neighbours, God's only asking you to give him back what he gave to you in the first place. So for heaven's sake stop grumbling! Death and taxes are both paths to God.

### All-age worship

*Make rubbings on paper with a soft pencil or crayon of some modern coins. Who owns that money?*

### Suggested hymns

*God of mercy, God of grace; Lord, while for all mankind we pray; O God of earth and altar; Take my life and let it be.*

# Twenty-second Sunday after Trinity
## Second Service    Test the Spirits
Ps. 142 I cry to the Lord [143:1–11 None is righteous]; Prov. 4:1–18
A father's instruction; 1 John 3:16—4:6 Test the spirits; *Gospel at
Holy Communion*: Mark 10:35–45 A ransom for many

*'Beloved, do not believe every spirit, but test the spirits to see
whether they are from God.' 1 John 4:1*

## Customs and excise

It sounds like an instruction to a customs and excise officer, who's
been sent to a pub to check that nobody's been watering down the
whiskey: 'Test the spirits!' But when St John uses that phrase in his
first letter, that's not what he means. He's talking about people who
give messages wrapped up in religious language, claiming that they
come with the authority of some spirit or other, perhaps the Holy
Spirit of God. St John is telling his readers, including you and me,
to be discriminating. Don't give your credence to everything that's
told you in the name of religion.

## False prophets

In St John's day there were false prophets who were leading the
inexperienced Christians astray. The message of John's first letter is
that Jesus is central to everything, and that Jesus brings love, light
and forgiveness. He's writing, he says, so that we may know that
God loves us, that we have eternal life, and that we may respond to
God's love by loving God and loving our neighbours. So what were
the false prophets saying? We don't know; but obviously it was
something very different from this message of love.

## The nature of sin

Perhaps these false prophets were teaching wrong ideas about sin.
Maybe they taught that morality doesn't matter. Maybe they taught
that sin is all about religion, and that our failure to observe certain
religious rituals is what really annoys God. Maybe they missed out
on love altogether, and encouraged Christians to be narrow-minded,
intolerant and judgemental. They forgot that a failure to love our
neighbours is at the root of sin, and judging others is usually a far

greater sin than the little naughtinesses that we condemn them for. Love covers a multitude of sins.

## Forgiveness

Perhaps the false prophets were denying God's love and forgiveness. They were claiming to know better than Christ's Apostles. If you want to be forgiven, they said, you must go through certain religious rituals, offer sacrifices, deny yourself pleasures and inflict suffering on yourselves. That's the only way to earn God's forgiveness, they said. But the Apostles said that all we need to do is trust Jesus – God's only too anxious to forgive us as soon as we turn back to him. We can never earn God's forgiveness, according to the Apostles; we don't have to, because he gives it to us, even when we could never deserve it.

## God's unconditional love

The main thing to hold onto, according to St John – the centre of the Christian faith – is the message of God's unconditional love. Any teaching which goes against that comes from a false spirit. Test the spirits, he says, to see whether they are of God.

## Today

And so today, too, there are false prophets around. Believe this, they tell you, don't believe that, do this, don't do that. 'The only way to come to God is to join our group,' they say, 'there's no other way.' They wrap it up in religious language to make it sound fancy, and gullible people are led astray. Jesus told us to love God, with all our heart and mind and soul and strength, and to love our neighbours as ourselves. That's all that matters. Surely 'loving God with all our mind' means using the intelligence he's given us to think about what we believe. To know God we need faith; but faith doesn't contradict reason. There's nothing unreasonable in what Christians believe, though faith takes us beyond reason into areas which reason can never reach. Unfortunately, when non-Christians hear these superstitious distortions of Christianity, they reject them as illogical nonsense, which they are. Then they think that this proves that true Christianity, which they may never have met, is false also.

## Test the spirits

So St John's not talking about alcohol when he warns us to test the spirits. He means, when people start talking about religion, don't believe everything they tell you. Use your minds, check what they say for reasonableness, and check it against the tradition of the Church and the teaching of the holy Scriptures. God is love, says the Apostle; he gives us his Holy Spirit to help us be more loving. Test the words of people who claim to have spiritual understanding; nothing which is contrary to the Spirit of Love can possibly be from God.

### Suggested hymns

*Dear Lord and Father of mankind; Gracious Spirit, Holy Ghost; Let there be love shown among you; Love divine, all loves excelling.*

## Last Sunday after Trinity (Proper 25)   26 October
## (*Alternatively Bible Sunday or the Dedication Festival*)
## *Principal Service* Love for God and Neighbour

(*Continuous*): Deut. 34:1–12 The death of Moses; Ps. 90:1–6, 13–17 Our refuge; *or* (*Related*): Lev. 19:1–2, 15–18 Love for the needy; Ps. 1 Law and righteousness; 1 Thess. 2:1–8 Paul's love for the Church; Matt. 22:34–46 Love God and love your neighbour

> 'One of them, a lawyer, asked [Jesus] a question, to test him. "Teacher, which commandment in the law is the greatest?" '
> Matthew 22:35–36

### Charity

This is a story about two people. The woman was called 'Charity' and the man was called 'Pius'. The story's fiction, and the character of these two is suggested by their names. Charity was a good woman; always busy in good works. She reached out to the people around her: the poor and needy in her home town, and the starving people in other countries. She raised large sums of money to buy them food, clothes and shelter. Whenever there was a natural disaster, she sent trucks full of relief supplies to those who'd suffered. Charity really cared for needy people, but her love seemed to be entirely *horizontal*. I'll explain what I mean. She never seemed to enter emotionally into the depths of people's suffering. She never thought about their higher aspirations and hopes; their needs for dignity and respect. So there was no depth and no height in her love; nothing vertical at all. After a while, her care for others began to wear a bit thin. They never seemed to be grateful for what she gave them, and it's hard to go on loving people like that. She knew something was missing in her life. She didn't believe in God. Unreasonably, she blamed the God who doesn't exist for causing all the natural disasters in the world.

## Pius

The man in this story, called Pius, had never met Charity. He was a good man: every day he spent a long time before breakfast on his knees in prayer. He sincerely asked that his sins might be forgiven, and prayed that he might be allowed to go to heaven when he died. Pius was a very religious man, but his faith was entirely *vertical*. When he thought about other people, it was only to condemn them for not being good enough. Yet he, too, felt there was something missing in his life.

## The cross

Then Charity organized a fundraising meeting in the hall of Pius's church. When Charity rose to open the meeting, Pius leapt to his feet and told them he was going to open with prayer. Before she could get her breath, he launched into a long prayer, telling God that they were all sinners, and a lot of other things that you would have thought that God knew already. Charity was furious. She came up to him afterwards to berate him for not mentioning the needy people the meeting was all about. He was furious with her for never starting their meetings with prayer. In fact, they were so cross with each other that they promptly fell in love! It was a turbulent courtship, but they gradually learnt to respect and admire each other's views, and eventually they got married. So Charity and Pius became 'one flesh', and the horizontal and the vertical dimensions in love were joined in one. Do you know what it makes when you join a horizontal line with a vertical line? Yes, a cross, the symbol of the Christian religion.

## Changes

Following the marriage there were changes in Charity. She came to believe in God, and accept that there are many things which she would never understand. Knowing she was loved by God helped her to go on loving all the ungrateful but needy people for God's sake. Her love was now vertical as well as horizontal, like the cross. There were changes in Charity, and improvements in Pius. He was no longer narrow and judgemental. He realized you can't love God, then ignore all the people that God loves. So he began to reach out to others. A cross was at the centre of his life, too.

## The great commandment

Jesus was asked what the great commandment is, and he replied, not with one but two commandments. Love God, said Jesus, but also love your neighbour. You can't have one without the other; they're inseparably joined, like the vertical and the horizontal in the cross. Loving God forces you to love your neighbour whom God loves; loving your neighbour forces you back to God, to ask for strength to keep going. Pray that the cross may be at the centre of your life, too, and ask for strength to love God and love your neighbour in equal measure, to the end of your life.

## All-age worship

*Make a collection of love poems. Which are about loving your family; your friends; your enemies; and starving people in other countries? Which are about loving God?*

## Suggested hymns

*Come down, O love divine; Love divine, all loves excelling; Morning glory, starlit sky; The God of Abraham praise.*

# Last Sunday after Trinity
## *Second Service*  Crowning an Athlete

Ps. 119:89–104 How I love your law; Eccles. 11, 12 Youth and age;
2 Tim. 2:1–7 Crowning an athlete; *Gospel at Holy Communion*:
Mark 12:28–34 Love God and love your neighbour

> *'In the case of an athlete, no one is crowned without competing according to the rules.'* 2 Timothy 2:5

## Three metaphors

In the first few verses of the Second Letter to Timothy, chapter 2, three metaphors are used for the Christian life. The Christian is pictured as a soldier, an athlete and a farmer. The metaphors are lined up one after the other. 'Metaphor' is a Greek word meaning 'carrying across'; in fact the removal vans in Greece today are all labelled *metaphores* because they carry your furniture across from one house to another! In grammar, a metaphor is a word conveying a picture which is then carried across to another idea, for example 'food for thought'. Metaphors are very useful in poetry and poetic prose, and the Bible's full of them.

## The soldier

The first metaphor in this passage is the comparison between a Christian and a soldier: 'Share in suffering like a good soldier of Christ Jesus. No one serving in the army gets entangled in everyday affairs; the soldier's aim is to please the enlisting officer.' Soldiers know that forced marches, hard rations and sleepless nights are part of their lot, and they accept them as the price they must pay to be soldiers. We may regret that the world needs soldiers, but it's a fact of life that those who join the army accept the necessity of suffering. The Bible compares that with the life of the Christian. We all know that there'll be hard work and self-sacrifice, and sometimes physical pain and sickness in the years that lie ahead. So we shouldn't grumble, or go back on our promise to follow Jesus, when bad times come. As they say, 'When the going gets tough, the tough get going.' Our 'enlisting officer' is Jesus Christ, and we should be just as disciplined as the soldier is, in our efforts to please him.

## The farmer

The third picture – I shall come back to the second in a minute – is of a farmer. Townies don't realize the long hours and back-breaking toil that are required if you're to make a success of agriculture. The cows can't take a day off from being milked, the harvest has to be brought in before the weather breaks. Compared with the farmer, most of us are very half-hearted in tilling the part of God's vineyard that has been allotted to us. God's got work for each one of us, whether it's in counselling our friends, preaching his word, making music to his glory, or the less glamorous tasks of church administration. What do we say to God? 'Sorry, I haven't got time for all of that.' Farmers know their lives depend on their hard work; are we rejecting the chance of eternal life if we refuse to work for Christ?

## The athlete

So, returning now to the metaphor of the athlete. Anyone who wants to succeed in sport or athletics knows they must dedicate themselves to it completely. They must be quite blinkered and narrow-minded in rejecting the temptations of other pleasures which might come between them and success. Practising first thing every morning for many hours a day; no late nights; no drugs. As the Bible puts it, 'no one is crowned without competing according to the rules'. Now this may mean the rules of the game: you'll soon be disqualified if you break those. But there were also rules about training: competitors in the Olympic Games in ancient times had to swear before the statue of Jupiter that they'd been in strict training for at least six months. If they had to make such a promise before a mere statue – which was no god – what about our promises to Jesus Christ? Shouldn't we be disciplining ourselves and avoiding distractions? Our bodily appetites are not wrong in themselves, they are good things given to us by God. But like the athlete we need to learn self-control, so that over-indulgence doesn't make us unfit to run the race of Christian service to others. The athletes today aim for a gold, silver or bronze medal; in the old days the winner was given a circlet of wild olive leaves around their brow as the victor's crown. Here the metaphor breaks down, for only the winner was given a crown. The Bible's telling us that *every* Christian who strives as hard as an athlete does in living a Christian life, and doing the work God wants them to do, will be rewarded with the crown of eternal life. Isn't that worth disciplining yourself for?

*Fight the good fight with all thy might; Oft in danger, oft in woe; Onward, Christian soldiers; Soldiers of Christ, arise.*

## Fourth Sunday before Advent   2 November
*(For use if the feast of All Saints was celebrated on 1 November, see page 352.)*
**Principal Service   The End is Not Yet**
Micah 3:5–12 Judgement on society; Ps. 43 I will go to God's altar; 1 Thess. 2:9–13 A call to righteousness; Matt. 24:1–14 Predictions of the coming of Christ

> '[Jesus said,] "You will hear of wars and rumours of wars; see that you are not alarmed; for this must take place, but the end is not yet."' Matthew 24:6

### Are we there yet?

It is a fact well known to all parents that if you take children on a long car journey, before long they'll start calling out from the back seat, 'Are we there yet?' They may not be very clear where 'there', their destination, actually is. But they're quite certain that they're bored with the process of getting there. Now, the wise parent resorts to one of the age-old car games: 'I spy with my little eye, something beginning with B.' Or for those who are a little older, pub-sign cricket: you score a run for each of the legs in the picture, but if there are no legs you're out.

### The end

Grown-ups, too, can become impatient with a long wait. For instance, waiting for days for a plumber to mend your dripping tap. Even more so, we get impatient waiting for the big things that are wrong with the world to be put right. The 1914–18 war was optimistically called 'The war to end wars'. Some hopes! Will the end to violence never come? Jesus warned us that we may hear of wars near at hand and reports of wars far away; but, he said, 'The end is not yet.' Greed and violence are human nature; at best we may be able to limit and contain their effects. But there'll be no end to war until everyone changes the selfish workings of their hearts.

Are we there yet? No, we're still a long way from that ideal state of affairs. Jesus said that the 'gospel of the kingdom' must first be proclaimed to every nation. That is, the good news that God can take charge of the world, but only if we let him. Many countries still haven't heard this message; many people in our own country remain unaware of what Jesus promised.

## Hearts grow cold

And so, because we're still not there yet, still not at the point when all evil's brought to an end, we grow impatient, like the children in the car. As Jesus put it, because wickedness grows stronger, most people's love grows cold. We begin by being full of enthusiasm for Jesus and his message, and then the heart goes out of us because we have to wait so long for its fulfilment. Love can grow cold in a marriage, but it needn't. Of course you never can 'recapture that first fine careless rapture' of when you first fell in love, but that's not what staying in love is about. To stay in love requires that both partners should decide to do everything in their power to make the other happy and fulfilled. Married love's more an act of the will than an emotional feeling; though if you work at it, the loving feelings will keep breaking through. But if hearts can grow cold in a marriage, they can positively freeze over in our love affair with God. God never stops loving us, but unless we work at it, our love for God can cool down, because of the long wait until his promises are fulfilled.

## Enduring to the end

We mustn't lose hope. Jesus made a firm promise: those who endure to the end will be saved. It's a wonderful aria from Mendelssohn's oratorio *Elijah*: 'He that shall endure to the end shall be sav-ed.' If you work at your love for God, patiently obey his command-ments, and avoid the peril of the heart grown cold, then you *will* be saved. Saved from the guilt and power of sin and the fear of death. Saved from impatience, saved from endlessly moaning 'Are we there yet?' When we see the wickedness around us, the pain and suffering in the world, we could easily be tempted to give up the struggle. Don't give up, says Jesus. Keep the faith. There *is* a destination, and we *shall* come to it eventually. It's called heaven, and it'll make all the trials of the journey, and even the boredom of waiting, worthwhile.

### All-age worship

*Read a summary of* Pilgrim's Progress, *and draw a map of Christian's journey.*

### Suggested hymns

*All my hope on God is founded; He who would valiant be/Who would true valour see; Lord of all hopefulness; Thy/Your kingdom come, O God.*

## All Saints' Sunday   2 November
### Beatitudes
**(*These readings are used on the Sunday, or if this is not kept as All Saints' Sunday, on 1 November itself, see page 352.*)**
Rev. 7:9–17 The crowd before God's throne; Ps. 34:1–10 Happy are those who find God; 1 John 3:1–3 A child of God does not continue to sin; Matt. 5:1–12 The Beatitudes

'[Jesus said,] "Blessed are the poor in spirit." ' Matthew 5:3

### Attitudes

Gilbert and Sullivan's comic opera *Patience* makes fun of rather precious poets 'uttering platitudes in stained-glass attitudes'. There's some very beautiful medieval stained-glass in our old churches, but you could hardly say that the saints who are so stylistically portrayed in them look like real people. The stained-glass pictures of the saints can symbolize their importance. But they can hardly inspire us to imitate their example, because we could never twist ourselves into the unnatural attitudes they're standing in. Yet the saints *were* real people. Their *mental* attitudes are something which we *can* imitate. In fact, imitating the saints is all a matter of mental attitude. We can't do exactly what they did, because we live in a different world from theirs. But we can look at things the way the saints did, and adopt, like them, an attitude of obedience and love to God, and care and compassion for our neighbours.

## Beatitudes

There's another word that sounds a bit like 'attitude'. Jesus began his Sermon on the Mount with eight sayings describing the ideal Christian life, and the path to happiness. Each of the eight begins with the word 'Blessed', and, from the Latin word for blessed, we describe these sayings as the eight 'Beatitudes'. Together they form a description of the lives of the saints. Listen:

> Blessed are the poor in spirit,
> Blessed are those who mourn,
> Blessed are the meek,
> Blessed are those who thirst for righteousness,
> Blessed are the merciful,
> Blessed are the pure in heart,
> Blessed are the peacemakers,
> Blessed are those who are persecuted.

Think of any saint in the calendar, and the eight Beatitudes describe their character.

## Directions

You notice that the Beatitudes aren't laws. They don't tell you exactly what to do. They're more about your approach to life. Your mental attitude, in fact. I wouldn't want you to think I was swearing if I describe the Beatitudes as 'B–attitudes', for the 'B' here stands for 'blessed'. But it does help us to imitate the lives of the saints, and in fact to imitate Jesus himself, if we remember that we aren't being asked to follow a set of detailed instructions for living. We're called on to adopt the same attitude to God and the people around us as the saints did. The Sermon on the Mount's not a pernickety set of directions, like the instruction leaflet for a piece of Japanese electronic wizardry. They point out the direction we travel in, and then leave us free to find the best way for ourselves in the light of the circumstances. The Beatitudes, like the whole of the Sermon on the Mount, are directions in which to set out on a journey. God pays us the compliment of giving us free will. He allows us to choose for ourselves what to do at each step of the way. God trusts us to find our own way through life, provided we start out with the right attitudes.

## Poor in spirit

So for instance, Jesus says we're happy if we're poor in spirit – by which he means having simple tastes. There's nothing particularly happy in being penniless if you're starving to death. But those who live on low incomes often have a freedom and simplicity in their lives which richer, more sophisticated people envy them. The poor know that they're dependent on others to help them through, and so they help others by sharing their meagre resources with them. Jesus isn't telling everyone to live in poverty like St Francis; the world would grind to a halt if they did and everyone would starve. We can follow Francis's spirit of simplicity and his unselfish attitude, however, whether our income is high or low.

## Read them

When you get home, find your Bible – I hope there's at least one in the house – and read the Beatitudes in Matthew chapter 5. Then ask yourself, how could I live my life in that sort of way? You'll be on the way, then, to becoming a saint: not those ridiculous people who utter 'platitudes in stained-glass attitudes', but those who share the saintly approach to life, devoted in your attitude to God, and selfless and loving in your attitude to those around.

## All-age worship

*Copy stained-glass pictures of a saint, with crayons or appliqué. In a 'scroll' design underneath, write one of the Beatitudes which you think applies to that saint.*

## Suggested hymns

*Blest are the pure in heart; For all the saints who from their labours rest; Seek ye first the kingdom of God; Take my life, and let it be.*

# Third Sunday before Advent  9 November
*Principal Service*  **Bridesmaids**
(*For a service which is not a Service of Remembrance.*)
Wisd. 6:12–16 Wisdom described; *Canticle*: Wisd. 6:17–20 Divine
wisdom; *or* Amos 5:18–24 Let justice roll down; Ps. 70 A prayer for
help; 1 Thess. 4:13–18 The resurrection from death; Matt. 25:1–13
Wise and foolish bridesmaids

> '[Jesus said,] "Keep awake therefore, for you know neither the
> day nor the hour."' *Matthew 25:13*

## Wedding customs

What a flurry there is before a wedding. Especially concerning the
bridesmaids. Who will you choose; who might be offended if they're
not bridesmaids? What are they going to wear; where will the
dresses come from? Then they must be sure of getting to the church
on time. We're talking here of the wedding customs in Europe and
North America during the past two hundred years. But other times
had other customs. In the Holy Land the ceremonies began with a
great procession from the bride's house to the bridegroom's home.
The bridegroom would come to the bride's home at a prearranged
time, and lead his bride, accompanied by her bridesmaids, across to
his home, where the ceremony was to take place.

## A parable

Jesus told a parable about bridesmaids. The story was about a wedding that went wrong – every parent's nightmare. There were ten
bridesmaids, or 'virgins' as they were called in the older translations.
Five of them were sensible girls, and five were scatterbrained and
flighty. Remind you of anyone you know? Because the procession
was to be after dark, each of them was equipped with an oil-lamp to
light their way. But the bridegroom was late. Each bridesmaid had
enough oil to burn for several hours. The sensible ones saved their
oil and sat in the dark, but the silly ones lit their lamps and enjoyed
the light until their oil ran out. At last, hours after they'd expected
him, the bridegroom arrived. But the five stupid girls had no oil in
their lamps. Anyone could have predicted that. Plan ahead, they'd
have warned them. Think of the consequences of your actions. Be
prepared. Sacrifice short-term pleasure for long-term benefit. That's

what the people who first heard the parable would have said, as they chuckled over the girls' foolishness. Then, as in so many parables, they would have realized that the joke was against themselves and their own lack of preparedness for life's crises.

## The Second Coming

Jesus said, 'Keep awake therefore, for you know neither the day nor the hour.' The traditional Christian interpretation has been to assume that he was talking about the Second Coming. The Bible nowhere uses that phrase, though the angels at the ascension say that Jesus will come again, and St John's Gospel talks about 'the last day'. The first disciples expected the Second Coming to happen in their lifetime. Now that two millennia have passed and he still hasn't come, it's hard to summon up the same sense of urgency. 'Keep awake therefore,' says Jesus, 'for you know neither the day nor the hour.' There may still be a Second Coming, and it may be today. Be prepared. But Jesus may also have been talking about other things as well. Jesus, the Son of God, came to earth to save people from sin and death. Would they recognize him? Would they welcome him? When he was crucified, they would have to decide which side they were on. Then, a mere forty years later, the Roman soldiers would destroy Jerusalem. Would they be ready to face these crises in their lives? Jesus said, 'Keep awake therefore, for you know neither the day nor the hour.'

## Moments of crisis

There are times of crisis in the life of each one of us. There are so many times when our plans unravel. There are so many times when we have to make moral decisions, to stand up and be counted. We should ask ourselves, 'Shall I be ready?' Then death comes to us all. The best way to be ready for death, when it comes, is to live every day as though it was our last day on earth, so that we can look back at it with pride. We each hope we shall live for many more years, but it's not too soon to ask, 'Am I ready to die?' When all these moments of crisis come, are you like the wise bridesmaids, looking to the future and planning accordingly? Or are you like the silly children who lived for the moment and forgot that the moment of decision must inevitably come. Jesus said, 'Keep awake therefore, for you know neither the day nor the hour.'

### All-age worship

*Act the story of the bridesmaids. Print a card to hang on the wall reading*

But write the letters so big that there's no room for the last two on the same line and write them small underneath. See who gets the joke.

### Suggested hymns

*Awake, my soul, and with the sun; Sleepers wake! A voice is sounding; The Lord will come and not be slow; Once to every man and nation.* (see http://www.cyberhymnal.org/htm/o/n/oncetoev.htm)

## Remembrance Sunday   9 November
## Remembering Sacrifice
**(These readings are for the Second Service on this day. Those for 'In Time of Trouble' or 'The Peace of the World' can also be used.)**
Ps. [20 Your heart's desire] 82 Judge the earth; Judg. 7:2–22 Reduced forces; John 15:9–17 To lay down one's life

> '[Jesus said,] "No one has greater love than this, to lay down one's life for one's friends."' John 15:13

### The Poseidon Adventure

In the original film of *The Poseidon Adventure* there was a short scene near the beginning when two Christian ministers were arguing about the death of Jesus on the cross. The younger one said that all the old talk of sacrifice was outdated, we should think of the cross as an example of love. The older minister replies that there's no love, and no salvation, without sacrifice. The older man is drowned when the liner turns turtle; the younger minister tries to lead a group of survivors to safety, and finally has to sacrifice

275

his own life to save them. There's no love without sacrifice; the old man was right.

## Gideon

There's a strange story in the Old Testament. A general called Gideon was going into battle with thirty-two thousand men. God told Gideon, first of all, to let those who were afraid go home: two-thirds of the army left. The remaining ten thousand men were told to drink from the nearby water source. Some knelt and put their faces in the water, but three hundred scooped it up in their hands. On this purely arbitrary basis, God told Gideon to reduce his forces and take a mere three hundred into battle. They hid their torches inside earthenware jars, then suddenly revealed their presence by breaking the jars and blowing trumpets. The enemy thought a huge army was attacking them, and ran away in panic. But the purpose of reducing the army like this was to teach Gideon humility. If he'd beaten the enemy with a large army, it would have gone to his head, and he'd have imagined he could cope on his own. Because he succeeded with a handful of troops, he realized that nobody can win without God's help.

## Agincourt

When Henry V triumphed at Agincourt, according to Shakespeare, he told his soldiers to sing the one-hundred-and-fifteenth psalm:

> Not to us, Lord, not to us,
> but to your name give the glory.

We should always remember when a war is won that we couldn't have done it on our own, but that we were successful because God helped us. That doesn't mean that God takes sides. God is as saddened by the death of one of the enemy as he is by that of one of our own troops. Even if we've carefully thought out the doctrine of the just war, and decided that this particular campaign was necessary to protect the weak, we'll never succeed if we forget to call on God. *Everyone* who dies as a consequence of war, whether they willingly decided to put their lives at risk or not, can be counted among the martyrs who've sacrificed their lives for others. Jesus said, 'No one has greater love than this, to lay down one's life for one's friends.' There's no love without sacrifice.

## War poets

At the beginning of the 1914–18 war there were many poets among the soldiers who went down into the trenches. Some of them, like Rupert Brooke, were patriotic and regarded their sacrifice as made willingly for their country:

> There's some corner of a foreign field
> that is for ever England.

Towards the end of the war, however, others like Wilfred Owen realized that their self-sacrifice had been unjustly demanded of them by ignorant superiors. 'The poetry', he wrote, 'is in the pity.' He reversed the story of Abraham sparing the life of Isaac, so that Abraham

> raised his hand and slew his son,
> and half the seed of Europe one by one.

## Remembering sacrifice

On Remembrance Sunday we must remember all those who sacrificed their lives in wartime. Both those who willingly laid down their lives for their friends, and those who thought it was all a waste, but still obediently did their duty. For if we don't remember those whose lives have been sacrificed so that we can live, we shall be very ungrateful. By remembering them, we remind ourselves to live lives worthy of their sacrifice. We remind ourselves to work for peace so that more lives don't need to be sacrificed. And we remind ourselves that we could never have won if we hadn't made sure our cause was just, and prayed to God to help us.

### All-age worship

*Look at the names on the local war memorial. Are those families still living in the neighbourhood? What do you imagine the soldiers felt as they went into battle? What did their families feel when they didn't come back? What can we do to prevent war?*

### Suggested hymns

*All people that on earth do dwell; Make me a channel of your peace; O God, our help in ages past; Son of God, eternal Saviour.*

## Second Sunday before Advent    16 November
*Principal Service*    **Talents**

Zeph. 1:7, 12–18 The day of judgement; Ps. 90:1–8 [9–11] 12
Prayer, providence and faith; 1 Thess. 5:1–11 The day of the Lord;
Matt. 25:14–30 The parable of the talents

*'I went and hid your talent in the ground.' Matthew 25:25*

### Auction of talents

Some churches raise money by holding an auction of talents. The
idea is that members of the congregation fill out a list of what they're
talented at, and offer to put that talent at the disposal of somebody
else. This is an excellent way of fundraising. It involves all the
congregation in doing what they're good at, but they only have to
dig into their pockets to pay for something which they'd otherwise
have paid more for in a shop. The only snag is that, as soon as you
mention the word talent, everybody in the congregation screams,
'But I haven't got any talents. I'm the most untalented person in the
universe. I'm not good at doing anything!' So it's wiser to call it an
'auction of promises'. Circulate a paper with a few examples: making mince pies, mowing the lawn, mending clothes, and so on; and
soon everybody's saying, 'Well, I could do *that,* if *that's* all that's
needed.' Then they come up with other ideas of what they could do.
'But I didn't realize *that* was what you meant by a talent,' they say.
So everybody discovers that they do have a few talents after all.

### The parable

Jesus told a parable about talents. The first thing to point out is
that the word's changed its meaning. In Jesus's day, a talent was
a sum of money, a huge amount. It would have taken a labourer
about fifteen years to earn that much. When Jesus told the parable
of the talents he was talking about high finance, not about gifts
and abilities. The story's about a wealthy man who invested his
money by loaning it out to members of his staff. Three of them
were lent huge amounts of capital and told to trade with it. Two
of the three were remarkably successful; they returned the capital,
and the profit, to the boss, but in return they were paid a salary to
administer a large section of the business and treated as responsible
executives. But one buried the money, made no profit and returned

it untouched. He was told off and punished for his timidity and lack of imagination.

## Knowledge of God

In the parable, the sum of money probably represents our knowledge of God. The Jews had learnt from their Scriptures about a God who loves us, saves us and cares how we treat each other. But they were given this knowledge, not just for their own benefit, but so that they could spread it to others, too. To keep your knowledge of God to yourself is selfish and mean; we need to spread around what we've learnt of God's love to our family and friends too. That's the basic meaning of the parable.

## Stewardship of money

The Christian stewardship movement points out to us that all the money we own has been lent to us by God. Using the word 'talent' in its original, financial sense they point out that when we give money to the church, we're actually only giving back to God what we had on loan from him in the first place. Some churches suggest tithing, giving back to God a tenth of your income; most others suggest that nowadays a twentieth part of your after-tax income is a realistic target to aim at. Twenty people on average incomes giving 5 per cent to the church would pay the entire stipend of the minister. But no matter how much you give, if it's as much as you can afford, God will honour your gift.

## Ability

But as soon as Jesus told the parable, people began to apply it to our gifts and abilities. So the word 'talent' took on a new meaning: what we're talented or clever at. We mustn't bury our talent, we must put it to work in the service of others, and serving the Church. Everybody can do something; perhaps not brilliantly well, but sufficiently to be appreciated. Think what your talents are: cooking, gardening, making music, sewing, word-processing – the list's endless. Then don't wait for an auction of promises. Think out, now, ways you could use your talents to help others, or to help your church. Don't bury your talents: use them to help your heavenly boss in the love business.

## All-age worship

*List the things you're good at. Draw the man burying money in the ground. How could you use your talents to make other people happy?*

## Suggested hymns

*From heaven you came (The Servant King); Let us talents and tongues employ; O God of earth and sky and sea; Take my life, and let it be.*

# Second Sunday before Advent
## *Second Service*   Zadok the Priest

Ps. 89:19–37 David's greatness; 1 Kings 1:15–40 (*or* 1–40) David chooses Solomon; Rev. 1:4–18 The heavenly Christ; *Gospel at Holy Communion*: Luke 9:1–6 Apostolic authority

> 'Zadok the priest [and] Nathan the prophet ... anointed Solomon ... And all the people said "Long live King Solomon!"' *1 Kings 1:38–39*

### Handel's anthem

In Handel's first coronation anthem the choir bursts in with a blaze of sound to the words: 'Zadok the priest and Nathan the prophet anointed Solomon King. And all the people rejoiced and said, "Long live the King. Long live the King!"' The anthem was written by Handel for the coronation of King George II, and it's been used at every coronation in Westminster Abbey ever since, when the United Kingdom has one of its periodic fits of patriotic fervour.

### Solomon's coronation

Yet King Solomon's coronation was a controversial occasion. Solomon was the offspring of King David's adultery with Bathsheba. David had legitimized him by the expedient of having Bathsheba's husband murdered, and Nathan the prophet had roundly rebuked David for this. David had already married at least six wives before Bathsheba, and there were many others afterwards. All David's other sons, therefore, would have claimed that they had a better right to the throne than the child who was illegitimate when he was conceived. One of them, in fact, had already claimed the crown as the next king of Israel while King David was on his deathbed. Zadok, Nathan and Bathsheba formed a deputation and called on the dying king, demanding that he keep his promise that Solomon should succeed him on the throne. Fortunately for Solomon, the people were on his side, and he soon became a popular monarch, famed for his wealth and wisdom.

## A Good Thing

The Old Testament praises King Solomon, for he was the ancestor of all the subsequent kings of Judah. Therefore he was also the ancestor of Jesus. Probably most of us, if we traced our family tree far enough back, could find some rather shady dealings somewhere in the family. That's no reason why we shouldn't rejoice in the good things that happened, and the coronation of Solomon was undoubtedly a Good Thing. Its consequences for the Jews were good, because he brought prosperity and good government to their nation. Its consequences for us were good, for he was the ancestor of Jesus. Next Sunday we shall be thinking more about Jesus as 'Christ the King', and the hymns and readings will focus on Jesus as Son of David. This week, let's think about Jesus as the descendant of King Solomon.

## Wisdom

Solomon was famous for his wisdom. After the bloody times under David, Solomon introduced law and justice: his wise decision in the case of the two women both claiming that the baby was theirs is famous. Jesus also gave wise teaching about just behaviour. St Paul wrote to those who were claiming that the Greek philosophers had greater wisdom than the Christians, that Jesus is 'to those who are called … Christ the power of God and the wisdom of God'. He also wrote that Christians who have the gift of wisdom mustn't boast, because their wisdom comes from the Holy Spirit.

## Wealth

Solomon was famous for his wisdom, and famous for his wealth. Jesus doesn't automatically make us rich, and he said it was blessed to be poor. But he does bring us a wealth of spiritual gifts to make us joyful in this life, and makes us heirs of the kingdom of heaven, so that we can inherit eternal happiness. To know that God loves you is more precious than all the money in the world.

## A greater than Solomon

'The fear of the Lord is the beginning of wisdom,' says the book of Proverbs. The fear of the Lord doesn't mean terror, but the respect which comes from knowing how great is the God who loves us. Jesus said:

> The queen of the South will rise up at the judgement with this generation and condemn it, because she came from the ends of the earth to listen to the wisdom of Solomon, and see, something greater than Solomon is here!

Jesus came to earth to bring us the knowledge of God our loving heavenly Father, to invite us to love him and to become citizens of the kingdom of God. If you think how the people rejoiced at the coronation of King Solomon, just imagine how the citizens of heaven rejoice when you crown Jesus, who is greater than Solomon, as the king of your life, and promise to obey him as your king for ever. What a coronation day that is!

## *Suggested hymns*

*Disposer supreme, and Judge of the earth; Immortal, invisible, God only wise; The kingdom of God is justice and joy; To God be the glory.*

# Christist the King   23 November
*Principal Service*   **Sheep and Goats**
Ezek. 34:11–16, 20–24 God the shepherd; Ps. 95:1–7 We are his
sheep, he is our shepherd; Eph. 1:15–23 Christ the head of all;
Matt. 25:31–46 Sheep and goats

> *'All the nations will be gathered before him, and he will separate
> people one from another as a shepherd separates the sheep from
> the goats.' Matthew 25:32*

## Bible translation

*used HK 08*

Translating the Bible is a difficult art. It's not enough to find the
words in one language which correspond to the words in another.
You have to find words which convey an equivalent meaning, in the
mind of the readers, to what was understood by those who wrote
the originals. For instance, when they tried to translate the phrase
'separate the sheep from the goats' into Chinese, they discovered
that Chinese uses the same word for both sheep and goats. Eventually the translators decided to write about separating the mountain
sheep from the valley sheep. But in Papua New Guinea, where
sheep are unknown, I'm told they needed an even more complicated phrase about pigs! For us, where sheep and goats are usually
kept in separate flocks, we need to remember that in the Middle
East they usually graze their way across the countryside in mixed
flocks, sheep and goats together, and only at shearing time are they
separated. Even so, all too many readers miss the main point of the
parable altogether.

## Faith, not works

The words about sheep and goats are a tiny graphic image to
introduce some teaching about judgement. The animals are not
mentioned after the first two verses; after that Jesus is talking about
separating people, which will be done *like*, or *as*, a shepherd divides
his flock. The dividing of the people is done on the basis of their actions. Those who've been kind to the poor and needy are rewarded,
those who've ignored them will be punished. But when you stop
and think, that's a very disturbing message. How much good do we
have to do to outweigh the millions of poor people we've neglected?

What about Jesus's parable of the tax-collector, who was a very bad man, and the Pharisee who was full of good deeds, yet only the taxman was justified? What, indeed, about St Paul's teaching on justification? We are justified by the grace of God alone, on the basis of our faith and trust in Jesus, not on the basis of the good works we've done. The separation of people in the parable of the sheep and goats, based on how much good they've done, seems at first to be in flat contradiction with the rest of the New Testament. But that's because we fail to notice the first few words.

## The nations

The message of the Bible is clear: for those who believe in Jesus, we can be saved, no matter how many wrong things we've done, provided we admit to them and genuinely try to do better. God in his kindness will forgive the sins of those who have faith. But what about those who don't believe in Jesus? Followers of other religions, or those with no religion at all? Why, people often complain, doesn't the Bible tell us anything about them? Well it does. Right here, in the parable of the sheep and the goats. Because the parable begins by describing the Son of Man, that's Jesus, sitting on his throne, and before him are gathered *all the nations*. Then they'll be judged on the basis of the care they've given to those in need. Now this could mean that the United Kingdom, France and the United States are judged on how much they contributed to world development, but the parable sounds more personal than that. So we need to remember that the words 'the nations' were what the Jews called all the rest of the world, the non-Jews. In Hebrew the word translated as 'nations' is *goi-im*, in Greek it's *ethnoi,* and in Latin its 'Gentiles'. During the lifetime of Jesus, all his followers were Jews; this is teaching about the foreign nationals who had had no chance to hear his teaching. There was no way non-Jews could be saved by their faith in Jesus, so he offers them another way to heaven.

## The little ones

The Gentiles, says Jesus, will be judged on how they responded to human need when they met it. In particular he mentions their treatment of 'one of the least of these my sisters and brothers'. This probably refers to the first Christians, who were put in prison or left to starve because they proclaimed the gospel of Jesus. If the non-Jews were moved by the Christian message of love, and treated the

284

missionaries well, that would be enough to make up for their lack of understanding of the Christian God, and book them a place in the kingdom. Two thousand years later, it would be a fair interpretation of the message of Jesus in this parable to say that atheists and agnostics, Muslims, Buddhists and Hindus, who've had no chance to hear the universal love of Jesus attractively presented, may still find a way to heaven on the basis of their compassion. The fact that they've never heard the gospel lovingly told is a judgement on us, not on them. But we can be forgiven for that, if we repent, because of our faith. One way or another, God's loving welcome is extended to all.

### All-age worship

*Make a map of the world, showing the majority religions, and find out from a missionary society what the Christians in one country are doing to share the good news of Jesus with those who have not heard it.*

### Suggested hymns

*God is working his purpose out; Hills of the north rejoice; In Christ there is no east or west; When I needed a neighbour, were you there?*

## Christ the King
### Second Service   Revolt of the Maccabees
Morning Ps. 29 Enthroned, 110 The king at your right hand; Evening Ps. 93 An ideal king [97 The Lord is king]; 2 Sam. 23:1–7 The last words of David; *or* 1 Macc. 2:15–29 The beginning of the revolt; Matt. 28:16–20 Ascension authority

> 'We will not obey the king's words by turning aside from our religion to the right hand or to the left.' *1 Maccabees 2:22*

### The Apocrypha

The last book of the Hebrew Old Testament to be written was probably Daniel in about 163 BC; the first book of the Greek New Testament was probably Paul's Letter to the Thessalonians in about

AD 50. In the intervening two hundred years, many religious books were written by Jews, but none of them found their way into the Hebrew Bible. Some of these late books, however, were included in the Greek translation of the Old Testament, and are therefore included in the Bible of the Greek Orthodox Church and the Roman Catholic Church. At the Reformation, Martin Luther decided to separate out these books which were in the Greek Bible but not the Hebrew Bible, and call them the Apocrypha, meaning the 'hidden' books. The Anglican Church followed his arrangement, but many Protestant Bibles leave them out altogether. Yet although they may not have the full authority of the Hebrew Scriptures, there's a lot we can learn from the books of the Apocrypha.

## The Maccabean revolt: importance

One of the set readings for today is from the First Book of Maccabees; though always when a book from the Apocrypha is suggested, an alternative is provided for those who don't have it in their Bible. Maccabee means a hammer: the best beer you can buy in Israel today is Maccabee beer, with a symbol of a hammer on the label. The revolt of the Jews against the occupying Greeks between 166 and 163 BC was led by the family of Judas Maccabeus, Judas the hammer. The famous chorus 'See the conquering hero comes' is from Handel's oratorio *Judas Maccabeus,* which tells the story of the Maccabean revolt. This bit of history's important to Christians, because it was the first time Jews began to understand the importance of sacrificing your life as a martyr for a cause, and that martyrs would be rewarded at the resurrection.

## The Maccabean revolt: history

God had delivered the Jewish people from their exile in Babylon in about 538 BC. But freedom didn't last long; in about 323 they were enslaved, as they saw it, by the Greek descendants of Alexander the Great, who occupied Israel until 63 BC when the Romans took their place. The Jews revolted against the occupying Greeks, beginning with the story told in today's reading. Mattathias the Hasmonean refused to sacrifice to the emperor, and led the resistance. His son Judas Maccabeus, together with his brothers, took over the leadership of the rebels. In one hilarious story, a rebel stabbed the king's elephant to death, but it fell on top of him and killed him! They defeated the Syrian armies who fought for the Greeks, and re-dedicated the Jerusalem Temple. Judas formed an alliance with the Romans, but after his defeat and death, his brother Jonathan, by wheeling and dealing, got himself appointed High Priest. The revolt was successful in setting up a line of Hasmonean kings to rule the Jews, even though they were mostly puppets doing the bidding of Greece and Rome. King Herod the Great, though he was an Arab, not a Jew, was related to the Hasmonean line by marriage.

## Loyalty to the king

It's unlikely that any of us will have to face being killed for our loy-alty to King Jesus, as the early Christian martyrs were, and which Christians in some countries are still threatened with. But there are many other forms of Christian martyrdom, like being penalized at work, or excluded from certain social gatherings, or mocked by your friends because they know you're a Christian. The message of the books of Maccabees, like that of the Christian martyrs, is 'Be loyal'. Stand up and be counted, put your reputation on the line, and keep the faith. There's no need to 'court martyrdom', as they say. It's wrong to take unnecessary risks. And you must always be cour-teous and tolerant in the way you present the Christian gospel. But when the crunch comes, it's important to know which side you're on. War's no way to spread the kingdom of God, though force may be necessary in resisting an aggressor. But whenever and however the challenge comes, your loyalty to Jesus must come first.

## Suggested hymns

*Christ is the king, O friends rejoice; Crown him with many crowns; He is Lord, he is Lord; Rejoice, the Lord is king.*

# Sermons for Saints' Days and Special Occasions

## SAINTS' DAYS

When his friends describe the martyrdom of St Polycarp in about AD 156, they declare their intention of 'celebrating the birthday of his martyrdom' every year in the future. When churches could be built to enshrine the bodies or relics of the martyrs, they were often dedicated on the anniversary of their death, and an annual dedication festival was held on that date. Other churches dedicated to the name of a saint soon celebrated the saint's day as their 'patronal festival'. The Bible describes the heroes of the Old Testament as a 'cloud of witnesses' around us, and all believers as being united in the body of Christ, as 'fellow citizens of the saints, and of the household of God'. Since the time of the Maccabees it had been held that those who had died heroically are praying for those who are alive, the Church Triumphant interceding for the Church Militant. It seemed natural to ask the departed for their prayers, and to talk to our dead friends just as we did when they were alive. But superstition grew up around devotion to the saints in the Middle Ages, and it was rejected by most Protestants. Yet many congregations wished to continue honouring the saints, especially on their own patronal festival. When the Book of Common Prayer was printed in two colours, the more important saints' days were listed in the calendar as 'Red-Letter Days'. This book provides sermons for all the 'Festivals' in the modern calendars, including the patron saints of England, Scotland, Wales and Ireland, and Corpus Christi; as well the 'Principal Feasts' commemorating the Epiphany, the Annunciation and All Saints' Day; Harvest Festival and sermons for Baptisms, Weddings and Funerals. *The Christian Year: Calendar, Lectionary and Collects* (with later amendments) gives rules for transferring the observation of Festivals when they coincide with Principal Feasts, as well as suggesting colours for the hangings and vestments in church; in general, feasts of martyrs are red, all others are white, with an option to use gold on Principal Feasts.

# St Stephen, Deacon, First Martyr
## 26 December 2007
**Persecution** 2 Chron. 24:20–22 The stoning of Zechariah; *or* Acts 7:51–60 The death of Stephen; Ps. 119:161–168 Persecuted without a cause (*if the Acts reading is used instead of the Old Testament reading, the New Testament reading is* Gal. 2:16b–20 Crucified with Christ); Matt. 10:17–22 What you are to say

> *'Princes persecute me without cause, but my heart stands in awe of your words.' Psalm 119:161*

## Bullying

Why is it always the nice children who get bullied at school? The answer's obvious: their very niceness makes the bullies jealous. The bully's unconsciously aware that comparisons will be made. He or she can't stand the thought that the nice, tolerant child is showing up how horrid the intolerant bully is. So they pick on the weaker child. Sadly, tolerance in some people seems to beget intolerance in some others. Jesus knew that his love and kindness would lead evil men to pick on him. It had happened before, and it would happen again.

## Stephen

After the crucifixion of Jesus, the pattern of judicial murder continued with the persecution of his followers. The first Christian to be martyred was Stephen, whom we commemorate today. Stephen was a Jew who spoke Greek as his first language. Because of an argument between two language groups, seven Greek-speakers, including Stephen, were appointed to be in charge of the charitable work. But Stephen was also a brilliant debater. There were several synagogues in Jerusalem where Greek-speaking Jews gathered, and there Stephen was persuading many of them to become Christians. The authorities, who'd conspired to crucify Jesus, didn't like this. So they put Stephen on trial.

## His speech

Stephen made a long speech in his own defence. It's a brilliant piece of rhetoric. He began by praising the Jewish people, to whom God had chosen to reveal his love and justice. That would have put his Jewish listeners on his side to begin with. But gradually Stephen showed how good Jews had always been persecuted by their bullying neighbours. In a crescendo of accusation he mentions Joseph and Moses; and concludes by accusing them of murdering Jesus, who'd been sent to them by God: 'Which of the prophets did your ancestors not persecute? They killed those who foretold the coming of the Righteous One, and now you have become his betrayers and murderers.'

## Getting rid of the whistle-blower

The Jewish authorities didn't like that. So they decided to eliminate the whistle-blower. It was all legal and above board, of course: they formed a kangaroo court and held a travesty of a trial, then they executed Stephen for blasphemy, by stoning him to death, as the law laid down. So the bullies formed a lynch-mob to persecute the innocent. 'Twas ever thus.

## The blood of the martyrs

Which all sounds pretty depressing until you remember what was the result of Stephen's death. Many other Greek-speaking Jews joined the Christian community until before long they became the majority. But the most surprising of all was the conversion of the chief persecutor. To free themselves for their sport, those who did the stoning placed their clothes at the feet of the umpire, Saul of Tarsus. What he'd seen that day worked on his mind until eventually, on the road to Damascus, he gave his life to Christ and became Paul the Apostle. So from the place where Stephen's blood was shed, there sprang up a great growth of new Christians. As a Christian in the third century called Tertullian wrote, 'The blood of the martyrs is the seed of the church.' Those who suffer may not always see the results of their suffering. The bullies may go scot-free while the bullied are punished, the whistle-blowers lose their jobs, the honest politician is deselected. But people remember, and in the long term they're inspired by the examples of those who've been persecuted, and gradually things change and improve. We're followers of a crucified Messiah. If we speak up in his name, we can't avoid suffering as he did. But the world will be a better place for our children if we do. Remember Stephen. Remember Jesus.

## Suggested hymns

*How bright these glorious spirits shine; Lo, round the throne, a glorious band; Palms of glory, raiment bright; Soldiers, who are Christ's below.*

# St John, Apostle and Evangelist  27 December
## The Tent of Meeting

Ex. 33:7–11a The Tent of Meeting; Ps. 117 Praise God, all nations; 1 John 1 The word of life; John 21:19b–25 The Beloved Disciple

> *'Everyone who sought the* Lord *would go out to the tent of meeting.' Exodus 33:7*

### No fixed abode

When God's people were nomads, God himself was of no fixed abode. God lived in a tent, which could be struck and repitched elsewhere. Or rather, he focused himself in the tent when people wanted to meet him. In the book of the Exodus we read, 'Everyone who sought the Lord would go out to the tent of meeting.' You can't pin God down, God's everywhere in the universe he created; he's also outside and beyond his creation. But in his mercy God's appointed meeting-places. You can't talk to a God who's all around you; you don't know which way to turn. But God wants us to talk to him, so he gives us places where we can imagine him standing before us, giving us his total attention. Yet he wants us to focus our minds on him, not on the place where we meet him. When the Jews thought the Temple was the one and only place where you could talk to God, the prophets reminded them that God's of no fixed abode, and originally he met them in a movable tent. It's very misleading that all the old translations refer to it as a tabernacle, which sounds like something special, but it's only the Latin word for a tent.

### Tents

Anybody who's ever slept in a tent, in the garden on a hot night, or at scout or guide camp, or on a camping or caravanning holiday, or in the army, knows that it's a very odd experience. There may be 'long-leggety beasties and things that go bump in the night'. You certainly feel close to nature, but sometimes too close for comfort! And always there's this feeling of the temporary nature of your home, its impermanence. James Montgomery's old hymn, 'For ever with the Lord', treats the whole of life as a pilgrimage back to heaven:

> Here in the body pent,
> Absent from thee I roam,
> Yet nightly pitch my moving tent
> A day's march nearer home.

There was, incidentally, a nineteenth-century cartoon which made fun of the Anglican ritualists, and their love affair with the Roman Catholic Church, representing them as singing 'I nightly pitch my moving tent a day's march nearer ... Rome'!

## St John's Gospel

In the first chapter of St John's Gospel, the author struggles to put into words the mystery of almighty God becoming a human being when Jesus was born, 'the Word made flesh'. At one point he writes, as most translations put it: 'The Word became flesh and lived among us', or 'dwelt among us'. But the actual word that John wrote was, 'he tabernacled among us,' or 'he pitched his tent among us'. Jesus came into the middle of our campsite, and pitched his tent beside ours. That's how close Jesus came to us; St John wants us to know that Jesus was not too proud to come right alongside us, where we are. Jesus knows what it's like to be human, because he's been human too. Jesus knows what it's like to love, to suffer and to grieve, because Jesus has loved, and suffered, and grieved like us. Jesus was the new tent of meeting. If you want to talk to God, go to Jesus, because in him the fullness of the Godhead dwells.

## Moving on

But tents are temporary, they're for people who don't want to stay in one place, but are always moving on. You can come to church to talk to Jesus; it's a useful place to remind ourselves of his presence. But he's not restricted to the church, you can talk to him anywhere. And you can't pin Jesus down; if you want to keep up with him, you've got to hurry after him, facing new challenges, new opportunities. He said to Mary Magdalene at the resurrection: 'Don't cling to me.' There's nothing static about being a Christian, you have to be moving on. There's no room for nostalgia; you can never re-create the past – then was then, and now is now, and things are different. But if we keep travelling on in our pilgrimage, Jesus travels with us, always pitching his tent, the tent of meeting, very close to us if we want to talk to him. Give thanks today for St John, who wrote of Jesus pitching his tent next to ours for the night, the God of no fixed abode, remembering that as the Israelites travelled across the wilderness, 'Everyone who sought the LORD would go out to the tent of meeting.'

### Suggested hymns

*Disposer supreme, and Judge of the earth; For ever with the Lord; How lovely is your dwelling place; One more step along the world I go.*

# Holy Innocents  28 December
## God Chose What is Weak  Jer. 31:15–17 Rachel weeping for her children; Ps. 124 When our enemies attacked us; 1 Cor. 1:26–29 God chose what is weak; Matt. 2:13–18 The massacre

*'God chose what is foolish in the world to shame the wise; God chose what is weak in the world to shame the strong.' 1 Corinthians 1:27*

### Corinth

Corinth was a wealthy city, and we know there were a few rich Christians who opened their homes so that the church members could worship there. But most of the Christians were anything but rich; many of them, in fact, were slaves who were allowed to possess nothing. Erastus, who was clever enough to be appointed town clerk of Corinth, and left an inscription by the theatre to say that he'd had the pavement relaid at his own expense, was a Christian and is mentioned in the Bible. But most of the Christians could lay no claim to intellectual prowess. So some of them grew discouraged, thinking that what they did was insignificant. But the eyes of the city were on the tiny Christian minority, and they'd judge the new religion by the way the ordinary members behaved.

So St Paul encouraged them: they did matter, every one of them had a part in God's plan.

> Consider your own call, brothers and sisters: not many of you were wise by human standards, not many were powerful, not many were of noble birth. But God chose what is foolish in the world to shame the wise; God chose what is weak in the world to shame the strong; God chose what is low and despised in the world, things that are not, to reduce to nothing things that are, so that no one might boast in the presence of God.

## Bethlehem

The babies whom King Herod massacred at Bethlehem mattered, too. Murder was nothing to Herod. When he came to the throne he had many members of the Sanhedrin, the Jewish Supreme Court, killed lest they opposed him. He murdered his wife Mariamme, and her mother Alexandra, and his three sons Antipater, Alexander and Aristobulus, because they might become a threat to his authority. Bethlehem was a small place, so he may have only had to kill twenty to thirty babies, which to him was nothing. No other historian than St Matthew thought it was important enough to write about it. All the children were under two years old, yet they changed the course of history by their death. Herod thought he'd included the newborn Messiah in the slaughter, and eliminated Jesus, his baby rival as King of the Jews. So he called off the persecution. But he hadn't, and by their deaths those innocent children helped Jesus to survive to become the Saviour of the world. Maybe they also made it harder for later tyrants to murder babies with impunity. It would have been cold comfort for their grieving mothers to know this, but even the death of a tiny child can bring good consequences in the long term.

## Children

By commemorating the Holy Innocents on this day, we remind ourselves that even weak and helpless children can have a part in God's plan. They must do, for God himself became a puling baby for our sake. So we shouldn't brush aside the importance of children, nor keep on telling them not to be a nuisance. There's always something we can teach them which will be useful to them when they grow up, and there's always something we can learn from them, too, if we'll only be patient and humble enough to pay attention to what they say. 'God chose what is foolish in the world to shame the wise; God chose what is weak in the world to shame the strong.'

## Insignificant people

Maybe you yourself thought you were insignificant in the great scheme of things. You don't have great strength to do things for others, you don't have 'loadsamoney' to buy things for them. You don't have a string of exam results to prove how clever you are, so that other people will turn to you for advice. But it doesn't matter; God loves you, and you're important to him. Don't despair. On the other hand, don't relax. Other people are watching you, to see whether you're a good example of Christian love. And God's watching you, so don't let him down. You matter to God, and by your humility and your love you have a vital role to play in building God's kingdom.

### Suggested hymns

*In vain the cruel Herod's fear; Lully, lullay, thou little tiny child; Unto us a boy is born; Ye servants of the Lord.*

# Naming and Circumcision of Jesus   1 January 2008
**Jesus the Jew** Num. 6:22–27 Aaron's blessing; Ps. 8 From the mouths of babes; Gal. 4:4–7 Born under the law; Luke 2:15–21 Naming and circumcision

> *'When the fullness of time had come, God sent his Son, born of a woman, born under the law, in order to redeem those who were under the law, so that we might receive adoption as children.'* Galatians 4:4–5

## Circumcision

William Norman Ewer, an English writer, once expressed what many people in the 1920s must have felt; he wrote:

> How odd
> Of God
> To choose
> The Jews.

The correct reply to such prejudice was written by an American, Cecil Browne:

> But not so odd
> As those who choose
> A Jewish God,
> But spurn the Jews.

Christians have a Jewish God and a Jewish Saviour; it's easy to forget that. When Jesus was eight days old he was circumcised. Circumcision, the little operation of removing a baby boy's foreskin, was given to Abraham as the sign of God's covenant with Abraham's descendants. Because Jesus was circumcised, he knew and his family knew that he was one of God's chosen people, the covenant community.

## Jesus the Jew

What does it matter to us that Jesus was a Jew? First, it puts what he was doing in context. His birth was the culmination of a long period of preparation. We can only understand what he did when we read the Old Testament. Just as God saved the Jews from slavery in Egypt, so Jesus saves us from slavery to sin. God gave the law to show his people that he cared how they treat each other. When they sinned, he gave them a system of sacrifices, so that they could be forgiven. The death of Jesus on the cross means that Jesus was sacrificing himself so that we all can be forgiven. Second, we misunderstand many of the things Jesus said if we forget that he said them in a dialect of Hebrew. That doesn't mean that we all have to learn to read Hebrew; it's enough if we read the Bible, and books about the Bible, to catch hold of the Jewish way of saying things. If we're to understand what Jesus said, we need to know what Jews in his time believed about the afterlife; how they used ironic humour; how they hated the Romans occupying the land where they'd been born, and how they were brewing up towards rebellion. Of course, Jesus speaks directly to us in the Gospels. But it's dangerous, as well as arrogant, to claim that our own interpretation of his words is more correct than that of experts who have spent their lives studying the context in which they were spoken. Jesus was a Jew.

## Saving the Jews

St Paul, who was also a Jew, wrote a letter to Christians in Galatia, where there was a row going on between Jews and non-Jews: 'When the fullness of time had come,' wrote St Paul, 'God sent his Son, born of a woman, born under the law, in order to redeem those who were under the law, so that we might receive adoption as children.' After all those centuries of preparation, God sent Jesus, a Jew because he had a Jewish mother. He was one of the Chosen People, covenanted to obey the law of Moses, but he had come to set his own people, the Jews, free from slavery to the law. Those were shocking words for any Jew to hear; they still are today.

## What Gentiles must learn from Jews

The rest of us, who are not Jews, are referred to as Gentiles. While we must work and pray for the conversion of our own people to a living faith in Jesus, we must also pray for the Jews, who are still God's chosen people. We Gentiles have a lot to learn from the Jews. Their passionate devotion to discovering God's will and doing it, their belief that their faith must apply to the whole of life, and their joyous expectation of a Messiah, are all needed by Gentiles too, if we're to be truly Christians.

## Adoption as children

God's purpose was not that the Jews should become un-Jewish, but that we Gentiles should be grafted into the Chosen People. Then we become brothers and sisters of Jesus, and so brothers and sisters with the Jews. We're all adopted children of God. Not slaves, who have to be told what to do, but God's children, who do what he wants because we love him. It wasn't odd of God to choose the Jews at all, because through Jesus the Jew, all the world, Gentiles as well as Jews, can be saved. Praise God!

## Suggested hymns

*How sweet the name of Jesus sounds; Long ago, prophets knew; Lord, for the years your love has kept and guided; The God of Abraham praise.*

# Epiphany

*(Celebrated on Sunday 6 January 2008, see page 43.)*

## Week of Prayer for Christian Unity  18–25 January
### If Two Agree

Jer. 33:6–9a Judah and Israel; Eph. 4:1–6 Maintain the unity;
Ps. 100 All lands praise God; Matt. 18:19–22 If two agree

> *'[Jesus said to his disciples,] "Truly I tell you, if two of you agree on earth about anything you ask, it will be done for you by my Father in heaven. For where two or three are gathered in my name, I am there among them."' Matthew 18:19–20*

### Children and parents

Children soon become adept at playing their parents off against each other.

'Kylie, don't do that!'
'Why not, Mummy? Daddy said I could.'
'Oh well, if Daddy said so, I suppose I'll have to let you.'

And little Kylie devoutly hopes that by the time Daddy comes home, Mummy will have forgotten all about it, because Daddy never said anything of the kind. Children will also try to get an advantage over their brothers and sisters, by winning their parents over to their side:

'Mummy, please tell little Wayne not to do that, he's annoying me.'
'Mummy, I know you said we were none of us to have any chocolates, but I can have one, can't I, because I'm your favourite little girl?'
'Mummy, I should be allowed to watch the TV programmes *I* want, because *I've* been good today.'

It's understandable, but it's pernicious. What Mummy and Daddy want most of all is the unity of the family. They want all the children to get along together, and to get on equally well with both parents. That's more important than giving any child what they ask for.

## Christians and God

Now translate those little dialogues into the form of Christians praying to God, their loving heavenly Father. How many times we pray for special privileges for ourselves, over and above those given to other people. How many times we actually pray that God will punish other people, but not punish us. How many of our prayers, if they could be heard by the people we're praying for, would make them feel very threatened by our resentment. What do you imagine God thinks about those self-centred prayers? He must feel rather like a parent would about a child who asks for special privileges. There's a story about a Protestant, a Catholic and a Jew who were each offered the chance to ask one prayer which God would answer. 'Well, God,' said the Protestant, 'I'd like you to remove every Catholic from this land.' Hearing this, the Catholic said, 'God, please remove every Protestant from our nation.' God turned to the Jew and asked him what he wanted. 'Nothing for myself,' answered the Jew. 'I'd just like you to attend to both these gentlemen's prayers.'

## Jesus wants unity

Jesus said to his disciples:

> Truly I tell you, if two of you agree on earth about anything you ask, it will be done for you by my Father in heaven. For where two or three are gathered in my name, I am there among them.

Those words carry a promise, but also a warning. They tell us that 'Jesus loves to answer prayer.' God really wants to give us what we ask for. But he can't, because we ask selfishly, without considering the needs of others. The hiker can't have a sunny day for his walk, when the farmer needs rain for her crops. Far more important to God than answering our individual requests is that we should learn to love each other. So although Jesus told us to go into a room by ourselves, free from distractions, when we're learning to pray, we must progress from there and learn to add to our private prayer the habit of praying with others. It's only when we've learnt to subordinate our private wishes to the needs of others that he's promised to answer our prayers. Above all, Jesus wants unity among his children.

## That includes unity in the Church

That includes unity in the Church. Of course God is pleased whenever we pray to him. God is pleased whenever and wherever we go to worship him in church. But has it ever occurred to you how much pain it must give to God to see that his children pray in different denominations and can't meet altogether in one building Sunday by Sunday to pray to him together? Some of the problems which divide us into denominations are very important, and go very deep. But they could all be solved if we really wanted to solve them. If only we realized how much Jesus wants us to be united, and how much our divisions pain him. Maybe one reason why so many of our prayers go unanswered is because we're still divided. If only we made them together Jesus would keep his promise to answer them.

### Suggested hymns

*Come, my soul, thy suit prepare; God is love, and where true love is, God himself is there; Great Shepherd of thy people, hear; In Christ there is no east or west.*

## Conversion of St Paul   25 January
**The Reward of Eternal Life** Jer. 1:4–10 The call of a prophet; Ps. 67 Let all the peoples praise you; Acts 9:1–22 Saul's conversion; *(if the Acts reading is used instead of the Old Testament reading, the New Testament reading is* Gal. 1:11–16a Called me through his grace*)*; Matt. 19:27–30 The reward of eternal life

> *'Jesus said to them ... "Everyone who has left houses or brothers or sisters or father or mother or children or fields, for my name's sake, will receive a hundredfold, and will inherit eternal life."'*
> Matthew 19:28–29

### What a life!

St Paul led one of the most dramatic lives in ancient history. He was born in the city of Tarsus, a Greek university town on the coast of what we now call Turkey, into a strictly observant Jewish family which was, however, important enough to be given Roman citizenship. He had a privileged upbringing, and was educated at the feet of Rabbi Gamaliel, one of the leading Pharisees in Jerusalem. Saul, as he was then called, spoke Greek nearly as well as he did Hebrew. He was probably one of those who debated with the Greek-speaking Jew called Stephen who'd become a leader in the new Jesus movement in Jerusalem. He was in charge of the execution squad who stoned Stephen to death. Then he had sufficient influence with the Sanhedrin, the governing council, to obtain letters of authorization from them. He was to go to Damascus and destroy the Jews there who followed Jesus. But on the road over the Golan Heights he had an experience which changed his life – turned him right round, which is what 'conversion' means.

## What he gave up

Saul gave up so much. He gave up his privileged background, the support of the Jewish authorities and most of his former friends, and probably the support of his family also. He had no regular income, but supported himself as a travelling tent-maker. He became first a recluse in Syria while he sorted his ideas out, then an adviser to the new church in Antioch. He was invited by his friend Barnabas to go on a preaching tour through the synagogues in Cyprus. There he met the Roman Governor, and went so far as to give up his Jewish name and adopt the Latin name of the Governor, Paulus. He sailed to the Turkish coast, where he probably suffered the first of many bouts of malaria. He then went on preaching journeys halfway across the known world, the Roman Empire, and back again, not once but three times. He built up new Christian communities from scratch, and left them in the care of leaders whom he himself had trained. As Paul wrote, in his Second Letter to the Corinthians:

Three times I was beaten with rods. Once I received a stoning. Three times I was shipwrecked; for a night and a day I was adrift at sea; on frequent journeys, in danger from rivers, danger from bandits, danger from my own people, danger from Gentiles, danger in the city, danger in the wilderness, danger at sea, danger from false brothers and sisters; in toil and hardship, through many a sleepless night, hungry and thirsty, often without food, cold and naked. And, besides other things, I am under daily pressure because of my anxiety for all the churches.

Finally he was taken under arrest to Rome, and shipwrecked again on the way there. Tradition tells us he was later rearrested and beheaded with a sword.

## What he gained in return

Paul gave up so much. But he gained so much in return. He gave up his old friends but gained many new ones. In the church he found a new family, and he watched the churches he'd founded grow and spread their influence to the towns around. He translated the Hebrew thought of the new faith into Greek ways of expression, and saw it appeal to some of the finest minds in the Roman Empire, as well as attracting thousands of humble people and slaves. He successfully fought off an attempt to impose on the non-Jewish converts the full weight of Jewish tradition, and won for Christianity a policy of racial and cultural tolerance.

## Eternal life

The centre of Paul's preaching was 'Christ, and him crucified', and the message of the resurrection, first of Jesus, then of his followers. He took up the teaching of Jesus on eternal life, and taught his followers to hope for life in a better world after death. And then, as the reward for all he had given up, the reward for his hardships and labours, he himself entered into that glorious new life. For hadn't Jesus promised: 'Everyone who has left houses or brothers or sisters or father or mother or children or fields, for my name's sake, will receive a hundredfold, and will inherit eternal life'?

### Suggested hymns

*Disposer supreme, and Judge of the earth; For all the saints who from their labours rest; We sing the glorious conquest; Will you come and follow me?*

# Presentation of Christ in the Temple (Candlemas)
## 2 February (*or may be celebrated on Sunday 3 February*)
## A Watershed
Mal. 3:1–5 The Lord shall come to his Temple; Ps. 24:[1–6] 7–10 Open the gates for the Lord; Heb. 2:14–18 Jesus became like the descendants of Abraham; Luke 2:22–40 The presentation of Christ in the Temple

*'When the time came for their purification according to the law*

*of Moses, they brought [Jesus] up to Jerusalem to present him to the Lord.' Luke 2:22*

## A watershed

If you drive through the Black Forest in Germany, you may be surprised to come to a sign which says that rain falling to the right of the road drains into the River Danube and thence into the Black Sea hundreds of miles to the south-east. Rain falling to the left of the road drains into the Rhine and thence into the North Sea, hundreds of miles to the north. You're at what's called a watershed. Today's a watershed in the Church's year: until today, we've been looking back to Christmas; from now on we look forward to Easter.

## Mary visits the Temple

Today we think of baby Jesus visiting the Temple in Jerusalem when he was just over a month old. Three separate parts of the Old Testament are woven together into this story.

## Purification

First, when a mother gives birth to a baby, she's vulnerable to infection. So it was decided in olden times that she shouldn't leave the house for forty days. They weren't clear how infection was given or received, so they said vulnerable people were 'unclean' and when they were no longer vulnerable they were 'purified'. Ardent feminists needn't get in a tizzy about calling this day, forty days after Christmas, 'The Purification of the Virgin Mary'! Put it down to good intentions coupled with biological ignorance.

## Redemption

Second, at the Exodus, when all the first-born of Egypt were killed, it was decided that the first-born male child of any Israelite and of their animals belonged to God, and had to be bought back, or 're-deemed'. So when Jesus was presented in the Temple, the Redeemer of the world was himself redeemed!

## Judgement

Third, Psalm 24 suggests that the Israelites celebrated an annual festival, when the ark of the covenant was carried into the Temple. The ark was a symbol of the presence of God with his people. But the prophet Malachi foresaw a day when God would come to his Temple in judgement. The first to be judged are the Levitical priests; religious people must always ask ourselves, do we practise what we preach? The rest of the people are judged, according to Malachi, by a surprisingly modern checklist, which if you translate it into modern terminology means:

- Are we superstitious?
- Do we support and encourage our families?
- Do we cheat in business?
- Are we fair employers?
- Do we provide pensions for the needy?
- Have we a fair immigration policy?
- Is God important in our lives?

## Purification, redemption and judgement

Those three themes are brought together when Jesus is brought to the Temple: purification, redemption and judgement. The judgement of the priests went off well; God picked a good one, an old man called Simeon. Simeon had waited years for the Redeemer to come; he had the astonishing insight to recognize that he had come in baby Jesus. He warned Mary that Jesus would suffer, and that she would suffer with him. Then he sang what we call the Nunc Dimittis. It's the song of a servant when he reaches retirement age: 'Master, let your servant go in peace.' Simeon said that Jesus was 'a light to lighten the Gentiles'. Light's a good symbol for justice: frightening for oppressors, good news for the oppressed. Oppressors are like cockroaches scuttling away from the light. The oppressed are like a frightened child at night, when the light's turned on, showing that the grizzly bear behind the door is only your dressing gown.

## Candlemas

In the days before electricity, light was very precious; while people were singing the Nunc Dimittis, which is all about light, on this day, they used to bless the year's supply of candles. So they called the day Candlemas. It's the watershed between Christmas and Easter.

So it looks back to the birth of Jesus, but it also looks forward to his suffering on the cross. It's a reminder that each one of us has a part to play in spreading the light of Christ and the good news that he's brought us justice. There's no justice without suffering, of course. But if we've repented of the things we do in the dark, Jesus has borne the suffering for us, to bring us joyfully into the light. The good news we have to spread is of a suffering Redeemer.

## Suggested hymns

*Faithful vigil ended; Hail to the Lord who comes; In a world where people walk in darkness; Lord, the light of your love is shining (Shine, Jesus, shine).*

# St David, Bishop of Menevia, Patron of Wales
## *c.* 601   1 March
**A Life Worthy of God** Ecclus. 15:1–6 Whoever holds to the law will obtain wisdom; Ps. 16:1–7 I have a goodly heritage; 1 Thess. 2: 2–12 Entrusted with the gospel; Matt. 16:24–27 Take up your cross

*'As you know, we dealt with each one of you like a father with his children, urging and encouraging you and pleading that you lead a life worthy of God, who calls you into his own kingdom and glory.' 1 Thessalonians 2:11–12*

## A gentle bishop

St David was a monk and bishop in Wales. He was famous for his preaching, and he founded the cathedral in Menevia, which is known today as St David's. He died in about AD 601, and has been venerated as the patron saint of Wales since at least the twelfth century. As a monk he was very strict with himself, living a life of self-denial. Yet he was loved by the ordinary people for his kindness and compassion to the poor and the sick. Strict with himself, gentle with others – St David could be a model for each of us to imitate.

## St Paul

The Apostle Paul was also very strict with himself. Sometimes he had to be strict with those he wrote his letters to, particularly if they came from the self-indulgent society of the cities in the Roman Empire. What attracted many non-Jews to Christianity was the high moral principles of the Jewish Christians. But they were not always easy to live up to in practice, and Paul, at times, had to rebuke his hearers for their failures. But he much preferred the gentle approach whenever he could. He describes himself, in his first letter to the Christians in Thessalonica, as dealing with them like a loving father bringing up his children. He urged them, and encouraged them, and pleaded with them to live a life worthy of God, he said. The highest standards are required of those who are called into God's glorious kingdom.

## Parenting

But you don't create high standards in your children if you browbeat and threaten them. The only way is to encourage them. You have to say to them, 'You did that really well. Now try something a little harder.' Or, 'I don't think what you did then was in line with your usual high standards of behaviour.' Or even, 'I love you, and nothing will ever stop me loving you, but I really dislike what you've just done, please don't do it again.' The gentle approach doesn't rob others of their self-respect, and gives them a motive for doing better. If you're always criticizing other people, they'll probably give up trying.

## St David's preaching

It seems that St David knew the importance of encouraging others in his preaching. His biographer writes that he was 'the supreme preacher, from whom all received the content and structure of virtuous living'. The biography goes on to tell us that St David corrected the people, warning them when their behaviour was not worthy of a Christian. He absolved them, sharing with them God's forgiveness when they repented for their wrongdoing. And he blessed them, bringing them God's grace to help them to do better.

## Excuses

A recent survey showed that many people in Britain who've stopped going to church blame their lapse on the standard of the preaching. They said that the sermons were all about politics, and didn't tell them how to live a Christian life. This sounds like a jolly good excuse, invented by people who are feeling guilty, in order to justify themselves. For a start, the care of the orphans and widows, the sick and the poor, which St David thought was so important a part of the Christian life, are achieved these days through the democratic process of government. The most practical thing that Christian voters can do for the needy is to let our representatives know that we care more about the needs of the poor than about our own interests. But second, if preachers tell their congregation what to do and what not to do, the people will say, 'I didn't come here to be preached at!'

## We know how to live

You see, we all know already how we should live. We know we should be loving and unselfish in the service of others. Sometimes it's quite difficult to work out what the loving thing is to do. You can only find that out by discussing your particular problem with someone; blanket condemnation from the pulpit doesn't help at all. We need to learn from St David to set ourselves the highest standards, and to be gentle with others. Preachers need to learn that too, and Christians should be as eager to hear what their preachers are saying as the Welsh people were to listen to St David.

### Suggested hymns

*Captains of the saintly band; Guide me, O thou great Redeemer; Lord of all hopefulness; Jesu, lover of my soul.*

# Annunciation of Our Lord to the Blessed Virgin Mary   31 March (*transferred from 25 March*)
**Virgin Birth** Isa. 7:10–14 The sign of Immanuel; Ps. 40:5–11 I love to do your will; Heb. 10:4–10 I have come to do your will; Luke 1:26–38 The angel's message

> *'Mary said to the angel, "How can this be, since I am a virgin?"'* Luke 1:34

## Impossible

A virgin birth is impossible. Humanly speaking. And that's the whole point. The angel said to Mary, 'Nothing will be impossible with God.' Jesus said, talking about salvation, 'For mortals it is impossible, but for God all things are possible.' So if the virgin birth is humanly impossible, but actually happened, that's a sure sign that God's at work. But until I started researching for this sermon, I hadn't realized that the science is not as clear as many people imagine. Bees and ants regularly produce their male offspring, or drones, by parthenogenesis, which is the name that scientists use for virgin birth. Mice and rabbits have been artificially reproduced in the laboratory by a-sexual means. In February 2005, a monkey embryo was produced by this method, from which stem cells were extracted which could possibly be used to cure human diseases. We may be a long way from creating a human virgin birth, but it's not as impossible as we'd thought. In Mary's case, the factor which no scientist could predict was the involvement of almighty God. For God, all things are possible.

### Fulfilment of prophecy

So what's the point of the virgin birth? First, as I've said, it's to show that God's involved. Second, to show the fulfilment of prophecy. When Isaiah spoke of a woman conceiving a child called Immanuel, he may not have meant a virgin in the modern sense, simply a young woman, King Ahab's wife perhaps. She was expecting a baby, and by the time she gave birth, Israel would be victorious in battle, and she'd be able to call her child 'Immanuel', which means 'God is with us – God's on our side'. But God had had an idea in his mind for a long time – for ever, since the creation of time, in fact. God wanted to send his Son into the world. So whether he put that form of words into Isaiah's mind, or took advantage of the words when Isaiah had spoken them, they formed a perfect prophecy of the incarnation: God in Jesus would be literally with us, God moving about his world robed in fleshly form. So the virgin birth completed the argument from prophecy. It showed that Jesus was a very special baby, the long-expected Saviour.

### God's initiative

But there's a still more important reason for the virgin birth. It showed that the initiative in the birth of Jesus lay entirely with God. He was born 'not of blood or of the will of the flesh or of the will of man, but of God'. It was God's decision to save the world through Jesus. It wasn't something that human beings had planned or calculated. Though Joseph was important in Jesus's upbringing, he wasn't the prime mover: God was the one who set everything going. The birth of Jesus was like no other birth, because the baby who was born was like no other baby – he was both human and divine.

## Still doubtful

These are compelling reasons for believing in the virgin birth. Nobody need fear that they're being unscientific or illogical by accepting what the Bible says as true. But are you still doubtful? Don't worry. A small number of devout Christians have always had doubts about it. They'll say that the nativity narrative's a sort of poem whose meaning goes deeper than prose, a myth where what's revealed about the personalities and their motives is more important than historical accuracy. What really matters is whether you believe that in some way God took the initiative in the life of Jesus, in order to save the world from the grip of sin and the fear of death. It's the incarnation that really matters, not how it came about. If you believe in that, you can call yourself a Christian, and know that Jesus is alive and listens to your prayers. And if you've never had any problems in believing in the message of the angel to Mary, spare a little sympathy for those who wrestle with the doctrine of the virgin birth. It's important that the Church should teach clearly the message that God loves and saves us. But individual Christians follow their own path to a relationship with their loving Saviour, and the Church has no interest in making it more difficult for them by insisting on the acceptance of a particular set of words. The one whom Mary conceived in her womb is the Word of God, and no human words are adequate to describe how he came to earth.

## Suggested hymns

*For Mary, Mother of our Lord; Her Virgin eyes saw God incarnate born; Sing we of the blessed Mother; The angel Gabriel from heaven came.*

## Joseph of Nazareth   1 April
## (*transferred from 19 March*)
**David's Descendants** 2 Sam. 7:4–16 Descendants of David; Ps. 89:26–36 David's line; Rom. 4:13–18 Abraham's descendants; Matt. 1:18–25 Joseph's dream

> '[The Lord said to King David,] "When your days are fulfilled and you lie down with your ancestors, I will raise up your offspring after you, who shall come forth from your body, and I will establish his kingdom."' 2 Samuel 7:12

### Family trees

It's become a popular pastime to research your family tree. Anyone who's willing to interrogate their grandparents, and look up a few birth certificates in the Public Records Office, can find out something about their ancestors a few generations ago. We're also interested in our descendants. Fathers like their sons to have sons, so as to carry on the family name. There aren't many family businesses left these days. If you're hoping your descendants will carry on the family firm after you're gone, you could be disappointed; they may be interested in some other career, and want to be independent. King David was desperate to know what would happen to his descendants. He had struggled to the throne of the newly united clans of Israel, and he was anxious lest the whole show should fall apart when he died. So God promised him that David's son would succeed him. King Solomon sat on David's throne after David died, but the break-up of the tribal federation had begun. Around the time the Jews were exiled in Babylon, the direct line of succession from David seems to have died out. But a thousand years after David's reign, there were many people who could claim to be indirectly descended from him. That's hardly surprising. One of these was Joseph of Nazareth; a member of the old firm of David and Sons.

### The Messiah

Of course, Joseph wasn't a king, and he wasn't interested in kingship. Yet there was a widespread belief in his time that one of the descendants of King David would be the promised Messiah. God promised: 'He shall build a house for my name, and I will establish the throne of his kingdom forever. I will be a father to him, and he shall be a son to me.' For ever? Solomon reigned for less than forty years. So we're talking about a superhuman Messiah here, one who'll rule in eternity. And the relationship between the Messiah and God would be like that between a son and his father. Joseph didn't think he himself was going to be the Messiah. But he was very concerned that he should have a legitimate son, who might inherit the throne of David.

## Jesus

So you can see why he was so worried when he discovered that Mary was expecting, but he wasn't the father of her child. Fortunately he had a dream, in which God told him everything was OK, and Mary's son would be the long-expected Saviour. So Joseph married Mary, which meant that Jesus was Joseph's adopted son; so he was legally a descendant of King David, as far as the promises God had made were concerned.

## Father and son

So Jesus did go into the old firm, after all: the firm of Joseph and son, carpenters of Nazareth. I'm sure that, being human, Jesus had to learn a lot from his parents before he realized who he really was. From Joseph, Jesus learnt how fathers treat their children. Jesus spoke often about loving, caring fathers; I wonder where he got that idea from? From Joseph, Jesus learnt how sons treat their fathers. Sons, ideally, should love and respect their fathers, co-operate and work with them. It's not always like that; some parents do little to earn their children's respect. So Joseph must have been a Dad in a million. But if that's what it meant to be son of Joseph, what does it mean to be Son of God? Jesus worked alongside his heavenly Father, to construct a community of people who would accept God's love and pass it on to others. Jesus has pretty ropey materials to do his building work with: you and me, for instance. But he learnt from Joseph that it's the quality of the workmanship that counts, and with his skills Jesus can turn even you and me into saints. For Joseph was a descendant of King David, and when Joseph adopted him, Jesus became not only Son of God, Son of Man and Son of Mary, but Son of David as well. The old firm of David and Sons is in the business of leading God's people towards a world of peace and justice. That's a skill Jesus is now the chief exponent of, and just as he learnt from Joseph his carpentry skills, so he learnt from his heavenly Father that love and self-sacrifice are the only way to teach your children how to live.

### Suggested hymns

*As Joseph was a-walking; Joseph dearest, Joseph mine; Lord of the home, your only Son; Rejoice in God's saints, today and all days.*

## St Patrick, Bishop, Missionary, Patron of Ireland
### c. 460  2 April (transferred from 17 March)
**Treasure in Clay Jars** Deut. 32:1–9 Remember the days of old; *or* Tob. 13:1b–7 In the land of exile; Ps. 145:2–13 Make known to all people; 2 Cor. 4:1–12 Treasure in clay jars; Matt. 10:16–23 Warnings for missionaries; *or* John 4:31–38 Ripe for the harvest

> *'We have this treasure in clay jars, so that it may be made clear that this extraordinary power belongs to God and does not come from us.' 2 Corinthians 4:7*

### A clue

'Treasure in clay jars.' It sounds like a clue from an adventure story – in fact Enid Blyton did once use it as such in one of her children's stories. If you know there's a treasure to be found, where would you look for it? In some splendid treasure chest in a secure vault, probably. But sometimes treasure's hidden in places which surprise us. In past centuries, rich people fleeing from an invading army would bury all their coins in an inconspicuous earthenware pot; if they were unable to come back for it, it might be found later by archaeologists. Or even a lucky hobbyist with a metal-detector. You can't judge a book by its cover, and you can't judge the priceless contents by the ordinariness of the container.

### St Paul

The Apostle Paul used this as a metaphor to defend himself against his critics. He admitted he wasn't much to look at. He never claimed to be perfect; he was just a human being like the rest of us. Don't look at the container, he pleaded, look at its contents! Never mind the faults of the messenger, listen to the message. He'd been through all sorts of physical hardships and faced many types of opposition to bring this message to Corinth. These experiences had left their scars on his body, and may have made him rather quick-tempered. Ignore it, he said. Look at the treasure, the message of the gospel. Not the fallible missionary who's brought it to you, who's only a clay jar.

## St Patrick

St Patrick had been through many hardships, too. Taken as a slave from England to Ireland when he was sixteen; escaping in a shipful of dogs; taken to France, and eventually making his way back home to England. There his nominal Christianity became a burning faith, and he decided to share the gospel with his former captors. Making the risky journey back to Ireland, he made his base in Armagh and walked all over the emerald isle. His mission was ridiculed, he tells us in his autobiography, and he was persecuted and imprisoned. 'Who am I, Lord,' he asks humbly, 'that you should use me to display your power?' Yet by his persistence and his humility he brought the whole Irish nation to the feet of Jesus Christ. He didn't point to himself, but to the message he brought. Once again we find 'treasure in clay jars'.

### *Eminent Victorians*

We must honour the saints of old, and hold them up as our heroes, for people to imitate their faith and their determination, and the generosity of their self-sacrifice. But we do ourselves no favours if we pretend they were perfect. The Victorian age idolized their heroes and heroines, only to have them knocked off their pedestals by Lytton Strachey in his book *Eminent Victorians*. If only they'd been honest about the faults and failings of the people they venerated, they needn't have been disturbed by the truth when it came out. 'Treasure in clay jars', they could have answered. It's not the fallibility of the messengers but the importance of their message which should claim our attention. Together with the courage they showed in defending the rights of others.

## Honouring the saints

So it's important that we should honour the saints of old, but not be blind to their human failings. There's a word, 'hagiography', which literally means writing the lives of the saints; but it's come to imply a flattering description of somebody as a perfect super-hero. God doesn't look for Superman and Superwoman to do his work; it's just as well, because perfect people are in short supply! Instead, God uses ordinary people who are a mixture of good and bad, just like you and me. Which is a great encouragement, because if God can use them, perhaps God can use us as well. We should honour the saints, but not pretend that they were perfect. Neither St Paul nor St Patrick claimed that for themselves. But they were determined to share the good news of God's love with others, and for that we should honour them and imitate them. We ourselves are only plain, undecorated clay jars. But we can be used to carry the treasure of the gospel to those who don't realize that God loves them. Then, like Paul and Patrick and all the other saints, we must tell others to ignore the messenger and just listen to the message.

### Suggested hymns

*Disposer supreme, and Judge of the earth; For all the saints, who from their labours rest; I bind unto myself today; Rejoice, rejoice, Christ is in you.*

# St George, Martyr, Patron of England
*c.* 304    23 April
**Romantic Love** 1 Macc. 2:59–64 Be courageous; *or* Rev. 12:7–12 Michael fights the dragon; Ps. 126 Restore our fortunes; 2 Tim. 2:3–13 A soldier of Christ; John 15:18–21 They will persecute you

> *'Share in suffering like a good soldier of Christ Jesus.'* 2 Timothy 2:3

### The dragon

The well-known legend tells of St George as a knight in armour riding up on horseback to rescue an unfortunate maiden, who was tied up to be sacrificed to a dragon. St George kills the dragon and everyone lives happily ever after. It's a marvellous story, and it's inspired centuries of Christian men and boys to be willing to risk their lives in the defence of women, and numerous women to expect that their menfolk would care for them tenderly. That may sound a bit sexist today, but courage and valour, courtesy and chivalry, mutual care and trust, are noble emotions and should be encouraged. If the story of George and the dragon can promote feelings like this, it should be told over and again. It doesn't matter a whit that it's completely unhistorical; this is romantic fiction, and stirring up romantic ideals is what that sort of story is for. And a good thing too.

## History and legend

Historically, George was a Christian martyr, dying for his faith during the third century AD in Lydda, in the Holy Land. Not far from there is the seaport of Joppa. At the mouth of the harbour rises what's known as 'Andromeda's Rock'. In Greek mythology, Andromeda was chained to the rock, and left there to be devoured by a great sea monster, the Kraken. The Greek hero Perseus flew by on the winged horse Pegasus, fell in love with Andromeda, and asked for her hand in marriage. Her father agreed, and Perseus slew the monster. The legendary story of Perseus was attached to the historical St George in Christian times.

## The crusades

The story of George and the dragon was heard by the crusaders when they fought the Saracens in that part of Palestine. They adopted him as a pattern of courage, painted his red cross on their shields, and brought the story back to England. There was much that was terrible and bad about the crusades, but also a few things that were good and noble. Beginning as a movement to defend Christian pilgrims to Jerusalem, it quickly turned into a bloodbath, where Muslims, Jews and other Christians were slaughtered indiscriminately. In many wars, good intentions are lost sight of when violent means are chosen to achieve them. But many knights, accompanied by their squires, left this country with high ideals in a search for honour and glory.

## Romantic love

And the period of the crusades was marked by the growth of the ideal of romantic love. There are traces of this concept in the Bible; think of Jacob working for fourteen years for Rachel because

315

he loved her. But it was not at all widespread. Jesus contradicted the patriarchal view of marriage when he emphasized that 'a man shall *leave his father and mother* and be joined to his wife, and the two shall become one flesh'. St Paul balanced the accepted rule that a wife must obey her husband with the novel suggestion that a husband should care for his wife. Kenneth Clarke, in the television series *Civilisation,* pointed out that the third most read book in the Middle Ages was one instructing husbands how to beat their wives, and was only exaggerating slightly when he said that marriage, then, was entirely to do with property and not at all to do with love. But many young men, not yet old enough to go to the crusades, formed a romantic and for the most part innocent attachment to the wives, widows and daughters who'd been left at home by the crusaders. The troubadours sang songs of passionate and fruitless love for unattainable females, for whom the knights would be willing to risk their lives. Since the knights rode on horseback, this movement became known as 'chivalry', from the French word, *cheval,* for a horse. The stories of King Arthur and the Knights of the Round Table were retold to fit the new romantic mood. So was the story of St George risking his life to defend the maiden from the dragon.

### The romantic hero

The romantic ideal influenced literature, music and life for many centuries. It's easy to make fun of absurdly romantic legends, but they encouraged young men to be brave and young women to be virtuous. Every nation in every age needs its heroes, whether in fact or fiction. Generations of English people have been inspired to work hard for their families, and defend their nation when necessary, by the legend of St George and the dragon. Let's honour them, and the ideal of romantic, self-sacrificing love which they followed, while we honour our patron saint today.

### *Suggested hymns*

*And did those feet, in ancient time; Onward, Christian soldiers; Soldiers of Christ arise; When a knight won his spurs.*

# St Mark the Evangelist  25 April
## The Deserter

Prov. 15:28–33 Good news; or Acts 15:35–41 Paul rejects Mark; Ps. 119:9–16 How shall the young keep their way pure?; Eph. 4:7–16 The gift of an evangelist; Mark 13:5–13 Staying power

> 'Then Paul and his companions set sail from Paphos and came to Perga in Pamphylia. John, however, left them and returned to Jerusalem.' Acts 13:13

## Deserters

In the 1914–18 war, any soldier who panicked and ran away was shot as a deserter. That, at least, was the theory, though many officers lied on behalf of their men in order to get the accusation of desertion reduced to a lesser charge. It was a serious matter, though. If one man turns and runs away from the enemy, the infection of cowardice may spread to others; then the battle will be lost, and all of them will die. The French dramatist Voltaire, in his satirical comedy *Candide,* says that in England 'it is thought well to kill an admiral from time to time to encourage the others'. The joke is that in French *'pour encourager les autres'* means to give the other admirals courage, in other words to stop them cravenly sailing away. Deserters led to disaster. So what are we to make of young John Mark, the nephew of the Apostle Barnabas? He travelled as their assistant with his uncle and the Apostle Paul, from Antioch all the way through Cyprus until they reached the southern coast of what's now called Turkey, and then 'left them and returned to Jerusalem'. Was he a deserter? Did St Paul think this was cowardice?

## What Paul thought

Paul had a very short fuse. When the former persecutor of the Church was converted, his short temper took a little longer than the rest of him to give in to Christ! He was probably very, very angry with Mark for running away. It led to a rift in the old friendship between Paul and Mark's uncle: when Barnabas wanted to take Mark with them on their next journey,

> Paul decided not to take with them one who had deserted them in Pamphylia and had not accompanied them in the work. The

disagreement became so sharp that they parted company; Barnabas took Mark with him and sailed away to Cyprus. But Paul chose Silas and set out.

Paul had no patience with anyone who began work as a missionary, and gave up when the going got difficult, and that's exactly what Mark had done.

## Poor Mark

Poor Mark! You have to feel sorry for him. He thought he was going on a holiday. Tagging along with dear old Uncle Barnie for a nice trip round the synagogues of Cyprus. There they'd be among friends, old chums of his uncle's, who'd welcome him as one of themselves and listen politely to what he told them about Jesus. All Jews together. And then his uncle's friend Saul of Tarsus, as he was known then, met the Roman Governor of Cyprus, called Sergius Paulus. Saul changed his name to Paul, and from then on he was a changed man. They sailed across to Pamphylia, then Paul wanted to strike inland from the coast, up into the wild Taurus mountains and on to the remote high Anatolian plain. This just wasn't what Mark had signed up for; no wonder he felt homesick. So he ran off on his own, leaving everybody angry with him. He must have had a miserable homecoming.

## Redeeming himself

But nobody's beyond hope, and when he realized what he'd done, poor young Mark spent the rest of his life trying to make up for it. He offered himself for another journey, though Paul wasn't ready for that yet. According to a reliable tradition, he then travelled with Peter, translating his sermons for him from Hebrew into Greek, and writing down what Peter said in the form of a Gospel. And eventually he was reconciled to Paul – but that's another sermon.

## Take courage

We should take courage from the story of John Mark, however. He wasn't perfect: neither are we. He let his friends down: so do we. He gave up when things went badly; aren't we tempted to do the same? But he was sorry for what he'd done wrong; and he was forgiven by Paul, and also, we believe, by Jesus. We can be forgiven, too, if we say sorry. Then Mark redeemed himself completely, when God called him to write the first ever Gospel, and so to spread the good news of God's love. We, too, can spread God's love, by our words and by our actions, if we're humble enough to admit our mistakes, like Mark did. He was a walking disaster as a Christian, yet God forgave him 'to encourage the others'. Mark shows us that nobody, absolutely nobody, is ever beyond hope of redemption. Not Mark; not me; not you.

### Suggested hymns

*Awake, my soul, and with the sun; Disposer supreme, and Judge of the earth; Lord, thy word abideth; Take my life, and let it be.*

## SS Philip and James, Apostles  2 May
## (transferred from 1 May)
**This is the Way** Isa. 30:15–21 This is the way; Ps. 119:1–8 The way of the Lord; Eph. 1:3–10 The mystery of forgiveness; John 14:1–14 Show us the Father

> *'When you turn to the right or when you turn to the left, your ears shall hear a word behind you, saying, "This is the way; walk in it."' Isaiah 30:21*

### Waymarks

The Ramblers' Association lists over two hundred footpaths in different parts of Britain that walkers can easily follow, because they're 'waymarked'. This means that they're distinguished by small signs, usually a circle of plastic with a coloured arrow on it, nailed to every stile and gatepost on the way. Diligent walkers need to keep their eyes peeled, because if you fail to notice one of the waymarks and follow a wrong turning it may take you miles out of your way. I want to suggest to you that our path through life is also a waymarked route. We may go for days along a straight road through life, then suddenly we're faced with a choice. We look for some guidance, some sign which will point out to us the correct choice to make. The prophet Isaiah suggests that the pointers are there in the Bible, either in words or by example: 'When you turn to the right or when you turn to the left, your ears shall hear a word behind you, saying, "This is the way; walk in it."'

## Laws as pointers

The Bible's full of laws and commandments. Some of them are suited only to a nomadic tribe, and can no longer be applied to the society of today. St Paul warned that obedience to the letter of the law doesn't earn you a place in heaven. Jesus, in the Sermon on the Mount, gave us instructions which go beyond the Ten Commandments, because he went to the heart and the spirit of them – 'You were told in the past ... but *I* say to you ...' Yet neither Paul nor Jesus allows us to jettison the law altogether. Every one of those laws is a pointer. Maybe we can't apply them literally. Laws may be in conflict, forcing us to choose the lesser of two evils. The commandments of Jesus, to love God and love our neighbour as ourselves, override all loveless slavery to a moral code. But the laws still indicate areas in which we have to make moral choices. The commandments of the Bible are waymarks along the journey of life.

## The example of Jesus

More important than the words we find in the Bible, however, is the example of Jesus. '*I* am the Way,' said Jesus. If we follow his example, we'll know what choices to make, because we can ask ourselves, 'What would Jesus have done in this situation?' We shall have to think about it deeply, because Jesus was never in many of the dilemmas in which we find ourselves today. But if we read the Gospels carefully, we'll discern the character of Jesus, learn to know him as our best friend, and be able to work out what a loving person like him would have done in most of the dilemmas of modern life.

## In quietness and in trust

But though you have to use all the brainpower God has given you in working out what choices to make, you don't have to worry about it and get yourself in a state. Isaiah also said, 'In returning and rest you shall be saved; in quietness and in trust shall be your strength.' There's a sort of Quaker simplicity about the Christian way of life, where you don't bother the Lord with hundreds of questions but listen in silence till God speaks to you, then do what he tells you and trust the outcome into God's hands.

## Philip's question

On the first of May each year we celebrate St Philip and St James's Day; though when Ascension Day falls on the first, we may have to postpone 'Pip and Jim' to the next day. For the Gospel we read from one of the passages where Philip's mentioned. At the Last Supper, Jesus talked about the way to heaven. Thomas asked Jesus how we could know the way. Jesus replied, 'I am the Way.' In other words, the way God wants us to live is found in the example of Jesus. Philip asked Jesus to show them his Father. Jesus's answer was that whoever's seen Jesus has seen our Father God, compressed into a human personality. So the life of Jesus points out the way that we, too, should live. The path of life is fully waymarked. The waymarks appear whenever we ask ourselves, 'What would Jesus have done?' Then you hear God's voice saying, 'This is the way; walk in it.'

### Suggested hymns

*Be still, for the presence of the Lord; O Jesus, I have promised; Let me have my way among you, do not strive; Thou art the way, by thee alone.*

## St Matthias the Apostle    14 May
## Appointed to Go

Isa. 22:15–25 Eliakim replaces Shebna; Ps. 15 Who shall dwell in your house?; Acts 1:15–26 Matthias replaces Judas (*if the Acts reading is used instead of the Old Testament reading, the New Testament reading is* 1 Cor. 4:1–7 Stewards of God's mysteries); John 15:9–17 I have appointed you to go

> '[Jesus said,] "You did not choose me but I chose you. And I appointed you to go and bear fruit, fruit that will last."' John 15:16

## Courtship

Courtship's an amazing process. To the detached observer, it's also quite amusing. Let's assume a man chooses a woman whom he likes, though it could equally well be the other way round. If he tries the unsubtle method of winning her, like a pirate boarding a ship, he's likely to get a slap in the face. So he uses the subtle approach, bringing her gifts, doing things together which she enjoys, flattering her, helping her to feel good about herself. Then, because she enjoys being in the company of a man who makes her feel like that, she chooses him. Though, as I said, often it's the woman who makes the choice first. Who did the choosing? If both of them think they did, they'll get along just fine.

## Matthias

It's rather like when Jesus said to his disciples, 'You didn't choose me, but I chose you.' The disciples chose to become followers of Jesus, or so they thought. But actually they were responding to his choice of them. He made himself attractive to them because he loved them. And so it goes round and round, as all relationships do, by a process of mutual attracting and choosing. The Twelve maybe thought they'd applied for positions of leadership within the fledgling community of disciples. Actually, Jesus picked out twelve who had the potential that he needed to turn them into leaders. Then Judas Iscariot hanged himself, and Matthias was chosen to replace him in the team who were to lead the growing Church. He was chosen by 'casting lots', which means throwing pieces of wood with writing on onto the ground, rather like tossing a coin, and seeing which turned up heads. The Twelve wanted to show that human politics played no part in the choice. The outcome might look like random chance to us, but God's in control of everything, even of the laws of probability. Matthias didn't choose to be an Apostle; God chose him.

## Bearing fruit

What's the job description of an Apostle? Well, Jesus had already told them at the Last Supper: 'I chose you and I appointed you to go and bear fruit, fruit that will last.' The first thing was that they were to go. The word 'apostle' means someone who's sent. The twelve thrones that they'd been promised were purely metaphorical. They weren't supposed to sit down on the job, but to get up and go. It seems to have taken the Twelve a while to understand this; at first they all stayed in Jerusalem until persecution forced them to leave. But when they left and started travelling on the Lord's business, what a difference they made! Because the second thing Jesus had told them to do was to bear fruit. Now every Christian bears the fruit of the Spirit, and the fruit of good works, but that's not what Jesus was talking about. You remember how many times Jesus spoke of making new converts as being like gathering in the harvest? That was what the Apostles were to do: bring new believers to follow Jesus.

## The Chosen People

When God chooses people, it's not to give them special privileges, but to demand of them special commitment to service. The Jews were and are God's Chosen People: chosen to know him and to tell the rest of the world about him. You and I have been grafted into the Chosen People; but you and I, also, are chosen not for privilege but for service. This means there can be no pride: we mustn't think we're better than our neighbours because we've chosen to go to church. No, we've been chosen by Jesus to be members of his Church so that we can serve him. And it's not because we're specially clever or virtuous that Jesus has chosen us; Jesus often chooses people who are basically useless, because he can start from scratch and make something of them! If you hold an office in the church, it's not because you've chosen to do it, but Jesus has chosen you to do it for him. And even the ordinary church member is chosen to bear fruit: the fruit of the Spirit, love, joy and peace; the fruit of good works, helping other people; and the harvest of other people brought to believe in Jesus through your word and example. How much fruit have you borne for Jesus this year?

## *Suggested hymns*

*Jesus, take me as I am; O thou who camest from above; Strengthen for service, Lord, the hands; Thy way, not mine, O Lord.*

# Day of Thanksgiving for the Institution of Holy Communion (Corpus Christi)  22 May

**Melchizedek** Gen. 14:18–20 Melchizedek brought bread and wine; Ps. 116:10–17 The cup of salvation; 1 Cor. 11:23–26 The Last Supper; John 6:51–58 Living bread

> *'King Melchizedek of Salem brought out bread and wine; he was priest of God Most High.'* Genesis 14:18

## Prophecy and typology

Supposing you watched a film in 2005, without understanding what it meant. Then in 2008 the events began to unfold exactly as you'd seen them in the film. You'd feel that something extremely spooky was going on. That must have been the feeling of the friends of Jesus, when they saw how many things that happened to him seemed to mirror the words that were written in the Hebrew Scriptures, from four hundred to two thousand years previously. The gospel-writers keep saying, 'This happened to fulfil the prophecy of ...' so and so, and Jesus himself said, 'You search the Scriptures ... and it is they that testify on my behalf.' The predictions proved to the disciples that God was at work, for how could the prophets know how to prophesy the future unless God had given them the words to write? Later Christians used the word 'typology', like a typewriter impressing the image of keys made in the past on the blank paper of the present. We don't use the 'argument from prophecy' so much these days, preferring to point out that God's consistent, and God's behaviour today is how he's behaved in the past. But some of the verbal parallels between the Old Testament and the New Testament are, to say the least, a remarkable coincidence.

## Melchizedek

So let's look at the bizarre story of Melchizedek, who was both priest and King of Salem, and who brought forth bread and wine. What's this got to do with Jesus at the Last Supper? 'Melchi-Zedek' means 'King of Righteousness'. 'Salem' is assumed to be the same word as 'Shalom', and is part of the name of the city of Jeru-Salem, the city of peace. So the King of Salem is the Prince of Peace. He's a priest, but instead of sacrificing an animal he brings forth bread and wine, and blesses Abraham in the name of the Most High God. Then Abraham pays him tithes. Curiouser and curiouser. The

324

inhabitants of Jerusalem at this time were a Canaanite tribe called Jebusites, who worshipped God under the name of El. Later, after King David captured Jerusalem, it became a centre for worship of the Lord, called something like Yahweh. Worship of El passed to the north, after the twelve tribes split into two kingdoms. So perhaps an old story was updated to try and reconcile the southern and the northern kingdoms, and bring them both to worship in Jerusalem, the city of King David's descendants, and pay tithes to the Jerusalem priesthood. Psalm 110 says to the king in Jerusalem, 'You are a priest forever, after the pattern of Melchizedek.' The ingenious explanation fits together, but why 'bread and wine'?

## The Last Supper

The writers of the New Testament thought that the true meaning of the Melchizedek prophecy only became clear at the Last Supper, where Jesus gave bread and wine to his disciples. They were a standard element in the Passover ritual, when Jews ate and drank to remember their deliverance, when they escaped from slavery in Egypt. Jesus gave them a new meaning, referring them to his body and blood. The Israelites often used to eat the flesh of their sacrificial animals, such as the Passover lamb. The blood of the sacrifice was sprinkled on the worshippers to take the place of signing a contract or covenant. So when you receive bread and wine in the church service, you are claiming the forgiveness brought to us by the sacrificial death of Jesus on the cross, and signing your name to the New Covenant, promising to obey Jesus as your response to his love for us. Jesus is our priest, who brings us God's blessing, and our king whom we obey in faith.

## Fulfilment

When you join in this sacrament, you're fulfilling a pattern which was set four thousand years ago, when Melchizedek brought forth bread and wine. Maybe the words are just a coincidence. But somehow, I don't think so. If God's the maker of time, he can see the past and the future at the same time. God could easily cause things to happen in one age, whose full meaning wouldn't be understood until far in the future. And events in the present, like this service, can only be understood when we see them in the context of what God has done in the past. It isn't spooky, after all. It just means, 'Look out, God's at work.'

## Suggested hymns

*Alleluia, sing to Jesus; Author of life divine; Broken for me, broken for you; Now, my tongue, the mystery telling.*

## Visit of the Blessed Virgin Mary to Elizabeth
### 31 May

**Sing!** Zeph. 3:14–18 Sing, daughter Zion; Ps. 113 Making her a joyous mother; Rom. 12:9–16 Hospitality; Luke 1:39–49 [50–56] Magnificat

> *'Sing aloud, O daughter Zion; shout, O Israel! Rejoice and exult with all your heart, O daughter Jerusalem!' Zephaniah 3:14*

### Can you sing?

Can you sing? Do you sing? In church, at home, in the bath, or never? Many people sing, but never pluck up the courage to sing in public. Others have been told they can't sing, but in fact they could, for their own pleasure if not for anybody else's, if they were encouraged. It's only a question of listening to the sounds that come from your mouth and correcting them till they're right. According to St Luke, the Blessed Virgin Mary, when she visited her cousin Elizabeth, suddenly started to sing. She sang the song which we now call the Magnificat:

> My soul magnifies the Lord,
> and my spirit rejoices in God my Saviour.

### Is that how it was?

Do you think that's how it really happened? For all that it was based on the Song of Hannah in the Old Testament, it was an original composition. Do you suppose she came out with it spontaneously, fully composed in the form we now have it? Or has Luke written it up a bit to make a good story, and actually she spent the whole of the three months she was with Elizabeth writing the poetry and composing the melody? Some people think it's so unlikely that a peasant girl from Nazareth could write such a beautiful thing, that they've speculated that it was written by somebody else, maybe even by St Luke himself. There are three songs in Luke's Gospel: Zechariah's song which we call the Benedictus; old Simeon's song, the Nunc Dimittis; and Mary's Magnificat. They're all in the style of Hebrew poetry, with the second half of each verse reflecting the first half, many quotations from the Old Testament, and a very Jewish vocabulary, which it's unlikely that Luke, a Greek, could have written himself. They don't have any of the teaching of developed Christian theology, about the cross and the resurrection, the Son of Man or the Son of God. Instead they seem to reflect the Jewish expectation of a Messiah who would rescue Israel from its enemies, which must have been characteristic of the time when Jesus was born. All three songs, and the Magnificat especially, are what we'd call today politically very revolutionary: 'put down the mighty from their thrones, and lifted up the lowly' indeed – you'd be arrested for preaching that sort of thing at Hyde Park Corner! So perhaps, just perhaps, Mary was indeed the author of the Magnificat. In which case she was a very remarkable teenager.

## Poets and songwriters

Perhaps a lot of teenagers do write poetry, but keep it to themselves. Maybe many of them compose pop songs, but never perform them in public. If so, they should be encouraged. Everbody should be encouraged to be creative. God's a creator, and he made us in his image, so we ought all to be creative. Maybe if you learnt to look at things with an artist's eye, you would find that you can paint. Maybe if you made up words in your head and wrote them down, you could be a writer. If you expressed your feelings in poetic language, and thought a little about words that rhyme, maybe even learnt about how many syllables to put in a line, you could write verse which occasionally blossoms into poetry. The American poet Emily Dickinson wrote hundreds of verses for her own pleasure, none of which were published in her own lifetime. Few of us have the skill to write musical notes on a page; but perhaps we could make up little tunes and hum them to ourselves while we go about the housework. Or even sing words we've made up ourselves when nobody else is around. You never know what you can do till you try.

## Sing to God

The prophet Zechariah wrote:

> Sing aloud, O daughter Zion;
> shout, O Israel!
> Rejoice and exult with all your heart,
> O daughter Jerusalem!

Perhaps the prophets sang their prophecies? Perhaps Mary was encouraged by these words to become a songwriter? Surely it's the most natural thing in the world, if you feel happy about what God has done, to want to sing about it. If we follow the Virgin Mary's example, we might all sing a bit more joyfully in church than we usually do, and hum God's praises as we go round the house when we're at home. That would make life much more tuneful and joyous, and it might make God as happy as it would make us.

### Suggested hymns

*How shall I sing that majesty?; I will sing, I will sing, a song unto the Lord; I will sing the wondrous story; Ye watchers and ye holy ones.*

# St Barnabas the Apostle   11 June
# One Who Comforts

Job 29:11–16 Like one who comforts; Ps. 112 Generous; Acts 11:19–30 Barnabas encourages Saul (*if the Acts reading is used instead of the Old Testament reading, the New Testament reading is* Gal. 2:1–10 Barnabas and me); John 15:12–17 Love one another

'*I chose their way, and sat as chief, and I lived like a king among his troops, like one who comforts mourners.*' Job 29:25

### Job's goodness

The book of Job's a story about a good man who suffered the loss of his family, his home and his health. His friends come to visit him, and tell him that if he's suffering, he must deserve it – he *must* be wicked. They are often called 'Job's comforters', but it's only cold comfort that they bring him. Job knows he doesn't deserve what's happening to him. So he argues with his friends, and he argues with

God. Eventually Job realizes that God's much greater than we are, and we shall never fully understand his ways. When at last Job gives up, and says sorry for being so presumptuous, he realizes that 'my Redeemer lives'. It's only in the cross that we see that God suffers with us, which is the answer to the problem of innocent suffering. But I'm running ahead of myself; in chapter 29, Job's argument with God is in full swing. Job makes what's become known as his 'negative confession'. He doesn't confess his sins to God, as the friends urged him to: he confesses his virtues. It sounds arrogant, but the so-called comforters have driven him to it. Job said:

> I delivered the poor who cried,
> and the orphan who had no helper ...
> I was eyes to the blind, and feet to the lame.
> I was a father to the needy,
> and I championed the cause of the stranger ...
> like one who comforts mourners.

The chief point in Job's favour was that he was one who comforted others.

## The 'son of encouragement'

The Apostle Barnabas was another one who comforted other people. In Acts, he's nicknamed 'son of encouragement', or 'son of consolation'. Who could ask for higher praise? Barnabas was an early convert, when the Christian Church was small and struggling. He sold a farm which he owned, brought the money it had fetched and gave it to the Apostles. This was a great comfort to them, and encouraged them to keep going. He encouraged Saul of Tarsus, later known as St Paul, when the rest of the church were suspicious of this former persecutor. He encouraged Saul to come to Antioch, to minister to the Greek-speaking Christians there. Barnabas encouraged Saul to travel, to spread the gospel to other Greek-speakers, but he made sure the first journey was an easy one. They set off for a tour of the synagogues in Cyprus, where Barnabas was born, and where he already knew most of the Jews. They'd be among friends, which would be a comfort for them.

## Staying loyal

Of course, it didn't work out as Barnabas had planned. Saul met the Roman Governor of Cyprus, Sergius Paulus, and changed his name to Paul. They probably spoke about the Roman Empire, and how it needed a new religion of love to bring together the many different races, each with its own religion, which were tearing the Empire apart. So as soon as they reached the shore of what's now called Turkey, Paul set off into the interior, Gentile territory. Barnabas's nephew, John Mark, was so horrified that he deserted and went home. But Barnabas stuck with his friend Paul and went with him, shared the preaching, and shared the suffering when their fellow Jews rejected them. The people of Lystra thought Barnabas was Zeus, the father of the gods, come to earth to visit them, he was so fatherly and god-like. He took Paul's side when the first synod of the Church met in Jerusalem to discuss whether non-Jewish Christians needed to be circumcised and follow the customary Jewish way of life. Later they went their separate ways because Barnabas wanted to comfort and encourage his nephew John Mark. He appears to have been successful, because Mark was later reconciled to St Paul, and wrote the first of the Gospels.

## One who comforts

St Barnabas is an example to us all. He wasn't bothered about his own achievements. Like Job, all Barnabas cared about was to encourage and comfort others, who gave him the nickname 'son of encouragement'. He was quite prepared to bask in Paul and Mark's reflected glory, knowing that in a quiet way he'd helped them to achieve what they did, and brought out their full potential. We, too, could ask for no higher praise than to be known as someone who encourages others, lifts them up when they're down, and brings out the best in them.

## Suggested hymns

*Brother, sister, let me serve you; Disposer supreme, and Judge of the earth; O for a heart to praise my God; Take my life, and let it be.*

# The Birth of John the Baptist  24 June
## A Baptism of Repentance

Isa. 40:1–11 A voice in the wilderness; Ps. 85:7–13 Salvation is at hand; Acts 13:14b–26 A baptism of repentance; *or* Gal. 3:23–29 The law our schoolmaster; Luke 1:57–66, 80 Birth of the Baptist

*'Before [Jesus's] coming John had already proclaimed a baptism of repentance to all the people of Israel.' Acts 13:24*

## Translation

Anyone who's been on holiday to a foreign country knows that translating from one language into another's not easy. Words have a nasty habit of meaning something subtly different in one language from the word which usually represents them in another. So pity the poor Bible translator, who tries to make an accurate translation of the Holy Scriptures into a new language, for a people who've never read it before. A phrase which means one thing in the Bible may mean something quite different in another language. Translators say the hardest Bible verse of all to translate into any language is the description of John the Baptist, who 'came proclaiming a baptism of repentance for the remission of sins'. Every single word in that sentence, except 'a', of', 'for' and 'the', presents a problem, and sometimes needs a whole sentence to explain it.

## Came proclaiming

'Came' is not too bad, except that it doesn't mean coming from one place to another, it means coming into the focus of public attention. But 'proclaiming'? It's the word used about a herald when he brings the good news that a victory has been won. The same word is used for preaching – remember that, every time the sermon begins: the preacher's there to give you good news.

## Baptism

What did John the Baptist mean by baptism? The word simply means 'washing'; remember that today, when you baptize the dishes! The Jews in those days were always washing themselves; not for hygienic reasons, but because, unless you were physically clean, they thought you weren't spiritually pure enough to approach the holy God. So when somebody who wasn't a Jew wanted to follow the Jewish religion, they had to be baptized, washed, to be purified of all their Gentile evil thoughts and bad habits. When John the Baptist said to his fellow Jews, 'You must be baptized', he was warning them that birth and race were not enough. You may have a good Jewish mother, but that doesn't make you one of the Chosen People; you're no better than the filthy Gentiles: you need to be washed; you must choose to be chosen. You can imagine what he'd say to us Christians when we say, 'I come from a Christian family and I live in a Christian country, I was christened when I was too small to know anything about it. What else do you want?' John would say, 'You've got to choose for yourself to be a Christian.'

## Repentance

The next word's the hardest of all to translate: 'repentance'. Because it doesn't mean 'remorse'. We all know that saying sorry is important, that it's the hardest word to say, and you can't be forgiven until you've owned up and taken responsibility for your own actions. We were taught that at our mother's knee, though most of us aren't very good at doing it. But that's not what John was talking about. The word which we mistranslate as 'repentance' actually means changing your mind. Changing your attitude. Making a fresh start. It's the difference between the Pharisee who said in his prayers, 'I've done this and I've done that, so I deserve to be saved,' and the tax-collector who prayed, 'Lord, have mercy on me, a sinner.' John's message was all about not boasting of our own achievements, but starting all over again in utter dependence on God.

## Remission

The words get a bit easier now. 'John came proclaiming a baptism of repentance for the remission of sins.' 'Remission' means 'sending away'. A penitent challenged a priest, 'How do I know that God hears your prayers?' The priest replied, 'Ask God what sins I confessed to him today.' The penitent came back crestfallen the next morning. 'I asked God what sins you'd confessed,' he said, 'and God said he's already forgotten!' That's what 'remission' means: God sends your sins away, forgives and forgets. In fact God's probably the only one who's capable of forgiving you and totally forgetting what it was he forgave. So don't go reminding him because you can't lose the habit of feeling guilty.

## Sins

That only leaves the word 'sins'. Basically it means 'falling short', as when an arrow fails to make it as far as the target. The target for each of us is to be as loving as Jesus was. Anything less is sin. But if we repent, our sins can be sent away into oblivion. John the Baptist was born so that he could proclaim a baptism of repentance for the remission of sins. Listen to him; change your attitude, and depend entirely on the loving mercy of God.

### Suggested hymns

*Hark! A herald voice is calling; Lo, from the desert homes; The great forerunner of the morn; When Jesus came to Jordan.*

## SS Peter and Paul, Apostles  29 June
*(See page 184.)*

## St Thomas the Apostle  3 July
**Faith** Hab. 2:1–4 The righteous live by faith; Ps. 31:1–6 I trust in the Lord; Eph. 2:19–22 The foundation of the Apostles; John 20:24–29 Doubting Thomas is convinced

> *'Look at the proud! Their spirit is not right in them, but the righteous live by their faith.' Habakkuk 2:4*

### Doubt and certainty

A man was once described in *Private Eye* magazine in words that could have been applied to Doubting Thomas: 'He used to be fairly indecisive, but now he's not so certain.' The prophet Habakkuk called his people to have faith in the certain truth of God's promises. It's the conflict between certainty and doubt which makes this appropriate for St Thomas's day.

### Habakkuk

Habakkuk – one 'b', three 'k's – was a prophet in Judah about 600 BC. The struggle between the great powers of Babylon and

Egypt was at its height, and Judah was caught as piggy-in-the-middle. Some people in Judah were pro-Egypt, and others thought it safer to support Babylon. The nation was in chaos, and there was no justice. The prophet spoke for the ordinary people, whom he calls 'the righteous'; they felt themselves threatened on all sides, and defenceless.

## Watchman

The city of Jerusalem was surrounded by walls, and every few hundred feet there was a watchtower, in which a watchman stood looking out for enemies. His job was to cry out when the enemy appeared, a bit like the sailor in the crow's-nest. Habakkuk wrote: 'I will stand at my watchpost, and station myself on the rampart; I will keep watch to see what he will say to me, and what he will answer concerning my complaint.' He says that he's like a watchman on the walls, crying out when God's people are under attack. But in his case, it's to God that he cries out, pleading for God to come to their aid.

## God's answer

In reply, God gives the prophet a vision of the future. It's a vision of 'the end'. Probably this simply means the end of the people's sufferings, which will come at 'the appointed time'; when God thinks the time is ripe. Some Christians have taken this to refer to the end of the world, and that, too, will be an end of suffering for those who are suffering from injustice. The prophet's vision was rather like Martin Luther King's, when he said 'I have a dream ...'. Habakkuk dreamt of a day when justice will come for the ordinary powerless people; that day will come, he said, because God's promised it. In fact, God's commanded him to write it down so that everybody can see it, in great big letters so that somebody running past wouldn't even have to slow down to read it: 'So that he who runs may read.' The message is that though justice seems to be delayed, we must be patient and wait for it.

Then the LORD answered me and said: Write the vision; make it plain on tablets, so that a runner may read it. For there is still a vision for the appointed time; it speaks of the end, and does not lie. If it seems to tarry, wait for it; it will surely come, it will not delay.

## The righteous will live by faith

So, Habakkuk concludes, 'the righteous live by their faith'. By being faithful and patient, God's people will survive the times of hardship. This verse is quoted three times in the New Testament, because the first Jewish Christians and Gentile Christians found themselves in conflict with Jews who hadn't become Christians. How can you be righteous, asked the Jews, except by keeping every detail of the Jewish laws? No, wrote the Apostles, we're justified, made righteous, by God's free gift of grace, which we accept when we have faith and trust in God. Faith's not the same as certainty. We can't be certain that there is a God, and that he'll save us at the end. But he's promised and we trust him. The alternatives are all so improbable, that we learn to accept the truth of God's promises as the most likely explanation. St Thomas had to learn this lesson: to put aside his doubts, stop looking for certainty and learn that the righteous shall live by faith.

### Suggested hymns

*Firmly I believe and truly; In the Lord I'll be ever thankful (Taizé); Jesu, my Lord, my God, my all; Lead, kindly light, amidst the encircling gloom.*

# St Mary Magdalene   22 July
## As Deer Long for Water S. of Sol. 3:1–4 Seeking and finding; Ps. 42:1–10 As deer long for water; 2 Cor. 5:14–17 A new creation; John 20:1–2, 11–18 Go and tell

> *'As a deer longs for the water brooks, so my soul longs for you, O God.' Psalm 42:1 (Common Worship)*

### Mary Magdalene

Mary Magdalene was distraught and distracted. She was torn apart by different voices when she was possessed by seven devils. Then Jesus healed her, and set her to work caring for the domestic needs of his disciples, which kept her hands full. She was one of the women who watched Jesus being crucified, and felt her heart being ripped in two. She gathered some spices to anoint his dead body, the least she could do for the man who'd given meaning to her life; and the tomb was empty, the body had gone. She fell to her knees. The gardener came up behind her, as she thought. She cried out through her tears, 'Tell me where you've put him!' Then, when she realized it was Jesus, she reached out to grasp his legs. But he told her, 'Don't touch me now, but go and tell.' She was sent, or 'apostled' as they say in Greek, to tell Jesus's brothers, the other disciples, and the whole world that Jesus was alive. She was the first witness of the resurrection, and her life from then on would be busy bearing witness to everybody and everyone. Not a restful vocation. Yet she'd come to Jesus to find some peace.

## Peace

Many people come to Jesus to find rest. In the midst of a busy life, they come to church to wind down and find an atmosphere of calm. There must be many people like that in this church today. Surrounded by a changing world, we come to the unchanging Church to find Jesus, 'the same yesterday, today and for ever'. And the love of Jesus never changes – 'with whom there is no variation or shadow due to change', as Mary Magdalene found out. But the Church is constantly changing and adapting to new ways of spreading the love of God, and some people feel let down by this. Whether it's the loss of Latin, or women in the pulpit, or new hymns, many people are averse to change and long for the simple unchanging faith of their childhood. If they'd listened to the older people when they were children, they'd have realized that people have always been lamenting some lost paradise from long ago. If we want a peaceful life, Christianity is the wrong place to look. But when you surrender your heart to Jesus, then he'll give you that inner peace through which you can walk serenely amid the turmoil all around you. 'Peace, perfect peace, in this dark world of sin?' asks the hymn, incredulously, and answers, 'The blood of Jesus whispers, "Peace within".'

## 'Like as the hart'

That's why Psalm 42 is such a favourite with many people:

> As a deer longs for the water-brooks,
> so my soul longs for you, O God.

The mountains on both sides of the Jordan valley are a dry and thirsty land; the wild deer must have had to go without a drink for long stretches of time. Then they would catch sight of water in the distance, and hurry towards it to find refreshment. The Psalmist may have been thinking of a deer-hunt, as the hymn suggests:

> As pants the hart for cooling streams
> when heated in the chase.

Then the psalm compares our longing for 'the peace of God, which passes all understanding' to the intensity of thirst felt by the hunted animal. Our longing for God's not supposed to be a casual thing, like a hobby; the desire to know God should be a raging thirst which consumes our whole life and all our energy.

## 'I thirst'

Jesus on the cross cried out, 'I thirst'. It was not just physical thirst; by becoming human, even though he was the Son of God, he'd learnt how human beings can feel the absence of God: 'My God, my God, why hast thou forsaken me?' Almost everybody's had patches of dryness in their prayer-life – sometimes it lasts for years. Prayer becomes like talking on the telephone without knowing whether anyone's listening at the other end. One of the great writers on prayer, St John of the Cross, called it 'the dark night of the soul'. He said you should thank God for it, because it means that God trusts you to go on praying to him without the prop of lovely emotions. I wonder whether Mary Magdalene went through something like that. She longed to cling to Jesus for support, but he sent her away from him to be a witness to his unchanging love. No matter how distraught and distracted we may be, 'the blood of Jesus whispers, "Peace within"'.

## Suggested hymns

*As pants the hart for cooling streams; Good Joseph had a garden; Great is thy faithfulness, O God my Father; Peace, perfect peace?*

337

## St James the Apostle   25 July

**James the Martyr** Jer. 45:1–5 Seeking greatness; Ps. 126 Sow in tears, harvest in joy; Acts 11:27—12:2 Herod kills James (*if the Acts reading is used instead of the Old Testament reading, the New Testament reading is* 2 Cor. 4:7–15 Treasure in clay pots); Matt. 20:20–28 Seeking greatness

*'About that time King Herod laid violent hands upon some who belonged to the church. He had James, the brother of John, killed with the sword.' Acts 12:1–2*

### A martyr

Although there are other Jameses mentioned in the Bible, the one we commemorate today is James the Great. He and his brother John, the sons of Zebedee, were among Jesus's closest friends; Jesus nicknamed them the 'Sons of Thunder'. He was the James mentioned in the Acts of the Apostles, whom King Herod Agrippa I had killed with a sword. Although St Stephen was the first Christian martyr, James was the first of the Twelve to die – apart, that is, from Judas Iscariot. When James and his brother John had asked whether they could be seated next to Jesus in his kingdom, Jesus replied with words which, the others later realized, referred to the manner of their death:

Jesus said to them, 'You do not know what you are asking. Are you able to drink the cup that I drink, or be baptized with the baptism that I am baptized with?' They replied, 'We are able.' Then Jesus said to them, 'The cup that I drink you will drink; and with the baptism with which I am baptized, you will be baptized.'

Only thirty years later James proved the accuracy of that prediction when he, like Jesus, died as a martyr to human cruelty.

### He didn't realize

James didn't realize what he was letting himself in for when he accepted Jesus's call to be a disciple. It's probably as well, because if he'd known he was on the path which would lead him to death by the sword, he'd have turned back before he started. We none of us know what we're letting ourselves in for when we call ourselves Christians. Probably none of you will have to die for your faith, though if a thing's worth living for, it's worth dying for. But there are probably other painful episodes to undergo or sacrifices to make – you may have already made them. If you'd known about them when you first started to follow Jesus, you'd have given up. If you've already had a rough ride, you'll know that being a Christian isn't easy, but it's amazing how God gives you his grace to help you through. In which case, you needn't worry about future troubles, because you now know that with God you can cope with whatever comes your way.

## Ready for anything

The Christian must be ready for anything. The US Navy ran a series of cautionary training cartoons in which a character called Murphy could be relied on to get things wrong. It's not known for certain, but this may be the origin of the expression 'Murphy's Law', which states that 'anything that can go wrong, will go wrong'. Fortunately, it doesn't apply to the whole of life. But you can be sure that one or two of the things you most dread will happen to you sometime. In which case, it's just as well to start preparing yourself mentally. The first thing to remember is that God will give you grace to come through them. As St Paul said:

No testing has overtaken you that is not common to everyone. God is faithful, and he will not let you be tested beyond your strength, but with the testing he will also provide the way out so that you may be able to endure it.

The second thing is that suffering for your faith, even if it's only mildly, brings you a reward in heaven. And the third is that heaven lies at the end of the road anyway, so death is not a thing to be dreaded, but looked forward to as the gateway into eternity.

## St James knew this

St James the Martyr knew this. So when death came to him, he was probably proud to share the same baptism of suffering as his Lord. Following his example, we must prepare ourselves, by trusting in God's help, to endure the unendurable, to accept the unacceptable, and to suffer the insufferable, if that's what God calls us to. The Romans used to say that all roads lead to Rome. Well, for the Christian, all paths lead to heaven. Whichever path becomes the path of our life, we can endure it bravely, like St James, because we know that glory and love are at the end of it, and God will be with us every step of the way.

### Suggested hymns

*For all thy saints, O Lord; How bright these glorious spirits shine!; Lord, it belongs not to my care; Who are these like stars appearing?*

## The Transfiguration of Our Lord   6 August
**Déjà Vu** Dan. 7:9–10, 13–14 The Son of Man; Ps. 97 Clouds are around him; 2 Peter 1:16–19 We saw; Luke 9:28–36 The transfiguration

> *'Suddenly they saw two men, Moses and Elijah, talking to [Jesus]. They appeared in glory and were speaking of his departure, which he was about to accomplish at Jerusalem.' Luke 9:30–31*

### Exodus

In Britain, we call the place you turn off a motorway an 'exit'. But that's a Latin word, so in Greece you see by each of the motorway exits a word every Bible reader will recognize, though it's spelt slightly differently. The Greek word for an exit is *exodos*. *Odos* is Greek for a road, so *exodos* means 'the road out'. That's why 'Exodus' is the name given to the book in the Bible which describes the Israelites' road out of Egypt, their great exit from slavery. It was God who led them out, and this great act of salvation showed them what sort of God they were dealing with: a God who saves. Whenever God spectacularly saved the Israelites, after that, they would describe it as another victory like the first – another exodus which God had accomplished. Those were the words which Moses and Elijah used to Jesus, when they appeared at the transfiguration. It's a slightly complicated metaphor, and most Bible readers wouldn't understand it, so many Bible translations use a different word, which is a shame: 'Moses and Elijah ... were speaking [to Jesus] of his *departure*, which he was about to accomplish at Jerusalem.' How do you 'accomplish' a departure? But Jesus was about to save all of those who come to him from the guilt and power of sin and the fear of death. That was an even greater act of salvation than the road out of Egypt. So what they were really talking about was the 'new exodus' which Jesus was about to accomplish when he died and rose again in Jerusalem.

## God is consistent

God is consistent. If he saves us once, he'll save us again. Coming events cast their shadows before them. So Christians have seen the Exodus of the Israelites from Egypt as a foreshadowing, or prefiguring, of the salvation which Jesus wrought on the cross. As God saved the Israelites from slavery by leading them through the Red Sea waters to the promised land, so Jesus leads us from slavery to sin, through the waters of baptism and the deep waters of death, to freedom in the land of heaven. Before they went out, the Jews became united as God's people by eating a meal of bread and wine, and a sacrificial lamb; we commemorate the sacrifice of Jesus, our Passover Lamb, by eating bread and drinking wine together, and so we're formed into the people of God.

## Transfiguration

All this was explained by the words that the disciples heard Moses and Elijah speaking during their vision on the Mount of Transfiguration. They were covered by a cloud, like the pillar of cloud that symbolized the presence of God at the Exodus. Usually when you're in a cloud you can't see very well. In this case, the disciples saw more clearly than they ever had before, that Jesus was about to complete a salvation greater than the Exodus. The transfiguration was when the meaning of the cross was explained to them – not that they understood it till later.

### Déjà vu

There's a phrase we use about events which remind us of what happened before. Most English-speakers, who can't pronounce French very well, call it a sense of 'Day-jar voo'! The words actually mean 'seen already'. 'When I saw that house,' we say, 'it looked so like the house I grew up in that I had a real sense of *déjà vu*.' Or, 'When I first saw you, my darling, I had the feeling that I'd seen you already long ago in my dreams.' So the conversation at the transfiguration was meant to give us a sense of *déjà vu* when we think about the cross and resurrection: 'We've been here before,' we should say, 'at the Exodus. God's done it again! He never changes. He's always a God who saves.'

## God saves us

Every salvation carries echoes of previous salvations, because God is the same yesterday, today and for ever; you can depend on him. The more you hear about Jesus, the more he reveals to us the glory of the God who saves. Don't get caught up in the fog of doubt, but in the cloud of the transfiguration which shows you the glory of Jesus. If you see clearly that Jesus is glorious, then you can rely on God to rescue you, too, when you get into a scrape; for God is, and always has been, a God who saves.

### Suggested hymns

*Come, ye faithful, raise the strain; Immortal, invisible, God only wise; Lord, the light of your love is shining; 'Tis good, Lord, to be here.*

## The Blessed Virgin Mary    15 August

**As a Bride** Isa. 61:10–11 As a bride; *or* Rev. 11:19—12:6, 10 A woman in heaven; Ps. 45:10–17 You shall have sons; Gal. 4:4–7 Born of a woman; Luke 1:46–55 Magnificat

> *'I will greatly rejoice in the LORD, my whole being shall exult in my God; for he has clothed me with the garments of salvation, he has covered me with the robe of righteousness, as a bridegroom decks himself with a garland, and as a bride adorns herself with her jewels.' Isaiah 61:10*

## Wedding preparations

Everybody wears their best clothes for a wedding. The guests put on their glad-rags as a tribute to the bride and groom. And the bride and groom – who do they dress up for? Maybe the bride makes herself look beautiful for her own sake, because she enjoys it – after all, it's probably the only chance she'll get to wear a bridal gown. And she wears her finest clothes for her family, who'll enjoy the reflected glory. But most of all she wants to look her best for the sake of the man she loves, so that he can say, 'Darling, you do look lovely.' And the groom wants to look smart for the sake of his beloved. No, the age of romance is not past. So we know what the Bible's talking about when we read: 'God ... has clothed me with the garments of salvation, he has covered me with the robe of righteousness, as a bridegroom decks himself with a garland, and as a bride adorns herself with her jewels.'

## The bride of God

On this day we think about the Blessed Virgin Mary, who is often spoken about as God's holy bride. But that passage from the book of Isaiah was talking about Holy Zion, the hill in Jerusalem where the Temple stood. Earlier in the chapter we read about 'those who mourn in Zion'. The best of the population of Jerusalem had been taken into exile in Babylon. But God promised that the city would have new glory when God brought the exiles home. They will rejoice that God has saved them, and through God's grace they will achieve a new standard of righteousness. God loves his people, as a bridegroom loves his bride; the people of Israel came to think of themselves as the bride of God.

## Abu Gosh (pronounced with a long 'o')

Nowadays, we Christians count ourselves as having been grafted into the original people of God. God loves us, the people who make up the Christian Church. We are his bride. And Mary is a symbol of the Church. At a place called Abu Gosh, in the Holy Land, a huge statue of the Madonna and Child towers high above the village. Abu Gosh is one of the possible sites of Emmaus. But it's also the place where the Ark of the Covenant rested for twenty years before King David took it into Jerusalem. The ark became the symbol of the presence of God; it contained God for them. And the church is called Our Lady of the Ark of the Covenant, because when Mary conceived Jesus in her womb, she contained God within her, and became the symbol of God's presence. God took Mary as his bride, and she became the Mother of God's Son. Now all this talk of brides and sons is symbolic language. But we can rejoice in this honour paid to Mary, because she symbolizes the Christian Church, which also contains the body of Christ in its midst.

343

## Obedience

The angel said, 'Greetings, favoured one! The Lord is with you.' God in his grace took this simple peasant girl and made her the Mother of God. She replied, 'Here am I, the servant of the Lord; let it be with me according to your word.' Her response to God's grace was the offer of her complete obedience. Here, too, she is a symbol of the Christian Church. We receive God's grace in our lives, Jesus dwells within the Church, we become a symbol of the presence of God to the world, and the Church offers to God its total obedience. We thank Mary for having given us an example of what it means to be the bride of God, in simple trust and total obedience. When you receive the sacrament of bread and wine, Jesus dwells with you as surely as he dwelt in Mary. Will your response be one of glad obedience to all that God asks you to do for him, like hers? Will you say, as Mary said,

> I will greatly rejoice in the LORD, my whole being shall exult in my God; for he has clothed me with the garments of salvation, he has covered me with the robe of righteousness, as a bridegroom decks himself with a garland, and as a bride adorns herself with her jewels.

### Suggested hymns

*Her virgin eyes saw God incarnate born; Shall we not love thee, Mother dear?; Ye watchers and ye holy ones; Ye who own the faith of Jesus.*

## St Bartholomew the Apostle   24 August
*(See page 223.)*

## Holy Cross Day   14 September
*(See page 237.)*

## St Matthew, Apostle and Evangelist   21 September
*(See page 242.)*

# St Michael and All Angels  29 September
## Angels Descending on the Son of Man

Gen. 28:10–17 Jacob's ladder; Ps. 103:19–22 Bless the Lord, you angels; Rev. 12:7–12 Michael fought the dragon (*if the Revelation reading is used instead of the Old Testament reading, the New Testament reading is* Heb. 1:5–14 Higher than the angels); John 1:47–51 Angels descending on the Son of Man.

*'[Jesus] said to [Nathanael,] "Very truly, I tell you, you will see heaven opened and the angels of God ascending and descending upon the Son of Man."' John 1:51*

### Be an angel

Sometimes, in very polite families, one member of the family will say to another, 'Would you be an angel and make me a cup of tea?' In not very polite families … well, let's not talk about that! We talk about 'being an angel', referring, presumably, to the belief in guardian angels who protect and take care of us. Jesus said, 'Take care that you do not despise one of these little ones; for, I tell you, in heaven their angels continually see the face of my Father in heaven.' Since angels are spiritual beings, we know very little about them, but Jesus seems to suggest that you and I, each one of us, has a guardian angel individually assigned to care for us, warn us when we're about to do something wrong, and speak to God on our behalf.

### Messengers

The word 'angel' simply means a messenger. Over and over in the Bible, angels are said to bring people messages from God, warning them of danger, or instructing them in the way they should go.

### God himself

In some of the oldest books in the Bible, to say that 'the angel of the Lord' spoke to someone is almost the same as saying that God spoke to them. It's as though God is so desperate to communicate with us, that he'll appear to us in any form that we're willing to listen to.

## Male or female, wings?

So what form do angels take? The Bible gives us no clear answer. As pure spirit can have no gender, we can't say that they are either male or female. Although modern pictures of angels almost always show them as women, that was quite a late development in the history of art. In Lichfield Cathedral a splendid Saxon carving has been recently rediscovered of an angel with an impressive beard. Carved cherubs with wings were placed over the Ark of the Covenant in the Temple of Jerusalem. Isaiah calls them seraphs and says that 'each had six wings: with two they covered their faces, and with two they covered their feet, and with two they flew'. In the Psalms, God rides on a cherub and flies through the air. But there's nothing about angels having wings when they appear to people.

## Angels unaware

In fact, the Letter to the Hebrews warns us: 'Do not neglect to show hospitality to strangers, for by doing that, some have entertained angels without knowing it.' This is probably a reference to the book of Tobit in the Apocrypha, where young Tobias is accompanied on a long journey by the Archangel Raphael without realizing this was not a human companion. Sometimes it may be that angels appear in the form of an ordinary human being, if that's the best way for us to hear God's messages.

## Jacob's ladder

In Jacob's dream at Bethel, he saw a ladder reaching to heaven, with angels ascending and descending on it. This was intended to show him that communication is a two-way process. God has messages to send down to us, and he wants us to communicate to him in our prayers our requests and our questions, our praise and our love. The place where we pray is 'the house of God'; it's holy ground.

## Jesus

Jesus said to Nathanael, 'Very truly, I tell you, you will see heaven opened and the angels of God ascending and descending upon the Son of Man.' By this he meant to tell us that he himself is like Jacob's ladder. God dwells in Jesus; God communicates with us through the words that fall from Jesus's lips, and wants us to communicate with God by making our prayers through Jesus.

## God wants communication

So whatever you think about angels, they're a vivid symbol to us that God is in the communications business. He wants to give us information about how we should live, and he wants to hear information about us in our prayers. Next time you ask someone to 'be an angel', remember that God has many ways of showing his love for us. When members of our family show us kindness, they may be acting as the messengers of God without realizing it.

### Suggested hymns

*Angels voices, ever singing; Around the throne of God a band; Hark! hark, my soul! angelic songs are swelling; Ye holy angels bright.*

## St Luke the Evangelist   18 October

**Luke's Loyalty**  Isa. 35:3–6 Healing in the new age; *or* Acts 16:6–12a The Macedonian call; Ps. 147:1–7 God heals the broken-hearted; 2 Tim. 4:5–17 Only Luke is with me; Luke 10:1–9 Sending out the seventy

'Only Luke is with me.' 2 Timothy 4:11

### Who wrote the Gospel according to Luke?

Who wrote the Gospel according to Luke? The text of the Gospel nowhere names the writer, but the very earliest copies give it the title: 'The Gospel according to Luke'. Three times in his letters, St Paul mentions someone named Luke, and it's probably the same person in each case. To the Colossians, Paul writes 'Luke, the beloved physician, and Demas greet you.' Writing to Timothy, Paul sighs that 'Only Luke is with me.' And in his short letter to Philemon, Paul, who's in prison, includes Luke among his 'fellow-workers' who send their greetings. Luke wasn't one of the Twelve Apostles; he's not mentioned in the Gospels at all. If anyone had wanted to pass off an anonymous Gospel as being by somebody important, they wouldn't haven't chosen anyone as obscure as Luke. So the first clues lead inevitably to the most obvious solution: the Gospel according to Luke was written by Luke, the beloved physician.

## Who wrote the Acts of the Apostles?

But there's a second stage to our investigation. Who wrote the Acts of the Apostles? Well, that's easy, too. St Luke begins his Gospel by dedicating it to someone he calls 'most excellent Theophilus'. The Acts begin with the words, 'In the first book, Theophilus, I wrote about all that Jesus did and taught from the beginning.' So the Gospel and the Acts are evidently two parts of the same work, by the same author. Acts was written by Luke; in many places he writes '*we* set sail'; '*we* met to break bread'; '*we* came in sight of Cyprus'; '*we* were shipwrecked'; and so on. He was present at some of the events he described.

## Was he a doctor?

Is there any evidence from his writings that Luke was a doctor, as Paul describes him? Well, it's not conclusive, but he does seem to report very clearly the methods that Jesus and the Apostles used when they were healing people. He's particularly compassionate towards women, the outcast and the weak, as you'd expect from anyone with a good bedside manner. Physicians in those days weren't very scientific, and they were often mere slaves; Luke is a name adopted by several freed slaves.

## Jew or Gentile?

It's usually assumed that Luke was a Greek, because Lukas is a Greek name; but many Jews in those days adopted Greek names in addition to or instead of their Hebrew names. Many doctors were Greek, but there were excellent Jewish doctors, too. Luke takes a particular interest in the way that Jesus and the Apostles reached out to foreigners with the gospel, and they accepted it. That would be natural if he wrote his two books to be read by Greeks like Theophilus, or even to be used in connection with defending Paul and other Christians against the charge that they were a threat to the Roman Empire. He is describing the ministry of Paul, his boss, who'd taken on the task of reconciling Jewish Christians with Gentile Christians. Such an interest in the multiracial aspects of our faith would be natural if Luke were himself from a non-Jewish race; but it would be even more impressive if he was a Jew.

## Reconciliation

For the effort towards reconciliation has to come from both sides. As St Paul said, we've been given a ministry of reconciliation, reconciling human beings to God and to each other. You can't be a friend of God while you harbour hatred in your heart for a fellow human whom God loves. Jews and Greeks loathed each other, and Luke, whatever his background, was at the heart of the struggle to teach all races to love one other for Christ's sake. It was the most important task facing the Church then, and it still is now.

## Loyalty

One aspect of love which is often overlooked is that of loyalty. Paul was very lonely when he wrote to Timothy that 'only Luke is with me'. His other friends had gone away for one reason or another, but Luke had remained loyal. He stuck by his friend Paul through thick and thin, in shipwreck and in prison. A friend in need is a friend indeed, and Luke had proved himself a true friend to Paul. Jesus, according to St Luke, called us all to be loyal to God. We can demonstrate our faithfulness to God by being loyal to our friends, even when it's inconvenient. We have a lot to learn from Luke: from the ardour for reconciliation with which he wrote, and from the loyalty by which he lived.

## Suggested hymns

*Disposer supreme, and Judge of the earth; Give us the wings of faith to rise; How beauteous are the feet; Let saints on earth in concert sing.*

## SS Simon and Jude, Apostles   28 October

**Names on a List** Isa. 28:14–16 A foundation stone; Ps. 119:89–96
I am yours, save me!; Eph. 2:19–22 The foundation of the Apostles;
John 15:17–27 You have been with me

> '[Jesus said to his apostles,] "You also are to testify because you
> have been with me from the beginning."' John 15:27

### Celebrated together

Saints Simon and Jude are celebrated together on 28 October. Probably there was a church in Rome which was dedicated to both of them, and which was consecrated on this day. Simon's referred to in the Gospels of Matthew and Mark as Simon the Cananaean. In St Luke's Gospel he's called Simon the Zealot. Cananaean doesn't mean someone from the land of Canaan, that's a Canaanite. Probably 'Cananaean' was an Aramaic word for what Luke calls a Zealot. The Zealots were the extreme Jewish nationalists, the revolutionaries, what we would call today freedom fighters. A nationalist warrior's an unlikely person to find in a list of the twelve closest friends of Jesus. Simon must have been a reformed terrorist. Jesus must have convinced him there was a better way to bring in the kingdom of God than by fighting.

### Namesakes

Many people called Simon are mentioned in the New Testament. The name of Jude is more confusing. Jude's an English form of the Greek name Judas. Judas is the Greek form of Judah. So Jude was a common name; there were two of them among the Twelve Apostles, and the one we commemorate today is not the same as Judas Iscariot. What makes it more confusing is that the name Jude doesn't occur in all the lists of the Twelve; some of them put in place of Jude the name of Thaddeus or Lebbeus. They were probably different names for the same person. Unlike with Simon, at least we know something that Jude said. In John's Gospel we read that 'Judas (not Iscariot) said to Jesus, "Lord, how is it that you will reveal yourself to us and not to the world?"'

## Names on a list

We know very little about Saints Simon and Jude, then. They're both just names on a list, the list of the Twelve who were closest to Jesus. Jesus chose twelve men, so that they could represent the twelve sons of Jacob. They were symbols of the twelve patriarchs, the ancestors of the twelve tribes of Israel. The Twelve Apostles were chosen to show that the Church is the new Israel. Sometimes people ask why Jesus didn't choose women to be among the Twelve. The answer's that he couldn't, because it would have spoilt the symbolism. He gave to women several positions of leadership and importance in the Church, and he even chose Mary Magdalene and sent her to go and tell the Apostles that Jesus had risen, so that they could tell the world. But women couldn't represent the twelve sons of Jacob. The Twelve weren't the only people to be called 'apostles'. The word 'apostle' simply means somebody who's sent out; what we'd call a missionary. St Paul and many others were called apostles, though they weren't members of the original Twelve. St Paul, in his Letter to the Romans, even sends greetings to 'Andronicus and Junia, my relatives who were in prison with me; they are prominent among the apostles, and they were in Christ before I was'. Junia is almost certainly a woman's name.

## Willing helpers

There were no Christian priests in New Testament days, no hierarchy. The Twelve were missionaries, willing helpers in spreading the good news that God loves us and wants us to live with him for ever. They were not proud prelates, but willing to fade into the background when their job was done. The Church is built on the foundation of the apostles and prophets, including Simon and Jude, though they're only names in a list. If someone was turning over the records of your church in a hundred years from now, would your name appear in any list? Would you be listed among the willing helpers? Like Saints Simon and Jude, you're called to be an apostle, sent out by God to be a witness to the resurrection. You know from your own experience that Jesus, who died two thousand years ago, answers your prayers. So Jesus must be alive, you've proved it yourself. Then be an apostle, sent by Jesus to tell the world that Jesus is alive. Are you one of the firm foundations on which the Church today can rest? Even if you're only a name in a list, we've all got a job to do, if we're willing.

### Suggested hymns

*Captains of the saintly band; Christ is made the sure foundation; Christ is our cornerstone; Ye watchers and ye holy ones.*

## All Saints' Day  1 November
*(If 2 November is not kept as All Saints' Sunday, the readings on page 270 are used on 1 November. If those are used on the Sunday, the following are the readings on 1 November)*
**Rejoice, You Righteous** Isa. 56:3–8 My house for all people; or 2 Esd. 2:42–48 Crowned by the Son of God; Ps. 33:1–5 Rejoice, you righteous; Heb. 12:18–24 Come to Zion; Matt. 5:1–12 The Beatitudes

> 'Rejoice in the Lord, O you righteous.' Psalm 33:1 (Common Worship)

### Heaven is fun

Heaven is fun. No, that's not just my opinion, it's the teaching of the Bible, which describes heaven under the image of the best sort of wedding reception. I would have said that heaven's like a party, except that some people don't enjoy parties, and I wouldn't want them to feel out of it. So think of the most enjoyable experience you can imagine, multiply it tenfold and use that as your image of heaven. Some Christians make heaven sound a rather gloomy sort of place, with only the pious and devout being admitted – the sort of people who never have any fun in this life and don't expect it in the world to come. But that's quite the opposite of what the Bible says.

### Peter Abelard

There are many hymns about the joy of heaven. One which is not sung quite so often begins:

> Oh what their joy and their glory must be,
> Those endless sabbaths the blessed ones see!

It's a hymn written by Peter Abelard in the twelfth century, and the nineteenth-century translation doesn't really do it justice. The word 'sabbath' itself sounds gloomy, whereas a more modern translation begins 'Oh, what high holiday …'. Peter Abelard taught about the love of God in the University of Paris, and upset some people by his jubilant approach and his failure to emphasize sin and penitence. Then he fell in love with his cousin Eloise, was castrated on the orders of her furious uncle and driven into exile. He had no further contact with his beloved except by letter. But in spite of his pain, the delights of heaven kept breaking through in his writings: ' "Vision of peace" that brings joy evermore!'

## All good children go to heaven

Our idea of heaven depends very much on whom we expect to meet there. They used to teach children to count with rhymes like:

> One two three four five six seven,
> All good children go to heaven.

The trouble was that the children whom the teachers described as good seemed to some of the rest of us not very fun people to know at all. 'Goody-goody' or 'Little Miss Goody Two-shoes' we called them, and the idea of spending eternity with them was far from attractive. Not that we ever dreamt that we should, because we knew we just weren't good enough. Yet Jesus taught that sinners who were sorry for what they had done wrong would enter the kingdom of God ahead of those who thought they were good.

## Saints

We also think of heaven as being full of saints and angels. It's true that all the saints are there, but there are many other people who would never have thought of themselves as saints. In the Roman Catholic Church, nobody can be prayed to as a saint until their name has been judged worthy and they have been canonized by the Pope. But St Paul wrote to 'the saints in Corinth' and went on to accuse them of the most terrible sins you can imagine, and a few that you'd rather not! Yet the Christians there had been chosen by God, and God was helping them to grow into saints. All Saints' Day is for remembering all those who never made it into a dictionary of saints, but were welcomed with trumpets into the courts of heaven. That includes some quite ordinary people like you and me.

## Rejoice, you righteous

Psalm 33 begins:

> Rejoice in the LORD, O you righteous,
> For it is good for the just to sing praises.

It's a description of the joy in heaven, based on the worship of the Temple in Jerusalem, with its lyres and ten-stringed harps. And when it talks about the righteous, it doesn't mean the impossibly good and saintly. Christians claim that when we die, even if we have no righteousness of our own, the righteousness of Jesus is credited to our account. So there's hope for me yet, and for you. One day we too shall join with all the saints in enjoying the fun in heaven, for ever and ever. Amen.

### Suggested hymns

*Give me the wings of faith to rise; Hark the sound of holy voices; Oh what their joy and their glory must be; There is a land of pure delight.*

## Commemoration of the Faithful Departed
## (All Souls' Day)
### 3 November (*transferred from 2 November*)
### The Dead Will Hear His Voice

Lam. 3:17–26, 31–33 New every morning; *or* Wisd. 3:1–9 Souls of the righteous; Ps. 23 The Lord is my shepherd; *or* 27:1–6, 16–17 He shall hide me; Rom. 5:5–11 Christ died for us; *or* 1 Peter 1:3–9 Salvation ready to be revealed; John 5:19–25 The dead will hear his voice; *or* John 6:37–40 I will raise them up

> *[Jesus said,] "Truly, truly, I say to you, the hour is coming, and now is, when the dead will hear the voice of the Son of God, and those who hear will live."' John 5:25*

### Sheol

There's a story that a group of Cockney workers was gathered in the porch of St Paul's Cathedral in London, while Dean Inge was preaching. One of them overheard part of the sermon and came rushing out calling to his mates, 'Cheer up, lads, you can carry on sinning; Dean Hinge says there ain't no 'ell!' I very much doubt whether the Gloomy Dean said anything of the sort, though it's easy to be misunderstood on this subject! Maybe he began by pointing out that there are two words in the Bible translated as hell, in both the Old and New Testaments. The first is a neutral term and means where all dead people go. In the Old Testament it was called 'sheol', and it's described as somewhere beneath the earth where dead people sleep. It has been compared to a great railway terminal on a foggy day: nothing much is happening, many people are arriving but nobody's going anywhere! In the New Testament the Greek equivalent is Hades. It's not a place of punishment.

## Gehenna

The other word's derived from the Valley of Hinnom, Jerusalem's municipal rubbish tip, to the south and downwind of the city. Any prophet, preaching in Jerusalem, could point to the smoke rising from the burning garbage in Hinnom, or Ge-henna as it's called in Greek, where the fire never goes out and the maggots never go hungry. The prophets could challenge their hearers, and tell them that from God's point of view they were a load of rubbish. They deserved nothing better than to be destroyed in the fires of the rubbish tip. Jesus sometimes uses such language himself, but it's metaphorical. God takes no pleasure in watching damned souls writhing in everlasting torment. Some people are amazed at the wideness of God's mercy and forgiveness, and believe that he's forgiven everyone. Others, amazed at the depth of God's tolerance, consider that if someone chooses to reject God's offer of eternal life, he'll allow them to, and that'll be the end of them. Medieval murals were full of demons with pitchforks thrusting sinners into the flames; there's nothing in the Bible that requires us to believe in that. In that sense the cockney was right: 'there ain't no 'ell'. A lot of muddled thinking has been caused by the unfortunate fact that both Sheol or Hades, and Hinnom or Gehenna, are translated into English as 'hell'.

## The Apostles' Creed

In the fourth century, the church in Rome made candidates recite a statement of faith before they were baptized. Because they claimed that it was based on the teachings of the Apostles in the Scriptures, they called this the Apostles' Creed. In this, it's stated that, after he died on the cross, Jesus 'descended into hell'. This wasn't a place of punishment. This is Sheol, or Hades, where the dead sleep and wait for the resurrection. What's taught by the Apostles' Creed is that the same thing happened to Jesus, when he died, as happens to everybody else: he went to the same place as everybody else goes to. That's the official teaching of the Church, though your salvation doesn't depend on your believing this, or even understanding it.

## A comfort to the bereaved

Jesus said, 'Very truly, I tell you, the hour is coming, and is now here, when the dead will hear the voice of the Son of God, and those who hear will live.' St Peter wrote: 'This is the reason the gospel was proclaimed even to the dead, so that, though they had been judged in the flesh as everyone is judged, they might live in the spirit, as God does.' The doctrine that Jesus descended into hell is a great comfort to the bereaved, for it's the doctrine of the second chance. If anyone deliberately turns their back on God, their end may be total destruction. But if they had no chance to believe in Jesus in this life, Jesus may meet them in the afterlife, and allow them to accept him. We mustn't presume on God's mercy for ourselves, but we can depend on it for those we love.

### Suggested hymns

*Christ, the Lord, is risen again; Give rest, O Christ, to thy servant with thy saints; I danced in the morning; Sweet is the work, my God, my king.*

## The Saints and Martyrs of (our own nation)
8 November
## The Marriage Supper of the Lamb
Isa. 61:4–9 Build up the ancient ruins; *or* Ecclus. 44:1–15 Let us now praise famous men; Ps. 15 Who may dwell in your tabernacle?; Rev. 19:5–10 A great multitude invited; John 17:18–23 To be with me to see my glory

*'Blessed are those who are invited to the marriage supper of the Lamb.' Revelation 19:9*

## Mixed metaphors

I'm going to remind you of some grammatical terms you probably already know. If you compare one thing to another; that's a simile: 'My love is like a red, red rose.' If the comparison is implied, but not stated, it becomes a metaphor: 'He carried a heavy burden of responsibility.' It would be absurd to take literally the poet's metaphor about the skylark: 'Hail to thee, blithe spirit, bird thou never wert.' Sometimes a metaphor is used so often that people forget that it's a picture. Then it becomes a cliché, or 'dead metaphor': 'The beefy bowler windmilled his arm and the ball came whistling down the wicket.' But the worst trap of all's the mixed metaphor, where you use two comparisons in the same sentence and create a nonsense:

'I shall put my foot down with a heavy hand.'
'The arrival of the wet blanket added fuel to the fire.'
'They got the wrong end of the stick because they weren't all singing from the same hymn-sheet.'
'You'll have to take the plunge if you want to keep your head above water.'

And so on!

## The Bible

The Bible's full of metaphors: poetic statements which convey a vivid picture, but which were never meant to be taken literally:

'Take my yoke upon you.'
'I will make you fishers for people.'
'If your eye offend you, pluck it out.'

Surely the most famous mixed metaphor in the Bible is in the book of Revelation, where it speaks about 'the marriage supper of the Lamb'. But here the combination of two entirely different pictures in one sentence is justified, because it makes you think. What has describing heaven as a marriage feast got to do with comparing Jesus to a sacrificial lamb?

## The wedding feast

Jesus himself compared the afterlife to a wedding reception. Sometimes such occasions can be fraught with tensions and problems, the biggest being deciding whom to invite and whom to leave out. But Jesus spoke of a king, who could afford to invite everybody, and did so, even including the tramps in the streets. So heaven's a place of celebration and enjoyment, not, of course, at a literal table with physical food, but metaphorically speaking. We shall see God and receive his forgiveness; we shall meet Jesus and know that he loves us; we shall meet our loved ones and remember happy times together; we shall meet our old enemies and discover that each of us has been transformed. What happy times those will be!

## The Lamb

That happiness, however, has been won at a cost. Lambs were used in sacrifices in the ancient world, as a token payment for the forgiveness of sins. The Passover lamb built the Israelites into a close-knit community. All lovers have to make sacrifices for the ones they love. So Jesus was described as the Lamb of God, who takes away the sin of the world, because in his willingness to sacrifice his life on the cross for us, he showed that God's love knows no limits in the price it will pay to win our love. Heaven's a happy wedding reception, but that joy's been won at the cost of Christ's death on the cross.

## Invitations

How pleased we are when we receive an invitation to a wedding reception. It's good to know that among those who are already celebrating in heaven are many saints who lived in our own nation. Today's a day for remembering with pride the sacrifices they made for our own people, and for the world. The saints of our nation start with the hermits and missionaries of the misty days of ancient legend, about whom little is known except that they gave their names to country villages and shrines. Then there were the monks and nuns of the Middle Ages, facing the challenges of living in community, healing the sick, welcoming travellers, taming the wilderness, standing up to monarchs and teaching the faith. At the time of the Reformation there were heroic lives on both sides of the religious divide, willing to be burnt at the stake or beheaded rather than deny their understanding of the faith. In more recent times there have been social reformers, bishops and teachers, statesmen and women, and humble pastors, who've lived their lives sacrificially for the benefit of others. If we're fellow citizens with the saints on earth, we shall meet them face to face when we ourselves come to heaven. For everyone's invited to the marriage supper of the Lamb.

### Suggested hymns

*God, whose city's sure foundation; In our day of thanksgiving one psalm let us offer; Judge eternal, throned in splendour; Lord, while for all mankind we pray.*

## St Andrew the Apostle   1 December
## (transferred from 30 November)

*WW 26/11/08*

**Immediately** Isa. 52:7–10 The messenger who announces peace; Ps. 19:1–6 The heavens declare God's glory; Rom. 10:12–18 God's messengers reconcile Jew and Greek; Matt. 4:18–22 The call of the fishermen

*'Immediately they left their nets and followed him.'* Matthew 4:20

### A Round Tuit

Do you know how to tease somebody who's just a teensy bit lazy? You make a big fuss about giving them something they've always wanted. Then you hand them a circular piece of card with some wording on it. Occasionally you even see the same words on a dinner plate, which is even funnier. It's called a 'Tuit', spelt T U I T. Because it's circular, the heading reads, 'A ... Round ... Tuit'. With luck, the recipient will have read half way through it before they realize what those words actually mean. The inscription goes like this:

A Round Tuit. At last we have a sufficient quantity for each of you to have their own! Guard it with your life. These tuits have been very hard to come by, especially the round ones. This is an indispensable item. It will enable you to become a much more efficient worker. For years we have heard people say 'I'll do that as soon as I get a round tuit'. Now that you have a round tuit of your very own, many things that have been needing to be accomplished will get done.

## Prevarication

Who's the target of this joke? Surely the idle person to whom you've presented the gift, who never seems to 'Get ... around ... to ... it', whatever 'it' is that they've been asked to do! But just a moment. Isn't there a bit of that in each one of us? We're all pretty good at prevaricating. We all make excuses for never doing today what we can possibly put off until tomorrow. We dither, we delay, we equivocate. We stall, we shift and we shuffle to avoid coming to the point. We beat about the bush. We dodge the real challenge, we hedge. We introduce quibbles, cavils, and deceptions to delay addressing the real challenge. We dissemble. We may even tergiversate. We speak a lot of words which don't really mean anything – just as I've been doing. All to make excuses for not coming to a decision. In other words, we never 'get around to it'. If this is only about unwelcome tasks at work, or chores about the house and garden, it doesn't matter too much. You can even make a joke about it. But if God challenges you to do something, it's no excuse to say, 'I never got around to it.'

## Andrew

So it's quite remarkable that when Jesus called St Andrew and the other fishermen, as we read in the Gospel, 'Immediately they left their nets and followed him.' Immediately! No prevaricating, no delay. They didn't wait until they got around to it. At once, they abandoned their fishing nets, and started on a new life. Why did they obey so promptly? They'd previously been followers of John the Baptist, so perhaps they'd met Jesus before. But the simple answer is that they recognized in Jesus an authority that they couldn't ignore. When Jesus tells you to do something, they must have felt, you do it. At once. Immediately. And not grudgingly, either. Because as soon as you recognize what sort of a man Jesus is, obeying him comes as naturally and inevitably as singing does to a songbird. You can't help it.

## Leaving behind

What did the fishermen leave behind when they followed Jesus? They left their nets; the tools of their trade, the means by which they earned their living. They left the comfortable security of a known way of life, to follow the unknown way of discipleship. Perhaps they recognized that the nets were just that, nets, which entangled them. Security and familiarity are dangerous traps, when they come between us and wholehearted discipleship. So is the demand for careful scientific reasons before coming to a decision. We get enmeshed in a network of logical doubts and hesitations, and when Jesus calls us, we somehow never get around to it. Thereby we miss the chance for a satisfying life of joy and purpose, here on earth, and the promise of eternal happiness in the world to come. Maybe you promised at your confirmation to follow Jesus all your life, and you've been backsliding. Or there's something God wants you to do, for your church or your neighbour or our suffering world. And you make excuses: too busy, you need to think it over a bit longer. Thank God St Andrew didn't prevaricate. 'Immediately they left their nets and followed.' Please God, give us the grace and the obedience to respond as cheerfully and immediately to the challenges that face us today.

## Suggested hymns

*Jesus calls us, o'er the tumult; When I survey the wondrous cross; Who would true valour see; Will you come and follow me?*

# Sermon for Harvest Festival

**Ps and Qs** Deut. 8:7–18 Do not forget the Lord; *or* Deut. 28:1–14 Blessings for obedience; Ps. 65 Thanks for earth's bounty; 2 Cor. 9:6–15 Generous sowing, generous reaping; Luke 12:16–30 The rich fool; *or* Luke 17:11–19 The thankful leper

> *'[Jesus asked,] "Was none of them found to return and give praise to God except this foreigner?"' Luke 17:18*

## Mind your Ps and Qs

When children were going out to a party, they used to be told, the last thing before they went out, 'Now be sure to mind your Ps and Qs.' You don't hear the expression so often these days, which is a pity. Ps and Qs, what on earth does it mean? The answer is: Ps and Qs stands for 'Please' and 'Thank you'. If you say them quickly and a little carelessly the words please and thank you sound a bit like the letters P and Q: 'Pease, Mummy'. 'Than–KYOU.' So 'Mind your Ps and Qs' means 'Don't forget to say "please" when you ask for anything, and "thank you" for everything you're given.'

## Blessings of courtesy

That's an important lesson to learn when you're growing up. Some grown-ups could do with a refresher course in minding their Ps and Qs, too. Because if you just say 'Give me that', it sounds rude and selfish. But the magic word 'Please' works wonders; it makes people so happy when you're polite, that they're much more likely to give you things than if you're rude. It's the same with 'Thank you'; if you forget to say it, it sounds as though you don't really care about what you've been given. So if it wasn't important enough for you to say thank you, then the person who gave it feels that they're not very important to you either. Let's hope they're too grown-up to sulk about it, but they're not very likely to give you anything else for a while.

## The thankful Samaritan

Jesus was walking from his home in Galilee to the city of Jerusalem. Jesus was a Jew, and the people in Galilee and Jerusalem were all Jews. But to get from one to the other they had to pass through the area where the Samaritans lived. They were different from the Jews; not very different, but sometimes people who are almost like you, but not quite, are the hardest to get on with. Usually Jews and Samaritans wouldn't even speak to each other. But ten people who were unwell were travelling around together, hoping to find some-one who could make them better; nine of them were Jews, and one was a Samaritan. But the fact that they were all sick was far more important to them than what race they came from. When Jesus came along the road, these ten people asked him to make them better. But the skin disease that they had meant that people were frightened to touch them in case they caught it from them. So they stayed a little way away from Jesus and called out, 'Jesus, Master, have mercy on us.' But Jesus wasn't afraid of falling ill; he usually went right up to people like that and touched them. Probably he did that this time too, and told them to go to the priests to prove that they'd been healed. They did that, and then one came back to say thank you. Only one, and he was the Samaritan, the foreigner, the one the Jews didn't like. Jesus told him that he had more faith in God than those who forgot to say thank you.

## Saying thank you to God

Harvest Festival's a time to say thank you to God. Thank you for our food, and all the other good things he's given us. There's a song that children sometimes sing before they eat; the usual tune's called 'Buckland', and it's in some hymnbooks to the words, 'Loving Shepherd of thy sheep'. The words go like this:

> Thank you for the world so sweet,
> Thank you for the food we eat,
> Thank you for the birds that sing,
> Thank you, God, for everything.

It's quite easy for even young children to learn it; it has been known, if anybody forgot to sing it before eating, for the youngest one to shout out insistently: 'Birds that sing, birds that sing!' That's the right idea, but it misses some of the finer points about politely minding your Ps and Qs! It's important to say thank you to God, the same as it is to someone who invited you to their party. It reminds us that if it wasn't for God making the crops grow, we wouldn't have anything at all to eat. And it reminds God that we don't take him for granted, but we love him because he's so kind to us. When you're talking to God, mind your Ps and Qs.

## All-age worship

*Act the story of the thankful Samaritan.*

## Suggested hymns

*Come, ye thankful people, come; Fear not, rejoice and be glad; For the fruits of his creation; We plough the fields, and scatter.*

# Sermon for a Wedding
## Mutual Submission
Eph. 5:21–33

*'Be subject to one another out of reverence for Christ.'* Ephesians
5:21

## What is Christian love?

Couples get married because they love each other, and they want to
form a loving family unit. But what does it mean, to love one another? What *is* love, and especially, what's Christian love? St Paul
must have often been asked this question. After all, there must have
been many married couples among the congregations he ministered
to, and they'll have wanted his guidance on how they should live in
the new situation created by their belief in Jesus.

## Starting where they are

When beginning a discussion on Christian behaviour, Paul
was always careful to get his readers on his side to begin with.
He often quoted a popular opinion, which everyone could agree
with, and started the discussion from there. The Roman Empire
was a very patriarchal society, far more than anything we know
now: the man was the boss, and women had almost no rights. But
everyone accepted this; they didn't know anything different. So
if Paul quoted the popular injunction, 'Wives, be subject to your
husbands', nobody'd disagree. Then, very subtly and before anyone
had noticed what he was doing, Paul would turn the argument on
its head: 'If you believe this, then it follows logically that you must
believe that.' Thus they'd find that, starting from the traditional
view which they all agreed with, they'd come to a quite unexpected
conclusion.

## Christ the husband of the Church

Jews often referred to God as the husband of his people; Hosea
wrote: 'On that day, says the LORD, you will call me, "My husband."' Then it followed that wives must obey their husbands, just
the same as Israel must obey the Lord. When Jesus came, his disciples
wanted to Christianize this, so they said that Jesus is the husband of

the Church. Hence, just as the Church obeys Jesus, so wives obey their husbands. So far everybody's in agreement. Then Paul makes his unexpected move. Jesus is the husband of the Church, he says. But Jesus gave his life on the cross as a sacrifice for the Church. So if the married relationship is modelled on the relationship between Jesus and the Church, it follows that husbands must love their wives in the same way as Jesus loves us, completely and sacrificially. 'Husbands, love your wives, just as Christ loved the Church and gave himself up for her,' says St Paul. This means sacrificing everything for your wife: giving up your time, your money, your comfort, your right to plan your own life without thinking about others, your independence, everything. This wasn't what the husbands had expected to hear. It wasn't what they wanted to hear! But Paul had made it follow logically from what they already believed, and they couldn't escape. Ouch!

## Mutual submission

Now, having stuck the knife in, St Paul didn't want to twist it. He could have said, to sacrifice yourself completely for somebody is much more demanding and difficult than obeying them. But Paul didn't want to lose the sympathy of the husbands in his congregation completely. So he then toned down his demands until they were the same for husbands as for wives. 'Be subject to one another out of reverence for Christ.' Mutual submission. Marriage is a relationship of equality: mutual obedience, equal self-sacrifice for the sake of the other. That's what Christian love means, for Jesus told us all to love one another in the same way as he loves us: the way of total self-sacrifice: Jesus said, 'This is my commandment, that you love one another as I have loved you.'

## Looking together towards Christ

Antoine de Saint-Exupéry was the author of that famous children's book *The Little Prince*. He wrote in another of his books, 'Experience shows us that love does not consist in gazing at each other but in looking together in the same direction.' It's very easy for newlyweds to become so wrapped up in each other that they forget everybody else. They're so busy looking into the eyes of the person they love that they don't notice the people all round them. True love consists in standing side by side, holding hands and looking at the world from the same point of view. Then you can get on with changing the world. But the Christian would want to go further. Love doesn't consist in gazing at each other, says the Christian, but in standing together hand in hand and looking together into the eyes of Jesus. Jesus, by his self-sacrificing love for us, has won the right to be obeyed. In fact, in Christian marriage, wives *don't* obey husbands, husbands don't obey wives; instead they find out together what obeying Jesus means and get on with it together.

## Suggested hymns

*Lead us, heavenly Father, lead us; Lord Jesus Christ, you have come to us; Praise, my soul, the king of heaven; The Lord's my Shepherd, I'll not want.*

# Sermon for a Baptism or Christening
## Wonderful Water
John 7:37–39

> *'Jesus ... cried out, "Let anyone who is thirsty come to me, and let the one who believes in me drink."' John 7:37*

### Wonderful water

Water's amazing stuff. Wonderful water, you can do so many things with it. Water will clean you when you're dirty and refresh you when you're tired. Water will power hydraulic machines, and it creates some of our most beautiful scenery. If there were no water on earth, there could be no life. Water makes up more than half your body; without food you can live several weeks, but without fresh water you'd be lucky to survive a couple of days. The first step towards solving the problem of starvation in Africa is to bring to each village a water supply. Wars have been fought, and could be fought again, over rivalry for a limited water supply. Don't despise water; it's valuable stuff.

### Christening

In this service we're going to pour some water over a baby's head. It's a strange thing to do. But water, as we've seen, is full of symbolic meaning. Jesus told his friends to go out into all the world, teaching people and baptizing them. Jesus used plain ordinary down-to-earth water as a way of showing us that God loves us. That's because the God that Jesus told us about is a very down-to-earth God. Jesus himself came down to earth when he was born as a baby in Bethlehem. God isn't too high-and-mighty to be interested in humble material things like water. God isn't too high and mighty to be interested in humble material things like you and me. God loves people – ordinary down-to-earth people like us. He even loves tiny insignificant babies. Of course every baby's the most important person in the world to its parents. God wants us to know that babies are important to him, too. So he gives us christening services to show that he welcomes babies into his arms, and into his family the Church, before they're even old enough to understand what's happening to them. And that's the first symbolism: baptism is God's way of welcoming children into the world.

## Clean

Second, baptism is God's way of telling us that he will make us clean. A lot of people go round feeling guilty. Some people don't, though they should. But God doesn't want us to *go on* feeling guilty; God wants us to come to him so that we can be forgiven. We come to God feeling dirty, and God makes us feel clean. So we give babies a symbolic washing with water, even before they've done anything wrong, to show that God's ready and waiting to forgive anything we feel guilty about, as soon as we say sorry.

## Refreshed

Third and finally, water refreshes us when we're tired. Everybody feels a bit tired and run down at times: being a human being's an exhausting job. But if you're feeling depressed, and you pray to God and ask him to help you, God will give you the strength to carry on. So we baptize babies to show them that God's refreshing power is available to us as soon as we ask him for it.

## Tell them about it

Christening shows us that every child is welcomed and promised God's cleansing forgiveness and refreshing power as soon as they're born. Of course they're not able to understand all that yet. The job of the parents and godparents is to explain it to them as soon as they can grasp it. Tell them that God loves them. Teach them to love God, and to pray to him as soon as they can talk. It's never too soon to share the love of God with any of God's children. That's why we baptize babies.

## Suggested hymns

*Give me oil in my lamp, keep me burning; Guide me, O thou great Redeemer/Jehovah; He's got the whole wide world in his hands; When Jesus came to Jordan.*

## Sermon for a Funeral or Memorial Service
## We Miss Them
John 11:25–44

> 'When Jesus saw [the sister of the man who had died] weeping, and the Jews who came with her also weeping, he was deeply moved in spirit and troubled; and he said, "Where have you laid him?" They said to him, "Lord, come and see." Jesus wept.' John 11:32–35

### Friends

Jesus was a loving person. Like all loving people, he formed close friendships. So when his good friend Lazarus died, Jesus was heartbroken. He knew, as all bereaved people know, that life on this earth from thereon would be the poorer for the absence of such a good friend. Not that Lazarus was perfect – nobody is. But Jesus and his other friends were prepared to live with Lazarus's faults, because they enjoyed his company. Then Jesus wept for the death of his friend. That, surely, is a comfort to all the bereaved who weep for the death of those they love. Jesus was not above human emotion; even Jesus knew how to cry, and he sympathizes with those who weep today.

### Resurrection

Then Jesus did a surprising and totally unexpected thing. He brought Lazarus back to life again. He's never done such a thing before or since. Why should he have done it in this case? It won't do to say it was because he loved Lazarus so much, because he loved other people too; why didn't he bring them back to life? The Bible says he loves everybody; why doesn't he bring everybody back to live for ever on this earth? Why doesn't Jesus raise the person we mourn today? Well, when you think of it, it would be impossible and undesirable to have the world filled with all the people who've ever lived – there wouldn't be room. Jesus has something better in mind: to raise us to new life with him in heaven, where, he's told us, there's room for everyone. So why did he bring Lazarus back to earth?

## Heaven

Well, I can only guess, but I think it was to teach us that death's not an end, but a beginning. Heaven's hard to imagine. We can't see heaven; how do we know it exists? So Jesus gave us a visual aid, in the form of his friend Lazarus. If Jesus can do the impossible by bringing one dead man back to life on earth, surely we can trust him to do something much easier: raising everyone who dies, to enjoy new life with him in the invisible world of eternity.

## Missing them

Missing our friends who've died is a perfectly natural and right thing. Although nobody's perfect, anyone who loved their friends and family will feel that this world will be a much poorer place for us because they've left it. But let's try to look at it from the point of view of the deceased. Of course there's unfinished business, and people they would like to look after. But God's given them the gift of eternal life. Their failures have been washed away, their good points have been made better, there's no more pain, and they've met up again with people who went to heaven before them. What's even better, they can look forward to being for ever together again with you and me, their friends from the time they spent on earth. But not just you and me as they've known us, with all our faults, but the new improved model, with all the failures forgotten and the imperfections put right. Just imagine, a perfect you or me, meeting in heaven with a perfect version of those we love, and enjoying their company for ever! Doesn't that make our brief period of mourning on this earth worthwhile?

## Grief

So it's perfectly OK to grieve – Jesus grieved too; Jesus wept. But our grief must be mingled with hope – hope that the promises of Jesus will be fulfilled; that God really does love us; that he'll support and sustain us through our grief. Then, one day, when he has no more jobs for us to do on earth, Jesus will lead us through that gloomy gateway we call death into the beautiful world of heaven. What happy greetings, what joyful reunions then, when we meet again with those for whom we've mourned! May God bless you and care for you until that happy day.

### Suggested hymns

*Jesus lives! Thy terrors now; Soon and very soon; The Lord's my Shepherd, I'll not want; Thine be the glory, risen, conquering Son.*

# Hymn for a funeral

Sung to the slow movement from Dvorak's *Symphony from the New World,* see facing page.

Christ the Way, every day,
we will walk with you.
No more fear, you are near,
loving us anew.
Friend of all, when we call,
bring us, as we roam,
all our days filled with praise,
nightly nearer home.

Those we love, now above,
live in rapture there;
happy they, night and day
in your love they share.
When they leave, while we grieve,
they are free from cares;
we rejoice in your choice
that your home is theirs.

All we do is for you,
Jesus, Lord most high;
So must we, therefore, be
unafraid to die.
Till that day, come what may,
when no more we roam,
let each breath sing till death
'We are going home.'
Then on high, when we die,
we shall be at home,
*(hum)*
in our Father's home.

*Michael Counsell* © 1984

# Christic the Way

words © 1984 Michael Counsell

*p* 1.Christ the Way, ev'- ry day, we will walk with you.
*p* 2.Those we love, now a- bove, live in rap- ture there;
*p* 3.All we do is for you, Je- sus, Lord most high;

No more fear, — you are near, lov- ing us a- new.
hap- py they, night and day in your love they share.
so must we, — there- fore, be un - a- fraid to die.

Friend of all, when we call, bring us, as we roam,
When they leave, while we grieve, they are free from cares;
Till that day, come what may, when no more we roam,

*verses 1, 2*

all our days filled with praise, night- ly near- er home.
we re- joice in your choice that your home is theirs.
let each breath sing till death

*verse 3*

'We are go - ing home,' Then on high, when we die, — we shall be at
*mf*

home, (hum) in our Fa- ther's home.
*p*        *pp*

Dvorak, Symphony from the New World, arrangement © 2006 Michael Counsell

# Scripture Index to Sermon Texts

# Subject Index

Entries in *italics* are sermon titles

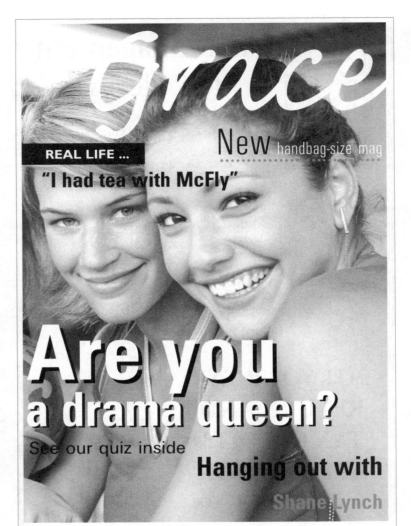

*Grace* is a cool, new, glossy, handbag-size mag for teenage girls – full of fashion, beauty, health, **real-life stories**, interviews, reviews, QUIZZES, problem pages and more! In addition, readers can get involved with **campaigning** on the issues they're passionate about, and grab some support in their relationship with GOD.

Give *Grace* to girls aged 11-16 in your community. Bulk orders available to youth groups, churches and youth organisations at a discounted rate.

## www.gracemag.co.uk

# Author Index

# Notes

# Notes

# Notes

# Notes

# Notes

# Notes

# Notes

# Notes

# Notes

# Notes

# Notes

# Notes

# Notes